A Tolerant Nation?

A Tolerant Nation?

Revisiting Ethnic Diversity in a
Devolved Wales

Edited by

Charlotte Williams, Neil Evans
and Paul O'Leary

UNIVERSITY OF WALES PRESS

www.uwp.co.uk

British Library Cataloguing-in-Publication Data
A catalogue record for this book is available from the British Library.

ISBN   978-1-78316-188-1
eISBN   978-1-78316-189-8

Printed by CPI Antony Rowe, Chippenham, Wiltshire

Contents

Foreword
    Vaughan Gething   vii
List of Contributors   ix
List of Illustrations   xv
List of Abbreviations   xvii

Introduction: Race, Nation and Globalization
   in a Devolved Wales
    Neil Evans, Paul O'Leary and Charlotte Williams   1

1. Immigrants and Minorities in Wales, 1840–
   1990: A Comparative Perspective
    Neil Evans   24

2. Slaughter and Salvation: Welsh Missionary
   Activity and British Imperialism
    Jane Aaron   51

3. The Other Internationalism? Missionary Activity and
   Welsh Nonconformist Perceptions of the World
   in the Nineteenth and Twentieth Centuries
    Aled Jones   69

4. Apes and Cannibals in Cambria: Literary
   Representations of the Racial and Gendered Other
    Kirsti Bohata   85

Contents

5. Wales and Africa: William Hughes
   and the Congo Institute
   Neil Evans and Ivor Wynne Jones   106

6. Through the Prism of Ethnic Violence: Riots
   and Racial Attacks in Wales, 1826–2014
   Neil Evans   128

7. Playing the Game: Sport and Ethnic
   Minorities in Modern Wales
   Neil Evans and Paul O'Leary   153

8. Changing the Archive: History and Memory as
   Cultural Politics in Multi-Ethnic Wales
   Glenn Jordan and Chris Weedon   175

9. Religious Diversity in Wales
   Paul Chambers   206

10. Extending the Parameters of Social Policy
    Research for a Multicultural Wales
    Roiyah Saltus and Charlotte Williams   224

11. Experiencing Rural Wales
    Charlotte Williams   251

12. 'This is the place we are calling home':
    Changes in Sanctuary Seeking in Wales
    Alida Payson   277

13. Getting Involved: Public Policy Making
    and Political Life in Wales
    Paul Chaney   305

14. Claiming the National: Nation, National
    Identity and Ethnic Minorities
    Charlotte Williams   331

Index   353

Foreword

I am very pleased to be able to write a foreword to the updated version of this pioneering book of essays. When the first edition was published over a decade ago it was the first publication of its kind to document and debate in a sustained way the contribution of black and ethnic minority groups to the history, culture and modern society of Wales. It was the first overview of around 200 years of ethnic diversity in the country and it demonstrated the significance of that diversity for modern society. At the time of its publication devolution was still in its infancy. Since then the devolution settlement in Wales, Scotland and Northern Ireland has been embedded and the distinctiveness of each society has become more obvious, as well as what they share with a wider world.

As the contributions to this book show, Wales is becoming an even more diverse society than it has been in the past. That pattern of diversity is subtly different to the picture to be found elsewhere in the UK and this book provides informed guidance on the nature of those differences, both past and present. Understanding the roots and nature of our diversity as a society and the extent to which some groups are disadvantaged or experience inequalities is an urgent task. At the same time, the book locates developments in this small country in a broader international context. The impact of

Foreword

globalization is to be found here as in other countries, with all the complexities that involves.

In this context, there is a powerful argument for up-to-date research on ethnic diversity in the devolved nations. This fully updated and augmented edition of *A Tolerant Nation?* provides new data and fresh analyses to help inform policy makers and the wider public in Wales and beyond. I welcome this book because systematic research is essential for an understanding of contemporary developments. We need informed and challenging debate rather than comforting plat-itudes if we are to meet the challenges that face us.

Vaughan Gething AM
Cardiff South and Penarth,
National Assembly for Wales

Contributors

Professor Jane Aaron teaches Welsh writing in English at the University of South Wales. Her publications include the monographs *Pur fel y Dur: Y Gymraes yn Llên Menywod y Bedwaredd Ganrif ar Bymtheg* (1998), which won the Ellis Griffith prize in 1999, *Nineteenth-Century Women's Writing in Wales* (2007), which won the Roland Mathias Award in 2009, and *Welsh Gothic* (2013). With others, she co-edited the essay collections *Our Sisters' Land: The Changing Identities of Women in Wales* (1994), *Postcolonial Wales* (2005) and *Gendering Border Studies* (2010). She is also co-editor of the series Gender Studies in Wales and Writers of Wales, both published by the University of Wales Press, and editor of Honno Press's reprint series, Welsh Women's Classics, for which she has edited five volumes, the latest of which is Allen Raine's *A Welsh Witch* (2013).

Kirsti Bohata is Associate Professor of English and Director of CREW, the Centre for Research into the English Literature and Language of Wales, at Swansea University. She is the author of *Postcolonialism Revisited: Writing Wales in English* (2004) and her most recent publication is *Rediscovering Margiad Evans: Gender, Marginality, Illness* (2013), co-edited with Katie Gramich.

Contributors

Paul Chambers is a Senior Lecturer in Sociology at the University of South Wales. He is the author of *Religion, Secularization and Social Change in Wales* and numerous articles on aspects of religion, both in Wales and Europe. His current research interests include desecularization, migration and faith-based social action.

Paul Chaney is Reader in Public Policy at Cardiff University School of Social Sciences. His books include *Women, Politics and Constitutional Change* (2007; co-authored), *Equality and Public Policy* (2011) and *Public Policy-Making and the Devolved State* (forthcoming). He is co-editor of *Contemporary Wales: An Annual Review of Economic, Political and Social Research*.

Neil Evans is a Fellow of the Royal Historical Society, an Honorary Research Fellow in History at Cardiff University and vice-chair of Llafur: The Welsh People's History Society. He has published work on many aspects of Welsh and British history, including urban history, protest movements, on ethnic minorities and most recently on the British Empire and its impact on Wales. He is working with Paul O'Leary on a study of processions and urban culture in south Wales *c.*1870–1914 and has just edited a book (with Huw Pryce): *Writing a Small Nation's Past: Wales in Comparative Perspective, 1850–1950* (2013).

Dr Aled Jones is Chief Executive and Librarian at the National Library of Wales at Aberystwyth. Until 2013 he was the Sir John Williams Professor of Welsh History and Senior Pro-Vice Chancellor at Aberystwyth University. He is the author of *Powers of the Press: Newspapers, Power and the Public in Nineteenth-Century England* (1996), *Press, Politics and Society: A History of Journalism in Wales* (1993) and co-author of *Welsh Reflections: Y Drych and America, 1851–2001* (2001). He is associate editor of the *Dictionary of*

Nineteenth Century Journalism (2009) and a contributor to *Banglapedia: The National Encyclopedia of Bangladesh* (2003). His research encompasses the history of journalism, the writings of Welsh missionaries and travellers in the British Empire and the connections between British and North American journalism.

Ivor Wynne Jones (deceased) was a local historian and international authority on the Congo Institute and its founder. He authored numerous books, including the pioneering *Shipwrecks of North Wales* (1973, 1978, 1986); *Llandudno, Queen of the Welsh Resorts* (1976); *Colwyn Bay, A Brief History* (1995); *Gold Frankenstein and Manure* (1997); *Money for All* (1969); and many smaller but seminal booklets. Ivor Wynne Jones was a member of the Welsh Academy/ Yr Academi Gymreig.

Professor Paul O'Leary teaches History at Aberystwyth University, where he is Director of Welsh Language and Culture in the Institute of Geography, History and Politics. He is co-editor of the *Welsh History Review* and has written widely on Irish migration and urban history. He is author of *Claiming the Streets: Processions and Urban Culture in South Wales, c.1830–1880* (2012), which was shortlisted for the Katherine Briggs Award for 2013; *Immigration and Integration: The Irish in Wales, 1798–1922* (2000); and editor of *Irish Migrants in Modern Wales* (2004). The projects he is currently working on deal with the interactions between Wales and empire and technological transfer between Britain and the European Continent during the Industrial Revolution.

Alida Payson is a PhD candidate in the School of Journalism, Media and Cultural Studies at Cardiff University. Her research is about how migrant women in Cardiff engage in creative practices of belonging and cultural citizenship. Prior to her PhD, she worked with young people from Somalia, Sudan,

Contributors

Rwanda, Burundi and Cambodia as part of a community gardening and food justice project in the United States. Her research interests include gender and migration, refugee rights, foodways and food justice, and everyday creativity.

Dr Roiyah Saltus is a Principal Research Fellow in the Faculty of Life Sciences and Education at the University of South Wales. Her research activities include qualitative studies to explore the personal and collective histories of the migratory experience of older ethnic minority people in Wales, with a focus on their social networks, help-seeking behaviour, understanding of notions of personal and social dignity, and anticipated social care requirements. Resilience, recovery pathways and mental wellbeing of people from racialized groups in Wales remains another ongoing focus. A key aspect of her research and publications has been to draw out the voices of people from ethnic minority population groups, to explore and map the responsiveness of public services, to spotlight issues of access, engagement and participation in a range of health and social care settings, and to explore and spotlight gaps between policy and practice.

Dr Glenn Jordan is a Reader in Cultural Studies and Creative Practice and Director of Butetown History & Arts Centre. His research and publications are in cultural studies, especially where that field intersects with history, ethnography and photographic practices. He has written on themes and issues in African-American intellectual history; the formation of African-American subjectivity from the middle passage to the Civil Rights Movement; and the histories of immigrants and minorities in Wales and Ireland, particularly in Cardiff docklands. His practice-based research, which results in exhibitions as well as academic writing, brings together photographic and curatorial practices with oral history and post-positivist ethnography. His photographic work combines large portraits, life stories and ethnography and has been shown in museums and galleries in the UK, Ireland and the USA. His photographs have also appeared on the covers of academic books and journals, including each of the bimonthly covers of the journal *Cultural Studies* during 2011.

Professor Chris Weedon is Honorary Director of the Centre for Critical and Cultural Theory at Cardiff University. She has published widely on feminist theory, cultural politics and women's writing. Her books include *Feminist Practice and Poststructuralist Theory* (1987 and 1996); *Cultural Politics: Class, Gender, Race and the Postmodern World* (with Glenn Jordan, 1994); *Postwar Women's Writing in German* (ed. 1997); *Feminism, Theory and the Politics of Difference* (1999); *Identity and Culture: Narratives of Difference and Belonging* (2004); and *Gender, Feminism and Fiction in Germany 1840–1914* (2006). She is currently working on multi-ethnic Britain and cultural and collective memory.

Professor Charlotte Williams OBE is Deputy Dean of Social Work at RMIT University, Melbourne, Australia. She has over twenty-five years of experience in social work education in the UK and internationally, previously having worked at Bangor University and Keele University in Staffordshire. Charlotte has held public appointments in both Wales and England and served on numerous advisory boards and task groups for the Welsh Government. Charlotte has an ongoing research interest in issues of cultural diversity, migration and multiculturalism within social work education and practice. She has published widely on issues of race, ethnicity and equalities, in particular in the Welsh context. She is editor of *Social Policy for Social Welfare Practice in a Devolved Wales* (2011) and author of the award winning memoir *Sugar and Slate* (2002). In 2007 Charlotte was awarded an OBE in the Queen's New Year's Honours List for services to ethnic minorities and equal opportunities in Wales.

Illustrations

Fig. 1 Butetown History & Arts Centre, Cardiff Bay © Glenn Jordan.

Fig. 2 Seamen from different ethnic backgrounds © Butetown History & Arts Centre archive.

Fig. 3 Marriage of Mohamed Hassan and Katie Link, Butetown, c.1924 © Butetown History & Arts Centre archive.

Fig. 4 Marriage of Stella Hersi to Milton Howard, American Serviceman, early 1940s © Butetown History & Arts Centre archive.

Fig. 5 Founding members, Butetown Community History Project, February 1988. Back row: Selma Salaman, Olwen (Blackman) Watkins, Kevin Haines, Marcia (Brahmin) Barry, Vera Johnson, Nino Abdi. Front row: Glenn Jordan and Tony DeGabriel © *South Wales Echo*.

Fig. 6 Interviewing Gerald Carey, retired merchant navy man from Jamaica, for a BBC radio programme made by oral historian Stephen Humphreys, 1987 © Glenn Jordan.

Fig. 7 Pedro Martinez Brito (from Cape Verde) and Eleanor Rosino, Cardiff – on their wedding day, 17 January 1926 © Butetown History & Arts Centre archive.

Fig. 8 Portrait of Somali seaman Said Ishmail Ali with his war medals, 2001 © Glenn Jordan.

Fig. 9 Jack Sullivan, *Home to Tiger Bay* (oil painting) – at the Dock Gate, near where the Wales Millennium Centre is now © Butetown History & Arts Centre archive.

Fig. 10 Page from John Doe Wesley's certificate of identity © Butetown History & Arts Centre archive.

Fig. 11 Gloria Evans (from Jamaica) with daughter Pauline Andam. From Glenn Jordan's 'Mothers and Daughters Portraits from Multi-ethnic Wales' project © Glenn Jordan.

Fig. 12 (a) and (b) Saeed Adan Yusuf and Ibrahim Ahmed Hassan. From Glenn Jordan, *Somali Elders: Portraits from Multi-ethnic Wales* (2004) © Glenn Jordan.

Fig. 13 A Muslim/Catholic Wedding, Butetown, 1930s © Butetown History & Arts Centre archive.

Abbreviations

ABMU   American Baptist Missionary Union
AM   Assembly Member (i.e. Member of the National Assembly for Wales)
AWEMA All Wales Ethnic Minority Association
BEST   Black and Ethnic Minority Support Team
BME   black and minority ethnic
BMS   Baptist Missionary Society
BNP   British National Party
CEEHD Centre for Evidence in Ethnicity, Health and Diversity
CIACS Cardiff International Athletics Club
CMS   Christian Missionary Society
CRE   Commission for Racial Equality
CSI   Core Subject Indicator
CYTÛN Churches Together in Wales
EALAW English as an Additional Language Association of Wales
EHRC   Equality and Human Rights Commission
EIAs   Equality impact assessments
HRP   Household Reference Person
NAW   National Assembly for Wales
NGO   non-governmental organization
NHS   National Health Service
NISCHR National Institute for Social Care and Health Research

Abbreviations

PEDW   Patients' Episode Database for Wales
PRIAE   Policy Research Institute on Ageing and Ethnicity
SDLP   Scottish Democratic Labour Party
TSPC   Third Sector Partnership Council
UNHCR   United Nations High Commissioner for Refugees
VSPC   Voluntary Sector Partnership Council
WARD   Wales Asylum Seeking and Refugee Doctors
WRC   Welsh Refugee Council
WRO   Wales Rural Observatory

Introduction

Race, Nation and Globalization in a Devolved Wales

NEIL EVANS, PAUL O'LEARY AND CHARLOTTE WILLIAMS

When the first edition of this book was published in 2003 we identified three key themes of significance for the understanding of minority ethnic groups in Wales: race, nation and globalization. These were the key concepts around which the book was organized, and they remain of cardinal importance in thinking through this revised and updated second edition, which includes three entirely new chapters as well as others that have been extensively rewritten in the light of new research. Some of that new research was stimulated by the discussions inaugurated by the first edition of the book. One idea of key importance to our discussions that has become increasingly contested since the first edition is multiculturalism. In 2003 we noted that the Parekh Report on the future of multicultural Britain, published in 2000, argued that there was a need to 'rethink the national story' and for nations to review their understanding of themselves and to 're-imagine themselves'. Nations needed to explore the cultural fabric of society and consider 'what should be jettisoned, what revised, what reworked?'[1] This remains an important task.

At the time of the Parekh Report the full impact of devolved government in the United Kingdom had yet to be felt – possibly it has still yet to be felt. Certainly, the question of how

1

narratives of nationality are reshaped to include minority ethnic groups – expressed through literature and the arts, sport and public life more generally – remains in flux. In the meantime, developments in the wider culture have changed the context for our discussions. While multiculturalism has been associated with a black British identity, the apparent decline of Britishness as the primary identity of most people in England, Scotland and Wales during the first fourteen years of the twenty-first century raises difficult questions about the long-term viability of black Britishness as an umbrella identity. This decline of Britishness as a cohesive identity is evidenced by the population census of 2011, which, although unable to provide a definitive picture of identity formation and reliant on a tick-box methodology, nevertheless provides an indicative snapshot of how people in the different nations expressed their national identity when asked to do so. While various permutations of single and combined identities were recorded, the striking figures related to those who reported that they had 'No British identity'. Some 73.7% of people in Wales placed themselves in this category, compared to 70.7% in England. In Scotland the figure was more than 80%. Such exceptionally high figures appear to be supported by data from social attitude surveys.[2] This would appear to belie the otherwise powerful, if often confused, imagery of the London Olympics of 2012, as well as claims that Englishness *should not* be divorced from Britishness.[3] Perhaps the superdiversity identified by some authors also increasingly militates against a single overarching British narrative.

While context and trends over time are of great significance for understanding how people frame and report their identity, the snapshot provided by the census reveals a crucially important point: as unifying historical experiences like the Second World War recede beyond the memory of the majority and erstwhile unifying institutions such as the National Health Service are eroded by piecemeal privatization, the fabric and memories of a unitary British identity are being eroded.

Perhaps we are experiencing the decline of Britishness as a unitary 'imagined community', to use Benedict Anderson's terminology.[4] The implications of this for how minority ethnic groups relate to ideas of national identity more generally have yet to be fully examined.

At the same time as widespread identification with Britishness was in decline, the idea of an officially sanctioned multiculturalism as public policy has been under attack, both from progressive and conservative standpoints. There are different definitions of multiculturalism, of course, sometimes complementary and sometimes competing. At its most basic, the fact of ethnic diversity – both historically and in contemporary society – is undeniable but the meaning of multiculturalism in public discourse and policy making has become a contested feature of academic and public life.[5] Following the 9/11 attacks on the Twin Towers in New York and events such as the race riots of 2001 two connected developments fuelled debates about the viability of a multicultural society. The first of these was the increasing visibility of Islam as a marker of cultural difference for some groups, which has inflected the broader debate in important ways. It raised questions about the compatibility of a particular minority community with the fundamental values of a culturally diverse liberal democracy, especially regarding attitudes to the freedoms of women. These concerns were at the root of David Cameron's 'war on multiculturalism' in 2011,[6] but they have also created dilemmas for progressives.

Cultural difference – especially as expressed through particular forms of dress connected to religious practice – is related to the second factor that challenged multiculturalism, that is the perceived separateness of minority ethnic communities. In this context, one writer has discerned the emergence of an 'ascendant majoritarianism' that threatens the viability of multiculturalism as state policy, not just in the United Kingdom but in other liberal democracies too.[7] Against this background, even prominent black figures such as Trevor

Phillips, a former chair of the Equality and Human Rights Commission, argued that multiculturalism as a state policy was no longer viable because it encouraged the separation of minority ethnic groups rather than their integration. His response to this problem was to promote Britishness as the primary identity of such groups, which – as we have seen – is a problematic proposal under current conditions in which Britishness is of decreasing salience as an identity in England, Scotland and Wales.[8]

Where does this leave Wales at the beginning of the twenty-first century? Devolved governments in Scotland, Wales and Northern Ireland provide new contexts for addressing questions relating to ethnic diversity and multiculturalism. We are witnessing the emergence of new ethnicities at home and, indeed, across Europe. The second edition of this book is therefore extremely timely. World events, the impact of globalization, migratory movements and the European Union's strategic attention to issues of racism, xenophobia, religious diversity and institutional racism since the 1997 Amsterdam Treaty all imply the need for deliberation, debate and action.

There are two key factors that make Wales distinctive in the context of this wider debate. The first is the existence of a strengthened representative body, the National Assembly for Wales, which acquired primary law-making powers in twenty policy areas in 2011 and – following the report of the Silk Commission – has the possibility of acquiring tax-raising powers. While the referendum of 1997 that created the Assembly was won by a wafer-thin majority of 50.3%, the referendum conferring primary law-making powers in 2011 was won more emphatically by a majority of 63.5%. Although turnout in these votes was low in relative terms, the principle of securing popular consent for these changes has been crucially important, and evidence indicates that there is greater popular confidence in the public institutions of government in Wales (and in Scotland) than in England. The fact that Wales is a stateless nation that is gradually acquiring the institutions of self-government as a result of two referenda has implications for new narratives of the nation: the Assembly has become the focus for the officially sponsored celebration of an ethnically inclusive civic national identity.

A study of the Italians in Wales has demonstrated how a white minority ethnic group has been incorporated in a national history for nation-building purposes, although it also shows how such a process entails forgetting inconvenient aspects of the past.[9] The idea of an ethnically inclusive nation is not without its challenges, as shown by contributions to this book. Racial descriptions of incomers to rural Wales as well as the use of racial language by Labour politicians and the media to attack Welsh speakers as an electoral strategy following the creation of the Assembly underline this point.[10] But it takes us beyond the idea of the toleration of minorities that dominated the concerns of the first edition of this book and which is critiqued by Charlotte Williams in the final chapter of this edition. A study of nation-building in Australia has demonstrated that an inclusive national identity can be 'an important source of cohesion and unity in ethnically and culturally diverse societies' and that multiculturalism can be central to this venture.[11] Wales and the other constituent nations of the UK face the same challenge, both in terms of fashioning national identities that reflect ethnic diversity and ensuring that social, economic and political inequalities are tackled.

The second of the key factors that make Wales distinctive from the standpoint of this book is the particular pattern of minority ethnic groups as revealed by the 2011 population census. It showed that the total population of Wales in 2011 was 3.1 million, an increase from 2.9 million in 2001. As in other parts of the UK, the number of people from minority ethnic backgrounds increased. In Wales the number of people from black and minority ethnic backgrounds (those other than white British, white Irish and white other, and including mixed ethnicity groups) increased from 1.5% (41,551) in 1991 to 2.1% (61,580) in 2001 and reached a total of 135,203 (approximately 4.0% of the total population) in 2011. By way of comparison, the size of the visible ethnic minority population in Scotland was just over 100,000 (2%) in 2001 and 192,900 (3.7%) in 2011. In Northern Ireland there was also a rise in the minority ethnic population (including Irish Travellers), from 0.8% in 2001 to 1.8% (32,400) in 2011. These changes in overall numbers and percentages have been accompanied by changes in the composition of the minority ethnic population. In Wales since 1991 there have been steady increases in the proportions of African, Indian, Pakistani, Bangladeshi and Chinese people, and increases in the number of people who classified themselves according to one of the several mixed ethnicities categories used in the census.

Another important particularity is the fact that the black and minority ethnic population in Wales remains highly concentrated geographically in the cities of south-east Wales. In 2001 the largest minority ethnic population was in Cardiff (with 42% of the minority ethnic population of Wales), followed by Newport (11%) and Swansea (8%). Of the twenty-two individual local authority areas in 2001 only Cardiff and Newport had significantly more than 2% of their population of minority ethnic backgrounds (8% and 5% respectively).[12] This pattern of residence has not changed, other than increasing in proportion. In each of these areas ethnic minority populations have more than doubled in the decade to 2011, with the biggest relative increase being in Swansea where the minority ethnic population rose from 4,800 to 14,200.[13] Perhaps unsurprisingly, the local authorities in Wales with the highest proportion of the population describing their ethnic group as white were Flintshire in the north-east (98.5%), Blaenau Gwent in the south-east (98.5%), Powys in rural mid-Wales (98.4%) and Caerphilly in south Wales (98.4%). Although the very dispersed nature of minority ethnic settlement continues, what is evident is that all local authorities have experienced rises in the numbers of residents identifying thcmselves as being from a minority ethnic background. The broad demographic profile of Wales is that it is small in size but increasingly diverse – indeed it can be described as 'super-diverse'[14] – and thus not easily readable as a conglomeration of discrete communities but is more an amalgamation of highly differentiated peoples that for the sake of convenience we categorize into ethnic minority groups.

Multicultural Wales

One meaning of multiculturalism, then, consists of a recognition of the existence of ethnic and cultural diversity. Wales has long demonstrated its ability to adapt, accommodate and shift in the face of wider social change and yet retain its essential values. As the historical essays in this book attest, Wales has always been a multicultural, multi-ethnic society, even if that has not always been recognized in official narratives of the nation. A number of contemporary novelists and artists have demonstrated that they are well in advance of many people in public life in this regard.[15] Multiculturalism, as ethnic diversity, is one element of historical continuity, an enduring quality of this small nation and a reminder that diversity is not a function of size. Nevertheless, recognition of the fact of multiculturalism and any systematic response to it has been patchy and contradictory. What has become identifiable in contemporary Wales is a patterning of neglect of the issues of 'race' and ethnicity and a consequent failure to address issues raised by a multicultural society. In the 'new' Wales there is evidence of a turnaround in this state of affairs and the emergence of the issue of minorities as a focus of public policy. Yet therein lies an immediate paradox. On the one hand, there is renewed interest at policy level, research and in the media, while a plethora of policy statements carry the statement 'and ethnic minorities'. On the other hand, there is growing awareness of disenfranchisement,

Introduction

compounded by marginalization, widening inequalities and widespread racism.

The notion of minorities/majorities is a complex one and provides an inadequate terminology for exploring the issues of central concern to this book. It is not simply that the terms imply some kind of fixed, unchanging and quantifiable entities but that they impute rather simplistic positionalities of superiority/inferiority, domination and subordination that are not borne out by the lived experiences of individuals. In reality, people may experience a number of minoritized positionings that are contextually given. Similarly the term 'ethnicity' is not without contention, notably because it is all too often used exclusively to denote people of colour with little acknowledgement of the fact that we all have an ethnic background. In this text we use the terms ethnic minority and minority ethnic interchangeably, recognizing the fact that terminology frequently undergoes change, and necessarily so. Transitions in our understanding of 'race', from its crude biological connotation to meanings that reflect social constructions, will be apparent in this book. Further terms frequently in use in policy circles such as 'black', 'black and minority ethnic', 'minority ethnic people', 'Asian people', have all been found wanting for their political connotations and their inadequacy in describing the subjective experiences of individuals. This is particularly apparent in Wales, where identifications of skin colour are not the only 'ethnic' marker for the many individuals of mixed descent.

This book focuses primarily on issues affecting visible ethnic minorities. This is not to deny the importance of the Irish, the Poles, the Greeks, Gypsy peoples, Eastern Europeans and others; nor does it seek to downplay religious minorities such as Jewish and Muslim communities or, indeed, linguistic minorities such as Welsh speakers. Their concerns and experience are central to any understanding of the key issues of nationhood, identity and difference. Indeed, in the context of devolution some literary scholars have demanded a

8

re-definition of multiculturalism to embrace autochthonous linguistic minorities such as Welsh speakers.[16] Here, however, we have focused mainly on the notion of the 'racialized' other and on the *processes* that produce that positioning of inferiority. Hence themes such as 'race thinking' are pursued through a consideration of historical and contemporary references, and attention is given to the *institutionalization* of processes of discrimination. It is, however, necessary to acknowledge a two-way process, and one strong ambition of this book is to mark up the significant contribution of the minority population to the development and profile of Wales as a nation both domestically and internationally, both historically and in a contemporary sense.

Given the range of issues discussed and the timescale covered (some 150 years) the book is necessarily multidisciplinary. It draws on the work of historians, literary critics, political scientists, social geographers, sociologists and social policy specialists. The book is richer for this diversity and, as the first edition demonstrated, it has broad appeal to individuals and groups in minority communities, to policy-makers and policy-shapers, as well as to the academic community. The first edition of this book initiated debates and established a bedrock of information that acted as a basis for further research and writing. The revised and updated second edition reflects those changes and seeks to focus them.

Themes and questions

The studies gathered together here cluster around two major themes. One is the nature and identity of the Welsh nation. The other is globalization and transnationality. They point towards a future in which we explore the intersections of these ideas, in the past and present, by analyzing what is particular to the Welsh experience in the light of global influences and developments. Between them they raise urgent questions about the nature of multiculturalism and citizenship in a rapidly changing society in which the constituent parts of the United Kingdom are developing distinctive and different governmental and civic cultures.

In Wales positive images of the nation have, in the past, drawn upon ideas of tolerance of difference and a welcoming approach to outsiders. This is frequently – if sometimes implicitly – contrasted with the attitudes of the English, who are perceived to be imperialist and domineering. In the first chapter, Neil Evans confronts this issue with the abundant historical evidence of conflicts and intolerance in Wales, as well as drawing attention to instances of open-mindedness and tolerance, but he argues that the point is to address the underlying circumstances that produce racism and xenophobia and those that act against it.[17] Identifying what is specific about Wales in this context means that more rigorous comparisons with other places have to be pursued, instead of simply adopting a broad-brush and impressionistic contrast with England. Locating the experiences of Wales against those of Merseyside, Scotland and Northern Ireland helps him to do this. Elsewhere he has shown that another problem with generalized comparisons is that they can be found in virtually all European nations and are frequently used to pass the responsibility for xenophobia from one country to another.[18] From the beginning, then, the idea of the nation carries us outside its bounds and into the realm of comparison.

The second theme, globalization and transnationality, is often seen as a purely contemporary phenomenon; most historians would reject this perspective.[19] While there have been major recent developments in instant communications and the collapse of distance, it is important to remember that the different parts of the globe have been connected for at least 500 years. It is essential to appreciate this fact in order to understand the importance of ethnic minorities within nations. To provide a specific and graphic Welsh illustration of this point we need to look no further than the multiracial community of Butetown (once known as 'Tiger Bay') in Cardiff, which dates from before the First World War and represents a clear and tangible indication of an earlier phase of globalization. The building of a community archive at the Butetown History and Arts Centre, analyzed by Glenn Jordan and Chris Weedon in chapter 8, underlines the complex historical legacy of this phase of globalization. They present a picture of a diverse place in contrast to the unified and threatening image presented by outsiders to the area.

Even before the European voyages of 'exploration' of the late fifteenth century, which inaugurated the era of proto-globalization, there was significant movement around the Eurasian landmass by overland routes. The Jewish diaspora that was enacted on this stage clearly touched Wales, and the Jews arrived in a medieval Welsh society that was ethnically diverse, comprising the native Welsh, Norman and English conquerors, and Flemish colonists. Gypsies probably arrived in Wales at the end of this era – which has been called 'archaic globalization' – around the time that European voyages outwards were beginning in earnest and the era of proto-globalization was starting.[20] This flow illustrates an interconnectedness between Wales and the wider world even in the remote past. Nor was there an ethnically homogeneous Wales with a simple and defined border with its English neighbour.

The era of proto-globalization made relatively little impact on Wales. It is in the era of modern globalization, coinciding with industrialization and the rise of the nation-state, that Wales was transformed and came to occupy a less marginal place in the world of the enlarged European empires. After the loss of the North American colonies in 1783 the centre of gravity of the British Empire shifted eastwards. It was in this context that more Welsh people came to have experience of the colonial encounter. In her analysis of the impact of missionaries on Welsh attitudes to the outside world, Jane

Aaron demonstrates that many children and adults had their ideas about other peoples shaped by the stories that came back in person and in print from these outposts of Western values and religious conversion. The major Welsh contribution to imperialism, she argues, was through missionary activity, which often ranged the missionary against commercial and military imperial interests. She finds at least a coincidence in the final demise of this activity in the 1960s and the growth of a nationalist movement in Wales. Aled Jones provides a parallel study by examining the work of the largest single Welsh missionary activity, the Calvinistic Methodist outpost in Khasia, and the way that this was refracted in Wales through the medium of the press. Like Aaron, he finds that the attitudes engendered by such work simultaneously helped foster enthusiasm for empire and celebrated the role of Wales in it. Yet they also led to discussions of racial and social justice. An unintended consequence of it was an internationalism which rivalled that of the labour movement and introduced discussions of colonialism to Welsh-speaking Nonconformist culture.

A crucial element of European expansionism in the period from the sixteenth century onwards was the slave trade that linked Europe with Africa and the Americas, imposing a triangular network across the Atlantic. Recent research has shown how some Welsh people were implicated in this hateful aspect of global trade as well as prompting radical and evangelical responses in protest against it.[21] The slave trade had a protracted death in the modern era. The peoples of the African diaspora came to retrace their roots via the movement known as Pan-Africanism. This reversed the triangular relationships of the slave trade by bringing back to Africa what Africans had learned in the New World. Religious leaders and politicians aimed at ending the imperial control of Africa and creating some degree of unity across the continent.[22] The chapter by Neil Evans and Ivor Wynne Jones shows the relationship that was forged between Wales and this movement. The missionary William Hughes feared that his African aides would not develop the full panoply of Western and Christian values if they were trained in Africa, where they would be open to local values. His solution to this problem was to bring Africans to Wales for training because of his perception of Welsh religiosity. Colwyn Bay had the added advantage of being close to Liverpool, one of the major ports of the African trade. Some Welsh people regarded the Africans as interesting exotica, while others saw them as threats to the dominant Nonconformist values. This fascinating episode provides another window into racial attitudes in Wales.

Kirsti Bohata's essay provides a means of assessing how much the ideas generated by imperialism entered the minds of people in Wales. Her close reading of three representative literary texts reveals how deeply racial stereotypes had entered the consciousness – and perhaps more so the unconscious. She also stresses the interconnections between different forms of social exclusion: racial discrimination overlapped in major ways with anxieties relating to gender, sexual orientation and class. Her essay is a reminder that these categories of analysis are relevant to an understanding of the experiences of ethnic minorities and complicate our understanding of race.

These essays provide the context for a group of three studies that focus on the changing nature of Welsh society and link the era of modern globalization with the post-colonial era. Neil Evans provides an overview of ethnic riots in the nineteenth and twentieth centuries, set against a background of wider communal violence. He finds cause for both optimism and pessimism in the current situation: optimism, because ethnic antagonisms can no longer mobilize large and representative portions of the population as they did in the nineteenth and early twentieth centuries; pessimism, because contemporary racial attacks are more murderous for being marginalized and lacking the constraints of wider community values. Communal violence in the past was more restrained and at some levels more symbolic than at present, where it is carried out by socially marginal groups and fuelled by the ideas of the far right.

Neil Evans and Paul O'Leary examine the experience of ethnic minorities in Wales through sport. Mass sport, like communal violence, is a central concern of social historians in Wales and it provides a different insight into the nature of society, identity creation and ways of negotiating cultural boundaries. An examination of the experience of ethnic minority sportspeople in Wales reveals both layers of discrimination and very positive achievements (at least as far as men are concerned), which have done much to enhance the self-esteem of minority communities. The achievements of key figures in both individual and team sports have provided highly visible examples of the presence of minority ethnic groups in Welsh society. The fact that at least some of these people were part of 'representative' national teams is a reminder of how sport can be a powerful aspect of the process of refashioning national narratives. Yet it needs to be remembered that many of them made their careers outside Wales, sometimes because they felt that their opportunities were blocked in their native land. And in the contemporary world a career in professional sport remains an ambiguous arena of achievement for ethnic minorities, both affirming achievement and reinforcing stereotypes.

Paul Chambers's essay provides an overview of the role of religion in Welsh identity and of its role in constructing ethnic 'Others'. He stresses the dominance of Nonconformity in nineteenth-century Wales, which allowed it to react to the Irish Catholic immigration from a position of strength.[23] Nonconformity has long lost its dominance, and it has reacted to this decline by embracing ecumenicalism. The census of 2011 showed a mixed picture of religious affiliation.[24] A significant number of the Welsh population indicated that they either had no religion (32.1%) or religion was not stated (7.6%). Of those who indicated they had a religion, over half

(57%) identified as Christians, followed by a rise in the number of Muslims from 24,211 (0.8%) in 2001 to 45,950 (1.5%) in 2011. In terms of what is known about particular subgroups, the Bangladeshi community in Wales is a largely homogenous ethno-linguistic group with the overwhelming majority being Muslim. The majority of the Indian ethnic group living in Wales is Hindu, while one fifth is Sikh. The majority of Chinese have no religion, while just over one fifth are of Christian faith and 15% are Buddhist. Christianity is the majority religion among people from Caribbean backgrounds. After that people tend not to be affiliated with any religion, and tiny numbers are affiliated with other religions. This is particularly important at a time when a perceived 'clash of civilizations' (rooted in religious cultures) is alleged to be the dynamic of the world order. In this context, the potential for culturally based racism is significant, but Paul Chambers shows that the impetus for it does not come from organized Christianity. As Neil Evans's chapter on ethnic violence shows, Islamophobia exists among marginalized social groups rather than being institutionalized in the mainstream. This point is reinforced by a research report by Race Council Cymru in 2012.[25]

These last essays straddle the divide between the modern and post-colonial eras of globalization and explore vital and interconnecting aspects of our time. As Alida Payson demonstrates, legislation by the British Government since 1999 has transformed the scope and diversity of asylum seekers in Wales, particularly because of its dispersal policy that led to an increase in the visibility of asylum seekers in local communities. Unlike previous waves of immigration it was not related to available economic opportunities but centrally directed. Furthermore, she shows that responses to refugees have been shaped in part by the civic networks established or enabled by devolution, which in turn have permitted a mobilization that has reshaped the idea of sanctuary in Wales. The refugee crisis that has grown out of the international uncertainty of the post-cold war era has renewed the ethnic minority population of Wales. This issue provides another intersection of our themes of nationality and globalization.

The theme of how ethnic minorities reflect the nation is explored by Paul Chaney through an examination of the experience of ethnic minorities in political participation in both formal and informal contexts. His sobering conclusion is that a rhetoric of inclusiveness has not been matched by practical achievements and that ethnic minority participation remains limited, with low levels of minority representation at all levels of the political process. The diversity of the minority populations in Wales has been a key issue here, and this diversity has made it difficult to establish the unity necessary for effective political action. While the new governmental structures clearly have the potential to make a difference, his chapter demonstrates that more needs to be done to mainstream race equality.

Low levels of political participation are matched by persistent inequalities in health and social care, housing, education and labour market participation among minority ethnic groups. Roiyah Saltus and Charlotte Williams explore how, in the context of devolution, social policy research might be harnessed to achieve the Welsh Government's aims for racial equality and improve the wellbeing of minority ethnic groups. They argue for the mainstreaming of concerns relating to social and economic inequality among minority ethnic groups in social policy research in Wales. Data collection in this area has improved but they argue that the reasons for the persistence of inequalities need to be addressed. Taken together, the chapters on political participation and social policy underscore the point that imagining a diverse and multicultural Welsh nation is not, of itself, enough.

Two chapters by Charlotte Williams return to the theme of the nature of the nation. In her chapter on rural Wales, she challenges hegemonic ideas of rurality. Our images of nations are often rural in nature, involving an implied or an explicit contrast with the alleged rootlessness of urban society, but this chapter subverts the formulaic dichotomies of rural/ urban divides. As shown above, the minority ethnic populations in Wales are overwhelmingly concentrated in the cities of the south, but the small, dispersed presence in rural Wales serves to complicate cherished notions of rural ethnic homogeneity. The existence of low-level and persistent rural racism is well documented, and ethnic minorities are marginalized in popular conceptions of rural society. Even so, members of these minorities are often active citizens in rural communities, and Charlotte Williams discerns the existence of 'transrural' relationships that are brought about by ethnic diversity and difference.

The second of these two chapters urges caution about being too eager to celebrate the rhetoric of diversity and expresses a concern that we do not gloss over the complexities of a diverse national community. She reprises an important theme that emerges in several contributions to this book – that the language of diversity needs to be matched by a willingness to resolve the problem of the unequal distribution of resources. She argues forcefully that in Wales we have 'gone for the easy win' by prioritizing claims relating to identity over the more difficult and less tractable challenge of removing inequalities. In this contest, she describes Welsh multiculturalism as 'a curious bundle of contradictions' and 'a project in the making'.

Contemporary Wales

How, then, do we assess the position of contemporary Wales in terms of our interacting themes? We can specify what is distinctive about Welsh identity and its connections with the wider world by means of some comparisons with the other nations in the British Isles. In England there is now a substantial ethnic minority population that is quite widespread geographically. This – along with the recognition of England's centrality in the British Empire – has forced issues of multiculturalism onto the political agenda and led to racial equality becoming a prominent issue, and one which has well-established institutional linkages. By contrast, in Scotland, where the role in the empire is well acknowledged and a source of pride and identity, there is only a small and concentrated minority ethnic population. Ireland has had even fewer representatives of ethnic minorities until very recently, but it has a broad awareness of its international connections through missionaries, functionaries of empire and the sustained emigration from Ireland in the modern period. Modern Irish identity is much shaped by these links. The situation in Wales is a distinctive blend of these elements. Unlike Ireland, emigration was never of massive proportions.[26]

Until recently the role of Welsh people in the British Empire was little explored. This situation has now changed and we have a clearer and developing sense of the complex interactions that have taken place over the centuries.[27] Although Welsh people were underrepresented among the servants of the empire, and some people would want to see the Welsh as the colonized rather than the colonizer, the military victories of imperial Britain were celebrated here and some Welsh politicians had well-developed imperial attitudes. There were complex cultural and religious relationships with the imperial project.[28] In addition, the place of ethnic minorities in Wales is much more limited than in England, though it is more prominent than in Scotland, which has no equivalent of Butetown's multiracial community. Both Scotland and Wales have largely avoided the racialized politics of England, partly because the Scots-English and Welsh-English ethnic issues have forced explicit discussions of race further down the agenda than in England. Only in the 1990s did the issue begin to make a serious impact on the political agenda, when a rise in racial attacks confronted the myth of tolerance, while television documentaries, newspaper articles and the Oscar-nominated film

Solomon a Gaenor examined aspects of cultural diversity and ethnic conflict in the past and the present.[29] At the same time, the institutional structures to promote racial equality were being more firmly established.

The problems we face in reconciling nationality with a globalizing world are not unique to Wales, nor are they unprecedented. We have resources to draw on from other countries and from our own past. Particular places everywhere are coming to be seen as distinct blends of elements from diverse origins rather than as hermetically sealed units. An important contribution to this task of re-definition, as well as the tackling of inequalities, will be research and analysis of the kind that is contained in this book. Creating links between our developing understanding of the past and our explorations of the present in a number of disciplinary fields provides a basis for thinking about ethnic diversity and the Welsh nation in new ways. That task will be difficult and contested, and it is about citizenship as much as scholarship, but we have some confidence that we have resources to prepare us for the task. These essays, we believe, make important contributions both to the way we understand the past and present, and to the way we build our common futures.

Notes

1 B. Parekh, *The Future of Multi-Ethnic Britain: The Parekh Report* (London, 2000).

2 C. Jeffery, 'A disintegrating union? Between Scotland's referendum and the emergence of England', Institute of Welsh Politics lecture, Aberystwyth University, 12 November 2013.

3 K. Kumar, 'Negotiating English identity: Englishness, Britishness and the future of the United Kingdom', *Nations and Nationalism*, 16, 3 (2010), 469–87.

4 B. Anderson, *Imagined Communities: Reflections on the Origins and Spread of Nationalism* (London, 1983; revised edn 1991).

5   C. Joppke, 'The retreat of multiculturalism in the liberal state: theory and policy', *British Journal of Sociology*, 55/2 (2004), 237–57; M. Hale Williams (ed.), *The Multicultural Dilemma: Migration, Ethnic Politics, and State Intervention* (Abingdon, 2013).

6   *The Independent* (5 February 2011). The significance of the attack on multiculturalism has been contested; see V. Oberoi and T. Modood, 'Has multiculturalism in Britain retreated?', *Soundings: A Journal of Politics and Culture*, 53 (2013), 129–42.

7   P. Pathak, *The Future of Multicultural Britain: Confronting the Progressive Dilemma* (Edinburgh, 2013), p. 7.

8   *The Times* (3 April 2004).

9   M. Giudici, 'Migration, memory and identity: Italians and nation-building in Wales, 1940–2010', unpublished Bangor University PhD thesis, 2012. See also P. O'Leary, 'Introduction: towards integration: the Irish in modern Wales', in P. O'Leary (ed.), *Irish Migrants in Modern Wales* (Liverpool, 2004), pp. 1–8.

10 G. Day, H. Davis and A. Drakakis-Smith, 'Being English in north Wales: in-migration and in-migrant experience', *Nationalism and Ethnic Politics*, 12/3–4 (2006), 577–98; G. Day, H. Davis, and A. Drakakis-Smith, 'There's one shop you don't go into if you are English; the social and political integration of English migrants into Wales', *Journal of Ethnic and Migration Studies*, 36/9 (2010), 1405–23; S. Brooks, 'The idiom of race: the "racist nationalist" in Wales as bogeyman', in T. Robin Chapman (ed.), *The Idiom of Dissent: Protest and Propaganda in Wales* (Llandysul, 2006), pp. 139–66.

11 A. Moran, 'Multiculturalism as nation-building in Australia: inclusive national identity and the embrace of diversity', *Ethnic and Racial Studies*, 34/12 (2011), 2153–72.

12 Wales Statistical Directorate, *A Statistical Focus on Ethnicity in Wales* (Cardiff, 2004).

13 Welsh Government, *2011 Census: First Results for Ethnicity, National Identity, and Religion for Wales* (Cardiff, 2012).

14 See S. Vertovec, 'Super-diversity and its implications', *Ethnic and Racial Studies*, 29/6 (2007), 1024–54, and S. Fanshawe and D. Skriskandarajah, *You Can't Put Me In A Box – Super Diversity and*

the End of Identity in Britain (IPPR, 2010): *http://visit.lincoln.ac.uk/ C7/C5/Equality/ED%20Annual%20Reports/You%20Can't%20 Put%20Me%20in%20a%20Box.pdf* (accessed 5 August 2013).

15 P. Corcoran, *Last Light Breaking* (Bridgend, 1998); T. Azzopardi, *The Hiding Place* (London, 2000); J. Williams, *Cardiff Dead* (London, 2000); C. Williams, *Sugar and Slate* (Aberystwyth, 2002); P. Pullman, *The Broken Bridge* (London, 1990, revised edn 2001); P. Aithie, *The Burning Ashes of Time: From Steamer Point to Tiger Bay* (Bridgend, 2005); R. Trezise, *Sixteen Shades of Crazy* (London, 2011).

16 D. G. Williams, 'Your multicultural nation is not necessarily mine', ClickonWales, *http://www.clickonwales.org/2012/11/your-multicul-tural-nation-is-not-necessarily-mine/* (accessed 1 November 2012).

17 This approach has been developed further in N. Evans, 'Comparing immigrant histories: the Irish and others in modern Wales', in O'Leary (ed.), *Irish Migrants in Modern Wales*, pp. 156–78.

18 N. Evans, 'Can we compare racisms? Regions, nations and Europe', in E. Bort and N. Evans (eds), *Networking Europe: Essays in Regionalism and Social Democracy* (Liverpool, 2000), pp. 235–62.

19 See A. G. Hopkins (ed.), *Globalization in World History* (London, 2002).

20 These variants of globalization are derived from Hopkins, *Globalization in World History.*

21 C. Evans, *Slave Wales: The Welsh and Atlantic Slavery, 1660–1850* (Cardiff, 2010); T. Burnard, 'From periphery to periphery: the Pennants' Jamaican plantations and industrialisation in north Wales, 1771–1812', in H. V. Bowen (ed.), *Wales and the British Overseas Empire: Interactions and Influences, 1650–1830* (Cardiff, 2012), pp. 114–42; A. Davies, '"Untainted with Human Gore"? Iolo Morganwg, slavery and the Jamaican inheritance', in G. H. Jenkins (ed.), *Rattleskull Genius: The Many Faces of Iolo Morganwg* (Cardiff, 2005), pp. 292–313; E. Wyn James, 'Welsh ballads and American slavery', *The Welsh Journal of Religious History*, 2 (2007), 59–86.

22 I. Geiss, 'Pan-Africanism', *Journal of Contemporary History*, 4/1 (1969), 187–200; G. Shepperson, 'Notes on Negro American

influences on the emergence of African nationalism', *Journal of African History*, 1/2 (1960), 299–312; G. Shepperson, 'Pan-Africanism and "Pan-Africanism": some historical notes', *Phylon*, 23/6 (1962), 346–58.

23 For an emphasis on the ways in which Irish Catholics integrated in Welsh society, see P. O'Leary, *Immigration and Integration: The Irish in Wales, 1798–1922* (Cardiff, 2000); idem, 'When was anti-Catholicism? The case of nineteenth- and twentieth-century Wales', *Journal of Ecclesiastical History*, 56/2 (April 2005), 307–25; idem, 'Processions, power and public space: Corpus Christi at Cardiff, 1872–1914', *Welsh History Review*, 24/1 (2008), 77–101; idem, *Claiming the Streets: Processions and Urban Culture in South Wales, c.1830–1880* (Cardiff, 2012).

24 Welsh Government, *2011 Census* (Cardiff, 2012).

25 H. Crawley, *A Report on Race Equality and Racism in Wales: An Exploratory Study* (Swansea, 2012).

26 Nevertheless, emigration has made a deep impact on Welsh consciousness; see W. D. Jones, *Wales and America: Scranton and the Welsh* (Cardiff, 1993); and his work on the Welsh in Australia, e.g. '"Going into Print": published immigrant letters, webs of personal relations, and the emergence of the Welsh public sphere', in B. S. Elliott, D. A. Gerber, and S. M. Sinke (eds), *Letters Across Borders: The Epistolary Practices of International Migrants* (Basingstoke, 2006), pp. 175–99.

27 H. V. Bowen (ed.), *Wales and the British Overseas Empire: Interactions and Influences, 1650–1830* (Cardiff, 2012); A. Jones and B. Jones, 'The Welsh world and the British Empire, c.1851–1939: an exploration', *The Journal of Imperial and Commonwealth History*, 31/2 (2003), 57–81; A. Jones and B. Jones, 'Empire and the Welsh Press', in S. J. Potter (ed.), *Newspapers and Empire in Ireland and Britain, c.1857–1921* (Dublin, 2004), pp. 75–91; N. Evans, 'Empire strides back: an unlikely revival in history, politics and culture', *Planet*, 187 (February–March 2008), 26–33.

28 N. Masterman, *The Forerunner: The Dilemmas of Tom Ellis, 1859–1899* (Llandybïe, 1972); J. Grigg, *Lloyd George: The Last Best Hope of the British Empire* (Caernarfon, 1999).

29 P. O'Leary, 'Film, history and anti-Semitism: *Solomon & Gaenor*
(1999) and representations of the past', *North American Journal of
Welsh Studies*, 7 (2012), 38–52; idem, 'Foreword to the new edition:
conflict and co-operation: *The Jews of South Wales* and the study of
Welsh Jewry', in U. R. Q. Henriques (ed.), *The Jews of South Wales:
Historical Studies* (Cardiff, 2013), pp. xii–xviii.

I

Immigrants and Minorities in Wales, 1840–1990: A Comparative Perspective[1]

NEIL EVANS

Václav Havel believes that a nation can be judged by the way it treats minorities.[2] Wales has often measured itself favourably by this standard and outsiders have also applied the same rule. It is an encapsulation of one of the subthemes of the Welsh idea of the *gwerin* – the Welsh people were the most upright, God-fearing, radical, moral, philosophical, cultured and tolerant in the world. The principled internationalism of the *gwerin* receives some academic support from one of the major studies in modern Welsh social history, Hywel Francis and David Smith's *The Fed: A History of the South Wales Miners in the Twentieth Century*.[3] Here the proletarian solidarity of the miners – most marked in their support for Irish independence in the 1920s and the Spanish Republic in the 1930s – is seen as being rooted in the plural experience of the coalfield: minorities are so well integrated that they contribute more than their mite to the radical tradition.

More recently, a dissenting tradition has arisen from the work of historians who have excavated the tangled history of ethnic conflict in Wales. For instance, Paul O'Leary has unearthed twenty major violent incidents against the Irish between 1826 and 1882.[4] Geoffrey Alderman and Colin Holmes have atomized the Tredegar anti-Jewish riots of 1911 and Jon Parry has examined the anti-Irish

24

disturbances of 1882. He eloquently understates the conclusion of the new line: 'The Welsh have never been immune to prejudice.'[5]

I

Riots were not weekly or even annual events in modern Welsh history. However, there is evidence that an ethnic ordering of society was apparent in everyday situations. Migrants to south Wales in the nineteenth century moved along ethnically laid tracks. Until the 1890s, English incomers went predominantly to the ports, while the Welsh headed for the Valleys. Similar segregation was discernible within Swansea. The English and the Irish tended to settle in the town itself, and to form separate communities. The Welsh went for the northern industrial fringe in communities such as Landore and Morriston. Such a distribution implied differences in occupations as well as in residence, for the jobs of the commercial core would be quite different from those of the industrial villages. In the south Wales ports similar hierarchies existed; the best seafaring jobs were the weekly ships to London that allowed the maintenance of family life, and these were dominated by the native-born. Diverse ethnic groups filled the bulk of Cardiff's tramp trade. This also applied in the coalfield, where those English people who arrived in the Valleys found that the best jobs – coal cutting – went to the native Welsh while they were left with haulage and surface work. The influx of English into nineteenth-century Wales also caused occasional friction, especially in the north Wales coalfield where this was one of the ways in which class solidarity was mobilized.[6] There was a tradition of running English managers out of town, culminating in the incident that gave rise to the tragic Mold Riots of 1869. Accusations of favouritism shown to English colliers had formed the background to the conflict. Less evidence of this has come to light in south Wales, but there were occasional suggestions of conflict and hostility.

Neil Evans

In 1874 Welsh workers backed locally based trade unions in preference to those from across the border in the 'Red Dragon' revolt, and later the Miners' Federation of Great Britain was often referred to as 'the English union'.[7]

The 1911 census showed that quite substantial foreign minorities were located in Wales. As south Wales in the previous decade had attracted incomers at a rate only surpassed within the Western world by the United States, this is not surprising. As far as the male population is concerned, areas of south Wales had high proportions of foreign-born. Cardiff was second only to London, while Swansea came fourth and Newport sixth. Merthyr trailed behind at thirty-fourth and Glamorgan at forty-third. The figures for women were quite different, with Cardiff coming seventeenth, Swansea twenty-first and Merthyr twenty-eighth. No figures were given for Newport and Glamorgan, which had insignificant proportions of foreign-born women. This implies that relatively few incomers emigrated as families, and meant that the potential for conflicts based upon sexual jealousy was always present. In marked contrast with this relative cosmopolitanism within Britain came rural Wales, the counties of which formed a solid phalanx from no. 6 to no. 11 in the table of counties with the highest proportion of native-born in Britain.

While some places in south Wales came to be quite cosmopolitan, they also had distinct cultural hierarchies. The Irish were often perceived as being less inclined to work than the native-born. Nor was the situation much different among the younger generation in the inter-war period. A survey of schoolchildren in different parts of Wales found a prevalence of stereotyped views of foreigners, often based on books and the cinema and which the authors thought offered little hope of fostering international understanding unless educational institutions intervened more directly.

Abercraf, at the head of the Swansea Valley, had diversity thrust suddenly upon it just before the First World War. In the space of a few years about 250 foreign migrants, mainly Spaniards, arrived. They were seen by many of the local populace as part of a devious ploy by coalowners to subvert the Minimum Wage Act of 1912 with cheap foreign labour. Their huts were said to be highly overcrowded, and the people themselves a moral threat. In July 1914 there were protest meetings that called for their expulsion from local pits, and an incident when native miners refused to work if they were allowed underground. M. Esteban defended his compatriots by claiming that the Spaniards were proportionately more unionized than the local miners and appealed to the international solidarity of the Welsh. The 'moral panic' in the agitation gives the lie to the claim by the chairman of a protest meeting (and the socialist newspaper *Llais Llafur*) that there was no hostility to foreigners as such in the campaign. In the end the issue seems to have been swallowed by the outbreak of war, and the growing prosperity that it brought.

Naturally, the bulk of such reactions came in industrial south Wales, but they were not confined to that area. One intriguing case of ethnic conflict occurred in mid-Cardiganshire at the turn of the century. The local lead industry had almost slipped into oblivion by then, but in 1899 a Belgian company bought the Frongoch mine near Ponterwyd. Some of the workers they engaged were Italians, who were placed in specially constructed barracks, and an old English Wesleyan chapel was converted as a Catholic place of worship. The employers sought to foster good feeling between the two sections of the workforce by providing a free tea, after which both communities sang their favourite songs. Yet the reputation of both countries as lands of song did not prove strong enough to overcome animosities that developed in the course of work. The whole enterprise was a marginal one, and the economic pressures exerted by management were intense. Resistance was conducted along ethnic lines with the Italians going out on strike on one occasion, followed by the Welsh on another. Once the Welsh bodily prevented the Italians from entering the mine. In one dispute dynamite was placed near the barracks of the Italians, and near the home of the mine captain. No-one was injured, and care was taken that this was the case, yet it is a scene more reminiscent of the American hard-rock mining frontier and the dynamiters of the Western Federation of Miners than of 'tranquil' rural Wales.

Not all settlements of ethnic minorities gave rise to pathological reactions, however. Jews, for instance, settled into Cardiff and formed a distinct but non-ghettoized community that seems to have suffered little overt hostility and to have been typical of the smaller Jewish settlements in British cities. The earliest Jewish settlements in Wales stretch back into the eighteenth century, and Swansea was probably the first town with a Hebrew community. In the late nineteenth century the influx of Jews fleeing East European pogroms pushed small numbers of them into scattered settlements in the Valleys. The chief rabbi visited south Wales and stressed that Jews were a community that had developed in parallel with the general development of Cardiff (and, by implication, of south Wales). A few worked underground but the strictly orthodox would not work the Saturday shift and were sometimes dismissed for this.[8]

The development of Italian settlements was similar. They came from a concentrated area of the country, Bardi in the Ceno Valley in Emilia-Romagna, escaping rural poverty to find a niche in the development of temperance bars in south Wales. Expanding prosperity drew them from Cardiff and other cities into the Valleys, and they became less clustered than the Italians who settled in England. They offered something new, even exotic, a welcome alternative to the pub. Many challenged the Sunday trading laws to provide a service and a profit – it was one of the more lucrative days of the week for takings. They recruited their labour from home along the *padrone* system and survived in a marginal trade by self and family exploitation. By 1938 they ran more than 300 cafes in south Wales. Because every cafe needed its catchment area, they never formed a concentrated community, and had few communal institutions. This meant that they were well integrated and formed only a loosely-knit community.[9]

Less edifying were the reactions to Gypsies. An encampment at Barmouth in 1901 drew the wrath of a local newspaper that demanded that it be cleared away, and in 1914 the *Welsh Outlook* published an interview with a Gypsy named Eli Burton who stressed that real Gypsies were not thieves, murderers or rapists and stressed the need for education. He argued that every town ought to have a field with proper conveniences and affordable camping fees. A hundred years on many of his descendants are still waiting.

Both world wars provide evidence of conflict and cooperation between ethnic groups in Wales. There was a rapturous early reception for Belgian refugees at the outbreak of the First World War, with crowds turning out on the streets in welcome, and hints that no society hostess was complete without at least one Belgian family to display. Large numbers were dispersed from Cardiff throughout south Wales, and offers of places exceeded the number of refugees. Many went to Swansea, where an existing community of metalworkers from Belgium provided the focus for settlement. Members of the Welsh intelligentsia foresaw a great cultural bonus for Wales because of the presence of so many distinguished writers and artists. Their talents were rapidly drawn upon in order to launch concerts that would finance the refugees' stay. However, when it became evident that the war would not be over by Christmas, tensions began to emerge. It was felt that Belgians could be either working or, better still, fighting. Yet trade unions were sometimes suspicious of their claims to work. The South Wales Miners' Federation was cool, but not hostile, when its opinions were sought. It did not oppose the claim of Belgians to jobs, but stressed that unemployment still existed in some areas of south Wales.[10]

A more sinister aspect of the wartime experience is a generalized hostility to aliens, encouraged by the governmental policies enshrined in the Aliens Act of 1914. The press emphasized the alien presence in south Wales, particularly in reporting court cases. For enemy aliens the situation could be frightening. At Aberystwyth a crowd set upon the septuagenarian Professor Ethé, who had given forty years of service to the University College of Wales. Much of the college and enlightened Welsh opinion was appalled, but this did not prevent him from being forced away from his chair (with a pension) in 1915. There was also an attack on German immigrants in Rhyl.[11] The intolerant side of the heritage did not disappear at the end of hostilities. The dislocations of the war and a generalized hostility to 'foreigners' provided the backdrop to the anti-black riots in the ports of south-east Wales in 1919.

In the Second World War, evacuees from England played the part that the Belgians played in the First World War. There was an early welcome, and there are many stories of lifelong attachments being formed, which cannot be discounted. In the coalfield, in particular, this seems to have been a fairly smooth process. Yet there were also tensions, as East-Enders and Carmarthenshire farmers experienced culture shock in encounters that they both felt were too close. In north Wales the problems arose from the unsympathetic billeting of Catholic Irish from Liverpool on a highly Protestant Nonconformist population: 'Bohemian Ideals versus the Puritan Ethic', as one newspaper headline had it; Catholics were disturbed to find that the Protestant Sunday denied them both their church *and* the pub! Friction arose mainly out of the attempts by Catholic priests to enter homes to look after the spiritual welfare of evacuees, and the decision of many locals to take children to chapel services rather than to leave them unsupervised or with long walks to Mass. Plaid Cymru was concerned that the whole process was a threat to the Welsh language and culture, an issue that foreshadowed the issue of in-migration of the 1980s. Yet it failed to rally any significant support. Perhaps the friction was exaggerated by the shortage of solid news in the 'phoney' war, yet there certainly was some localized concern as the multicultural nature of Britain was forcibly displayed.[12]

During the war, it was chiefly the Italians who were on the receiving end. In Swansea, on the night that Italy entered the conflict, large crowds roamed the streets and damaged the property of Italian cafe owners. A cafe owner living at Aberdare later remembered having had a window broken during the war and there were also some incidents at Tonypandy. This hostility does not seem to have been long-lasting or even especially widespread. Perhaps Italians were too well established in south Wales for the feelings to be really intense. In Swansea, a suspicion that Italians had been involved in fascist movements and were sympathetic to Mussolini's regime may have contributed to the outbreak. The deaths of many Italians from south Wales on the liner *Arandora Star*, which was taking them to wartime exile in Canada when it was sunk by a German U-boat, may have turned public feelings around. Italian and German prisoners of war were put to work in some parts of south Wales, particularly around Bridgend.[13]

After the war Italian workers were recruited to fill gaps in the workforce, along with other displaced persons from Europe. The census of 1951 showed a quite substantial rise in the numbers of foreign-born in Glamorgan and Monmouthshire as compared with the last pre-war census of 1931. At Llanelli there was some resentment at the Italian presence. Yet a clear legacy of the war was a general sentiment of hostility to fascism. In Cardiff, Butetown suddenly became respectable and a symbol of tolerance to the world, though actual behaviour towards blacks changed less than did the rhetoric. In the South Wales Coalfield there was a debate about the recruitment of black labour in 1948, though much of the comment was against the colour bar.

II

The momentous social changes of the nineteenth and early twentieth centuries were frequently punctuated by anti-immigrant riots, ranging from the first serious attack on the Irish in 1826 to anti-Jewish and anti-Chinese riots in 1911 and the assault on black newcomers in 1919. This ended a tradition of communal violence against outsiders, though this did not mean the end of ethnic violence.[14] Does this mean that the troubles of the mid-nineteenth century and early twentieth century were simply problems of adjustment – once the Welsh came to understand their guests they learned to live peaceably with them? There is certainly some mileage in this argument. It seems to fit the Irish best of all. A string of riots over almost sixty years gave way to growing cooperation over Home Rule and labour politics in the 1880s. Wales and Ireland increasingly marched together in political terms from 1868 to 1922. In Cardiff an Irish 'ghetto' broke down and at least some of its former inhabitants experienced increasing prosperity. In the 1890s Cardiff had an Irish Catholic mayor. Indeed, the Irish were integrated enough to be among the major assailants of blacks and Arabs in 1919, though perhaps this also shows the precariousness of the improved position of the community. An Arab or black invasion of 'their' quarter of the city threatened to place them back at the bottom of the pile. A West Indian with whom I discussed this issue once told me that Newtown was 'Irishmen's quarters' and 'this [Butetown] was our quarters'. When Jim Callaghan was selected as Labour candidate for Cardiff South, he (correctly) informed Protestants that he was a Protestant, but apparently omitted to do so in Catholic areas (where presumably his name made him seem like a Catholic). This suggests some ill ease over the issue, but there is no evidence of serious conflict either.[15] This integration presumably applies to the Spanish community by the 1930s, given the size of the Spanish Aid movement in south Wales, though some evidence from the

1920s suggests that if this is true it must have been a fairly recent change.

Other evidence suggests that for European immigrants the processes of adjustment were not too severe and that there was considerable integration. Some groups with immigrant origins found it difficult to maintain their identity in the post-war world. Italians complained that they were 'Bloody Italians' in Wales, and 'Bloody Inglesi' (*sic*) in Italy. Newcomers faced less fracturing choices: Greeks in Cardiff, for instance, could largely impose their home-country values on their children. But the most poignant story is that of the Jews. The numbers of the Orthodox declined throughout the post-war period, and already by the 1930s they were funnelling back from the Valleys to Cardiff and the other coastal towns. Contrary to popular belief, the pawnshop trade in which they were concentrated was devastated by the Depression and the Valleys communities never recovered. Politically it took Jews a long time to arrive, with Cardiff getting its first Jewish councillor in 1928 and its first Jewish lord mayor in 1987, though there were several Jewish deputy lord mayors in the meantime. They gained a collective voice for the first time since the turn of the century with the publication from 1951 onwards of *CAJEX* – the Journal of the Cardiff Jewish Ex-Servicemen and Women. It became the mouthpiece of all south Wales Jewry and an important repository of historical articles on their experience. Yet it tended to slip into nostalgia for departed Jewish communities and personalities, along with fears for the future as the birth rate fell, employment prospects took young people out of south Wales and they were not replaced by incomers.[16]

The problem was acutely felt by the Cathedral Road Synagogue in Cardiff, a symbol of the Victorian expansion of the faith. Yet their spokespeople stressed constantly the way in which they were integrated into Welsh society, and the lack of anti-Semitism. Recorded instances of grave desecration in Brynmawr in the early 1970s do not seriously challenge this

33

picture. Jews were so well integrated that they shared the central experiences of the majority population – the movement to the coast, an ageing population and secularization. Perhaps many felt less need for an all-embracing faith and culture in these circumstances.

The argument for integration over time carries us a little of the way forward, but it does not have a great deal of stamina. It falls at two major hurdles. Most importantly, there were, of course, few incomers in Welsh society in the 1920s and 1930s. The history of that period is one of devastating emigration, with somewhere between a fifth and a quarter of the Welsh population leaving Wales. We should hardly expect to find massive conflict between incomers and natives in these circumstances. Immigrant communities were not being created or, generally speaking, even 'topped up'; the Depression was too big to be explained by anyone as being the product of the fairly small minority groups that there were in Wales. In short, the *circumstances* for conflict did not exist to any great extent.

The second reason is in some ways the exception that proves the first rule. There probably were black newcomers to Cardiff in the 1920s and they faced unrelenting hostility from the local authorities and the trade unions. The absence of overt riot is misleading here, for there were far more effective ways of continuing the process that had begun on the streets in 1919 into the post-war period. Inverting Clausewitz we might describe it as the continuation of war by other means. After the publication of a hostile report by the chief constable on the 'coloured' population of Cardiff in 1929, Swansea did its own investigation, but decided it had nothing to fear. A Colonial Office investigator during the Second World War found the Barry black community to be less depressing than Cardiff and more united than South Shields. Yet he was not complacent and pointed out that people remembered the events of 1919 and they feared that they would not retain equality of opportunity at the end of the war. They were right to be concerned about the way that blacks were treated in south Wales. Colin Holmes, the most knowledgeable historian of the experience of immigrants and minorities in modern British history, after discussing the registration of black British seamen under the Aliens Order of 1925, concludes: 'Viewed in a sober historical perspective there are few clearer cases of the institutional oppression of minorities in early twentieth-century Britain.'[17] This points towards the need for comparison if the picture in Wales is to be understood. Belfast, Liverpool and Glasgow provide measures that allow us to find a scale for ethnic conflict in Wales.

III

Belfast could lull us into a false sense of security. Its ethnic conflict is so deep-rooted and persistent that no other city in the Western world compares with it. There was little in its situation that really compared with south Wales – a pre-existing pattern of segregation, rooted in the plantations of the seventeenth century, was disturbed by the rapid urbanization of Catholics in the earlier part of the nineteenth century. By mid-century Catholics accounted for a third of the population. The violence that followed from the 1850s onwards seems to have been a more-or-less conscious effort to force them out of Belfast – and Ulster – and one that was overwhelmingly 'successful'. By 1900, Catholics had been reduced to a quarter of the population of the city, and confined to a tight ghetto within it. Economic competition played a vital part in this whole process, but the occasion (rather than the reason) for the decisive political realignment (one that Ulster still lives – and dies – with) was the Home Rule split of the 1880s. Where politics had once been an alliance of Presbyterians and Catholics against the dominant Church of Ireland, it was now a Protestant common front against Catholics. At the risk of sounding antique, the superstructure somewhat tardily followed the base. The peak of violence came in the years of rebellion and civil war, between 1920 and 1922, but sectarianism remained a constant thread throughout the inter-war period, expressing itself most forcibly in the riots of 1935. There was also a strand of Protestant extremism that saw its own community as riddled with traitors, while Catholicism was united, aggressive and bent on domination. Since the 1960s these conflicts have been renewed; old conflicts have been reproduced in new settings, and the peace process seems to be a fragile instrument for breaking the vicious circle.[18]

Liverpool is different, but not by a great deal. Its sectarianism is also deep-rooted, and predates the Irish Famine. It has been constantly renewed by being one of the key centres of Irish immigration into Britain. Not only did this result in massive bloodletting on the streets, but it also infected social institutions and politics. Liverpool has Orange and Green divisions – and a Catholic community that returned an Irish Nationalist MP throughout the period 1885–1929. The issue took enough votes from the left to stop Labour from winning control of the city council until 1955; Tories needed the Orange card to win power. Liverpool had much closer connections with Ireland than did south Wales, but unlike Glasgow, it has few links with Ulster – apart perhaps from economic ones in the shipbuilding industry. Its fierce Protestantism seems to have been a native growth rather than an import. Lancashire was an area where the Reformation had not taken very deep root and fear of recusancy fuelled Protestant visions. Tories found that defence of church and state also made a good electoral rallying cry in the era of industrialization. The city's international trade drew in a diverse group of migrants from the British Empire as well. It became not just an Orange and Green city, but what Merfyn Jones has described as a rainbow city. Between 1909 and 1919 there were five major outbreaks of ethnic violence, not all of which have yet found their chronicler.[19]

Glasgow was not quite like either Liverpool or Belfast. There, in the other major reception area of Irish migration to

Britain, Orange and Green rivalries became set into social institutions, notoriously into its two football teams. Celtic, founded in 1887, gathered up existing Catholic support over the wider industrial area and its success in a society in which Catholics had few advantages was a symbol of achievement. Rangers was founded to counter this, and because it had a much larger pool of potential players could remain far more exclusively sectarian than Celtic could be without sacrificing success on the field. The teams were both champions and surrogates for wider Scottish/Irish, Protestant/Catholic divisions and helped channel bitter conflicts. The flow of people ensured that such institutions of civil society had a high longevity. Like Liverpool, it was part of an 'industrial triangle' that bound it to Belfast, but here there was also substantial contact with Protestant Ulster as well as with the Catholic majority of Ireland. Yet sectarianism did not dominate politics in Scotland in the way that it did in Lancashire. The redeeming factor was Scottish (and Glasgow's) Liberalism. It wavered in the 1880s with a swing to Liberal Unionism, but there was nothing like the Lancashire Tory tradition for sectarianism to feed upon. Indeed, in Glasgow it was probably the Tories who were the victims of sectarian division; Liberalism partly rested on the division of its opponents. Scotland's lurch to sectarian politics came in the period between the wars. It was a rapid rise and fall, originating in exaggerated fears of an Irish influx during the disturbances of 1920–2 and dying as the exponents of Protestant fundamentalism drifted too close to the flame of fascism and burned their wings. They plummeted into oblivion.[20]

How did south Wales differ from this experience? In the nineteenth century, it was never one of the major centres of Irish migration, even though it had a significant Irish presence. Only in a few communities were the Irish a central presence in the 1850s. In 1861 they were about a third of the population of Cardiff, and local opinion considered with alarm the prospects of a town that was fairly evenly divided between Welsh, Irish and English. These Irish were over-whelmingly from Munster, and therefore Catholics; unlike Glasgow there was no link with Ulster Protestantism and, unlike Lancashire, no pre-existing Catholic–Protestant tensions to draw upon. Anyway, the Irish soon lost much of their visibility in Wales. In Cardiff the Irish-born remained more or less constant in numbers for the rest of the century, while the city's size mushroomed until they became dwarfed by its growth. Outside the major south Wales ports the largest concentrations of Irish by the late nineteenth century were within a ten-mile radius of Tredegar, in the old iron-making district. In the Rhondda there were very few and the Sunday mass at Tonypandy needed to draw on all parts of the two valleys to sustain itself. For most of south Wales Joseph Keating's description of his native Mountain Ash as a colony would apply admirably. Adding the second and third genera-tion to this picture would, of course, enlarge the Irish population, but not change the basic argument. The minority became integrated into Liberal and Labour politics, and into trade unions. They caused none of the enthusiasm for Liberal Unionism that was a Scottish reaction to their presence.

In south Wales the Irish become increasingly 'invisible' from the 1880s, as they did in most parts of Britain, apart from London, central Scotland, Lancashire and the West Midlands, where their communities continued to grow signif-icantly into the twentieth century. They ceased to be serious competitors to the Welsh in the expanding areas of the econ-omy after 1850. This was partly the result of riots that prevented them from obtaining anything more than toeholds in the burgeoning steam coal areas. A series of riots in the early 1850s, the culmination of a very tense period through-out south Wales, bodily expelled them from the Rhondda; there was more than a shade of Belfast in this process. They seem to have been acceptable in established areas like Cardiff and Merthyr, where they were confined to a fairly narrow range of occupations. Merthyr probably had a more settled

Irish population than did Cardiff but it was mostly confined to jobs in the more poorly paid sections of iron-working. In Merthyr Vale and Aberfan, however, the Irish did become more integrated into the coalmining workforce. Tellingly, the riot in Tredegar in 1882 came when that community was undergoing the shift from iron-making to steel-making and coalmining. Again, the Irish were not welcome in an expanding sector. Occasionally, there were tensions at a later period, as in Pembrokeshire in the late 1930s, where a series of fights with locals took place. In Cardiff the ethnic conflicts did not intertwine in the way that they did in Liverpool. The tensions of the Irish were mid-Victorian and slowly faded away. European sailors were seen as competitors for jobs, holding the centre of the stage until the turn of the century, when they were displaced by people of diverse skin colours. There was a succession of issues rather than an entanglement of them. None of these issues became central to politics and society; religious and national freedom – and later class dignity – were much more compelling.[21]

IV

The story so far has taken us up to, and slightly beyond, the Second World War. What has happened in Wales in the period when Britain has become recognized as a multi-ethnic society? Have the Welsh been immune to prejudice? There were no riots in 1958 when Notting Hill and Nottingham experienced scaled-down versions of the disturbances of 1919. Nor were there major riots in the 1980s when the population of inner cities rebelled (rather in the manner of the American ghetto rebellions of the 1960s) against the way in which they were policed and their economic position.

Wales, in the post-war period, was not a major centre of black immigration. It took until 1961 for the overall population of Wales to regain the level it had been in 1921. Compared with many areas of Britain it had a persistent problem of unemployment. Black immigrants headed instead for the 'industrial coffin' – the south-east, the Midlands and the north of England. West Indians largely bypassed Wales. Some tried to come to Butetown, but on the whole they were not well received. It is not unusual for an urbanized minority to see a further rural influx as a challenge to whatever social position it has won for itself. Yet the relative lack of jobs was surely more important. The established black population began to make the transition from shipping to shore-based work in this period. Black newcomers went either for rapidly expanding areas like the south-east of England, where there was low unemployment, or for areas like the Midlands where the population was fairly stable, but where whites were abandoning certain jobs and areas of housing. Most of the later comers in Wales were from the Indian subcontinent. They came in a rush before the first Act to restrict Commonwealth immigration was passed in 1962 and overwhelmed the existing Asian communities. The result was more widespread dispersal than had been characteristic of West Indians. Only in Cardiff have they formed a very significant community, in terms of numbers.

Philip Jones's study of the dispersal of black immigrants in the decade 1961–71 does not consider any community with a black population of less than 1,500. Cardiff is the only place in Wales that he had to locate on his map. At the beginning of the 1980s there were 11,485 Commonwealth-born people in Wales, though the black population would have been considerably bigger, with an estimated 20,000 in the Cardiff travel-to-work area alone by 1989. Generally speaking, these people did not head for Butetown, but for the other inner-city areas of Cardiff, and Grangetown in particular. They formed clusters of different nationalities, each with its own place of worship, and largely apart from the city in their social and cultural life. One group that has been particularly studied – the Bhuttra Sikhs – have displayed this tendency to an unusual extent. Few of its 300 or so members in the 1970s could speak English comfortably. Since then there has been some further dispersal. Butetown and the Valleys both have some shopkeepers from the Indian subcontinent, but there are no large concentrations. In the 1980s the South Glamorgan Community Relations Executive found a good deal of discontent among the black population who were in touch with larger communities elsewhere in Britain, and were well aware of the lack of progress in south Wales in areas like multicultural education. It had taken ten years to persuade the police to appoint a liaison officer, and longer to gain a social worker with knowledge of Asian languages. It is no surprise that a survey in the late 1980s found blacks to be overwhelmingly concentrated in the unskilled, semi-skilled and basic clerical categories of employment, or that in Cardiff in 1987 only 3% of black school leavers found jobs, compared with 11% of their white contemporaries.[22]

The lack of any major concentration of blacks probably influences the degree of expressed racial prejudice in Wales. Studies of Britain generally show that propinquity to black immigrants increases hostility to them – or at least it did so in the 1960s – in the short run. On the other hand, casual contacts (as opposed to living close together) tended to reduce feelings of hostility. In the same period Liberal and Labour voters – the bulk of the Welsh electorate at that time – were less inclined to be racially prejudiced than were Conservative supporters. Two surveys of Welsh opinion, in 1966 and 1984, support this conclusion. The evidence shows that the Welsh came into the lowest segments of racial hostility in both the studies. This may not mean a great deal – it is after all just attitudes rather than behaviour – and in the case of most people, attitudes that are formed without there being much experience to root them in. Possibly the very idea of Welsh tolerance has helped to produce these results. There is less scope for optimism in a study of attitudes conducted in Swansea in 1983–4, where 44% of the population showed no overt prejudice, but 56% did so; among the young there was little middle ground with a clear split between tolerance and extreme prejudice as compared with older age groups.

41

Race has not entered Welsh politics to any large degree in the post-war period. Nor have there been any major disturbances. This may be the result of Cardiff's having a low percentage of its population in the most deprived categories, certainly as compared with Manchester and Liverpool. Butetown is also rather cut off from the rest of the inner city and this may have made a difference. When an incident did start there in July 1981, a media blackout was operated. The police were fearful of being drawn into an ambush and allowed the destruction of thousands of pounds' worth of property in Bute Terrace as a result. As riots were generally spread by word of mouth rather than television, local geography may have played a part. Anyway, in Butetown it appears that the established leadership has largely maintained its position and authority, whereas a key feature of riots that broke out elsewhere was the mounting of a challenge to leaders who were seen as too accommodating to the local authorities. Also, in a long-settled community there would not have been the rift between the experiences of first and second generation, which was crucial in many English cities. In 1981 the energies of Cardiff's Rastafarians were absorbed on a project to convert the old slipper baths into workshops and a centre for the unemployed. When they failed to gain government aid for the project, they wondered whether rioting would have been a more productive use of their time![23]

The Welsh context is illuminated by studies of race in Scottish politics conducted by Robert Miles and his associates at the University of Glasgow. Like Wales, Scotland parades the idea that it is exceptionally tolerant and thinks the English could learn a thing or two from them in this respect, as in others. In the surveys for which Welsh evidence was quoted above, Scotland's position is contradictory – high in one, low in the other. Miles, however, demonstrates that while racism is not absent in Scotland, and was fostered by a history that included participation in the slave trade and missionary activity, Scottish politics have not become racialized as English politics have become. The reasons for this are not tolerance but because of the nature of Scottish society and politics. Nationalism has been a major concern of the post-war period, with the result that many blame the decline of the Scottish economy on central control rather than upon immigrants, as can be the case in England. As there are relatively few immigrants they are not very conspicuous and tend not to come to the forefront in politics. Scottish civil society is also deeply divided into Orange and Green components, so that it is more difficult to see just what identity and culture black newcomers could be seen as threatening. Finally, there has been no strong tradition of fascism in Scottish society, and fascist groups have played a key part in putting race onto the political agenda in England. Most of this can be simply lifted from Scotland and applied to Wales. The main difference is the absence of Orange and Green divisions in Wales, but perhaps the growing divisions over language as this became a central political issue from the 1960s onwards have filled this particular gap. Language came onto the political agenda in Wales just as race was coming to prominence in England. The landmark BBC lecture *Tynged yr Iaith* (The fate of the language) was delivered in the very year that the Commonwealth Immigration Act of 1962 was passed.

In the 1980s both Scotland and Wales encountered the issue of different kinds of incomers – English in-migrants who seemed to challenge important aspects of local life and culture. They were instances of what have been called 'dominant minorities'. In Scotland the dispute was chiefly over the 'Englishing' of key institutions – education, art galleries, museums – and, though this has not been mentioned, one might add Rangers. Cultural imperialists running such institutions, it is charged, have failed to make distinctively Scottish aspects of their charges flourish. In Wales the issue is different, despite some attempts to link them. The domination of institutions by incomers is less apparent, if only because the requirement of speaking Welsh for many jobs reduces their impact. It is most marked in the University of Wales, outside its distinctively Welsh enclaves. The more serious issue in Wales is that of the impact of incomers on the heartland of the Welsh language. This is causing an anguish that is visible among many Welsh speakers. While it would be rash to make any real or sustained comparison with Loyalist and Republican terrorism in Northern Ireland, this was the only other sustained political campaign using violence in these islands in the 1980s. A recent opinion poll shows considerable support for the cause, if not for the methods. A dominant minority is, by its nature, a different thing from the poor and frequently despised immigrants who have figured more often in modern Welsh history. At least it forms a convenient place at which to conclude this survey.[24]

V

How do we conclude? In the past 150 years Wales has been the host to substantial numbers of immigrants in the period before the First World War, and relatively few thereafter. If there has been relatively little conflict with them – at least compared with Belfast, Glasgow and Liverpool – this must be the reason, rather than some inherent tolerance in the Welsh psyche. When there have been conflicts, they have been among the most vicious within Britain. It is only the peculiar historical circumstances of Wales that have ensured that these have not become ingrained as a tradition. The mechanisms that have sustained and escalated conflicts in other parts of the islands have – mercifully – been missing. There would seem to be little scope for self-congratulation in this. Breast-beating – or its converse, remorse – are not the most important things in the study of the history of minority groups and immigrants. The point is not to praise tolerance, but to uncover the causes of antagonism. Understanding is the thing

Immigrants and Minorities in Wales

we need most desperately. While Marx rightly stressed that understanding the world and changing it were different things, there is no need for him, or us, to conclude that the two are not closely related to each other.

Notes

1. This is an abridged and slightly revised version of an article that first appeared in *Llafur*, 5/4 (1991), 5–26.
2. The best general study of this topic for Britain as a whole is C. Holmes, *John Bull's Island: Immigration in British Society, 1871–1971* (London, 1988), which has much Welsh material.
3. H. Francis and D. Smith, *The Fed: A History of the South Wales Miners in the Twentieth Century* (London, 1980; new edn in paperback, Cardiff, 1998), chapter 1.
4. P. O'Leary, *Immigration and Integration: The Irish in Wales, 1798–1922* (Cardiff, 2000); P. O'Leary, 'Anti-Irish riots in Wales, 1826–1882', *Llafur*, 5/4 (1991), 27–36.
5. G. Alderman, 'The anti-Jewish riots of August 1911 in south Wales', *Welsh History Review*, 6/2 (1972), 190–200; C. Holmes, 'The Tredegar riots of 1911: anti-Jewish disturbances in south Wales', *Welsh History Review*, 11/2 (1982), 214–25; J. Parry, 'The Tredegar anti-Irish riots of 1882', *Llafur*, 3/4 (1983), 20–3.
6. P. N. Jones, 'Some aspects of immigration into the Glamorganshire coalfield between 1881 and 1911', *Transactions of the Honourable Society of Cymmrodorion* (1969), part I; J. R. Williams, 'The influence of foreign nationalities upon the social life of the people of Merthyr Tydfil', *Sociological Review*, 18/2 (1926); H. Francis, 'The secret world of the south Wales miner: the relevance of oral history', in D. Smith (ed.), *A People and a Proletariat: Essays in Welsh History, 1780–1980* (London, 1980), pp. 166–80; I. Gwynedd Jones, 'The making of an industrial community', in G. Williams (ed.), *Swansea: An Illustrated History* (Swansea, 1990), pp. 115–44.
7. E. Rogers, 'The history of trade unionism in the coalmining industry of north Wales', *Transactions of the Denbighshire Historical Society*, 16–18 (1967–9), 100–27, 147–76, 113–35; A. Burge, 'The Mold

45

riots of 1869', *Llafur*, 3/2 (1982), 42–57; A. Jones, 'The Red Dragon revolt', *Welsh History Review*, 12/2 (1984), 187–224; L. J. Williams, 'New unionism in south Wales, 1889–1892', *Welsh History Review*, 1/4 (1963), 413–29.

8   U. Henriques, *The Jews of South Wales: Historical Studies* (Cardiff, 1992); B. Goldblum, 'Swansea' (papers presented to the Jewish Historical Society Conference, 1975); N. H. Saunders, *The Swansea Hebrew Congregation, 1730–1980* (Swansea, 1980).

9   L. Sponza, *Italian Immigrants in Nineteenth-Century Britain: Realities and Images* (Leicester, 1988), pp. 17–18, 33, 58, 102, 110, 275; C. Hughes, *Lime, Lemon and Sarsaparilla: The Italian Community in South Wales, 1881–1945* (Bridgend, 1992).

10 J. R. Alban, 'The activities of the Swansea Belgian Refugees Committee, 1914–16', *Gower*, 26 (1975), 80–4; M. Vincentelli, 'The Davies family and Belgian refugee artists and musicians in Wales', *National Library of Wales Journal*, 22/2 (1981), 226–33.

11 C. J. Williams, 'An anti-German riot in Rhyl in 1915', *Flintshire Historical Society Publications*, 26 (1973–4), 170–4. For context see P. Panayi, 'Germans in Britain during the First World War', *Historical Research*, 64/153 (1991), 63–76.

12 P. Paterson, 'Freedom in Wales', *Spectator* (23 April 1983); A. Calder, *The People's War* (London, 1969); R. Inglis, *The Children's War: Evacuation, 1939–1945* (London, 1989), pp. 24–5, 30, 72; T. L. Crosby, *The Impact of Civilian Evacuation in the Second World War* (London, 1986), p. 40; C. R. Davies, 'Early educational problems of the Second World War in the Rhyl area', *Flintshire Historical Society Publications*, 27 (1975–6), 119–28; G. Wallis, 'North Wales receives: an account of the first government evacuation scheme, 1939–40', *Flintshire Historical Society Publications*, 32 (1989), 109–34.

13 Hughes, *Lime, Lemon and Sarsaparilla*, chapter 4.

14 See chapter 6 below. Also N. Evans, 'Across the universe: racial conflict and the postwar crisis in imperial Britain, 1919–1925', *Immigrants and Minorities*, 13 (1994), 59–88; G. Alderman, 'Into the vortex: south Wales Jewry before 1914', *Jewish Historical Society of England* (1975); P. N. Jones, 'Baptist chapels as an index of cultural transition in the South Wales Coalfield before 1914', *Journal of*

Historical Geography, 2/4 (1976), 347–60; D. Llwyd Morgan, 'The Welsh biblical heritage', *Transactions of the Caenarfonshire Historical Society* (1988); G. Tegai Hughes, 'Dreams of a promised land' (lecture to Meirionnydd Historical and Record Society, Towyn Branch, 26 November 1971). I am very grateful to Dr Hughes for letting me see his notes. J. Cayford, 'In search of John Chinaman', *Llafur*, 5/4 (1991), 37–50; J. P. May, 'The British working class and the Chinese, 1870–1911, with particular reference to the seamen's strike of 1911', unpublished University of Warwick MA thesis, 1973; J. P. May, 'The Chinese in Britain', in C. Holmes (ed.), *Immigrants and Minorities in British Society* (London, 1978), pp. 111–24.

15 J. V. Hickey, 'The origin and development of the Irish community in Cardiff', unpublished University of Wales MA thesis, 1959; J. V. Hickey, *Urban Catholics: Urban Catholics in England and Wales from 1829 to the Present Day* (London, 1967); P. Kellner and C. Hitchens, *Callaghan: The Road to No. 10* (London, 1976), pp. 5–6.

16 Williams, 'Foreign nationalities'; Francis, *Miners Against Fascism*, passim; Hughes, *Lime, Lemon and Sarsaparilla*.

17 B. Thomas, 'Wales and the Atlantic economy', in Thomas (ed.), *The Welsh Economy: Studies in Expansion* (Cardiff, 1962), pp. 1–29; N. Evans, 'Regulating the reserve army: Arabs, Blacks and the local state in Cardiff, 1919–1945', in K. Lunn (ed.), *Race and Labour in Twentieth-Century Britain* (London, 1985), pp. 68–115; K. Little, *Negroes in Britain: A Study of Race Relations in English Society* (second edn, London, 1972); M. Sherwood, 'Racism and resistance: Cardiff in the 1930s and 1940s', *Llafur*, 5/4 (1991), 51–70; P. B. Rich, *Race and Empire in British Politics* (second edn, Cambridge, 1990), chapter 6; C. Holmes, *A Tolerant Country? Immigrants, Refugees and Minorities in Britain* (London, 1991), p. 36.

18 S. Gribbons, 'An Irish city: Belfast in 1911', in D. Harkness and M. O'Dowd (eds), *The Town in Ireland* (*Historical Studies*, 13, Belfast, 1981), pp. 203–20; S. E. Baker, 'Orange and Green: Belfast, 1832–1912', in H. J. Dyos and M. Wolff (eds), *The Victorian City: Images and Realities* (London, 1973), pp. 789–814; A. C. Hepburn, 'Catholics in the north of Ireland, 1850–1921', in Hepburn (ed.), *Minorities in History* (*Historical Studies*, 12, 1978), pp. 84–101, and

Hepburn, 'Work, class and religion in Belfast, 1871–1911', *Irish Social and Economic History*, 10 (1983), 84–101; chapters by F. Heatly and B. Collins in J. C. Beckett et al. (eds), *Belfast: The Making of the City* (Belfast, 1983).

19   P. J. Waller, *Democracy and Sectarianism: A Political and Social History of Liverpool, 1868–1939* (Liverpool, 1981); F. Neal, *Sectarian Violence: The Liverpool Experience, 1819–1914* (Manchester, 1988); T. Lane, *Liverpool: Gateway of Empire* (London, 1987); M. Jones, 'Rainbow city: the Irish and others in Liverpool, 1820–1914', paper at the Lipman Seminar, 1991.

20   B. Murray, *The Old Firm: Sectarianism, Sport and Society in Scotland* (Edinburgh, 1984); Murray, *Glasgow's Giants: 100 Years of the Old Firm* (Edinburgh, 1988); T. Gallagher, *Glasgow: The Uneasy Peace* (Manchester, 1987); Gallagher, *Edinburgh Divided: John Cormack and No Popery in the 1930s* (Edinburgh, 1987); J. Smith, 'Class, skill and sectarianism in Glasgow and Liverpool, 1880–1914', in R. J. Morris (ed.), *Class, Power and Social Structure in British Nineteenth-Century Towns* (Leicester, 1986), pp. 157–203; S. Bruce, *No Pope of Rome: Militant Protestantism in Modern Scotland* (Edinburgh, 1985); G. Walker and T. Gallagher (eds), *Sermons and Battle Hymns: Protestant Popular Culture in Modern Scotland* (Edinburgh, 1990).

21   Hickey, 'Origin and development'; P. Jenkins, 'Antipopery on the Welsh marches in the seventeenth century', *Historical Journal*, 23/2 (1980), 275–93; Jenkins, '"A Welsh Lancashire"? Monmouthsire Catholics in the eighteenth century', *Recusant History*, 15/3 (1980), 176–88; D. M. MacRaild, *Irish Migrants in Modern Britain, 1750–1922* (London, 1999).

22   R. Miles and A. Phizacklea, *White Man's Country: Racism in British Politics* (London, 1984); I. Katznelson, *Black Men, White Cities: Race, Politics and Migration in the United States, 1900–30 and Britain, 1948–68* (Oxford, 1973); E. Pilkington, *Beyond the Mother Country: West Indians and the Notting Hill White Riots* (London, 1988); R. Miles, 'The riots of 1958: notes on the ideological construction of "race relations" in Britain', *Immigrants and Minorities*, 3/3 (1984), 252–75; P. Panayi, 'Middlesbrough 1961: a British race riot of the 1960s?', *Social History*, 16/2 (1991), 139–53; P. N. Jones, 'The

distribution and diffusion of the coloured population of England and Wales, 1961–1971', *Transactions of the Institute of British Geographers*, new series, 3/4 (1978), 515–32; C. Peach, 'The growth and distribution of the black population in Britain, 1945–1980', in D. A. Coleman (ed.), *Demography of Immigrants and Minority Groups in the United Kingdom* (London, 1982), pp. 23–42; L. Bloom, 'Introduction' to K. Little, *Negroes in Britain*; P. A. S. Guhman, 'Bhuttra Sikhs in Cardiff: family organisation and kinship', *New Community* (1980), 308–16.

23 R. T. Schaefer, 'Party affiliation and prejudice in Britain', *New Community*, 2/3 (1973), 296–300; idem, 'Contacts between immigrants and Englishmen: road to tolerance of intolerance?', ibid., 2 (1973), 258–71; idem, 'Regional differences in prejudice', *Regional Studies*, 9 (1975), 1–14; V. Robinson, 'Spatial variability in attitudes towards race in the United Kingdom', in P. Jackson (ed.), *Race and Racism: Essays in Social Geography* (London, 1987), pp. 133–59; V. Robinson, 'Racial antipathy in south Wales and its social and demographic correlates', *New Community*, 12/1 (1984–5), 116–24; H. Carter, 'Cardiff: local, regional and national capital', in G. Gordon (ed.), *Regional Cities in the UK* (London, 1986), pp. 179–90, at p. 184; *Arcade*, 20 (7 August 1981), and 33 (5 March 1982); M. Kettle and L. Hodges, *Uprising! The Police, the People and the Riots in Britain's Cities* (London, 1982). There is also a useful issue of the journal *Race and Class* on the 1981 riots (23/2–3, Autumn 1981–Winter 1982); C. Peach, 'A geographical perspective on the 1981 urban riots in England', *Ethnic and Racial Studies*, 9/3 (1986), 398–411.

24 R. Miles and A. Dunlop, 'The racialisation of politics in Britain: why Scotland is different', *Patterns of Prejudice*, 20/1 (1986), 20–33; idem, 'Racism in Britain: the Scottish dimension', in P. Jackson (ed.), *Race and Racism: Essays in Social Geography* (London, 1987), pp. 119–41; M. and L. Muirhead, 'Racism in Scotland: a matter for further investigation?', in D. McCrone (ed.), *Scottish Government Yearbook*, 1986 (Edinburgh, 1986), pp. 108–36; anon., 'The Englishing of Scotland', *Radical Scotland*, 35 (October–November 1988); A. C. Hepburn, 'Minorities in history', pp. 1–10, and

N. Canny, 'Dominant minorities: English settlers in Ireland and Virginia, 1550–1650', pp. 51–69, both in Hepburn, *Minorities in History*; 'Rift valleys' (Channel 4 television programme, transmitted 1991); D. Balsom, 'The smoke behind the fires: the recent survey examining the arson campaign', *Planet*, 73 (February–March 1989), 16–19.

2

Slaughter and Salvation:
Welsh Missionary Activity
and British Imperialism*

JANE AARON

Two centuries ago, on 19 October 1816, a young Welsh woman barely seventeen years of age embarked on the good ship *Alacrity* bound on a great adventure. Ann Jones from Llanidloes had married Evan Evans from Llanrwst just a fortnight previously, and she now set sail with her new husband for the Cape of Good Hope, which at that time was part of Britain's most recently established colony. Motivated by the need to secure for the merchant ships of the East India Company a safe resting place on the sea route to India, the British Crown, after a series of bloody engagements with both the indigenous people of the Cape and its Dutch settlers, was finally able to fly the Union Jack over Cape Colony in 1814. Where the soldiers went, the missionaries followed. Under the auspices of the London Missionary Society, Evan Evans, fresh from his Bala ordination into the ranks of the Calvinist Methodist church, was appointed to minister the gospel to the Hottentots, or rather to the Khoikhoi, to give the people of the Cape their real name (Hottentot, which apparently denotes 'stutterer', was the name the Dutch settlers gave to the natives they encountered, whose language included an expressive pattern of clicking sounds).

Eight months after she had embarked, Ann Evans, from her new home in Bethelsdorp, a small impoverished township east of Cape Town, set about the task of attempting to convey to her family at home some impression of the world in which she now found herself. Her long letter, which was subsequently published in Wales as a fundraising missionary pamphlet (though there is no suggestion in the letter that she herself intended it to be put to such use), vividly evokes the high romance of the enterprise. She makes little herself of the perils of the journey, but one passage in particular from the letter captures the intensity of her experience, not so much in her own words, but indirectly, through her report of another woman's speech. A missionary base already established at the High Kraal had provided one resting place on the Evanses' trek into the hinterlands, and she gives her parents a detailed account of her first prayer meeting there with the Khoikhoi:

> One of the women prayed after that, and it was enough to melt the hardest heart, I think, to hear how warmly and zealously she thanked the Lord for putting it in the heart of his people in the far country to send his servants to them, poor Hottentots, the most despised nation under the whole heaven, to teach them the way of eternal life; and, O!, how she laid out her amazement that it was possible for anybody on the surface of the whole earth to possess so much love for such black, poor and wretched creatures as they were, as to leave their country, their language, their fathers and mothers, their brothers and sisters, and everything dear to nature, to come to live in the desert-lands of Africa, as the means in the hand of God to save sinners from eternal damnation; and O!, how she marvelled that we had dared to cross the great stormy sea, and cross high mountains, and go through deep rivers, to come to live in their midst, poor Hottentots, who had nothing to give us after all our dangers and labour. My heart was ready to break as I listened to her, so that I could barely prevent myself from joining with them in weeping and calling out.[1]

For whom is Ann Evans's heart nearly breaking here? For herself? As well it might, prophetically, for her adventure was certainly to cost her dear. When she returned to Wales ten years later, she accompanied a dying husband, worn out at the age of thirty-five as much by his struggles with the obstructive Cape colonists as by his work among the indigenous people and the diseases and hard life of the hinterland. She buried him in Llanidloes shortly after their arrival home, along with one of their children who had sickened on the voyage; the bodies of two more of her children were left behind in African graves.[2]

Or is she here weeping for the Hottentots – a people with whom she seems, from the evidence of her letter, to have fallen in love as soon as she encountered them, with all the ardency of her seventeen years? It is unlikely that she would have been deaf to the phrases in the Khoikhoi woman's speech that point to a native history of dispossession and despair. By the time Ann Evans arrived in their midst the Khoikhoi people had already suffered nearly two centuries of colonization. At the beginning of the seventeenth century, before the coming of the white man, their nomadic tribes spread throughout the Cape provinces; today only scattered groups remain, and the Khoikhoi are nearly extinct as a race. Their experience of colonization reduced them to the condition of wretchedness and abject poverty the speaker describes, and taught them to conceive of themselves as 'the most despised nation under the whole heaven'. The 1973 revised edition of the *Shorter Oxford English Dictionary* still gives as one transferred meaning of the word 'Hottentot' 'a person of inferior intellect or culture'.

The Khoikhoi woman speaks of the pain of losing homelands and relatives; it is very likely that she herself had plenty of first-hand experiences of such bereavements. While the missionaries had at least chosen to leave their native habitations voluntarily, the lands and livelihoods of the Khoikhoi had been stolen from them, their 'fathers and mothers, brothers and sisters' slaughtered by weapons whose efficiency they could not previously have dreamt of, or killed by European diseases to which they had no immunity. The Khoikhoi were exploited as cheap labourers by the colonialists, who prized them as curiosities because of their short physique – few of them were taller than five feet. In the early nineteenth century, a woman of the Khoikhoi tribe, Saartje Baartmann, was exhibited in British freak shows as the 'Hottentot Venus', and became a topic of burlesque curiosity to the street balladeers and cartoonists of the period.[3]

The culture of the Khoikhoi suffered erosion, of course, along with their people and lands. In her prayer, the Khoikhoi woman itemizes 'their language' as one of the treasures 'dear to nature' that the missionaries have had to give up; she herself, however, cannot here have been speaking in her own language. The Cape missionary stations used the first settlers' language, Dutch, in their communication with the Khoikhoi, rather than the native tongue. It is unlikely that they did so out of any deliberate disinclination to foster the indigenous tongue, for the nineteenth-century missionaries had generally a good record for using native languages, and were frequently the first to inscribe, and create a grammar for, languages that had previously only existed as an oral tongue.[4] More probably, the Cape mission's language was Dutch because, after two centuries of colonization, that language was by now in common use in any exchanges between the Khoikhoi and the white settlers. Ann Evans herself, when she wrote her letter, does not even seem to have been aware that the Khoikhoi ever had a language of their own. It was the Dutch language that she and Evan studied in preparation for their mission, during the long months on board the *Alacrity*. With a poignancy made all the more acute by the fact that she is herself writing in a minority indigenous language, she tells her parents of the great pleasure it gave her to hear 'my dear husband preach to the Hottentots for the first time in their own language' – that is, in Dutch.[5] And, of course, the message that Evan Evans delivered to the Khoikhoi in the oppressors' language would have but further eroded their native culture and the basis of their native self-respect, if they accepted it. It would have taught them that they must abandon their own gods, and with them the myths, songs, dances and rituals central to their culture, and embrace as the only true religion the professed faith of all those Dutch and British settlers who, in material terms at any rate, had most effectively brought them not to eternal life but to the brink of annihilation. Well might Ann Evans weep for the Khoikhoi, then; perhaps her emotion here is also a marker of a more complex submerged grief about the nature of her meeting with them, shaped as it was by its place within a specific historical context that, for all the unquestionable sincerity of her dedication and her personal sacrifice, now makes it difficult for us to see in this encounter an unequivocal good.

That context was, of course, the rise of the British Empire. Recently, in English cultural studies, post-colonial critics have emphasized the fact that the empire, and all it stood for, must occupy a central place in our understanding of nineteenth-century British consciousness. According to Gayatri Chakravorty Spivak, for example, 'it should not be possible to read nineteenth-century British literature without remembering that imperialism, understood as England's social mission, was a crucial part of the cultural representation of England to the English'.[6] My subject in this chapter, however, is not so much the place of the British Empire in nineteenth-century English consciousness as its place in nineteenth-century Welsh consciousness, and its role in the cultural representation of Wales to the Welsh. I have dwelt on Ann Evans's letter at such length because, as a text arising out of the missionary movement, it is representative of that type of discourse in which we find by far the most numerous references to the British Empire in Welsh nineteenth-century writing.

Before the close of the nineteenth century, gospel-bearers had been sent out from Welsh chapels to every corner of the empire, to Cape Colony, as we have seen, and also to Natal, Sierra Leone, the Sudan, Ceylon, Malacca in South-East Asia, Australia, Fiji, Jamaica, Trinidad, the West Indies, British Honduras, Newfoundland, Gibraltar (to convert the Roman Catholics) and to so many Indian provinces that it would be tedious to list them. Major bases had also been established by the Welsh Nonconformists in territories – such as China, Madagascar, northern Africa and Tahiti – which were affiliated to Britain through trading agreements though not actually annexed under the British Crown. The numbers and the costs involved in such enterprises were substantial: by 1897, the Welsh Calvinist Methodists had sent out fifty-six ordained ministers to the Khasi Hills alone. And with the missionaries went, of course, their wives and children, and later doctors, schoolteachers and nurses as well. A well-developed late nineteenth-century missionary base contained schools, hospitals, domestic dwellings for the converts as well the British-born (for the converted were often rejected from their own families and had to be housed and supported by the mission) and maybe a printing-press too, as well as the church itself, of course, all of which had to be maintained by voluntary contributions from the congregations back home.[7]

In order to encourage their readers in the impetus to give, the Welsh denominational journals of the day filled their pages with letters and reports from missionaries, and articles, stories and poems about missionaries. The secular press, too, in so far as nineteenth-century Wales can be said to have had a secular press, also naturally enough reflected the same preoccupation. A collection of tales about Welsh village life published by Sara Maria Saunders in 1897, for example, and entitled *Llon a Lleddf* (Joyous and plaintive), is replete with references to India. A penniless girl sells her abundant hair in order to contribute her mite to the missionary collection; a widow so successfully dissembles her grief as she bids her only child Godspeed to the mission fields that he thinks she hardly cares, but the neighbours know that it has always been part of her generosity to give as if the gift meant nothing to her, and that she will never recover from this loss; a deacon who has never left the village is more familiar with every detail of the topography of the Khasi Hills than he is with his own backyard.[8] The imperial fields of the Lord were these villagers' romance, the missionaries their knights in shining armour, and each black convert a pearl that would shine forever in their heavenly crown.

References to the empire are just as rife, of course, in the English fiction of the period, but they are generally of a different order. Of course, there are missionaries in the English texts as well, but they do not usually enjoy the same kind of glamour as that which surrounds their Welsh counterparts; I am afraid that a Welsh Jane Eyre would have had to choose St John Rivers rather than Rochester as her husband if she was to retain her readers' sympathies. In typical English upper-middle-class domestic fiction, the empire features as the place to which the second son is sent to prove his manhood and repair the family fortune, not as a missionary, of course – he could hardly have repaired the family fortunes as a missionary – but as a military or civil officer. It is the place to which sad, unrequited lovers go only to reemerge later in the novel loaded with military honours and with much enhanced eligibility; or the place in which some colonial administrator dies bequeathing to his home-based heir a fortune that will bring about the novel's requisite concluding marriage. A Welsh-language novel, even had the genre been much more extensively developed in nineteenth-century Wales than it was, could hardly have included many examples of this type of reference because membership of the imperial officer ranks, whether military or administrative, was rigidly confined to the upper middle class, a group to which few Welshmen at this time belonged. A Welsh cottager's or labourer's son of exceptional enterprise might, after 1868, be imagined as becoming a Liberal MP or making a fortune in the dairy trade in London, but because of his parentage it would be difficult credibly to present him as joining the top-ranking empire club. Were he less ambitious, he would still statistically have been less likely than his Scottish or Irish equivalent to join the forces of empire as a voluntarily enlisted rank-and-file soldier, or as a lowly emigrant and settler, because the development of the south Wales industrial base offered the impoverished rural Welsh a new living closer to home. Consequently, in 1901, though the Welsh then made up 5% of the population of the British Isles, less than 1% of the British-born in Britain's over-seas colonies were Welsh.[9] But when it came to missionaries, there can be little doubt that, whatever the actual ratio for specifically Welsh as opposed to British gospel-bearers, the Welsh people at home thought of their own evangelists to the empire as constituting considerably more than 1% of the British total.

But the glamour that surrounds the figure of the mission-ary in nineteenth-century Welsh culture is too intense for it to be attributed merely to the fact that in statistical terms it constituted one of the few figures of imperial agency in which the Welsh could feel a personal involvement. Rather, I suggest, its potency arises from the missionary's redemptive role as saviour not only of the natives but also of Welsh pride in the face of the by now much-documented historical humiliations of the century. Given the awe-inspiring achievements of their English neighbours, and the mortifications induced by that neighbour's expressed disdain for the Welsh,[10] mid-nineteenth-century Welsh self-esteem would certainly have been in a very sorry plight had it not been able to take pride in the figure of the Welsh missionary as representing a far, far better mode of relating to the world at large than that of the English imperial officer. And yet the majority of the Welsh missionaries worked in fields that had only been made acces-sible to them by British guns, and the degree of security and prestige they enjoyed there was largely attributable to their identity as British subjects, as 'Christian soldiers' in the army of the Great White Queen.

The complex, at times contradictory, nature of the Welsh response to colonialism is apparent in some of the articles that Ieuan Gwynedd (the Reverend Evan Jones) published in the first Welsh-language journal for women, *Y Gymraes* (The Welsh woman), which he edited in 1850–1. In an article entitled 'Sais-addoliaeth' (The worship of the English), he pleads with his readers to resist identification with what he presents as very much the English, rather than British, ethos of imperialism. The article needs to be understood in the context of the anglicization of Wales in the nineteenth century, which Ieuan Gwynedd is here deploring. He fears that his audience will succumb to the allure of the increasingly powerful English, and reminds them that imperial glory is only gained at the expense of the colonized nations, who suffer just as the Welsh themselves did in the thirteenth century when they lost their sovereignty. His diatribe begins mildly enough. 'Personally, we have no reason to complain about the English,' he says, making use of the editorial 'we', 'but we venture to say that the spirit of the nation is such that we would not wish to see the Welsh imitating it.' Before the close of his article, however, after having listed in detail those atrocities that resulted from the aggressive 'spirit' of the English as a nation and their disparagement of other cultures, Ieuan Gwynedd is ferocious in his attack:

> Are we judging our brother harshly? Let his history answer from his landing on the island of Thanet, on the borders of Kent, to his present bloody slaughters in the Punjaub and Borneo in 1849. He is the arch thief of creation. He boasts of his learning, his civilization and his religion. His learning is butchery, his civilization is robbery, and his god is himself. We are not describing individuals, but the spirit of the nation, as it manifests itself on the pages of history.[11]

And yet in later numbers of *Y Gymraes* Ieuan Gwynedd reports approvingly on the Welsh missionaries' activities in

Jane Aaron

India and elsewhere.[12] There was clearly no necessary connection in his mind between English imperialism and the role of the missionaries.

Given the way in which the burgeoning empire was perceived during the first half of the nineteenth century, this is readily understandable. The slaughter of the Punjab Sikhs, to which Ieuan Gwynedd refers, was carried out not by Her Majesty's imperial army but by the militia of the East India Trading Company. Empire building was understood as being pre-eminently about increasing overseas trade. The ethos of trade was, of course, clearly distinguishable from that of Christian evangelism: in fact, there was open antagonism between the two interests. It was the evangelists largely who had aroused public protest in Britain against slavery and brought about the abolition of the British slave trade in 1807, and the freeing of slaves on British territory in 1833, with the loss, of course, of much trade revenue. Until 1813, when the evangelists in Parliament, under William Wilberforce, brought so much pressure to bear on the government that it threatened the East India Company with the loss of its charter if it continued to ban missionaries, no missionary presence had been allowed in India: the Trading Company had outlawed them. As the company saw it, any interference with their established religious practices was likely to provoke the Indian populace to rebellion against the white interlopers, and thus to imperil good trading relations.

For some decades after 1813, British soldiers in India continued to attempt to preserve the country's peace by checking the missionaries' endeavours to reform what they perceived as the most inhumane aspects of traditional Indian culture. A striking instance of one such collision between the interests of trade and that of the missionaries is given in _The Autobiography of Elizabeth Davis_, an oral record narrated by the intrepid traveller Betsy Cadwaladyr (to give her the name by which she knew herself) to her transcriber, the historian Jane Williams. The loyal daughter of a Calvinist Methodist

60

preacher, Betsy had a close affinity with missionaries and a strong dislike of soldiers. She closed her long adventure-packed career by serving as a nurse under Florence Nightingale in the Crimea, but makes a point in her autobiography of bluntly telling her audience that she did not volunteer out of any sympathy for the British army's plight but rather out of her insatiable wanderlust.[13] She attributes her prejudice against the military to an incident she witnessed in Madras in 1825 or thereabouts, while she was employed as a maidservant on board an independently owned merchant ship, trading between the various outposts of the empire:

> I had friends at Madras among the missionaries; and I went one day in company with Mr Elliott, Mr Cook, and Mr Benini, to see a suttee. The widow was . . . walking towards the pile [i.e. her husband's funeral pile], when Mr Cook and Mr Elliott met her, and asked her quietly whether it was her own will to be burned. She answered, 'No'. They next asked whether she would escape, if the opportunity were given her; and she answered, 'Yes'. The missionaries contrived to free a path for her, and she got off; but the English sentries stopped her. To avoid their bayonets, she threw herself into the river. The missionaries rescued her, and made an application to the governor; so that she was saved at last.[14]

Here, the chief enemy of the humane Christian viewpoint is presented as being the English soldiery, who should have known better than to allow the sacrifice of human life for the sake of preventing a possible disturbance among the native population. The interests of the empire understood as trade and those of the missionaries are poles apart; to participate in the work of the latter would not necessarily be to have to conceive oneself as in any way supporting the former.

But the Indian uprising of 1857, which nearly brought to an abrupt close Britain's rule in India, changed the way in which Britain conceived of its empire. The trading interest saw the mutiny as in part brought about by the natives' fear of the Christianizing presence, but the missionaries pointed out, with greater effect, that in those Indian provinces in which they had succeeded in making their presence felt less natives had rebelled. No Christian convert had raised arms against the British; had the Trading Company allowed them more scope, said the missionaries, and put Bibles in the hands of every Indian schoolchild as they had requested, the uprising might never have taken place. After Britain regained full control, India, in 1858, was placed under the direct rule of the British Crown, and the purposes of Britain in furthering its empire were now presented to the world in explicitly Christian terms. The British, it was now to be understood, ruled for the good of the colonized – those natives who had made their barbarous proclivities so disastrously clear during the uprising – and not for personal gain. According to one influential politician of the period, for example,

> the authority of the British Crown is at this moment the most powerful instrument under Providence, of maintaining peace and order in many extensive regions of the earth, and thereby assists in diffusing amongst millions of the human race, the blessings of Christianity and civilization.[15]

The missionaries, it would appear, had won the public opinion battle, but in another sense, from the point of view of someone like Ieuan Gwynedd, they had lost it, for from now on they and all they stood for would be seen as part and parcel of the ethos of British imperialism, and the providers of its overt moral justification. They would function to the public gaze as a coat of whitewash on what Joseph Conrad was later to term the 'whitened sepulchre' of imperialism.[16]

In devoutly Nonconformist nineteenth-century Wales, with the exception of some notable anti-English protesters such as Emrys ap Iwan and Michael D. Jones,[17] few voices were raised against this new version of the purposes of empire during the next decades. The travel writing of Margaret Jones of Rhosllanerchrugog, another Welsh Nonconformist maid-servant, serves to provide a view of the 'heathen' more typical, perhaps, of the majority opinion in late nineteenth-century Wales than Ieuan Gwynedd's more radical perspective. Margaret Jones found employment within the household of a family of converted Jews who participated in the Christian mission to the Jews, first in Paris, then Jerusalem and lastly in Morocco.[18] In a characteristic passage from the second of the two books she published on her travels and experiences, she comments on the people she observed through her Moroccan window:

> The influence of their tyrannical, degrading and corrupt religion (that is, Mohametanism) has worn away their civilization and their morals to a deplorable degree ... I saw them from the window of my room beating an offender for five minutes; they thrashed him like thrashing corn. My feelings were a mixture of sadness and rejoicing. Sadness at the punishment of the sinner, and joy because I knew of a better country, a better administration, because I was born and bred in that country, and educated in the religion which is the main spring of its justice. Britain for ever![19]

She closes her commentary by assuring her audience that the only hope for the restoration of law and order in Morocco is its speedy assimilation into the British Empire and a thoroughgoing Protestant Christian mission.

Even when, in the last two decades of the century, a Home Rule movement had started in Wales, in part in emulation of the Irish Young Ireland movement, not all its representatives were ready to forego their allegiance to the empire. As the leader of the Welsh Women's Liberal Association, and wife of the Liberal MP Wynford Philipps, a member of the Cymru Fydd or Young Wales group, Norah Philipps presumably espoused the two main aims of Cymru Fydd – the

Disestablishment of the Church in Wales and Home Rule. She was also in her own right a very active and effective propagator of liberal reform in Wales, particularly in the fields of women's education and women's suffrage. Yet, in an article published in *Young Wales*, the English-language mouthpiece of the Cymru Fydd movement, she has the following to say on nationalism:

> It would be easy to say, 'I am Irish, Welsh, or English, therefore I will be patriotic for Ireland, Wales, or England,' or it would be easy to say, 'I care and dare for the Empire, its greatness and glory. I will be no "little Englander".' But to be truly great is to care with a passionate patriotism for this great empire – great not only in extent but far more in the intent of her civilization – and yet with joy and pride and devotion strive for the country, that part of the great whole to which we, by special love and human linking of family, language, and religion, belong.[20]

Her concept of the 'intent' of the empire – that is, its Christianizing and civilizing aim – is such that she must applaud it, and proclaim her loyalty to it, even as she is here writing within the context of a movement intent on securing more devolved powers for the people of Wales.

One unusually circumstanced group of Welsh-born people were, however, provided by their experiences with a very different view of the processes of empire, and I will close with an anecdote from the works of one of that group's best-known spokespersons, the travel writer Eluned Morgan. Eluned Morgan was born in 1870 on board the ship *Myfanwy* that took a group of Welsh emigrants to what is generally referred to as the 'Welsh colony' of Patagonia. But, of course, Patagonia was never an imperial colony, or at least not a Welsh one; it was part of an Argentine-held territory, ruled and Christianized by Spanish colonists. The Welsh settlers had acquired the right to live according to their own religious beliefs and to use their own language, but they had no administrative control over the indigenous people of the area, and did not proselytize their religion to them. Nevertheless, according to Eluned Morgan in her accounts of her Patagonian childhood, close ties formed between the Welsh and their nomadic Indian neighbours, with the Indians frequently requesting the Welsh to intercede on their behalf against the Spanish authorities' attempts to drive them out of their traditional territories. In her book *Dringo'r Andes* (Climbing the Andes), Eluned Morgan describes a chance encounter with one such persecuted Indian, who had received support from her father:

> As we talked in the tent the word 'Cristianos' came up, and I asked him whom he meant by this 'Cristianos'.
> 'The Spaniards,' he said.
> 'But are not we [i.e., the Welsh settlers in Patagonia] also Cristianos?' I said.
> 'Oh no, you are *amigos de los Indios.*' . . .
> How painful to think that the word which used to be so sacred was coupled in the pagan's heart with every cruelty and barbarism . . . The Spaniard is not one jot worse than the Yank or the Englishman in this respect. Destroying natives and small nations is the characteristic vice of each of them.[21]

Clearly Eluned Morgan, for all her own devoutly Christian beliefs, had come to recognize through such encounters that coupling together Christianity and empire-building degrades the former while it does nothing from the colonized's point of view to redeem the latter.

Nevertheless, the Nonconformist chapels of Wales continued to send out their emissaries to the imperial fields for the duration of British rule. And the congregations at home continued, of course, to support them, financially and morally. I cannot be the only person over sixty brought up in small-town north and west Wales whose first introduction to racial difference came with those wistful Sunday school hymns that sang of far-away children with coloured skins and nobody to speak to them of God. And the answer, of course, was 'let's send the missionaries out over the sea, they will speak to them of God'. Nor perhaps was I the only child who first consciously experienced the shock of ideological difference when, on the annual round with the missionary collecting boxes, I realized, from some unexpectedly aggressive receptions, that not every-one in the early 1960s considered the missionary movement an unequivocally good thing. Later in the 1960s India finally expelled the remaining white missionaries from its provinces, as irredeemably tainted with the stains of imperialism. Perhaps it is no coincidence that that decade, the 1960s, which laid so low the formerly haloed figure of the Welsh missionary, also saw the rise in Wales of the Welsh language movement, and the first Plaid Cymru MP. One source of national pride and of identity had gone: the vacuum had to be filled, and those far-away children, suddenly grown adult, demanding their freedom and their own culture, taking down the Union Jack all over the globe, pointed the way. But by the late 1960s, of course, there were few committed Welsh Nonconformists left, as a percentage of the Welsh population as a whole, to feel the full impact of the trauma.

Notes

* An earlier article that was substantially revised for this chapter appeared as 'Slaughter and salvation: British imperialism in nine-teenth-century Welsh women's writing', in *New Welsh Review*, 38 (October 1997), 38–46.

1   A. Evans, *Llythyr Ann Evans* . . . (Bala, 1818), p. 16 (my translation).

2   G. Penar Griffith, *Hanes Bywgraffiadol o Genadon Cymreig i Wledydd Paganaidd* (Caerdydd, 1897), pp. 133–40.

3   For an account of the 'Hottentot Venus', see K. Bohata, 'The Black Venus: atavistic sexualities', in M. Stephens (ed.), *Rhys Davies: Decoding the Hare* (Cardiff, 2001), pp. 231–43.

4 See N. Jenkins, *Gwalia in Khasia* (Llandysul, 1995) for an account of this aspect of the missionaries' work; the Welsh missionary Thomas Jones, for example, is still esteemed in Khasia as the 'father of Khasi alphabets'; he gave the Khasi their 'written word' and in so doing kept their language alive (p. 143). But Jenkins points out that 'the missionaries' care for minority languages was often at odds with the homogenising inclinations of Empire' (p. 184).

5 Evans, *Llythyr Ann Evans*, pp. 17–18.

6 G. Chakravorty Spivak, 'Three women's texts and a critique of imperialism', in C. Belsey and J. Moore (eds), *The Feminist Reader: Essays in Gender and the Politics of Literary Criticism* (Basingstoke and London, 1995), p. 175.

7 In 1890, for example, in the year of the Calvinist Methodist Missionary Society's jubilee, Welsh Methodist chapels collected the sum of £37,326. 15s. 5d for the cause. See J. Hughes Morris, *Hanes Cenhadaeth Dramor y Methodistiaid Calfinaidd Cymreig, hyd Diwedd y Flwyddyn 1904* (Caernarfon, 1907), p. 259.

8 S. M. Saunders, *Llon a Lleddf* (Holywell, 1897), pp. 77, 56, 71.

9 For these statistics, see P. J. Marshall (ed.), *The Cambridge Illustrated History of the British Empire* (Cambridge, 1996), p. 265.

10 See the notorious 'Treachery of the Blue Books', the British government's *Report of the Commission of Inquiry into the State of Education in Wales* (London, 1847), which damned the Welsh as a lazy, drunken and sexually immoral people. For a commentary on the connections between this report and English imperial policy, see G. Tyson Roberts, *The Language of the Blue Books: The Perfect Instrument of Empire* (Cardiff, 1998).

11 [Evan Jones] Ieuan Gwynedd, 'Sais-addoliaeth', *Y Gymraes*, 1 (1850), 75–6 (my translation).

12 See, for example, 'Y Llong Genadol' (The missionary ship), ibid., 342–5.

13 J. Williams [Ysgafell] (ed.), *The Autobiography of Elizabeth Davis: Betsy Cadwaladyr, A Balaclava Nurse* [1857] (new edn; Dinas Powys, 1987), p. 153.

14 Ibid., pp. 78–9.

15 Earl Grey, quoted in Marshall (ed.), *Cambridge Illustrated History of the British Empire*, p. 30.

16 J. Conrad, 'Heart of Darkness' [1902], *Youth, a Narrative; and Two Other Stories* (London, 1957).

17 See, for example, Emrys ap Iwan, 'Bully, Taffy a Paddy', and 'Sylwadau am y rhyfel nad oedd yn rhyfel' (Comments on the war that was no war), *Y Faner* (1880) and (1882), in D. Myrddin Lloyd (ed.), *Erthyglau Emrys ap Iwan*, i (Dinbych, 1937), pp. 1–13, 82–9; and M. D. Jones, 'Ymfudo a threfedigaeth Gymreig' (Welsh emigration and colonialism), *Y Cronicl* (1850), in E. Pan Jones, *Oes a Gwaith y Prif Athraw y Parch. Michael Daniel Jones* (Bala, 1903), p. 63.

18 See, for a biographical study of Margaret Jones and a reprint of her first book, *Llythyrau y Gymraes o Ganaan*, E. Jones, *Y Gymraes o Ganaan: Anturiaethau Margaret Jones ar Bum Cyfandir* (Talybont, 2011).

19 M. Jones, *Morocco, a'r Hyn a Welais Yno* (Wrexham, 1883), pp. 54 and 133 (my translation).

20 N. Philipps, 'Notes on the work of Welsh Liberal women', *Young Wales*, 1 (1895), 39.

21 E. Morgan, *Dringo'r Andes* [1904] (new edn; Dinas Powys, 2001), pp. 37 and 44 (my translation).

3

The Other Internationalism? Missionary Activity and Welsh Nonconformist Perceptions of the World in the Nineteenth and Twentieth Centuries*

ALED JONES

Historians of modern Wales have, rightly and understandably, shown a keen interest, for example, in Welsh socialist and proletarian traditions of internationalism. What I will try to do here is to suggest that Welsh Nonconformity, too, fostered an internationalist perspective, one that is inescapably linked with, though not necessarily reducible to, the power of the British Empire. I wish to argue that evidence of such internationalism is to be found principally in writing produced by Welsh missionaries based in north-east India between 1841 and 1966. The mission, organized by the Calvinistic Methodist Presbyterian Church of Wales, was concentrated in a region of India sharply divided by religion as well as by its physical and administrative topography, and which sat astride the highly unstable frontier between Assam and Eastern Bengal,[1] an area which, in August 1947, was to be further and brutally divided by the new Partitionist international border separating India from what was then East Pakistan, and is now Bangladesh. Relatively small in scale – rarely were there more than fifty missionary workers in the field at any one time – it employed only a tiny proportion of the 10,000 or so British

69

missionaries who were on active service abroad in 1900. While other missionaries from Wales were at work in France, the islands of the Pacific, the Caribbean, parts of western and southern Africa, and China, those in north-east India formed the largest, most continuous project funded and organized by any Welsh-based denomination. They included evangelical preachers, doctors, nurses and teachers, and substantial numbers of them, constituting at times a clear majority, were lay women, mostly young and unmarried. The effects of their presence on the mission field were strikingly uneven, leaving a powerful and enduring mark on the Khasi Hills but making little impression on other areas of the field such as Sylhet. In Wales, too, the sounds of their evangelical fury have been strangely muted. Despite the extraordinary richness of the primary and printed records that they bequeathed to the home church, for much of the second half of the twentieth century their work attracted little sustained attention, other than from such retired missionaries as D. G. Merfyn Jones.[2] In part this may be due to the embarrassment caused by the mission's links with empire, and with the imperial arrogance associated with the idea of religious conversion in British colonies. Since the Second World War, these associations have sat uneasily with post-war constructions of Welsh national identity, whether among nationalists or the left. For both, missionaries represented the wrong kind of internationalism. I think it is time we reassessed those positions, and in doing so looked again, critically but openly, at the roles played by leading Welsh popular institutions in the expansion and consolidation of the British Empire.

The history of the Welsh mission in India has been well rehearsed, most recently in *Gwalia in Khasia* by Nigel Jenkins. The first missionary, Thomas Jones, from Aberriw, Montgomeryshire, arrived in the Khasi Hills in Assam in 1841. In the thirty years that followed his arrival, only around 500 Khasis were converted, but the extension of imperial control coupled with the growth of medical missions and schools led to greater success from the late 1870s onwards. The Khasi Christian community grew from just under 2,000 in 1881 to a little under 7,000 a decade later. By 1901 the figure had reached 16,000 and by 1905, the year of the Welsh Revival, the missionaries had established a following of some 23,000.[3] In the field, missionaries were charged with two major responsibilities. One was to take Welsh Calvinistic Methodism to the Assamese and Bengalis; the other was to keep the Welsh at home informed of their activities. This chapter will pay particular attention to the latter.

Transmission routes for missionary communications from the field back to Wales took a number of forms. Formal reports were submitted annually for publication in the *Report of the Foreign Mission*, but news also returned to Wales by means of letters, the contents of which at times were filtered through to the newspaper press. News coverage of events in 1857 in particular provides an intriguing illustration of the way in which editors used missionaries effectively as foreign correspondents. The monthly denominational journal *Y Drysorfa* (The treasury) included from 1847 a separate 'missionary chronicle' section, *Y Cronicl Cenhadol*, a periodical within a periodical, where reports from the field were regularly printed alongside other religious news and comment. Lectures and sermons given by missionaries on furlough, with occasional visits by converts, were widely publicized, as were special chapel events. Touring exhibitions of Indian villages and bazaars were intended further to excite the sympathies of their audiences. These were augmented in the 1920s by missionary films, shown in schools and chapels, such as the one shot in 1928 by Mostyn Lewis, son of the Liberal MP Sir Herbert Lewis.[4] The conversion of chapels into cinemas, albeit temporarily, signified a huge, even a shocking, shift in Nonconformist cultural sensibilities. Obituaries in newspapers also provided opportunities for the work of missionaries to be constructed as heroic, and allowed the church to appeal for more volunteers.[5] The most ubiquitous form of communication, however, was the missionary periodical press. It is certainly the most accessible to us today, yet it remains a surprisingly underused historical resource.

The Welsh mission field created its own communications media. John Pengwern Jones launched the *Friend of Sylhet* and *The Friend of the Women of Bengal* in 1899, and Helen Rowlands started *The Link* in 1933. But the most important missionary periodical was without doubt *Y Cenhadwr* (The missionary), published wholly in Welsh between 1922 and 1974, and aimed at a popular Welsh audience at home.[6] Initially edited by the Reverend J. Hughes Morris, and published as a monthly from the denomination's own press at Caernarfon, it printed a wide variety of articles, reports, essays and photographs from the mission field. Missionaries themselves contributed the vast majority of items. No circulation figures have as yet come to light, but we do know that the journal was distributed principally through the chapels and by subscription.

These forms of communication familiarized readers and audiences in Wales with images of India: one purpose was to raise funds to continue the missionary work. But what kind of world did these writings describe? The answer is more complicated than one might think. For example, there are numerous accounts in *Y Cenhadwr* where Indian religious practices, particularly Hindu beliefs, are caricatured and attacked. Take, for example, the article on Kali, one of a series on Hindu deities printed in 1924, where the author describes the goddess's nakedness, her drunken eyes, her delight in violence, her blood lust and her orgiastic dance on the corpse of her husband, condemning in so doing the corrupting effects of her image on the morality of those who worship her, and on Hindu family life in general. Other ethnographic accounts work in similar ways, particularly those that describe dress, social codes of behaviour, diet and occupation, though rarely, to be fair, with the same virulence. In 'The Indian barber', which forms part of an ambitious series on work and street life, the missionary Dilys Edmunds describes the social and religious significance of the *napit*, but it too 'fixes' the intellectual barber in an essentialist way, and attributes his social power to the Hindu 'superstitions' that, she seeks to persuade her readers, her school for Hindu girls in Karimganj was gradually eradicating.

But while some missionaries were deriding Indian religious beliefs and social practices, others were making available to readers in Welsh translation the work of Indian and Hindu poets and priests. There can be little doubt that texts were chosen which sought to emphasize the holiness, and the proximity to Christianity, of certain aspects of other religions, as Helen Rowlands explained in her introduction to her translations of Rabindranath Tagore. But Elizabeth Williams had also earlier translated the work of the Hindu priestess Chundra Lela into Welsh in 1908,[7] while in 1924 Helen Rowlands, with Hridesh Ranjan Ghose, published the sermons of the Sadhu Sundar Sing.[8] Readers in Wales were thereby invited to read certain approved Indian religious texts, in their own language and with the approval and authority of the church. Again, however, such translations are far more likely to have been forms of appropriation, or read as signs of redemption as the Hindu neared the Christian God, rather than evidence of syncretist deviationism within the mission.

Much of *Y Cenhadwr* contains what can only be described as news journalism, especially during the 1930s and 1940s, including articles on the progress of the Congress Party, the activities of Gandhi, the proliferation of symbols of nationhood and, in 1947, a series of extraordinary accounts of the human cost of Partition, the most notable being Helen Rowlands's reports from Karimganj, positioned on the new border between India and East Pakistan. In other accounts of journeys through the mission field, which included descriptions of landscapes, vegetation, animals, forms of transport, fields, street scenes, markets, and of the men, women and children they encountered, missionaries employed rhetorical strategies that both emphasized the otherness of India and which encouraged a sympathetic identification with it on the part of their readers. 'How different Sylhet is from Wales!' exclaimed Miss E. A. Roberts in 1902,⁹ yet the very contrast was intended to produce a closer affinity. The missionaries clearly wanted readers at home to care about their work, and about the people they were in contact with. Welsh and Bengali placenames are intertwined in these narratives, and comparisons are made between features of the landscape in the two regions. Such self-consciousness becomes most apparent when missionaries describe feelings of loneliness and of homesickness, of *hiraeth*, when they purport to see images of their home country projected on the landscape and the people around them. The employment of such tropes affirmed their sense of belonging to the physical as well as the mental world of their readers.

Other kinds of encounters demanded a different, more subtly nuanced use of language. An essay by Helen Rowlands entitled 'Y Glaw' (The rain), which describes a journey taken downriver with a group of her school pupils during the flood season in Sylhet in 1925, resonated with the vibrancy of colour, the scent of flowers, the softness of skin and the sensual textures of hair and cloth. Not what you would normally expect to find in evangelical Christian writing at this time.

Missionaries also developed and adapted Welsh cultural forms in the field. In 1901 John Pengwern Jones organized the first eisteddfod in Sylhet, while Helen Rowlands had later started in Karimganj an annual eisteddfod in Bengali.¹⁰ Hymns were written in, or translated into, indigenous languages, and these were used in much the same devotional way within the order of the service in the field as they were in the home church. J. Arthur Jones, sent to Shillong in 1910 by the *Manchester Guardian*, was struck by the combination of Indian landscape and Welsh religiosity:

While I sat at my dinner in the dak bungalow, a familiar strain came to my ears. Mingling with the fire-flies ... floated the minor cadences of an old Welsh tune. They were singing in the chapel which stood on the hill opposite. The timbre of the voices were a little strange, but apart from this I could have imagined myself in some Welsh village where the 'Seiat' was being held in Bethel or Saron. Yet the singers now were Khasis, a Mongolian hill folk of Assam, once worshippers of demons ... The Khasis have adopted Welsh Methodism with scarcely a variant.[11]

And in the first issue of *Y Cenhadwr* in 1922, Thomas Charles Edwards could confidently announce that the Welsh Calvinistic Methodists had 'to date created in India a Methodist Church in our own image'.[12] The recreation of a little Wales in India went beyond the strictly devotional. In an account of Christmas at her home for orphaned girls in Silchar in 1922, Miss E. M. Lloyd described how they had 'spent an evening in Wales!' Pictures and maps of the country had been pinned to the walls, the children were dressed in old Welsh costume and the choir sang *Hen Wlad fy Nhadau* and a number of Welsh folk songs, 'in Welsh'.[13] While such references to the use of the language and other symbols of Welsh identity are infrequent, this account does suggest another line was being crossed, which, in a very direct way, raises the question of the colonial context of the mission. Helen Rowlands herself used the term 'a colony of Welsh people'[14] to describe the mission field.

Whether the mission formed part of the broader British imperial presence in India, or whether it was engaged in a separate process of colonization of its own, in which case it did so by taking advantage of the colonial structures of the British Empire, the link between the mission and imperialism remains established and incontrovertible. J. N. Ogilvie's descriptions of Christian missions as 'the Empire's conscience' and the 'soul of the Empire'[15] in his Duff Lecture of 1924 have been echoed by historians,[16] even though many of them have emphasized the ways in which missionaries objected to its 'treatment of subject peoples'.[17] One could make three observations on the Welsh mission as a form of cultural imperialism. The key question here is why were self-conscious members of a linguistic and cultural minority prepared to undermine the cultural autonomy of others? Nigel Jenkins suggests that they did so because they had, during the previous century, so brutally remade their own culture. They were prepared to transform others because they had transformed themselves. This is a powerful argument, though the question could be approached differently. The ambivalent, even at times contemptuous, attitudes that some missionaries held towards the leadership of the church in Wales suggest that they regarded themselves as role models for evangelists at home. It was precisely the knowledge that they had not won the war in Wales that drove the missionaries, particularly in the early decades of the twentieth century, to regard themselves as the embodiment of the evangelist spirit of early Calvinism, the true voices of the faith, whose work would promote the continued evangelization of their home country as well as their adopted one. But if they appeared as remote, even formidably austere, figures among their brethren in Wales, they may have been equally incongruous in the mission field. The highly specific nature of their theology, and its cultural and linguistic packaging, is likely to have projected an oddly fragmented or even confused image of the imperial power. On balance, it appears to me that the history of the Welsh mission, certainly in the Sylheti plains but perhaps even in the hills, is broadly consistent with Andrew Porter's evaluation of missionaries generally as being weak agents of cultural imperialism.[18]

But if missionaries were 'weak agents' in that particular sense, what appears to be clear from the evidence is that they were quite significant agents of cultural communication. In this too they addressed the same two audiences, converts and potential converts in the mission field, but also their church and their readers at home. Missionaries formed the link between the two worlds of Wales and the field, and because it was they who played that pivotal role, the relationship between the two audiences was an asymmetrical one. While few Assamese or Bengalis toured Wales (and those who did were Christian), it was the missionaries themselves who introduced, through their journalism and their physical presence on furlough, cultural elements of the field. In the inter-war years, there are reports of pupils in Welsh primary schools being taught to sing folk songs in Bengali. Women-only meetings in chapels were known as zenanas. Poems and hymns were composed that eulogized the special relationship between the peoples of Wales and north-east India.[19] And, as we have seen, films, touring exhibitions and missionary journalism kept images of the field continuously in circulation.

It is possible to read this exercise in cultural communication in two ways. One is as a form of propaganda, not only for evangelization, both at home and abroad, but also for the British Empire itself. By simultaneously extolling the spiritual byproducts of empire, and by celebrating Wales's own collaborative role in Britain's imperial project, it could be argued that missionary activity was part of the ideological apparatus that sought not only to obtain the consent of Welsh Nonconformity for the empire, but also to obtain the consent of a key Welsh social institution for Wales's own colonization within it. Here, the 'multiple identities' that are embodied in missionary self-representations fold into an overarching British and imperial sense of belonging.[20] In other words, support for the mission implied support for the empire, and of Wales's collaboration with it. That is one way of reading the political fallout of missionary activity. But other readings are also possible. These spring from a fundamental element in the missionary belief system that implies that Christianity empowers both individuals and societies, and that its adoption generates social as well as ethical transformation and

improvement.[21] Gustav Warneck, in his study of the relationship between missions and culture, first published in English
translation in 1888, referred to Christianity, significantly, as
'the Magna Charta of humanity',[22] and James Dennis's sociological study of missions of 1897 identified this belief as a key
component of Christian missionary activity worldwide. It
also infused the writing of our Welsh missionaries. Only
Christianity, they argued, could liberate women, provide
useful education for children and free human beings from
poverty, caste and communalism, even from colonial depend-
ency. One does not have to share that view to admit its salience
as a motivating force in the Western Christian missionary
enterprise. From that fundamental conviction, in this particular case, three rather important issues arise in the missionary
literature that appear to have had some effect on political attitudes and forms of thinking in Wales, particularly in the
period up to the Second World War.

One is the modern evolution in Wales of the concept of
nationality. In the 1880s, the Young Wales movement had
drawn on U. Larsing's declarations of love for his Khasi Hills
during his tour of Wales twenty years earlier as a model of
patriotism for the Welsh to follow.[23] In 1922, in the opening
issue of Y *Cenhadwr*, Thomas Charles Edwards asked
whether nations could be 'moral agents'. Influenced no
doubt by the political rhetoric of David Lloyd George and
others during the First World War, his answer was unequivocally in the affirmative. 'The world owes more of a debt to
small nations than to the great empires', he wrote. And of
Wales's role as one of those 'small nations' he noted that
through its missionary activity 'our lines of communications
are gradually extending through the entire earth'. This, he
predicted, would in turn lead to 'a new International spirit
to kill the distrust and hatred of nations . . . The political
importance of the Foreign Missions will become more
apparent each day. On them depends the peace of the
world.'[24] Shortly afterwards, in lecture notes for a furlough

tour of Wales, the missionary Reverend Watcyn M. Price argued that

> The world must be treated as a unit and all the nations are equal ... We are as nationalists, as selfish as any group of politicians ... What would we be saying in Wales to-day if we were put in the position of India or Africa? ... India is challenging us to be revolutionary in everything.[25]

The emphasis in these texts on the creation of a world community through Christian missionary work was, in the following decade, reiterated even by elements on the Welsh left. In 1938, David Thomas, a leading member of the Welsh ILP, saw missionaries as having raised key international questions of social injustice and imperial oppression, and having paved the way for the League of Nations.[26] In the third reading of the Indian Independence Bill on 15 July 1947, W. R. Williams welcomed Indian Independence as a vindication, and in some respects as a culmination, of the liberating work of the Welsh mission, affirming that 'Wales will be second to none in its spirit of elation and thanksgiving on this great day in the history of India'.[27] A particular reading of the missionary experience had thus entered Welsh political thinking.

Secondly, and allied to this, one could argue that the mission provided a route into the culture for anti-imperialist ideas about race, difference and power. It is clear that the experience of some Welsh missionaries in India enabled them to respond positively to the work, for example, of the English missionaries J. H. Oldham and Basil Matthews, on race and the politics of inequality. These mounted critiques of Lothrop Stoddard's national and racial chauvinism[28] and sympathetically discussed leftist analyses of racial politics in the United States. For Oldham 'racial problems ... [were] to a large extent social, political and economic problems', and in that light he criticized the 'ethics of Empire'.[29] Both Oldham's *Christianity and the Race Problem* and Basil Matthews's *The*

Clash of Colour: A Study in the Problem of Race were published in 1924, and in 1926 the debate entered the pages of *Y Cenhadwr*, with articles on 'the colour problem' which endorsed and developed Oldham's general position.[30] I cannot find any other genre of Welsh-language writing at the time that addresses the international politics of race in this way.

Finally, and this has been discussed by Margaret Strobel, Aparnu Basu and others, the belief in the liberating potential of Christianity was held to apply particularly to the condition of women.[31] As early as 1887, Sarah Jane Rees (Cranogwen), as editor of *Y Frythones* (The British woman), had welcomed the church's decision to appoint single women as missionaries as a development that presaged a better future for Welsh women as a whole.[32] Missionary work not only provided women with greater professional opportunities than were available at home, it also gave them greater status, visibility and a degree of influence, both in the field and at home, than they might otherwise have enjoyed. It may be feasible to argue, then, that alongside the imperial message of the mission, it also helped develop new ways of thinking about nationhood, international relations and the politics of race and gender that acquired some currency, at least, in the inter-war years.

This brief exploration of the discourses of missionary writing suggests two matters of some significance. First, that we need to know much more than we now do about the Welsh mission in Assam/Bengal, and, secondly, that we need to consider not only the manner in which Wales, through its missionary work, affected Indians, but also how Nonconformist evangelization in India affected the Welsh. A fuller history of the mission, and the ways in which missionary work was articulated and received back home in Wales, may cast Nonconformist Wales in the nineteenth and early twentieth centuries in a more complex light, one where the empire, and the idea of Britain itself, may be subjected to new forms of scrutiny.

Notes

* A fuller version of this chapter may be found in A. Jones, *Welsh Missionary Journalism in India, 1880–1947*, Currents in World Christianity Position Paper 123 (Cambridge, 2000). For a fuller analysis of the spatial considerations involved in implanting the Welsh mission in Sylhet, see A. G. Jones, 'Sacred spaces: cultural geographies of mission in Welsh Sylhet, 1849–1940', *Welsh History Review*, 26/2 (2012), 215–45.

1 Eastern Bengal was separated from Assam and reunited with Bengal in 1912, *The Imperial Gazetteer of India*, xxvi, *Atlas* (Oxford, 1909), p. 30.

2 Most histories are by retired missionaries, the most informative being the following three-volume series: E. Thomas, *Bryniau'r Glaw* (Caernarfon, 1988); J. Meirion Lloyd, *Y Bannau Pell* (Caernarfon, 1989); D. G. Merfyn Jones, *Y Popty Poeth a'i Gyffiniau* (Caernarfon, 1990). See also A. Jones, '"Meddylier am India": tair taith y genhadaeth Gymreig yn Sylhet, 1887–1947', *Transactions of the Honourable Society of Cymmrodorion* (THSC), 1997, NS 4 (1998), 84–110, and J. Aaron, 'Slaughter and salvation: British imperialism in nineteenth-century Welsh women's writing', *New Welsh Review*, 38 (October 1997), 38–46 and chapter 2 in this volume.

3 B. C. Allen, CS, *Assam District Gazetteers*, vol. x, *The Khasi and Jaintia Hills, the Garo Hills and the Lushai Hills* (Allahabad, 1906), Part I, p. 66.

4 *Y Cenhadwr* (December 1928), 236.

5 R. J. Williams, 'Un o'r arloeswyr: Elizabeth Williams, Sylhet', *Y Goleuad* (7 September 1917), 5. See occasional series on 'Yr Oriel Genhadol', in *Y Cenhadwr* for biographies and photographic portraits.

6 Numbers of Welsh speakers in Wales over the age of three totalled 766,103 in 1921, peaking at 811,329 in 1931. For further details, consult L. J. Williams, *Digest of Welsh Historical Statistics*, i (Cardiff, 1985), pp. 86–8.

7 E. Williams, *Yr Offeiriades Hindwaidd: Hanes Bywyd Chundra Lela* (1908). This text was previously translated into English by Ada Lee in 1903.

8   H. J. Rowlands and H. Ranjan Ghose, *Sermons and Sayings of Sadhu Sundar Singh during his Visit to the Khasi Hills, Assam, March 1924* (Sylhet, 1924).

9   Miss E. A. Roberts, 'Y Cronicl Cenhadol', *Y Drysorfa* (December 1902), 570.

10 John Pengwern Jones introduced the eisteddfod to Sylhet in 1904, and Helen Rowlands later held eisteddfodau in Bengali in Karimganj, J. Meirion Lloyd, *Nine Missionary Pioneers: The Story of Nine Pioneering Missionaries in North-East India* (Caernarfon, 1989), p. 7.

11 *Report of the Foreign Mission* (1910), p. xiii.

12 Parch. T. Charles Edwards, 'Gair i Gychwyn', *Y Cenhadwr* (January 1922), 2.

13 *Y Cenhadwr* (December 1923), 189–90. See also S. Fleming McAllister, 'Cross-cultural dress in Victorian British missionary narratives: dressing for eternity', in J. C. Hawley, *Historicizing Christian Encounters with the Other* (Basingstoke, 1998), especially pp. 123–4.

14 *The Link* (March–April 1935), 18.

15 J. N. Ogilvie, *Our Empire's Debt to Missions: The Duff Missionary Lecture 1923* (London, 1924), pp. x, 253.

16 D. Harman Akenson, *The Irish Diaspora: A Primer* (Toronto, 1993), p. 146.

17 B. Stanley, *The Bible and the Flag: Protestant Missions and British Imperialism in the Nineteenth and Twentieth Centuries* (Leicester, 1990), p. 179.

18 A. N. Porter, 'Cultural imperialism and Protestant missionary enterprise 1780–1914', *Journal of Imperial and Commonwealth History*, 25/3 (1997), 367–91.

19 M. C. John, *Hanes Bywyd a Gwaith Mrs Esther Lewis – Cenhades, 1887–1958 (Swansea, 1996), pp. 15–16.

20 See L. Brockliss and D. Eastwood (eds), A *Union of Multiple Identities: The British Isles, c.1750–1850* (Manchester, 1997), especially p. 208 on the 'more positive' British identity that emerged in the late nineteenth century with the 'experience and management of

Empire'. In Scotland, '(m)issionaries unquestionably stimulated a belief in a profoundly Scottish contribution to empire-building', J. M. MacKenzie, 'Essay and reflection: on Scotland and the empire', *International History Review*, 15 (1993), 728.

21 J. S. Dennis, *Christian Missions and Social Progress: A Sociological Study of Foreign Missions* (London, 1897), p. 408.
22 G. Warneck, *Modern Missions and Culture: Their Mutual Relations*, trans. T. Smith (Edinburgh, 1888), p. xxii.
23 S. T. Jones, 'Cymry Cymreig', *Cymry Fydd* (April 1889), 381. U Larsing was, in 1846, among the first to be converted by Welsh missionaries in Khasia. He travelled to Wales in 1860, where he died in 1863. He is buried in Chester. See *Y Cenhadwr* (November 1922), 164.
24 Edwards, 'Gair i Gychwyn', 2.
25 Reverend W. M. Price, 'The call of India: notes for a lecture' (n.d.), National Library of Wales CMA GZ/53.
26 D. Thomas, *Y Ddinasyddiaeth Fawr* (Wrexham, 1938), pp. 79–82.
27 *Parliamentary Debates (Hansard)*, 5th series, vol. 440, col. 271. Williams was MP for Heston and Isleworth.
28 Stoddard (1883–1950) had proposed that 'civilization is the body, the race is the soul', L. Stoddard, *The Rising Tide of Colour against White World-Supremacy* (London, 1920). See also his *Revolt against Civilization: The Menace of the Under Man* (London, 1922).
29 J. H. Oldham, *Christianity and the Race Problem* (London, 1924), pp. 248 and 94. Oldham was Secretary to the International Missionary Council and editor of the *International Review of Missions*. See also B. Matthews, *The Clash of Colour: A Study in the Problem of Race* (London, 1924), published by the United Council for Missionary Education. For his treatment of W. E. B. DuBois and Marcus Garvey, see pp. 75–6. CMS 'Schemes of Study' are also revealing in this respect, see in particular *Indian Problems and the Christian Message: A Scheme of Study* (London, 1926) on 'the national ideal', and *India – Whither Bound? A Scheme of Study* (London, 1930), especially 'India's women: discuss "the women's movement in India holds the key to progress"', 8.

30 *Y Cenhadwr* (March 1926), 41–4.
31 M. Strobel, *European Women and the Second British Empire* (Bloomington, IN, 1991). Also N. Chaudhuri and M. Strobel (eds), *Western Women and Imperialism: Complicity and Resistance* (Bloomington, IN, 1992).
32 Cranogwen, 'Dyfodol merched Cymru', *Y Frythones* (July 1887), 202.

4

Apes and Cannibals in Cambria: Literary Representations of the Racial and Gendered Other[1]

KIRSTI BOHATA

The late eighteenth- and nineteenth-century imperial project to define the distinctive ethnological and 'racial' features of the peoples of empire (as well as the various types of European) had a profound influence on the way different races, nationalities, cultures and even classes were viewed. Fundamental to this project were the supposedly empirical sciences of physical anthropology, such as physiology, phrenology and craniology. The forms of 'knowledge' derived from these studies became part of the popular consciousness and, despite the complex characteristics of cultures and peoples, powerful stereotypes were constructed that often denied realities or, indeed, even worked to alter perceived realities.[2] While the theories behind the nineteenth-century project of ethnographic cartography have been discredited,[3] the images of racial and gendered 'Others' that were so enthusiastically taken up by the Victorian popular and periodical press remain in many respects meaningful signifiers into the present.

Gothic texts such as Mary Shelley's *Frankenstein* (1818) consciously or unconsciously draw upon stereotypes of race when portraying fearful or threatening characters or scenarios, as H. L. Malchow has shown in his study of 'British' literature.[4] But Malchow's work focuses on English literature. The present chapter reveals how anglophone Welsh literature is similarly informed by stereotypes of race and the discourses of colonialism and science, but argues that although the models discussed by Malchow are highly relevant, the case of Welsh writing in English and the position of a Welsh reader of this literature is rather more complex. The Welsh were complicit and instrumental within the British Empire as part of Britain. Yet as a nation within the United Kingdom Wales has generally been marginal to the centre – England (or perhaps more accurately, London). If the Welsh could imagine themselves as part of the imperial metropolis in colonial discourses that constructed the empire as exotically Other, Wales could also be constructed as a threatening Other in terms which were derived from the very same racialized discourses.

Negative stereotypes of race abound in the canonical texts of English literature, as the work post-colonial critics has shown, and it is not difficult to find a similar abundance of such material in Welsh writing in English. Much of this essay is concerned with Gothic literature since this form often is most obviously concerned with articulating cultural anxieties and fears. Arthur Machen's chilling tales of the Welsh borders, *The Great God Pan* (1894) and 'The Novel of the Black Seal' (1895), draw on *fin de siècle* ideas of racial degeneration and threat. Machen was a very popular writer in his own right and some of his stories were recently reissued as part of the Library of Wales series of classics, which is testimony to his enduring appeal. Margiad Evans's short story 'A Modest Adornment' is part of her wider interest in portraying female sexualities and same-sex desire and is illustrative of the way various images of Otherness (race, gender, sexuality) interact and inform one another.[5] It was selected as one of two stories by Evans for inclusion in the Honno Classics anthology of Welsh women's writing, *A View Across the Valley* (1999). The story with which this essay concludes, 'The Chosen One' (1966) by Rhys Davies, won the prestigious Edgar Allen Poe award in 1967 and has been included here for the way the author makes such pointed use of the racialized language of anthropology in the text. Before attending to the discourses of race, gender, sexuality and anthropology as they are present in these Welsh texts, however, we need first to briefly consider their wider provenance in the nineteenth-century discourses of race and empire.

Patriarchy and imperialism are connected and reinforce each other, firmly uniting on the site of the black female body. Black women of African origin were considered to be the lowest humans in the eighteenth-century hierarchy of crea-tion known as the 'great chain of being'[6] and in the nineteenth-century one may see the discourses of racism taken to their extremes in the medio-anthropological studies that pathologized their anatomies. The Black Woman became a highly sexualized construct and racial distinctness was asserted through the (mis)construction of black female geni-talia and secondary sexual parts, particularly the buttocks, as pathological, as grotesque *deviations* from the white norm. The case of Saartje Baartman (later known as Sarah Bartmann, although her original name is not recorded) is the paradig-matic example. Baartman, who came from South Africa, was exhibited in London and Paris between 1810 and her death in 1815 as the 'Hottentot Venus'.[7] She wore a costume that allowed the audience to view her buttocks and breasts, the size and shape of which generated great interest among scien-tists and the public alike. Although she firmly resisted genital examination while she was alive, Saartje Baartman was dissected in Paris after her death and Georges Cuvier found an 'overdevelopment' of the labia minora, which he described as the Hottentot Apron.[8] This genital formation was patholo-gized, in that it was seen to be abnormal and undesirable, yet it was also believed to be common to the racial group to which Baartman belonged and therefore this whole group could be considered to be pathological. Furthermore, this signifier of racial difference/pathology was linked to supposedly deviant manifestations of female sexuality, in particular those associated with an 'excessive' female libido, such as prostitution. Later in the nineteenth century, another variety of supposedly pathological female sexuality, lesbian-ism, came to be associated with Baartman's genitalia. Sander Gilman observes:

> The author, H. Hildebrandt [writing in 1877[9]], links this malformation [the 'Hottentot apron'] with the overdevelop-ment of the clitoris, which he sees as leading to those 'excesses' which 'are called "lesbian love'". The concupiscence of the black is thus associated with the sexuality of the lesbian.[10]

According to Lisa Moore the 'over-development' of the clito-ris, which Hildebrandt associates with lesbianism, was a common feature in 'the discursive representation of the [lesbian] body that came back from voyages of colonial explo-ration'.[11] Moore describes how the supposedly pathological sexuality of the lesbian was portrayed as a common charac-teristic of the 'Hindoo'. In an 1811 court case in which two women brought a libel case against the guardian of a former pupil of theirs who claimed she had witnessed the two teach-ers indulging in 'indecent and criminal practices',[12] the judgement finally rested on a belief that race was a primary factor in determining the sexuality of an individual. The court had to decide between two apparently unlikely scenarios, either the teachers were pleasuring each other in a bed occa-sionally shared by a pupil (bed sharing itself was common and unremarkable), or the girl had made up the story. In trying to account for how an apparently innocent girl might have imagined her story at all, the ' "Hindoo" background', or mixed race, of the witness (she was born in India to an Indian mother and a British father) was established as the cause of her vivid imagination and false testimony.[13]

Thus, we may see how the ostensibly unrelated discourses of race and sexuality inform and influence each other.

Rereading 'white' texts in the light of such intersecting has been one of the most significant contributions of post-colonial studies. For example, the discourses that construct upper- and middle-class white Victorian women as prone to madness, hysteria and irrationality are understood to be entwined with those that pathologized the non-white. It makes little sense, therefore, to discuss the construction of one manifestation of Otherness – be it homosexuality, race, class or gender and so on – without simultaneously recognizing the influence of a variety of interrelated or intersecting discourses of Otherness.

The interaction of the various images of cannibalism, witchcraft and lesbianism in constructions of white women as Other may be seen, for instance, in Margiad Evans's short story 'A Modest Adornment' (1948) and such interaction illustrates how racialized discourses intrude into areas that might formerly have been read in solely white gendered or lesbian terms.[14] The story focusses on the death of an elderly woman, a lesbian, in a state of apparent neglect and the way her lifelong partner deals with her demise. Miss Allensmore's reaction (or lack of it) to the slow death of Miss Plant is in sharp juxtaposition to the response of an elderly widow in the village who has begun to idolize Miss Plant – an affection that hints at the possibility of a less destructive same-sex desire. Despite a moving ending that testifies to the old love between Miss Allensmore and Miss Plant, it is difficult for the reader to sanction Miss Allensmore's apparent selfishness during the last days of her partner's life. Indeed, Miss Allensmore might easily be read as a typical representation of a witch, so drawing on old European constructions of female Others. She lives without male company, outside of the village. She is described as a 'fat black cauldron of a woman' (235). She keeps a hoard of black cats, and even Miss Plant takes on some resemblance to a cat, with her 'great silky green eyes' in which 'there was a curious sort of threat' (235). Suggestive of another traditional witches' familiar, her bare feet are 'as dark as toads' (238).

The chips she makes are 'long and warped and as gaunt as talons' (238) and her house is festooned with 'sagging black cobwebs' (238). Yet the interpretation of these features in terms of popular conceptions of the witch are complicated or perhaps extended by the subtle but persistent images of cannibalism in the story, and these are not divorced from the fact of Miss Allensmore's sexual orientation.

Black cauldrons may be typical of witches, but large, people-sized cauldrons are also the staple of popular portrayals of cannibals. Miss Allensmore's cooking habits suggest the fabled savagery of cannibals: from the kitchen comes the perpetual sound of 'furious frying or the grumpy sound of some pudding in the pot, bouncing and grunting like a goblin locked in a cupboard' (236). Miss Allensmore's appetite for food is emphasized at every opportunity, even her letters are sent by the baker, and our first glimpse of her sees her eating sweets. Elsewhere, Miss Allensmore drops grease on her naked, blackened feet (which are suggestive of the black 'savage' as well as of edible flesh); while she 'lick[s] away' an inappropriate half smile 'with the point of her tongue' (237); she regularly squats (a 'primitive' posture) or sits in front of a 'great fire' almost cooking her own body, her 'fat, soft flesh that looked as if it had been mixed with yeast, all naked and flushing' (248); even more explicitly, she is described by a villager as 'sit[ting] on top of a great fire a-frying [her]self' (245). There is the continual suggestion that Miss Allensmore has somehow devoured Miss Plant – Miss Allensmore is fat in contrast to the emaciated Miss Plant – although it is Miss Allensmore's body that is more obviously edible. The cannibalistic overtones are clear: this is a woman whose savage (sexual?) appetite is so voracious that she seems to have eaten her partner, a notion reminiscent of the purported behaviour of some South American women who were supposed to eat their lovers after sex, rather like some species of mantis.[15] The association of appetite and sexuality and the perceived excesses of these is clear. Moreover, the link between ambiguous sexuality, gender and food is established in the opening line of the story: '"Bull's eyes are boys' sweets," said Miss Allensmore and popped one in her mouth' (235).

Yet, if stereotypes of lesbianism, cannibalism, race and witchcraft may be seen to converge in this story, the 'authenticity' of such constructions is challenged. Miss Allensmore *is* constructed as thoroughly Other, and her refusal to conform to recognized feminine norms is accentuated by the contrast provided by Mrs Webb (Miss Plant's caring admirer) and the nurse who attends Miss Plant. Such gendered dichotomies are problematized, however, and the image of Miss Allensmore as Other is subverted not only by the romantic 'subplot' (which describes the young, sensually alert Miss Plant making a slow pilgrimage, on foot, to London 'just to say to her [Miss Allensmore], "I can no longer bear to live away from you"' (259)), but also in the way the reader is subtly encouraged to suspend judgement about the nature of Miss Allensmore's appetites. For example, the disapproval of the nurse when Miss Allensmore makes chips as Miss Plant lies dying upstairs apparently links her appetite for food with 'unnatural' feelings. She seems uncaring – cooking and eating at such a time is a rejection of the customs surrounding a death – but there is a strong suggestion that the nurse's disapproval is to do with the *way* that Miss Allensmore cares. After Miss Plant has died, Miss Allensmore sits alone in her cottage and plays her clarinet through the night. As in other stories by Evans, music is linked to same-sex desire and here Miss Allensmore knows her music, like her love, has never been understood. Hearing it drifting from her cottage, the villagers sternly disapprove.

The painful conclusion of the story confirms Miss Allensmore's love revealing the unreliability of the narrative perspective, which may have encouraged the reader to condemn Miss Allensmore's apparently heartless behaviour, and thus encouraging the reader to reflect on the distortive gloss of the language of stereotype. The reader is forced to recognize that we have only glimpsed Miss Allensmore as she

91

is characterized by village gossip – she remains throughout the story a distant, problematic and rather intangible figure. This is emphasized when returning to her cottage after Miss Plant's funeral at the end of the story Miss Allensmore papers over her windows and shuts herself off completely from the world, significantly excluding the reader, too.

Images of witchcraft, lesbianism, cannibalism and blackness can be seen to converge around notions of excess and deviancy in 'A Modest Adornment', yet the fear of female sexuality and racial difference extended beyond these intersecting categories. If the external physiology of black women provided the supposedly empirical evidence of their Otherness, then the internal organs of reproduction were no less a focus for the construction of the female body as pathological during the eighteenth and nineteenth centuries.[16] In this model of disease, the womb is seen as the cause of illness in the female body, perhaps the most extreme version of this being the phenomenon of the 'wandering womb' that could move freely around the female body and suck blood from the woman's brain (the connotations of vampirism/cannibalism are not insignificant here) rendering her weak and prone to insanity.[17] Yet in a racial context the womb poses perhaps the greatest threat of all in terms of its reproductive function, for it is the site of contamination, of miscegenation, of the corruption of the perceived purity of the races. While black women frequently, as slaves, bore the products of rape – the offspring of their white masters – it is the white woman's womb that is perceived as the greatest threat to racial purity, particularly with reference to the fears of 'black blood' going unnoticed in white society, of 'passing'.

There are all sorts of connotations attached to 'black blood'. For example, it was suggested in the eighteenth century that black people had black bile and even black blood, which caused the skin to appear black. That black bile had been considered a sign of illness since medieval times did nothing to undermine the idea that black skin was in itself a pathological indicator. Thus, black blood was believed to be the undesirable cause of black skin and, given the notions that black people were either a more primitive version of humanity or a degenerate form, the mixing of the races – the contamination of white blood – was to be feared. Thomas Jefferson, while noting the detrimental effects of slavery upon both slaves and slavers, justifies its continuation thus:

> Among the Romans, emancipation required but one effort. The slave, when made free, might *mix* with, without *staining* the blood of his master. But with us a second is necessary, unknown to history. When freed, he is to be removed beyond the reach of *mixture*.[18]

It is precisely this fear of 'mixture' that underlies and, indeed, provides much of the resonance of the work of Arthur Machen. Machen's fiction concerns itself with ancient evils that predate known history and perhaps even time itself. Many of Machen's stories are set among the border hills of Wales, littered with ancient, pre-Christian *meini hirion* (megalithic stones), or else in a polite London society infiltrated by ancient pagan forces or deities. Nevertheless Machen's stories of the 1890s are informed by very contemporary concerns of racial purity and degeneration. In 'The Great God Pan' (1894) evil is visited upon polite society in the form of an apparently beautiful woman who is in fact the grotesque product of a coupling between a woman and the devil (although the conception seems to have been 'immaculate' rather than physical). The real threat posed by this woman lies in the invisibility of her hybridity: she *passes*. A similar union between humankind and the beings of hell is the subject of another of Machen's stories, 'The Novel of the Black Seal' (1895), where a young woman gives birth to a demonic hybrid eight months after being discovered in a distressed state alone on top of a mysterious hill. The little boy is living proof of the protagonist's belief in

stories of mothers who have left a child quietly sleeping, with
the cottage door rudely barred with a piece of wood, and have
returned, not to find the plump and rosy little Saxon, but a
thin and wizened creature, with sallow skin and black piercing
eyes, *the child of another race.* Then, again, there were myths
darker still; the ... hint of demons who *mingled* with the
daughters of men.[19]

The sallow skin is suggestive of the unhealthy, but there is
also a strong hint of racial difference. The piercing eyes are
signifiers of the demonic in Gothic literature and here,
combined with the non-white skin, the description suggests
that races other than the healthy *Saxon* are themselves
demonic. Given the equation of the rational scientist with
colonial explorer and the fact that the story suggests the
mythology of the Celts may provide a link with the forgotten
people or powers sought by the scientist, the implicit suggestion is one of the English (Saxon) imperial rationalist risking
all among the dark, forbidding and thoroughly *Other* Welsh
(Celts). It seems clear that the reader is supposed to identify
with the rosy Saxon rather than 'the child of another race',
which may be problematic for Welsh readers who find themselves excluded from the implied audience. It might be
illuminating to read the ambiguity of this issue of identification as powerfully expressive of the fears of a 'border' or
'split' identity, which appears to aspire to identify with
Englishness while fearing the 'contamination' of an undesirable Welshness.

It is worth examining 'The Novel of the Black Seal' in
greater detail here, as it provides a good illustration of how
the Gothic genre, which relies heavily upon references that
are easily recognizable to the reader as significations of the
unnatural, the uncanny or downright evil, is heavily indebted
to racist colonial discourses that give meaning to these collective signifiers of terror. Significantly, the protagonist of 'The
Novel of the Black Seal' is not only a scientist, but 'an

authority of ethnology and kindred subjects' (3). The main part of the story is set in Monmouthshire and the portrayal of the countryside is central to the creation of a suitably oppressive and foreboding atmosphere. The landscape is described in terms immediately recognizable as reminiscent of colonial texts that portray foreign landscapes and peoples as strange and implicitly threatening: 'yielding in the north to even wilder country, barren and savage hills, and ragged commonland, a territory all strange and unvisited, and more unknown to Englishmen than the very heart of Africa' (15). The Professor's investigations themselves are referred to in the language of territorial exploration and discovery; he admits that 'I covet the renown of Columbus; you will, I hope, see me play the part of an explorer' (9). And later his quest is described as an attempt to find 'the undiscovered continent', which he believes to be peopled with 'a race which had fallen out of the grand march of evolution' (34). The nature of the 'lost' people is particularly fascinating – not only are they referred to in overtly colonial terms, these primitive people are located in the Welsh countryside. The Professor has sought clues in Welsh folklore being 'especially drawn to consider the stories of the fairies, the good folk of the Celtic races' (32).

Having repaired to a remote house in Wales to pursue his research, the Professor apparently does discover one of this strange race: the child of dubious paternity who was conceived on the hills. The boy is subject to fits during which his face becomes 'swollen and blackened to a hideous mask of humanity' (22) and he speaks an unintelligible language that is associated with a lack of evolutionary 'progress', being described as 'words ... that might have belonged to a tongue dead since untold ages and buried deep beneath Nilotic mud, or in the inmost recesses of the Mexican forest' (22). Here the conflation of the primitive and the colonial is explicit once more, and this is furthered by the later description of a bestial race that 'lagged so far behind the rest ... such a folk would speak a jargon but little removed from the inarticulate noises of brute beasts' (34). It is interesting, then, that one word the boy uses while speaking this 'primitive language' is repeated to the local Welsh-speaking parson in order to obtain a translation. The Professor does not think it *is* a Welsh word, yet the connection is made and it may be assumed that the implied (English-speaking) reader would not find the confusion between this demonic tongue and the exotic Welsh language, with its foreign sounding 'll's, at all incongruous.

Machen has been described as highly influenced by Darwinian notions of evolution,[20] and his stories are dependent on a notion of *progression*, and they play upon fears of racial *degeneration* that is portrayed as the opposite or reverse of (progressive) evolution. In 'The Great God Pan', Helen, the incarnation of evil, degenerates or regresses through the stages of evolution as she dies:

> Though ... an odour of corruption choked my breath, I remained firm ... [T]hat which was on the bed, lying there black like ink, transformed before my eyes ... I saw the form waver from sex to sex ... Then I saw the body descend to the beasts whence it ascended, and that which was on the heights go down to the depths, even to the abyss of all being ... I watched and saw nothing but a substance as jelly. Then the ladder was ascended again.[21]

Life forms are understood to be organized hierarchically (evolution is a ladder to be ascended) and human life is organized hierarchically according to race. For while the passage may not initially seem to be about race the imagery is influenced by fears about race and gender. The horror of a form wavering from 'sex to sex' is suggestive of contemporary fears of gender and sexual inversion. The New Women who wore trousers, wanted careers or took an active role as lover were understood as 'inverts' and gender inversion was a sign of sexual inversion – lesbianism (Helen's sexual excesses variously code her as lesbian and prostitute as well as femme fatale). We have already seen how racial Otherness is connected with sexual 'deviance', and the blackness of the form lying on the bed is an obvious indicator of racial difference, but so too is the malodorousness of the creature that is Helen. Bad odour is another example of the conjunction and conflation of many discourses concerned with Others/ Otherness. H. L. Malchow suggests that body odour was the focus of an obsession that failed to find a place in polite discourse and so emerges in Gothic fiction associated with constructions of Otherness:

> If one also considers the strong body odor associated in racist discourse with the animalistic African or with the unpleasant odors associated with the Jew . . . as well as that ascribed to prostitutes (owing, it was thought, to the retention of semen) and to menstruating women, it is clear that scent played a role in drawing together or bridging a surprising number of nineteenth century middle-class prejudices. The discourses of racism, homophobia, misogyny, class hatred, and religious bigotry were all corroborated by this most penetrating of the physical senses.[22]

It is no surprise, then, that Miss Allensmore's home in 'A Modest Adornment' is described as housing a 'prowling smell' (239), the adjective conjuring animalistic and predatory images. The strong smell remarked upon in Machen's 'The Novel of the Black Seal', which is associated with the boy/ demon, also has bestial connotations:

> There was a queer sort of smell in the study when I came down and opened the windows [relates the maid, after one of the boy's 'fits']; a bad smell it was, and I wondered what it could be. Do you know miss, I went a long time ago to the zoo in London . . . and we went into the snake house to see the snakes, and it was just the same sort of smell; very sick it made me feel . . . (28)

And if the boy and his malodourousness is, albeit tentatively, associated with the idea of the Welsh as racial Others in this story, the Welsh themselves were not above invoking bad smells in a racist context. In a study of racism and immigration in Wales, Neil Evans cites the instance of a Welsh miner who asserted the need for colour segregation (or more probably exclusion) in the mines on the basis that 'black people smelled so badly that even boys couldn't work with them!'[23]

Science, and the figure of the scientist, are important ingredients of Gothic fiction. The influence of racial/colonial discourses that relied heavily on science – from medicine through to anthropology and ethnology and even philology – to justify and rationalize the imperial project are also to be found in other genres. The final story examined here, a Gothic thriller 'The Chosen One', by Rhys Davies, is heavily and self-consciously informed by the language and practices of (colonial) anthropology. The now infamous image of the anthropologist equipped with calipers taking cranial measurements in order to assert a hierarchical evaluation of intellectual and moral capabilities based on skull shape and size might be seen as the epitome of the scientist as imperialist and patriarch; both non-whites and Western women were alleged to be intellectually inferior to white men in this way. In his anthropological study, *The Races of Britain* (1885), John Beddoe describes the so-called racial elements that exist in Britain through the cranial statistics and the colours of eyes and hair. From physical traits, Beddoe, like his contemporaries, moves seamlessly on to comment on the 'character' of the groups he studies. In these obviously subjective cultural values that are stated as objective scientific truths we may see an important aspect of the demonization of various constructions of Otherness.

The anthropological conflation of physical traits and behavioural characteristics are used and manipulated in Rhys Davies's typically curious story. In 'The Chosen One', a Welsh, working-class tenant of a cottage his family have inhabited for many generations is fighting to renew the lease with the anglicized (or possibly English) lady of the house. The way in which the working classes are constructed as Other by the more privileged classes is certainly an important issue here, but the significance of the racial, or rather national, implications of the story ought not to be overlooked. The tense historical relationship between Wales and England may be suggested in the details we are given about the way the cottage and some land was obtained rather deceitfully from a Welsh family by the owners of the larger estate. That the aristocratic family made money through such small-scale empire-building, through the expansion of the industrial railways that elsewhere were a vital component of the colonial project, and that they grossly underpaid for this land while making misleading promises about the cottage lease, places the story in a colonial as well as a class context. The tenant, Rufus, displays many simian characteristics and his Welshness is contrasted with the apparent anglicization of his landlady, an anthropologist, whose very class distances her from her Welsh surroundings. Rufus's dark curly hair, low brow and stocky build sound as if they come from a description of a Welshman in Beddoe's *Races of Britain*, and the lady of the house lives as remotely cut off from her neighbours as if she were a white settler in an African or Indian colony.[24]

Indeed, the racial and anthropological language of the story is explicit; Mrs Vines has 'lived among African savages, studying their ways with her first husband',[25] has African masks adorning her walls, keeps a sheep's skull because of the 'purity' of its breeding and views her tenant as a fascinating specimen, intensely observing his movements through binoculars. What is particularly fascinating are the descriptions of the tenant and his girlfriend in the overtly bestial terms so familiar from studies of African peoples. Rufus 'prowls' around his garden, he has 'full-fleshed lips' (1) and lives in a house Mrs Vines declares to be unfit for human habitation. She tells him, with contempt, 'You are almost as hairy as an ape' and shows great interest in his genitals, commenting that 'your organs are exceptionally pronounced' (31). His girlfriend, meanwhile, is distinguished by her tendency to shriek, and she is referred to by Mrs Vines as a 'jazz-dancing slut' with 'bare feet' (2). The combined reference to sexual promiscuity and the style of music and dancing that originated in black America suggest both the degeneracy of the working-class prostitute and the sensual black 'savage'. The connotations are of the primitive, the degenerate, and are described in the terms of physical anthropology:

> To her eye, the prognathous jaw, broad nose, and gypsy-black hair of this heavy-bodied but personable young man bore distinct atavistic elements. He possessed, too, a primitive bloom, which often lingered for years beyond adolescence with persons of tardy mental development. (12)

The prognathous jaw is associated with the mentally, racially and socially inferior; the broad nose draws parallels with the Negro, as does the racially ambiguous 'gypsy-black hair' (12). That these are racial, or hereditary, rather than accidental is emphasized by the fact that they are 'distinct *atavistic* elements' (12) (my emphasis).

In using an authorial narrative voice to describe what are effectively the anthropologist's observations, which typically run from physical appearance to assumptions of character and mental capacity, Rhys Davies draws attention to the complicity of literature with such constructions and parodies self-referential academic/scientific language used in such discourses to assert and maintain authority (Mrs Vines's letter giving notice of eviction uses language that is deliberately opaque in order to emphasize her power over her tenant). Furthermore, the story becomes almost a deconstruction of the methods of suggestion employed by some forms of literature, particularly, but by no means exclusively, the Gothic. By this I mean to suggest that the anthropologist reads physical 'signs' much in the same way that a reader interprets 'literary' signs littered about the text, signs that are interpreted according to fixed conventions such as, to give a simplistic example, the association of the colour black with evil or rural isolation with an 'uncivilized' or 'savage' threat – references that are not innocently contained within an arbitrary literary convention but which continually refer back to social and cultural discourses.[26]

The texts explored here suggest that there is an interdependent relationship between racial stereotypes, which were the product of supposedly empirical scientific research, and the 'domestic' discourses of imperial nations. The European colonialist's perception of non-whites is often reflected in disturbing and uncanny, even horrifying, literary figures, while such images themselves, and their fantastic exploration of European fears, reflect back upon notions of the racial Other, influencing in turn our collective 'knowledge' of the non-white. As the reader identifies against the Otherness constructed in the stories depicted here, s/he is constructed as white and, in these stories, as English (or at least not Welsh).

Interrelated stereotypes of racial, gendered and sexual Otherness are used in Welsh writing in English to mobilize (and indeed depend for their success upon) the preconceptions, prejudices and associated fears of the reader that are themselves informed by the belief in racial and patriarchal supremacy that underpinned imperial ideology. To some extent this use of racial Otherness performs the same functions as of similar constructions in English literature – Wales was, after all, part of the metropole of the British Empire and often shared its imperial vision. Yet, in Welsh writing in English the quasi-colonial status of Wales as a peripheral nation within the United Kingdom is reflected in the way the Welsh are themselves often cast in the role of racial Other. The Welsh reader, then, is faced with the somewhat schizophrenic experience of functioning/responding as part of the implied (metropolitan) audience usually assumed by the texts

– recognizing and responding to the literary motifs of the fearful Other in a certain way – while simultaneously realizing that they are excluded from the implied audience, from the metropolis, and often actually belong to the group being represented as grotesquely Other.[27]

Notes

1   This is a revised and shortened version of an essay that first appeared as 'Apes and cannibals in Cambria: images of the racial and gendered other in Gothic writing in Wales', *Welsh Writing in English: A Yearbook of Critical Essays*, 6 (Cardiff, 2000), 119–43.

2   See W. Schneider, 'Race and empire: the rise of popular ethnography in the late nineteenth century', *Journal of Popular Culture*, 2 (1977), 98–109.

3   See N. Stepan, *The Idea of Race in Science: Great Britain 1800–1960* (London, 1982).

4   See H. L. Malchow, *Gothic Images of Race in Nineteenth Century Britain* (Stanford, CA, 1996).

5   On Margiad Evans's lesbian writing, see K. Bohata, 'The Apparitional Lover: homoerotic and lesbian imagery in the writing of Margiad Evans', in K. Bohata and K. Gramich (eds), *Rediscovering Margiad Evans: Marginality, Gender and Illness* (Cardiff, 2013), pp. 107–28.

6   A. O. Lovejoy traces the history of the idea of the 'great chain of being' back to Greece. However, he notes that 'It was in the eighteenth century that the conception of the universe as a Chain of Being, and the principles which underlay this conception – plenitude, continuity, gradation – attained their widest diffusion and acceptance.' *The Great Chain of Being: A Study of the History of an Idea* (Cambridge, MA, 1957), p. 183.

7   See T. Denean Sharpley-Whiting, *Black Venus: Sexualised Savages, Primal Fears and Primitive Narratives in French* (Durham NC, 1999), and C. Crais, *Sara Baartman and the Hottentot Venus: A Ghost Story and a Biography* (Princeton, NJ, 2008).

8 This 'apron' was first 'observed' by Westerners in the seventeenth century and regarded as a deformity. By the late eighteenth/early nineteenth centuries there was still much confusion over whether its origins were congenital or cultural. This confusion still persists. Some academics assume congenital causes. Others suggest that cultural mores result in the manipulation of the labia to cause elongation. Some commentators also make the important point that pendulous labia – whether congenital or cultural – should not be regarded as abnormal in any way.

9 The *OED* lists the earliest use of the word 'lesbian' in the context of lesbian love in 1890 in *Billings Medical Dictionary*, II, 47/1. This passage is translated from German (presumably by Sander Gilman since no other is credited).

10 S. L. Gilman, *Difference and Pathology* (London, 1985), p. 89.

11 L. Moore, 'Teledildonics: virtual lesbians in the fiction of Jeanette Winterson', in E. Grosz and E. Probyn (eds), *Sexy Bodies: The Strange Carnalities of Feminism* (London and New York, 1995), p. 121.

12 L. Moore, '"Something more tender still than friendship": romantic friendship in early-nineteenth century England', *Feminist Studies*, 18/3 (Fall 1992), 514.

13 Ibid., 516.

14 M. Evans, 'A Modest Adornment', in *A View Across the Valley* (Dinas Powys, 1999), ed. J. Aaron. Subsequent references appear in parentheses in the text.

15 See E. Grosz, 'Animal sex: libido as desire and death', in E. Grosz and E.Probyn (eds), *Sexy Bodies: The Strange Carnalities of Feminism*, for a discussion of how attributes from the insect world have been projected onto female sexualities, pp. 278–98, especially p. 281; also B. Dijkstra, *Evil Sisters: The Threat of Female Sexuality and the Cult of Manhood* (New York, 1996).

16 See E. Showalter, *The Female Malady* (London, 1987), and J. M. Ussher, *The Psychology of the Female Body* (London, 1989).

17 See J. M. Ussher, *Women's Madness: Misogyny or Mental Illness?* (Hemel Hempstead, 1991), p. 74.

18   Thomas Jefferson, 'Laws', from *Notes on the State of Virginia,* repro-
      duced in *Race and the Enlightenment: A Reader,* ed. E. Chkwudi Eze
      (Oxford, 1997), p. 103; my emphasis.

19   A. Llewellyn Machen, 'The Novel of the Black Seal', in *Tales of
      Horror and the Supernatural,* with an introduction by P. van Doren
      Stern (London, 1949), p. 33; my emphasis. Subsequent references
      appear in parentheses in the text.

20   See D. Punter, *The Literature of Terror: A History of Gothic Fictions
      from 1765 to the Present Day, ii, The Modern Gothic (London,
      1996).*

21   A. Llewellyn Machen, 'The Great God Pan', in *Tales of Horror and
      the Supernatural,* pp. 111–12.

22   *Malchow, Gothic Images of Race,* p. 141.

23   N. Evans, 'Immigrants and minorities in Wales, 1840–1990: a
      comparative perspective', *Llafur,* 5/4, (1991), 5–26, 12.

24   The similarity between the descriptions of Rufus in 'The Chosen
      One' (see below) and David Gellatie and other villagers in *Waverley*
      (1814; Oxford, 1981, ed. Clare Lamont), Walter Scott's classic novel
      about the making of 'Britain' through the union of England and
      Scotland, are striking. Both are described in language that is borrowed
      from the discourses of anthropology and similar terms to those one
      would expect to find in the patronizing and derogatory texts of the
      colonizer referring to non-whites.

25   R. Davies, 'The Chosen One', *The Chosen One and Other Stories*
      (London, 1967), p. 8. Subsequent references appear in parentheses in
      the text.

26   Rhys Davies plays with such signifiers and uses them with some skill,
      although he never really subverts them. See K. Bohata, 'The black
      Venus: atavistic sexualities', and D. Williams, 'Withered roots: ideas
      of race in the writings of Rhys Davies and D. H. Lawrence', in
      M. Stephens (ed.), *Rhys Davies: Decoding the Hare* (Cardiff, 2001),
      pp. 231–43.

27   What the construction of the reader as white and non-Welsh means
      for a black Welsh reader is a question not addressed here, risking the
      implicit representation of Welsh readers as white. Charlotte Williams
      has written about the problematic displacement of 'reading white' in

'"I going away, I going home": mixed-"race", movement and iden-tity', in L. Pearce (ed.), *Devolving Identities: Feminist Readings in Home and Belonging*, Studies in European Cultural Transition, 8 (Aldershot, 2000). She has also explored in *Sugar and Slate* (Aberystwyth, 2002) the way her Welsh-speaking white mother could be perceived as a 'dark stranger' in England in ways that parallel or even surpass the otherness of her African-Caribbean father. The representation of Wales and the Welsh in terms of racial Otherness is clearly a topic that warrants further consideration. For a major new comparative study of Welsh Writing in English and African-American literature, which examines 'the ways in which African Americans and the Welsh have defined themselves as minorities within larger nation states', see D. G. Williams, *Black Masks, Blue Books: African Americans and Wales 1845–1945* (Cardiff, 2012).

5

Wales and Africa: William Hughes and the Congo Institute

NEIL EVANS AND IVOR WYNNE JONES[1]

When missionaries left Britain in the nineteenth century it was normal for church and chapel congregations to sing the missionary hymn, 'From Greenland's Icy Mountains' to speed them on their way. The following lines emphasized the size of the field open for conversion: 'From India's coral strand / Where Afric's sunny fountains / Roll down their golden sand.'[2] They were written at Wrexham in 1819 by the Reverend Reginald Herber at the behest of his father-in-law Dean Shipley of St Asaph, and while the words stress the immensity of the world and – hence the task of the mission-ary – their emphasis is upon simply spreading the message, wafting on the winds and across the seas.[3] The Reverend William Hughes, creator of the Congo Institute in Colwyn Bay, would have been very familiar with the words and we know that he heard them on his departure for a second visit to Africa in 1893. But by then the experience of his first African encounter had convinced him that the objective was much harder to achieve and needed different tactics from those of orthodox missionary societies. His life and work offer an insight into attitudes to race in late Victorian and Edwardian Wales.[4]

Hughes was the son of a tenant farmer, born on 8 April 1856 at a remote seventeenth-century long-house farm at

Ynys, two miles north of Llanystumdwy, in Caernarfonshire. The language of this sparsely populated community was entirely Welsh and he was expected to spend his life as a farm labourer, with neither the money nor the education to explore beyond the fields in which he worked. His parents failed to cultivate curiosity in the occasional activity at the small Baptist chapel – Capel y Beirdd – only 350 yards away at the southern boundary of the farm, and he was seventeen years of age before he was 'converted to Christianity' after he had walked to Garndolbenmaen with friends for his first visit to a church. 'An earnest prayer at the commencement of the service decided me for Christ', said Hughes nine years later, when writing to Alfred H. Baynes, secretary of the Baptist Missionary Society (BMS).⁵

Hughes joined Capel y Beirdd, which made him literate, and it was at the chapel, in 1875, that he listened to a lecture on Dr Livingstone's mission in Africa and Denbigh-born H. M. Stanley's famous greeting in 1871. Hughes became a lifelong admirer of Stanley. He was told he could not become a student at the Welsh Baptist College, Llangollen, until he learnt English. Never having ventured more than four or five miles from home, he set off in April 1875 'unable to understand the simplest English sentence', and found a job as a farm labourer in Cheshire. Eight months later he had learned enough English to move on to his finishing school – a large drapers' shop in Manchester. By 1877 he was sufficiently fluent to become a Sunday school teacher in Moss Side, where he bought a copy of *The Missionary Herald*. He was entranced by the heading 'Africa for Christ', and news of plans to set up a Baptist Mission in the Congo.⁶ It was two years before the BMS team arrived at Sao Salvador (in July 1879), and on 14 August H. M. Stanley turned up at the mouth of the Congo River to establish 'civilised settlements [where] justice and law and order shall prevail, and murder and lawlessness, and the cruel barter for slaves, shall for ever cease'.⁷

In the autumn of 1879 Hughes was admitted to Llangollen Baptist College. In May 1882 Principal Hugh Jones recommended the newly ordained Hughes to the BMS as 'a splendid young fellow', stating that he had linguistic limitations inhibiting his employment among the literate people of India or China, but that he was suitable for the Congo. Hughes was interviewed by the BMS in July and a month later embarked at Liverpool.[8] He stepped ashore at Banana on 22 September 1882 and travelled ninety-three miles up river by steamer, to the Underhill BMS base at Matadi. After a few weeks' instruction he was sent further up river and put in charge of Bayneston, which comprised a tent, a storehouse made of grass, a few fowls, some servants from the coast and one Congolese boy, Kinkasa, whom he had brought with him from down river. Lonely and surrounded by disease and death, Hughes found hope in the arrival at Bayneston of N'Kanza, a young slave boy belonging to the local chief.[9] Almost unable to walk because the soles of his feet were infested with boring parasites, N'Kanza was sent to the mission to be cured by Hughes, resulting in a bond that was later to take the boy to Colwyn Bay.

By 1884 Hughes, who had moved to the main Underhill base mission, was becoming disillusioned by the international politics surrounding his work. The Germans annexed the Cameroons, and their army attacked the BMS settlement accommodating Africans of many different tribes who had been liberated by the Royal Navy while being taken into slavery. The Berlin Conference opened in November, to carve up Africa among the Europeans, and by the time it closed in February 1885 Leopold II was king of the Congo – appointing as his first administrator Lieutenant-Colonel Sir Francis de Winton, of Maesllwch Castle, Radnorshire. Hughes was not alone in his disillusionment. In March 1885 the Reverend H. K. Moolenaar (who had sailed out with Hughes) wrote to the BMS in London citing cases of cruelty to native blacks by white missionaries, but the matter was hushed up. Hughes also wrote to Baynes but no hint of his letter was to be found in the report to the ninety-third annual general meeting of the BMS in July 1885.

Hughes was engaged to Katie, daughter of the principal of Llangollen College who wished to join him in the Congo, but he felt that it was too unhealthy and uncomfortable to allow such a course. He told the BMS that he wanted to leave the mission, accompanied by two boys, whom he would train at his own expense, for the benefit of their own people.[10] The BMS seemed content to leave Hughes to rot in the Congo and he was again struck down by fever. Fortuitously, Stanley's doctor was to hand and attended him for three days and nights, telling him his only chance of life was to leave Africa. Sir Francis de Winton used his steamer to take Hughes and the boys Kinkasa and N'Kanza down river to board a ship for Liverpool.[11] 'As soon as we cleared the river and got into the ocean, the sea breeze revived me', noted Hughes, and during the voyage he decided to create a Congo training college.

Baynes refused to accept Hughes's resignation, hoping he could be persuaded to return but retained him on the BMS payroll as a fundraiser to tour the Baptist churches of Wales.[12] While refusing to acknowledge the existence of Kinkasa and N'Kanza, the BMS capitalized on their star turn during Hughes's lecture tours. A Welsh poster for his 1885–6 tour announced that he would be accompanied by 'black boys', who would sing in Welsh, English and Congolese.[13] The BMS subjected Hughes to alternating threats and promises. He was told he could choose his station and be promoted to a senior missionary with better pay if he returned to the Congo, but he was warned he would be 'suppressed' if he did not go back.[14] In the autumn of 1885 he was told that the BMS did not consider the many white deaths from Congo fevers to be sufficient reason for a minister to abandon his flock. In January 1886 a friendly minister warned Hughes he would be crushed by the Baptist cause.

Under these pressures Hughes and Katie Jones were medically examined in January and February 1886 and pronounced unfit for service in Equatorial Africa: they were married in March. Hughes seems both to have brought to a head and symbolized long-standing conflicts between Welsh Baptists and the BMS. No firm and substantial relationship had ever been established nor had any structure to represent Welsh interests been created in the BMS. Its annual meetings in London were difficult and expensive for Welsh members to attend and by the 1880s the BMS had long since given up specific measures like a Welsh sermon to attract attendance from Wales. Occasionally Welsh people were elected to the committee but arguments were made that there ought to be specific Welsh representation, elected by Welsh members of the BMS. Such assertiveness was in parallel with the demands Welsh Liberals were making on the British state but they had little resonance in the BMS, partly because of the low level of support it enjoyed in Wales. Hughes focussed other Welsh discontents, particularly that the BMS did not adhere to the practice of closed communion in mission, which emphasized the divergence between English Baptists, where the New Theology was having an impact, and the more theologically conservative Wales.[15]

The BMS recruited the support of a fellow Welsh missionary, Thomas Lewis, when he arrived home on leave in April 1886 accompanied by a Congolese boy. He was sent on a lecture tour, promoting the Society's official line: 'Experience has taught us all better things for Africa. These poor lads looked in despair at the snow-covered country of the white man.'[16] The BMS formally reported the severance of its links with William Hughes in May 1886.[17]

However, invitations for Hughes's lecture and the trilingual singing of his 'black boys' poured in from all parts of Wales, attracting packed congregations. During each show Kinkasa and N'Kanza sold their photographs to raise money for their keep and for Hughes's dream of an independent Welsh-based Congo institute. In June 1887 he was appointed pastor of Llanelian Baptist Church, with the promise of a second pastorate for a new church being planned for Colwyn Bay.[18] The family took up residence in Bay View Road, Colwyn Bay, calling their home Congo House, two years before the first meeting of his Congo Institution Committee. In April 1890 he took over a house in Nant-y-Glyn Road, which he renamed Congo Institute.

Hughes's conception of the institute broke with most of the accepted wisdom of missionary thought. His experience in Africa interacted with his sense of Welshness to create a radically different approach, and one that reveals much about conceptions of racial and cultural difference at the time. On his voyage to Africa he had disembarked, briefly, at the old slave market port in Landana, a detached Portuguese enclave north of the Congo River associated with the Roman Catholic mission to Angola since the fifteenth century. He was impressed with the way in which former slaves had been trained as craftsmen but were also educated in the evenings. He saw this as a model of how indigenous missionaries might be trained and become rooted in a locality so that they could be more effective than itinerant white missionaries. He was prepared to learn from the Catholic Portuguese but resolved that a Protestant Welsh variant on this idea was necessary.[19]

The climate ruled out Africa as a field for missionary activity for Europeans, Hughes argued, not only from his own experience but from the general death rate of European missionaries in Africa: one missionary society, he claimed, lost twelve white men in the years 1882–5.[20] His solution was to train Africans for the task in Britain, where they would be removed from the 'superstitious and evil influences' of their fellow Africans, and because they would have a more profound influence than would Europeans. Hughes derived this idea from his experience of English rule in Wales: English people had been appointed as judges, preachers and magistrates but were ignorant of the language, culture and history of the people. So Wales served as a model for Africa.

111

Britain's climate was more suitable for Africans than the African climate was for Europeans. But why, then, locate the institute in Colwyn Bay? The practical answer to this question was its proximity to Liverpool with its extensive West African trade and the offer from the Liverpool shipping company Elder Dempster to give free passages to Africans training at the institute. This was around the time that Tom Ellis was proclaiming Liverpool as the capital of north Wales and a counterweight to the influence of Cardiff in the south. Hughes's plan was only workable because the institute was within the orbit of Liverpool. Colwyn Bay's elite included retired Lancashire magnates whose wealth ultimately rested on cotton grown by slaves and nominally free sharecroppers in the American south.[21] It was a place with a healthy climate, it was 'beautiful 'and 'rising' and a mere five miles from Llandudno by train, which, in turn, was two hours from Liverpool by steamer.[22]

But Colwyn Bay's key advantage was that it was in Wales and, according to Hughes, 'there is no country on earth with such religious surroundings as little Wales . . . a land of chapels, a land where there is a Bible in every house and everyone can read it.'[23] Wales was set into relief by Africa, which was seen as backward, superstitious and lacking in the work ethic, all things that could not be alleged about Wales. There could be few better illustrations of Catherine Hall's argument that empire was a vital aspect of national identity and that it permeated the culture of Britain:

> what is seen as outside an identity, other to it, is in fact constitutive of it. The fullness of identity depends on what it lacks . . . identities are always constructed in a process of mutual constitution – the making of the self through the making and marking off of others.[24]

'Cymru Lan' (Pure Wales) looked even purer when held up against 'dark' Africa. The clinching argument came when the

two came into confrontation: the beautiful town of Colwyn
Bay would 'compare very favourably in the eyes of our African
students with the miserable villages of their own country'.[25]
Hughes said that an African student had told him that he had
never thought so highly of white people until he came to
Colwyn Bay. He said that in Africa many white people were
immoral and there were few honourable examples. Hughes
added that he was appalled by the use of force (and the cruelty
entailed) in the aid of missionary efforts in Africa and saw the
BMS as being fatally compromised by its associates.[26] The
virtues of Wales could be transferred to England when Hughes
was in search for funds: in a short leaflet that seems to have
been be aimed at fundraising there (and containing the impri-
matur of a favourable comment in the *Leeds Mercury*),
England was praised as the most enlightened country in the
world and contrasted with 'the barbarous and degraded
heathen of India and Africa'.[27]

Wales had the advantage of being part of the British
Empire, which Hughes held to be the best of the colonial
powers, although a far from perfect one. Better government
in Ireland, he believed, would have averted the Great Famine
(1845–50), Ireland had been robbed in trade and blood had
been shed, and we have already seen his criticisms of the
government of Wales. However, generally Britain followed
the Bible and valued souls above large possessions. France
still treated Africa the way in which Britain had once treated
Ireland, he argued.

The struggle for converts was an uphill one. Hughes
produced a diagram that showed graphically the outnumber-
ing of Protestants (135 million) by Catholics (195 million) and
'Mohammedans' (173 million) and 'Heathen' (874 million).
Mission converts were a mere three million in the midst of
these 'heathens', and he argued that to change the balance
would require new methods such as those he was advocating.
A century before there had been only 200 million
Mohammedans and Heathens. He saw the world – or at least

appealed to people whom he thought saw the world – as a 'clash of civilizations' and he punctured Western ideas of racial supremacy with the threat of being overwhelmed.[28] Hughes's scheme had a fallback position for the eventuality of failure: even if his missionaries did not win converts they would civilize Africa through their skills. Africa needed industrial training, according to Hughes, as African men shirked labour, saw it as despicable and left it to women, so Africa needed secular as well as religious instruction. In this Africa was different from India and China. There was no better creed to inculcate the necessary values than that of the carpenter of Nazareth. Hughes was encouraged by the fact that merchants and traders had spread early Christianity and he clearly saw an analogous role for economic development in Africa.[29]

However, Hughes saw many aspects of Africa in a positive light: the country was 'wonderful', like America but with greater wealth and fertility. In the future it would be the finest country in the world, even if at the present it was behind Europe, China and India in the pecking order of progress. Moreover, Africans were good people if given proper treatment, knowledge and opportunity. They were 'keen, deep and sharp' as well as patient. Hughes did not espouse biological racism but he had a clear view that some civilizations and religions were better than others, although this was explained through history and development rather than race. It has been argued recently that such views predominated in nineteenth-century Britain as compared with continental Europe, yet we need to be aware of the counter-argument that race could be seen as a predisposing factor for development.[30]

Hughes revealed much of his outlook in an analogy he employed for the impact of British civilization on Africans: he compared it with the impact of the Crusades in helping to civilize Britain. There is little scope for biological racism in such a position. It was underlined explicitly in another comment: 'Our idea in training Africans as missionaries is that in all points they are like their brethren, of the same blood, the same colour, the same humour, the same language, the same in everything, excepting in education and training.'[31]

He saw Africa as one continent, containing one people but many tribes, and so his view was part of a pan-African vision that was to play a significant part in black liberation struggles in the twentieth century. As with many missionaries he was concerned to improve Africa by countering the activities of slavers. Slave traders wished to keep Africa degraded, whereas he argued that there were few such traders in the areas with which he was concerned and that it was exceptional for them to interfere in British colonies in general. However, on the continent as a whole, little progress had been made in this regard. He had a general vision of white oppression of black people, commenting that too many white men wanted to keep black people down, as evidenced in India, the United States and in Africa.[32]

In later years, Hughes protested about the imposition of hut taxes in Africa (intended to force Africans into waged work to obtain the cash needed to pay them) and in 1909 he wrote to the *Manchester Guardian* protesting against the provision for a colour bar that was written into the South Africa Bill, then before Parliament. 'It is an insult to 360 millions of coloured people who are to be found in different parts of our Empire', he said, adding that Britain was deserting the blacks by bending to the Boers' ideas of government. He argued that in the future the colour bar would be as much an object of shame as was slavery.[33] The Union of South Africa came into being in May 1910 and reflected a reconciliation of Boers and the settlers of British origin; it was based on white supremacy and the new constitution removed the political rights of black people who had often backed Britain in the Boer War, as well as laying the basis for racial segregation.[34] Hughes's comment invoked an image of a racially divided empire, and later black activists would invoke the overwhelming numerical supremacy of black people as a counter to their ill treatment in Britain.[35]

Congo House opened in 1890 and for much of the next decade enjoyed a modicum of success. There was a trickle rather than a stream of young men who came for training before returning to Africa; five of the students were to die in Colwyn Bay but we should not necessarily jump to the conclusion that this was the result of local environmental factors, as some died from conditions contracted in Africa and the student deaths need to be set against those of the four members of Hughes's own family who also made the journey to Llanelian Road Cemetery in the period.

The first student returned to Africa in July 1890. The fame of the very small Colwyn Bay operation spread up and down the West African coast, and students continued to arrive, including eight in 1891. Most of the students came via the American Baptist Missionary Union (ABMU), with which friendly and productive relations were established, in contrast to the continuing hostility of the BMS. In 1891 the hymn-writers Dwight Lyman Moody and Ira David Sankey, both prominent in the Congo work of the ABMU, visited the institute. 'Our American friends seem to appreciate this idea more than some of our friends nearer home', wrote Hughes. Another American visitor was the Reverend Daniel J. Jenkins, of Charleston, who had been born a slave soon after the Civil War began. The institute appears to have been the inspiration for the Jenkins Orphanage (now the Jenkins Institute for Children) in Charleston, and his son visited William Hughes at Colwyn Bay in 1916, when few people wanted to know him.[36]

The BMS's hostility continued unabated. The Reverend Benjamin Evans, of Gadlys, a Welsh member of the BMS committee, attacked Hughes in the columns of *Seren Cymru*, the Welsh-language Baptist newspaper. 'No missionary belonging to us in Africa, and especially in the Congo, is in sympathy with Mr. Hughes and his cause', he said in August

1893. The Reverend J. Spinther James replied robustly to Evans, and another critic, the Reverend A. Steffens, by publishing Hughes's letters of 1885–6 that had been suppressed by the BMS. On 20 March 1893 the Reverend Steffens of the German Missionary Society in the Cameroons had written to Hughes complaining of 'its' youth being stolen from them and refusing to employ any African who had been in a foreign country. Steffens's experience of such people was that they were corrupted by bad habits while away and came back dressed like gentlemen and ashamed of their native languages: 'If we hear of any more boys and girls going to England we will use other means', he threatened, and while we do not know what he meant he was clearly echoing Germany's ambition for an African empire. Steffens wrote in similar terms to BMS secretary Baynes, who gleefully printed his letter for general circulation.[37]

This posed a threat for Hughes's venture and he responded by setting off for West Africa at the end of June 1893. In Liberia, Cameroons, New Calabar and Sierra Leone he created a series of feeder and associated institutions for the venture in Colwyn Bay, something that had been one of his original intentions.[38] He was absent for four months and when he returned to Colwyn Bay, in October, he set about building his new African Institute, next door to the original Congo Institute, incorporating a printing room, tailoring workshop, classrooms, full immersion baptismal pool and dormitories. That was the month in which a prominent group of Liverpool Baptists travelled to Colwyn Bay to discuss Hughes's motives. Well satisfied with what they saw, they arranged for a public meeting in Liverpool to raise funds for the institute, but on the day before the well-advertised assembly Hughes received a telegram saying everything had been cancelled because of serious allegations by the BMS. Three members of the Colwyn Bay committee met the local BMS superintendent under the independent chairmanship of a prominent Liverpool merchant. The allegations were trivial and concerned the conduct of a returned student; and counter evidence was produced.[39]

On 9 December 1893 the *Lagos Weekly Record* carried a long feature in praise of the institute under the byline of the Reverend D. Brown Vincent, later to become an influential African nationalist, under his original native name of Mojola Agbebi. 'The effort may be regarded as the first prominent contribution of Wales to the redemption of Africa', he wrote. Further West African praise came in the *Sierra Leone Weekly News* on 2 June 1894, in a report of a meeting convened at the Freetown chambers of barrister (the future Sir) Samuel Lewis, CMG, a freed Yoruba slave. The gathering resolved: 'to take some definite step in shewing the world our appreciation of this noble work which already is in earnest progress with beneficial results to Africa'.

At home, however, the BMS was still trying to 'crush' Hughes. In April 1894 Baptist ministers were instructed to dissuade children from contributing to the African Institute by promising them a tea party if they switched their efforts to the BMS. In 1895 Hughes applied for the church he had established at the institute to be admitted into the Welsh Baptist Gymanfa (assembly), but he was refused and his name was removed from the list of ministers and erased from the Baptist cause two years later.

It was not to be the BMS, or even the Welsh Baptists, who ultimately were to topple the African Institute but a financial crisis that became apparent during a scandal. Two days before Christmas 1911 posters proclaiming: *BLACK BAPTIST'S BROWN BABY* peppered Colwyn Bay, drawing attention to a feature in Horatio Bottomley's notorious weekly magazine *John Bull*. For three months there had been rumours of a black baby born to an unmarried seamstress, which was attributed only to the presence in the town of the institute. As early as July 1907 Colwyn Bay residents had complained that four of the students had been seen in nearby woods with white girls, not to mention allegations that a student had been thrashed and expelled for 'improper' relations with white girls in the 1890s.[40] Hughes had denied the rumours, claiming they had been investigated, found baseless and he threatened legal action.[41] A copy of his warning was posted to *John Bull*, which sent a reporter to Colwyn Bay. It found that a twenty-six-year-old unmarried woman from Llandudno had given birth to a boy named Stanley, whose skin was dark. His father was a handsome Grenadian, John Lionel Franklin, who had come to Colwyn Bay in 1904 as lead actor in a performance of *Uncle Tom's Cabin* at the Public Hall. He attended a service at the African Institute and was subsequently used as a travelling fundraiser, though he was never a student at the institute.[42]

The *John Bull* feature was published in two parts. It opened with a reference to the text for a Bible class at the institute from chapter 1 of the First Book of Samuel, dealing with a man who had taken two wives, one infertile and the other giving him children. 'Anyone looking up this chapter in his Bible will be able to imagine the effect upon a mixed audience of European girls and "converted" Africans. Don't let me be misunderstood. I am not blaming these students. They are full-blooded men of fine physique,' wrote *John Bull*.[43] In the next installment, Franklin was named and described as a 'Black scoundrel':

> During the summer months at Colwyn Bay some of the lady visitors act in an astonishing manner towards these natives. They may be seen seated with them on the seafront, in earnest if not affectionate conversation. Afternoon tea parties are arranged, and when the dusk of evening arrives, 'black and white' may frequently be seen strolling together down the road behind the Institute.[44]

The articles allegedly led to creditors taking action to recover debts owed by the institute; a compulsory winding-up order was made and the African Institute closed on 21 March 1911.

On 14 March Hughes himself was declared bankrupt, with liabilities of £4,932. He initiated proceedings for libel against *John Bull* and the case was heard at Ruthin Assizes in June. The plaintiff said that the *John Bull* attacks were offensive and untrue, while the defendants replied that they published matters of fact in the public interest – to which the judge suggested a plea of fair comment might be more appropriate. Defending himself without the aid of counsel, Horatio Bottomley destroyed Hughes's credibility in cross-examination. Hughes had to concede the animosity of the BMS; his repeated issuing of cheques for which he had no funds; his expulsion of one unmanageable student yet retaining his name in the annual report as serving the institute mission in New Calabar; his inability to remember whether two others had also been expelled; slipshod book-keeping; no evidence of having funded any of the institute's declared forty-three out-stations in Africa; concealment from the institute's honorary solicitor of an unfavourable auditor's report for 1910, causing the solicitor's withdrawal; and the embezzlement of Ernestina Morford's personal fund from her Dutch father. The case ended abruptly when the judge asked the jury whether there was need to continue the trial, and the foreman said they had heard enough to reach a conclusion – in favour of *John Bull*. Bottomley reacted with a report stating: 'Colwyn Bay is delighted to be rid of Hughes and his niggers.'[45]

The institute had experienced some early funding problems but for most of the 1890s, following a lecture in Caernarfon by H. M. Stanley in aid of the institution, these seem not to have been severe.[46] The first hint of the institute's substantial financial problems appeared in the *African Times* of 2 July 1900, with an announcement that no new students could be accepted for the forthcoming school year. A year later the Colwyn Bay operation was registered as a charitable limited company, which bought the institute from Hughes, who used all the money to pay off his mortgage debts.[47] But the problems persisted: subscriptions had fallen during the Boer War

(1899–1902) the relief efforts for which made rival claims on subscribers. Fraud by an ex-student and a failed property speculation by Hughes added to the pressures. Sir Alfred Jones of Elder Dempster died in 1909 and the free passages for students back and fore to Africa ended. By 1909–10 there was an operating deficit of over £300. Also it is possible that rumours about Hughes's private life were in circulation.[48] The institute had always had enemies in more orthodox missionary circles but now it suffered from the failings of its friends. Hughes had been critical of the supporters of the BMS but his own supporters were found wanting. He had basked in the support of King Leopold of Belgium and Henry Morton Stanley, but both had had their reputations shredded by the revelations of slavery, brutality and exploitation in the Congo.[49] Clearly he could no longer stand on the moral high ground: deaths in the Congo outnumber those in the Holocaust. One of the earliest uses of the concept of a crime against humanity was during the exposure of the barbarism that was visited upon equatorial Africa.

The evidence of the local newspapers suggests that for the first twenty years of the institute's existence the people of Colwyn Bay warmly embraced its young black community; it was small, exotic and unthreatening. Not until 1907 did the image of black students walking in the woods with local girls cause concern. Even when *John Bull* turned up four years later to look for the rumoured black baby, it found local ladies happily seated on the promenade with, and inviting to tea, these 'full-blooded men of fine physique'. But clearly Bottomley sensed a vulnerable point and a story that was sensational enough to sell copies of his newspaper.

Black men in Britain inverted the usual racial and potential sexual relationships of imperialism: a black man in a sexual relationship with a white woman was much more transgressive of conventional values than a white man in a sexual relationship with a black woman. Yet it is clear that mixed race relationships were attractive to many people, whatever

the conventions of race and imperialism, and perhaps indicative of this is that the mother of the mixed race child in
Colwyn Bay never married because (she told her son) she had
never found another man to equal his father. Similarly, in
Cardiff's docklands white women often asserted the superiority of their black husbands. Issues like this fed into the
explosive mix that produced the race riots of 1919 in south
Wales.[50] Sexual tensions did not arise in any great measure in
Colwyn Bay but they did their damage in precipitating the
collapse of the already teetering African Institute. Hughes's
son believed that the 'Black baby' scandal was the catalyst
rather than the cause of that collapse.

Hughes briefly resurfaced when British and French troops
defeated his old German enemy in West Africa. He published
a pamphlet in 1916 under the simple title of *The Cameroons*.
He recalled the efforts of his African Institute to rescue indigenous students from German missionary tyranny and train
them for service in their homeland, where they had become
well-known preachers. 'We venture to state there would be
hardly any Christians in the Cameroons at the present time
but for the education and faithfulness of these men,' he wrote.

By 1917 Hughes had recovered sufficiently to contemplate
emigrating to Africa, black Baptists from the Cameroons
having sent him £30 for his fare. Fifty of the town's leading
citizens signed a splendidly illuminated farewell address,
which said: 'After a residence of 30 years among us, during
which you have rendered invaluable service to the town ... we,
the undersigned, exceedingly regret your departure.'[51] Except
for the events of 1911–12, the scroll gave a detailed recitation
of Hughes's career. 'Recognising your manifold services, we
bid you adieu', concluded the address, whose signatories
included sixteen ministers of various denominations, the
chairman of the town council, the editors of the local papers,
magistrates, general practitioners, teachers and the foreman
of the Urban District Council workmen. On 12 November
1917 Hughes circulated a farewell begging letter. He redated

it on 9 May 1918, and circulated it again, but never left.[52] His daughter Claudia died in December 1918, the last of Hughes's immediate family, except for his estranged footballer son Stanley. Hughes took to drink and was admitted to Penrhyndeudraeth workhouse as a pauper.[53] Later he was transferred to Conwy workhouse where he died of heart disease on 28 January 1924. Three quarters of a century later his name crops up on both sides of the Atlantic in any serious debate about the emancipation of black Africa, but he still awaits an entry in *The Dictionary of Welsh Biography*.

In its short history the Colwyn Bay Institute took in around 100 students from Africa.[54] Some of them travelled with Hughes on his fundraising exhibitions and were, of course, familiar sights in Colwyn Bay. It has been claimed that by the mid-nineteenth century most people in Britain would have seen a person of colour: this is unproveable but Hughes made his contribution to making it so in the years after 1886.[55] The institute was clearly part of a grid of institutions that linked the Western world and Africa, underpinning a pan-African network that reversed the polarities of the slave trade in a benign network that contributed to the promotion of change and freedom in Africa. William Hughes for a period had enlisted support for an approach to missionary activity that challenged some of the assumptions about race and Africa of his age. He demonstrates that there were divisions in such attitudes in the past and that at least some individuals could embrace ideas of equality, even if the overwhelming majority of people adopted opposing and more hostile positions.[56]

Notes

1   In the original edition of this book this essay appeared under the name of the late Ivor Wynne Jones (1927–2007) and it was his work alone. For the new edition it has been revised extensively drawing on the easily available printed sources and the research of Christopher

Draper, which is referred to in the notes. The judgements and analysis in this version are the responsibility of Neil Evans.

2 'The Hymns and Carols of Christmas', *http://www.hymnsandcarolsof-christmas.com/Hymns_and_Carols/from_greenlands_icy_mountains.htm* (accessed 22 December 2013).

3 L. F. Benson, *Studies of Familiar Hymns, First Series* (Philadelphia, 1924) in ibid.

4 C. Draper and J. Lawson-Reay, *Scandal at Congo House: William Hughes and the African Institute, Colwyn Bay* (Llanrwst, 2012), p. 75.

5 One of only two letters, with additional notes on the envelope, which make up Hughes's sparse personal file at the BMS, London.

6 H. M. Stanley, *The Congo and the Foundation of the Free State* (London, 1885).

7 BMS file.

8 BMS file; *The Missionary Herald* (August 1882).

9 W. Hughes, *Dark Africa and the Way Out: A Scheme for Civilizing and Evangelizing the Dark Continent* (London) p. 108.

10 *Seren Cymru* (3 September 1893).

11 Hughes, *Dark Africa*, pp. 10–13.

12 J. Spinther James, *Sefydliad Colwyn Bay wedi ei Brofi drwy Dân* (Carmarthen, 1894), pp. 18, 23.

13 A copy of this was shown to Ivor Wynne Jones at the printer's in Sussex Street, Rhyl, in October 1966.

14 James, *Sefydliad Colwyn Bay*, pp. 31–2.

15 T. M. Bassett, *The Baptists of Wales and the Baptist Missionary Society* (Swansea, 1991), *passim*, but especially pp. 17–24, 66.

16 T. Lewis, *These Seventy Years* (1930).

17 Minutes of BMS General Meeting, 11 May 1886.

18 T. Frimston, *Bedyddwyr Cantref y Rhos* (Blaenau Ffestiniog, 1924).

19 Hughes, *Dark Africa*, p. 4.

20 Ibid., p. 3.

21 T. E. Ellis, 'The national unity of Wales', *Young Wales* II 18 June 1896, pp. 153–6.

22 Hughes, *Dark Africa*, p. 18; Draper and Lawson-Reay, *Scandal*, p. 41.

23 Hughes, *Dark Africa*, pp. 10, 18.

24 C. Hall, 'Culture and identity in imperial Britain', in S. Stockwell (ed.), *The British Empire: Themes and Perspectives* (Oxford, 2008), pp. 200, 203 (quotation).

25 Hughes, *Dark Africa*, p. 10.

26 Ibid., p. 19.

27 *Congo Institute Colwyn Bay, North Wales: Reasons for Training the Most Promising of the African Converts in this Country* (Colwyn Bay, n.d., *c.*1893), p. 6.

28 Ibid. Hughes seems only to have recognized the monotheistic religions. All other beliefs were lumped together as 'Heathens'. He noted 85 million Orthodox Christians and 8 million Jews as well as the figures mentioned. S. P. Huntingdon, *The Clash of Civilizations and the Remaking of the World Order* (New York, 1996).

29 Hughes, *Dark Africa*, pp. 55, 60. It was common to differentiate India and China as being above Africa on the scale of civilizations because of their ancient civilizations. The BMS's decision that Hughes was more suitable for Africa than India or China because of his limited linguistic abilities is an example of this.

30 P. Mandler, *The English National Character: The History of an Idea from Edmund Burke to Tony Blair* (London, 2006); R. J. C Young, *The Idea of English Ethnicity* (Oxford, 2007).

31 Hughes, *Dark Africa*, p.

32 Ibid., p. 25; *Congo Training Institute Colwyn Bay, A Brief Account of the Secretary's Recent Visit to the West Coast of Africa* (Colwyn Bay, n.d., *c.*1894), unpaginated; *Reasons for Training*, pp. 7–8, 10.

33 *Manchester Guardian* (23 August 1909); Draper and Lawson-Reay, *Scandal*, p. 229.

34 S. Dubow, 'Colonial nationalism, the Milner kindergarten and the rise of "South Africanism", 1902–10', *History Workshop Journal*, 43 (1997), 53–85; D. Schreuder, 'Colonial nationalism and "Tribal Nationalism": making the white South African state, 1899–1910', in J. Eddy and D. Shreuder (eds), *The Rise of Colonial Nationalism: Australia, New Zealand, Canada and South Africa First Assert their Nationalities* (Sydney, 1988), pp. 192–226; S. Marks, 'White masculinity: Jan Smuts and the South African state', *Proceedings of the British Academy*, 111 (2001), 199–223.

35 N. Evans, 'Across the universe: racial conflict and the post-war crisis in Imperial Britain, 1919–1925', *Immigrants and Minorities*, 13/2 & 3 (1994), 59–88.

36 J. Chilton, *A Jazz Nursery* (London, 1980), p. 8.

37 Reprinted in *Seren Cymru* (28 July 1893).

38 Draper and Lawson-Reay, *Scandal*, p. 68; *North Wales Weekly News* (6 July 1894).

39 James, *Sefydliad Colwyn Bay*, p. 111.

40 Produced as evidence in court in Ruthin in 1912. Draper and Lawson-Reay, *Scandal*, p. 190.

41 *Colwyn Bay Times* (19 October 1911).

42 Ivor Wynne Jones, interview with Stanley Dale (1980).

43 *John Bull* (16 December 1911).

44 Ibid. (23 December 1911).

45 *North Wales Weekly News* (14, 21 1912); *Welsh Coast Pioneer* (13, 20 June 1912); *John Bull* (22 June 1912); account books shown to Ivor Wynne Hughes in 1966.

46 Draper and Lawson-Reay, *Scandal*, pp. 59–62, 103.

47 Information from the property deeds in the possession of Ivor Wynne Jones at the time of original publication.

48 Draper and Lawson-Reay, *Scandal*, chapters 8 and 10. In 1981 the Reverend Lewis Valentine (who conducted Hughes's funeral service) told Ivor Wynne Jones of Hughes' fondness for the wife of another Nonconformist minister.

49 A. Hoshchild, *King Leopold's Ghost: A Story of Greed, Terror and Heroism in Colonial Africa* (London, 1999).

50 N. Evans, 'The south Wales race riots of 1919', *Llafur*, 3/1 (1980), 5–29; Evans, 'Across the universe'; Ivor Wynne Jones, interview with Stanley Dale (1980).

51 This was shown to Ivor Wynne Jones in 1972 by Mrs Madge Bebbington, a granddaughter of Hughes's sister Elisabeth.

52 This was in the possession of Ivor Wynne Jones at the time of the publication of the first edition of this book.

53 Ivor Wynne Jones, information from Mrs Madge Bebbington.

54 J. Green, 'Hughes, William (1856–1924)', *Oxford Dictionary of*

National Biography (Oxford, 2004; online edn, Oct. 2006, *http://www.oxforddnb.com/view/article/76165* (accessed 7 January 2014).

55 Hall, 'Culture and identity', p. 201.
56 For a general argument along these lines (for which this essay provides further evidence), see N. Evans, 'Comparing immigrant histories: the Irish and others in modern Wales', in P. O'Leary (ed.), *Irish Migrants in Modern Wales* (Liverpool, 2004), pp. 156–77.

6

Through the Prism of Ethnic Violence: Riots and Racial Attacks in Wales, 1826–2014[1]

NEIL EVANS

Historical work on ethnic relations in Wales has frequently focussed on the riot. This has been the case for a variety of reasons. Often riots have drawn the attention of historians to an aspect of Welsh society that would otherwise have been hidden under the layers of the myth of tolerance. Secondly, major social conflicts frequently generate a large amount of comment and this enables a reconstruction of attitudes and structures of relationships to be undertaken for the past. This point shades into the third point, which is that such evidence allows the use of a social drama approach to the study of community and society. It is one in which historians have become well versed since 1945 as the study of crowds has become quite central to the subject and there is now a huge literature on crowd actions and riots.[2] It encompasses many different periods of history and is concerned with the compo-sition, values, beliefs and actions of crowds. By providing evocative accounts of ethnic riots, historians' preoccupation with social drama has served the purpose of puncturing the idea of Welsh tolerance rather well. It also helped to place studies of minorities nearer to the centre of the discipline's concerns and meant that there was a rich literature from which to draw insights. The main drawback was that most historians saw crowd actions more generally as a form of protest and therefore as in some sense 'progressive'. Far less attention was paid to reactionary crowds, like the 'Church and King' mobs of the eighteenth century. Racist crowds were rather more like these than the rioting ironworkers of Merthyr Tydfil in 1831 or the coalminers of Tonypandy in 1910.[3]

Such historical work has changed attitudes in the social sciences. Social scientists, at least in Britain, were hindered by a lack of such actions to study in the immediate post-war period. When riots did begin to erupt in Britain in the 1980s it was often historians who offered immediate commentary in the press and journalists who drew on the rich historical studies of crowd actions to set the present in perspective.[4] American social science, with a plethora of riots throughout the twentieth century to study, coped with the challenge more effectively. Some sociologists misread the present because they misunderstood the past.[5] By contrast the historical periods in which historians discovered ethnic riots were replete with riots of all kinds and it did not seem too difficult to interpret ethnic rioting as a variation in the broader landscape. Historians of crowd action have considered crowds to have varied repertoires of behaviour that changed in different periods. It was simply necessary to assimilate racial disturbances into this framework.[6]

Approaches to ethnic history based on conflict faced particular problems, however. They were always prone to the riposte that riots were untypical events and that they revealed little about day-to-day life in Wales. Was there evidence of harmony in ethnic relations outside the violent confrontation? This issue had to be addressed, and has been done elsewhere.[7] The purpose of this chapter is to provide a specific review of what we now know about ethnic violence in Wales.

The first substantial group of immigrants to arrive in modern industrial Wales were the Irish, whose numbers began to pick up in the early nineteenth century and then rose to a crescendo during the years of the famine migration of 1845–50. Over a period of almost sixty years, from 1826 to 1882, they were the targets of around twenty serious attacks. These fall into two broad categories. First, there were attacks that originated in the workplace; and, secondly, there were wider community attacks. Behind most anti-Irish attacks there were accusations of undercutting wages, but the evidence for this is patchy at best. More often, the workplace-based attacks were efforts to expel them from jobs in times of economic hardship. These attacks came in two clusters that were associated with work in the ironworks, such as at Rhymni in 1826 and 1834, Pontypool in 1834, Nantyglo and Blaina in 1843 and Brynmawr in 1850. The second crop was associated with the early days of steam coal in the Rhondda and clustered in the years 1848–57. A riot in Aberdare in 1866 may be regarded as a reprise to these outbreaks. The latter were much more 'successful' as they prevented the Irish from establishing a foothold in this expanding industry, and by 1914 there were very few Irish-born, or Catholics, in the Rhondda Valleys. Communal riots tended to be associated with the famine migration and were often the result of murders, religious bigotry or of economic grievances. In 1848 there were attacks on Irish communities in Llantrisant and Cardiff. The latter followed the murder of a Welshman by an Irishman and accusations that he was being hidden by the community. The Catholic Church and Irish homes were then assaulted with some venom. At Pontlottyn in 1869 a crowd of around 1,000 people attacked the Irish community with such ferocity that one man died. It was the result of long-established antipathies rather than transient wage issues and illustrates a broad hostility rather than a simple economic conflict.[8]

The most famous – and the last – attack on the Irish, at Tredegar in 1882, showed the layers of hostility that could accumulate. There were economic issues: the works was converting from iron to steel production and work was scarce. The outbreak happened some two months after the Phoenix

Park murders in Dublin when the Chief Secretary of Ireland and the Secretary of State were killed by Irish extremists. Also, there were some local conflicts between Catholics and the Salvation Army in Tredegar. As in many riots, the spark came in the pubs. Typical were the attacks on property, with fifty homes being wrecked and fifteen people seriously injured in physical attacks.[9]

The recent research of Louise Miskell locates such actions in the repertoire of the crowd. She stresses the element of regulation of morality within them, the expression of disapproval of an alien presence. Communities rarely expressed regret at what had happened but gave vociferous support in court to those who were charged with offences. Such riots adapted the methods of the rural *ceffyl pren* (the ritual mocking of moral offenders) to industrial locations and were a variant on the attacks of the Rebecca rioters and the Scotch Cattle in the 1820s–1840s. They bridged a period when such actions had declined in the industrial and agrarian spheres but still showed life in their ethnic variation.[10]

This framework of analysis provides a means of approaching the variety of riots against the diverse ethnic groups that entered Wales in the period 1880–1920. Some conflicts were clearly motivated by questions of employment. This was the case in the series of brawls that were fought on the streets of Butetown district of Cardiff in the late nineteenth and early twentieth centuries, which were associated with economic depressions in shipping and intense conflict over jobs. Accusations of undercutting abounded, as with the anti-Irish riots, but again the case is not clear-cut. It was not always black and foreign sailors who were accused of undercutting; it could be the native-born and much of the conflict may have been about signing on the ship rather than about wage rates. Shipping was too fluid an occupation for the locals to become established in one sector and keep outsiders at bay, as happened in the ironworks and coalmines. Ships signed on their crews by the voyage, and we need to think of a constant

and multifaceted struggle rather than the indigenous population defending their turf.[11]

The major riots against such incomers were communal
rather than workplace-based. That is not to say that there
were not elements of economic competition in them, but it *is*
to say that the issues were broader than that and often
involved a communal assault on an alien group. The focus of
such violence was the period 1910–20, which was on the cusp
of major changes. The growth of the international economy
in the period 1850–1914 had been massive, and south Wales
steam coal and its bunker trade had done much to fuel it –
literally. It is not surprising that a diverse group of incomers
became located in Wales in the process. To supplement the
European seamen who had begun to appear in the mid-
nineteenth century, black people and people of colour began
to appear. South Wales also attracted a small proportion of
the Jewish refugees from East European pogroms who began
to arrive in the 1880s.

This international economy was forced out of its grooves
by the world crisis of 1914–18 and it did not recover fully
until after 1945. The major riots in Wales came on either side
of this great divide. There were plenty of parallels elsewhere.
Liverpool had five major ethnic riots in the same period, while
the anti-black riots of 1917–19 occurred around the edges of
the Atlantic basin, including as far west as Chicago.[12]

In south Wales these outbreaks were concentrated in two
years, 1911 and 1919. In both there were associations with
industrial discontent. In the summer of 1911 the Cambrian
Combine strike in the Rhondda, which had started the previous autumn, was still proceeding and it was joined by the
international seamen's strike, which affected all the south
Wales ports. Just as this ended, a national railway strike
began. A number of people died in these confrontations: one
at Tonypandy and six at Llanelli in the railway strike. In
Cardiff during the seamen's strike warehouses were burned
down and violent picketing enforced the solidarity of the

strike. There was also considerable violence in Swansea, which has not received much attention from historians.[13]

The attacks on the Chinese in Cardiff were the first of the ethnic outbreaks. The seamen's strike was solid across ethnic lines, with the exception of some of the Greeks and the Chinese – the latter were not allowed to join the union anyway. In order to win the strike the seamen needed the support of the dockers and the union constantly harped on about the threat from the Chinese as a means of trying to win wider solidarity. On the day that the dockers downed tools, a Chinese crew was brought into Cardiff. There followed thirty attacks on Chinese laundries in Cardiff, located widely across the city. There had been accusations that these laundries were centres of white slave traffic in Cardiff and many other accusations of immoral behaviour were tacked on to this, such as opium smoking and gambling. Now the laundries were seen as the centres of strike-breaking. Windows were broken and property was destroyed in the attacks. This served the union's purposes as it helped maintain the solidarity of the strike, and ultimately helped the seamen to their victory. The small group of Chinese in the city – probably no more than 200 – had provided a useful scapegoat and a point around which opposition could rally.

One of the effects of the transport strike in Cardiff was to shut down the production of the eastern part of the south Wales coalfield within three days of the strike becoming general across the waterfront in Cardiff. This added to existing industrial tensions in the area, which were cross-cut by the railway strike. Industrial conflict thus served as the backdrop to the anti-Jewish riots that occurred in the eastern Valleys. They erupted from Tredegar, the locus of the anti-Irish riot of 1882, and spread across eastern Glamorgan and western Monmouthshire as far west as Senghennydd.

There is little real doubt that these were anti-Semitic riots, despite the efforts of some Jewish observers of the time to deny this, a strand of discussion now continued by a modern historian.[14] It is true that Jews were not the only targets and that certain splits were apparent in the local community, but the attacks started by selecting Jewish targets and only later did they involve non-Jews. Jews were attacked indiscriminately.[15] There was much condemnation of the outbreak and some expressions of philo-Semitism, but unanimity is not to be expected in such things. Much communal solidarity was expressed towards those rioters who were prosecuted, just as there had been in earlier anti-Irish riots. The fact that non-legitimated violence was used was bound to create divisions between the rioters and their supporters and the forces of order. Even the virulently anti-Irish *Cardiff and Merthyr Guardian* had condemned the riots in Cardiff in 1848 on the grounds that the Welsh should know better: they should not behave like Irishmen. The same divisions were apparent in the anti-Chinese riots in Cardiff; some observers had found the Chinese to be hard-working and law-abiding. In 1911 some people in the Valleys sheltered their Jewish neighbours rather than attack them.

Comparisons with other outbreaks at the time stress the way in which ethnic disturbances fit into a pattern. They were part of a repertoire of popular action that was being refurbished by the industrial conflicts of the period. Disputes over non-unionism in various parts of the coalfield had seen a revamping of the techniques of the *ceffyl pren* tradition in the form of whiteshirting (mockery of strikebreakers by parading them in women's petticoats). In Tonypandy in 1910 there was something of a communal uprising against the shopkeepers who were seen as taking the side of the coalowners. In Llanelli a wider community expressed its solidarity with the striking railwaymen in the mass picketing that led to tragic violence, and following this the property of unpopular shopkeepers and magistrates was attacked. In Cardiff the strike of 1911 led to two other major confrontations on the streets besides the attack on the Chinese. Immigrants were only one of the targets against whom crowd action could be deployed.

Perhaps to highlight the elements of ethnic conflict in these confrontations it is necessary to pick out just how unusual they were in a British context. While there was widespread hostility to Chinese seamen in Britain, the actions in Cardiff were the only recorded case of a riot against them. Similarly the anti-Jewish riots were the first since the readmission of the Jews in 1655 and the only others known of were in the East End of London in 1917. The riots that broke out in the south Wales ports in the summer of 1919 would be the worst of a wave of British outbreaks in that year.[16]

At the end of the war the economic situation again provided the context for attacks on black sailors in Barry, Newport and Cardiff. Because of shortages of merchant seamen in the First World War there had been renewed recruiting of men from the West Indies and Yemen. The black communities of the south Wales ports expanded significantly. At the end of the war white sailors were discharged from the Royal Navy and wanted their jobs back. In the main they got them and it was the newcomers who bore the brunt of unemployment. The outbreaks of 1919 were, therefore, only loosely related to the economic situation. There was a general context of industrial conflict – the post-war labour unrest, expressed in the railway strike of 1919, which was something of a dress rehearsal for the General Strike of 1926. But issues of morality once again stoked the fires of intolerance. Black men had white wives and girlfriends, and some commentators saw innocent girls as being seduced through service in boarding houses in Butetown. The black men were further accused of having shirked war duty – of having taken the high wages of merchant shipping, while white sailors fought. Certainly, wages in the merchant service were better than the paltry sums paid to the British armed services in the war, but the accusation of shirking danger was absurd. Merchant ships were just as much in the firing line as battleships and were more vulnerable. But the point is that black sailors were *seen* as profiting from the situation of others.

Neil Evans

The trigger of the riots in Cardiff was an attack on a brake containing black men and their white wives: it was not a dispute over signing on a ship or some direct economic cause, though such an incident had triggered the similar riots in South Shields earlier in the year. Religious pressure groups, such as the Cardiff and District Citizens' Union, and the police contributed to the situation. The huge crowds that made the assaults on the black community were not entirely local but contained discharged sailors and soldiers who happened to be in the port. But there is little doubt that these represented local feeling as much as that of outsiders. The riots in Cardiff redrew the boundaries of the black community to their pre-war shape. Those who had settled in areas north of the South Wales Railway bridge were forced to leave their homes. Such displacements of population had been a feature of nineteenth-century anti-Irish riots and of the anti-Jewish riots of 1911. Control of territory was an important dimension of them, and a clear, if tacit, expression of communality. Of course, many condemned the outbreaks. There were fears that there might be retaliation in the empire, where the balance of black and white was far different from that in Britain: indeed, there were some outbreaks in the West Indies that confirmed these forebodings. But much of the discussion condemned merely the methods of the rioters: it endorsed their principles of racial purity and jobs for the white British first. As in the past with other ethnic riots, it was violence that separated them from official opinion rather than objectives.

After 1919 there were only minor affrays in the south Wales ports. In the mid-Victorian period, violence against the Irish had persisted after more general manifestations of community violence declined, whereas the reverse was true in inter-war Wales. Ethnic violence ceased in 1919, while industrial violence continued up to the General Strike of 1926. However, the mass demonstrations of the 1930s – especially mass protest against the means test in 1935 – were

136

predominantly peaceful affairs and violence in general was removed from the repertoire of actions sanctioned by the community. Moreover, there was no echo in Wales of the disturbances associated with fascist demonstrations elsewhere in Britain, such as those that occurred in the East End of London in 1936. Fascist movements found little purchase in south Wales between the wars and failed to mobilize the kind of anti-Semitic feelings that had emerged explosively in Tredegar in 1911. Unlike the East End of London, south Wales had occasional examples of hostility to Jews but no deep-rooted tradition of anti-Semitism that could be exploited by fascist groups.[17]

By the post-war period there were few newcomers against whom to use such violence anyway. Across the Western world such ethnic riots entered a period of decline. There was a minor outbreak in Liverpool in 1948 and some of the American riots of the 1930s–1940s had this element in them. But most of the riots from the 1930s onwards in the US were ghetto rebellions in which the black population rebelled against their local exploiters in the ghetto shops and especially the police. They were very different from the riots of 1919. It took until the 1980s for such conflicts to occur in Britain. The first was in Bristol in 1980 and there were more widespread outbreaks in 1981 and 1985. There was little evidence of such an approach in Wales, though there was an outbreak in Butetown in 1981, which seems not to have spread because of a media blackout on reporting it. On that occasion, skinheads and black youths joined forces to try to lure the police into an ambush. The police anticipated this and allowed the rioters to destroy thousands of pounds' worth of property in Bute Terrace.[18] There was a more successful anti-police ambush in Butetown in 1986. This followed the pattern that had been established elsewhere: luring a police patrol into an ambush by means of a hoax 999 call and then attacking it with stones and petrol bombs.[19] Neither incident was significant on the scale of the Toxteth or Brixton riots. One reason for this is that the black community in Cardiff appears to have been less alienated from the dominant society. It was well established, intermarried, and there seems to have been far less of a rift between the generations within it compared with the English cities where such riots proliferated. Youth rebellion was less of a feature also, though it was the young people who initiated the actions that occurred. Cardiff also had less extensive areas of inner-city deprivation than many English cities.

By the 1990s violence in English cities had become concentrated in white communities and especially in outer estates rather than inner cities. The Ely riots of 1991 fitted into this pattern, but it contained one element that echoed the past. The confrontations with the police started with an attack by a white crowd on an Asian shop, following a dispute over the right to sell bread. The Pakistani family left the area and did not return. Yet much of the thrust of the events was hostility to the police and protest at deprivation. It was less straightforwardly an anti-black communal riot than those of the past had been, despite the central element of this in the outbreak.[20]

A more disturbing and threatening trend in the 1990s was the rise in the number of ethnic assaults in Wales. It is hard to compare this with the past when no systematic data were kept and only recently have they been taken seriously by the police. We find such incidents in newspaper reports, for instance, but there is no effective means of studying them. However, their prevalence in the present guards against an assumption that, just because riots seem to be mainly a thing of the past, all is well in the realm of ethnic violence.

A new chapter in the understanding of racism in Wales opened with the murder of Mohan Singh Kullar at Cadoxton, near Neath, in December 1994. The shopkeeper was killed by a small gang of drunken youths who threw a brick at him when he investigated the disturbance they were creating; one young man got a life sentence and two others got sentences of eight and three-and-a-half years in prison.[21] This created a sense of shock and outrage and did much to puncture the complacent attitudes that had dominated discussions of race in Wales. In this context, there was a popular reassessment of the history of race relations in Wales that drew the work of historians into the mainstream of discussion. Anti-racist[22] campaigners had been arguing that it would take a racial murder to make the authorities take the threat from neo-Nazi groups in Wales seriously and this awful event had proved them, tragically, to be right.[23] In the following years a number of television programmes and press discussions, as well as the Oscar-nominated film *Solomon a Gaenor* (which was set in the 1911 anti-Jewish riots), raised the profile of ethnic issues in political discussion and cultural awareness in Wales. It was in this context that the startling rise in the numbers of racist attacks in Wales came to be discussed.

Table 1. Racial incidents reported to the police

Police area	1988	1994–5	1995–6	1996–7	1997–8
Dyfed-Powys	0	3	23	18	17
Gwent	1	22	32	60	45
N. Wales	2	3	5	4	12
S. Wales	86	512	443	357	367
Provincial	2,169	6,398	7,211		
Metropolitan	2,214	5,480	5,011	5,621	5,862
Total	4,383	11,878	12,222	13,106	13,878

Source: Commission for Racial Equality factsheets, 1997, 1999.

It is clear that the number of attacks recorded rose significantly in this decade but it was often felt that this was the result of greater confidence in the police rather than any actual

increase in violence.[24] Between 1993 and 2012 there have been
five or six racist murders in Wales compared with around 105
in the UK. This is a disturbing figure, approximately in line
with its share of the UK population but far exceeding its share
of the minority population.[25] By the second decade of the
twenty-first century the numbers of racist attacks reported had
risen again though with no obvious trend in the recent figures.

*Table 2: Hate crimes relating to race and religion known to
police, 2009–13*

Police area	2009	2010	2011–12	2012–13
Dyfed-Powys	106	241	84	74
Gwent	403	241	190	193
N Wales	329	297	364	332
S Wales	684	760	784	838

Sources: *http:www.acpo.police.uk/asp/policies/Data/084a_Recorded_Hate_
Crime_-_January_to_December_2009.pdf*; *http://www.acpo.presscentre.
com/Press-Releases/ACPO-publishes-hate-crime-data-for-2010-111.aspx*;
*https://www.gov.uk/government/publications/hate-crimes-england-and-
wales-2011-to-2012--2*; *https://www.gov.uk/government/publications/
an-overview-of-hate-crime-in-england-and-wales*[26]

In 2012 the prevalence of such attacks was clearly in the
South Wales Police area where there was an attack per 1,531
of the population, followed by North Wales with one per
1,894, Gwent with one per 2,929 and Dyfed-Powys with one
per 5,810. There is probably some relationship with urban
deprivation displayed in these figures, with Dyfed-Powys, the
most rural area and with a very small minority population,
coming bottom of the list for numbers in relation to population. Gwent's low figure is perhaps surprising on these
assumptions, given that it includes parts of the Valleys.

One of the centres for racial attacks – though they are present throughout Wales – has been the south Wales Valleys. The journalist Steve Evans summed up the position in the 1990s well:

> Valleys racism, it seems, stems from particular factors. It is virtually invariably directed at local Asians rather than people from other ethnic backgrounds. The overall context is often one of deprived, run-down areas with very high unemployment but where the immigrant (black British from other areas of Britain) is relatively well off – perhaps a doctor or a pharmacist or a shopkeeper who has moved into the area precisely because he or she can see a living to be made ... [they] might have the trappings of money, say an expensive car, in an area where money is scarce.[27]

This analysis is confirmed by the words of some of the avowed racists: 'There's white people on the dole, when there's black people ... owning restaurants and working as doctors and taking all the money when white people should be.'[28] Such attitudes do not simply reflect economic decline and despondency – important as these are – they also involve issues of identity and social experience. The Valleys are now the least cosmopolitan part of Wales, with an overwhelming proportion of the population born locally. There is little to produce much awareness of difference or sensitivity to other cultures. Combined with this is the challenge of de-industrialization to a sense of Welsh identity. Heavy industry, and the wages it produced, was once a defining feature of Welshness.[29] In the Valleys some people have a strong sense of their Welshness but little that might provide them with any self-esteem. A sense of racial superiority fills the gap for some: 'We look after our race, you look after yours. I'm Celtic, I'm Welsh and proud. Our belief is we're pure; we're white and Welsh – being Welsh as well, that's a pride.'[30] This is supported by a victim of racial attacks and abuse in the area: 'The people around ŋere think that the Valleys are the heart of Wales. That is their home town. Not anybody else's. So we're like the outsiders coming in and it's like invading their territory.'[31]

In general terms the presence of far-Right groups and their agitations seems to provoke racist attacks. In areas like the Rhondda there were some neo-Nazi groups in existence in the late twentieth century and many signs of organized racism. Graffiti on the walls suggests that black people should leave the area ('Fuck off Coon') and some are prepared to make fascist gestures in front of the camera ('Rhondda Valley Skinheads – Sieg Heil').[32] Skinheads claim to have several hundred supporters in the Rhondda and there are suggestions that groupings of the Ku Klux Klan, Combat 18 and other equally vicious factions exist. Combat 18 has sent at least one death threat in Cardiff.[33]

Far-Right groups had had some presence in Wales for a couple of decades before that but they had never been very prominent. Most seem to have concentrated (if that is the word for small and fissiparous grouplets) around Cardiff. The growth of the National Front in the early 1970s hardly seems to have touched Wales: no candidates stood in Wales in the general elections of 1974, which proved to be its high tide in England. In the following election there were five candidates in Wales, who mustered a combined vote of 2,465 out of the 1,636,788 cast in Wales. Only in Cardiff West did the candidate poll over a thousand votes (4.1%). The next highest figure was in Newport with 454 votes (0.8%). In Barry, Pontypridd and Carmarthen they polled a maximum of 0.5% of the vote. The candidate in Carmarthen persisted into the following election in 1983, now running under the British National Party banner, a change that garnered him precisely five votes compared with his previous outing. In 1992 a BNP candidate gathered 121 votes in Cardiff North – a mere 0.3% of those cast.[34]

But the far-Right has maintained a presence in Wales through the whole of the period since the late 1970s.

Ideologically this has been rather easier because of the splits in the far-Right since 1979. Broadly the National Front headed in two directions. One of these was the traditional centralist British approach, which kept to its major themes of anti-Semitism and antagonism to blacks, who would be compulsorily repatriated. Others were influenced by ecological currents and learned to embrace the idea of a diverse (but white) Europe. This created the space for the recognition of ethnic differences within the UK, including support for the Welsh language, and for an attack upon English imperialism. It was the latter trend that influenced the National Front's deliberate targeting of Wales. In 1987 it invested £10,000 in work in Wales and produced some slick propaganda material. There were some articles in Welsh and support was expressed for Meibion Glyndŵr, a shadowy direct-action grouping responsible for burning second homes in rural Wales. These moves won a few dozen recruits – and quickly faced opposition on the streets from the South Wales Anti-Fascist Organisation, which disrupted concentrated recruiting drives in places like Merthyr and led to a switch to a guerrilla-like approach.

By 1990 Nick Griffin, a leading redistributivist, had moved to a smallholding in mid-Wales, and attempts were made to attach the movement to its nearest indigenously Welsh relative Cymdeithas Cyfamodwyr Cymru Rhydd (Covenanters for a Free Wales). Griffin saw potential in the 'white flight' from English conurbations: counter-urbanization driven by ethnic and racial concerns. During the BSE crisis attempts were made to recruit Welsh farmers by means of leaflets distributed at markets, with a little success. Griffin is trying to take the organization 'upmarket', with rural and respectable support, in imitation of Le Pen's Front National in France. This involves concealing much of the true nature of his party's beliefs.[35] His distaste for skinheads may explain why it is groups like the Ku Klux Klan and Combat 18 that seemed to be colonizing the south Wales Valleys. The Klan had a presence in Wales at least from the late 1980s when Alan Belshella, who was brought up in America and was a Klan member there, moved to live near Maesteg.[36]

In the early twenty-first century the far-Right has established a more prominent position, at least in electoral terms, but has failed to make a huge impact on the political scene in Wales. The BNP kept a deposit for the first time in a Welsh parliamentary election in 2010 when it fielded nine candidates in all. Its modest advance seems to be rooted in Assembly elections where it has fought a growing number of seats: in 2007 it fielded twenty candidates, garnered 4.36% of the vote and saved its deposits in North Wales and South Wales West. In 2011 it ran twenty-seven candidates with seven of these in first-past-the-post seats, though while it saved deposits in Swansea East and Islwyn, it secured a mere 1.6% of the vote. In local government it has recently found it difficult to run candidates because of the penalties imposed by the courts for its discriminatory membership policies.[37] But in most of Wales the membership of the BNP is low with fewer than ten members in many constituencies and rising to over thirty (but under forty) in Powys around Griffin's bailiwick. It has only a patchy presence in the south Wales Valleys and tends to be stronger in more coastal locations throughout Wales, with the exception of Powys and north-east Wales.[38]

There is also, as in previous decades, a more shadowy presence of other far-Right groups, notably the Welsh Defence League. Just how significant an organization this is is hard to say but it would appear to consist mainly of people who attend English Defence League demonstrations. The context for these groups is Islamophobia and the 'threat' from which England and Wales need to be protected is an Islamic state and sharia law. They are products of the post-9/11 situation, which along with the increase in refugees produced by the less stable post-Cold War world makes the present situation rather different from that of the late twentieth century. But the main manifestation of such attitudes is in a group known as the Casuals that has developed out of football hooliganism in Cardiff and allegedly has a female wing, the Casuals United News Team with an unprintable acronym. The WDL persistently claims it is not racist and is merely engaged in peaceful protest against Islamic extremism but members have been photographed making Nazi salutes, to include veterans of Combat 18 and to have a website that endorses the views of Enoch Powell as well as members who speak of killing black people and driving Muslims out of the Valleys. The Casuals held a white pride event with Nazi elements in Swansea in February 2013. But the impact of such groups is not huge: the demonstrations it has organized have been fiascos.[39]

But such groups do reflect opinions that are held by at least some people outside their circle and can contribute to microclimates of hostility that spark violent attacks. There is considerable evidence of more routine day-to-day racial abuse in Welsh society. Some actions were potentially lethal: shots have been fired through the windows of the Immigration Advisory Service and at premises owned by Asians and Jews in South Glamorgan.[40] That was another incident that suggested the possibility that violent groups based in disadvantaged communities of different races may clash with each other. This seems to have been the case in the riots in the north of England in 2001, and a running battle between white and Asian youths in Cardiff might have been a smaller version of this.[41] There is clearly a pattern of abuse of Muslims with women's headscarves being removed or pulled, accusations of being terrorists made (particularly on the anniversaries of the New York and London bombings), while in Llanelli drunken youths swore outside a mosque, broke a window and urinated on a doorstep, while in Wrexham a swastika was daubed on a mosque. Muslim graves have been desecrated with swastikas in Newport.[42]

But so far at least the new climate of Islamophobia has not produced any major incident like a riot. The major violent outbreak since 2001 has been a conflict between refugees and the indigenous population in Wrexham. Caia Park was built as a model estate in the 1950s but like so much social housing became a dumping ground for problem families. At the time of the outbreak in June 2003 it contained two of the 100 most deprived wards in Wales. The objects of hostility were Iraqi Kurds who fought back after experiencing abuse and attacks on their homes, leading to violent clashes in which baseball bats and metal rods were employed. This was a more serious version of the kind of incident experienced in Cardiff in 2002 and with some similarities to the more serious and rooted outbreaks in northern England in 2001. There were probably forty Kurds on the estate (rumour inflated this to 400) who were recently resident and largely driven away by the violence. Unlike in Oldham and Bradford it was not inter-communal violence by entrenched communities.[43]

Is such hostility and exclusion, however, the sum total of race relations in contemporary Wales? Clearly, this is not the case. Most people in the Valleys and in other deprived communities are not members or supporters of vicious racist groups. Many are appalled at their presence and exhibit tolerant attitudes. People interviewed in the Rhondda about the racist attacks on Asian shopkeepers and doctors have expressed disgust at the actions of a group they brand as a minority. Some of the victims have confirmed that they have much local support and that the 'good people' feel ashamed of what has happened. The perpetrators are seen as 'stupid . . . childish'. A landlord whose pub was adorned with racist graffiti was concerned that it would get the reputation of being a racist pub. As well as the abusers we have to remember the people who are prepared to brave hostility to pursue relationships with black people. In one case in Porth a white youth who verbally defended an abused Asian restaurant owner and insisted that all people are equal was stabbed and subsequently died. A police inspector stresses that in such attacks it is the 'pillars of the community' who are being abused by the mindless.[44] The Welsh Defence League has been met with much bigger counter demonstrations and one prominent opponent, Leanne Wood, argued that it was unacceptable to have such actions in Swansea: people wanted to live in harmony and to reject division. Even a WDL spokesperson commented that he would be ashamed to be Welsh if there was violence as there was in England and that Wales was friendly and peaceful. This was a comment that perhaps required an accompanying salt mine but it is an indication of the prevalence of an ideology that stresses the racial harmony of Wales and thus brands racist groups as outside the pale.[45]

In contemporary Wales, those who indulge in ethnic violence are more marginal to their communities than they were in the past. They are associated with political groups that are far outside the mainstream. They are frequently condemned not just by the forces of order but also by many ordinary people, who find their behaviour offensive and dangerous. It is difficult for them to claim the moral superiority that the ethnic crowd once did in Wales. There is now a substantial structure of anti-racist opinion and of political action to promote racial equality that did not exist in the past. It is harder to mobilize against ethnic minorities because of this.

This is not to be complacent about the current situation. Members of ethnic minorities frequently experience racial abuse, while racial attacks and murders also occur.[46] Perhaps the very isolation of this strand of opinion encourages violence. Terrorism, after all, usually grows out of political weakness. Certainly, the communal aspect of earlier ethnic riots had some impact in constraining violence within limits acceptable to that society, which was usually short of killing people. Yet it is hard to envisage a return of the communally based attacks of the past – unless they should grow out of the hostility of two disadvantaged communities, as suggested above. For the

Neil Evans

majority, there is no longer a repertoire of violence sanctioned by the community to draw upon. Since the 1920s communal violence in general has declined and even in the miners' strikes of 1972–85 the much vaunted mass picketing was mainly a controlled pushing and shoving match with the police. Those marginalized by the economic restructuring of the Valleys and other parts of Wales will continue their vicious attacks and draw some sustenance from extreme political groups.[47] But it is harder now than in the past to present them as representative of the underlying values of their society.

Notes

1   Thanks to Paul O'Leary for typically incisive comments on a draft and for the organizing framework that I have borrowed for the analysis.

2   From a huge literature, the following are central: G. Rude, *The Crowd in History* (London, 1964); E. P. Thompson, 'The moral economy of the English crowd in the eighteenth century', *Past and Present*, 50 (1971); B. Holton, 'The crowd in history: some problems of theory and method', *Social History*, 34 (1978).

3   E. J. Hobsbawm's *Primitive Rebels* (Manchester, 1959) was one of the few studies to show a concern for such reactionary violence.

4   The Welsh historian R. Merfyn Jones confidently predicted that the Toxteth riots of 1981 would have their logic and the selectivity of their targets displayed by subsequent research, a view amply confirmed in the event. R. Merfyn Jones, 'A land fit for Volvoes', *Arcade*, 19 (24 July 1981), 5–6.

5   N. Evans, 'Voices of the unheard: contemporary British urban riots in historical perspective', in I. Gwynedd Jones and G. Williams (eds), *Social Policy, Crime and Punishment: Essays in Memory of Jane Morgan* (Cardiff, 1994).

6   The idea of historically specific repertoires is central to the work of the historian/sociologist Charles Tilly. For a brief introduction to his work, see his 'Major forms of collective action in Western Europe 1500–1975', *Theory and Society*, 3/3 (Fall 1976); M. P. Hanagan,

148

L. Page Moch and W. Te Brake (eds), *Challenging Authority: The Historical Study of Contention* (Minneapolis, 1998), editors' introduction and essay by Tilly.

7   N. Evans, 'Immigrants and minorities in Wales: a comparative perspective', *Llafur*, 5/4 (1991), 5–26, and chapter 1 above.

8   P. O'Leary, 'Anti-irish riots in Wales, 1826–1882', *Llafur*, 5/1 (1991), 27–36.

9   L. Miskell, 'Reassessing the anti-Irish riot: popular protest and the Irish immigrant presence in south Wales, c.1826–1882', in P. O'Leary (ed.), *The Irish in Wales* (Liverpool, 2004) pp. 101–118.

10   Ibid.

11   M. J. Daunton, 'Jack ashore: seamen in Cardiff before 1914', *Welsh History Review*, 9/2 (December 1978).

12   N. Evans, 'Red summers 1917–1919', *History Today*, 51/2 (February 2001).

13   N. Evans, '"A tidal wave of impatience": the Cardiff general strike of 1911', in G. H. Jenkins and J. Beverley Smith (eds), *Politics and Society in Wales 1840–1922: Essays in Honour of Ieuan Gwynedd Jones* (Cardiff, 1988).

14   W. D. Rubinstein, 'The anti-Jewish riots in south Wales: a re-examination', *Welsh History Review*, 18/4 (1997).

15   This point is re-emphasized by G. Alderman, 'The anti-Jewish riots of August 1911 in south Wales: a response', *Welsh History Review*, 20 (2001).

16   D. Englander (ed.), *A Documentary History of Jewish Immigrants in Britain, 1840–1920* (Leicester, 1994), pp. 289–98.

17   H. Francis, *Miners against Fascism: Wales and the Spanish Civil War* (London, 1984); S. M. Cullen, 'Another nationalism: the British Union of Fascists in Glamorgan, 1932–40', *Welsh History Review*, 17/1 (1994), 105.

18   *Arcade*, 20 (7 August 1981), 2–3.

19   *Western Mail* (29, 30 August 1986); *South Wales Echo* (29 August, 1 September 1986).

20   B. Campbell, *Goliath: Britain's Dangerous Places* (London, 1993), chapter 1; A. Power and R. Tunstall, *Dangerous Disorder: Riots and Disturbances in Thirteen Areas of Britain, 1991–92* (York, 1997), p. 40.

Neil Evans

21 *The Times* (8 December 1994); *Western Mail* (26 October 1995).

22 *Wales on Sunday* (24 October 1993). P. Myers, 'Race attacks challenge idyll of welcome in Welsh valleys', *Guardian* (3 December 1994); *Western Mail* (9 June 1995); S. Evans, 'What's to be done about Welsh racism', *Planet*, 110 (April–May 1995), 115–16.

23 BBC Wales News (23 February 2000), *http://news.bbc.co.uk/1/hi/wales/654222.stm*

24 *http://www.walesonline.co.uk/news/wales-news/racism-wales-still-widespread-campaigners-2037282*; Institute of Race Relations, *http://www.irr.org.uk/research/statistics/racial-violence/*

25 I am extremely grateful to Mair Rigby of Race Equality First for her kind help with these figures.

26 Evans, 'What's to be done', 115.

27 National Library of Wales (NLW), S&VA, AM6989/3, 'Week-in-Week-out', 8 June 1999 – interview with skinheads in the Rhondda.

28 R. Merfyn Jones, 'Beyond identity? The reconstruction of the Welsh', *Journal of British Studies*, 31/4 (October 1992) 330–57.

29 NLW, S&VA, AM6989/3, 'Week-in-Week-out', 8 June 1999 – interview with skinheads in the Rhondda. The interviewees confirmed Steve Evans's view that the main focus of their anger was Asian people.

30 NLW, S&VA, AM 3268/3, 'The way it is', BBC2, 22 October 1996 – interview with 'Jimmy'.

31 NLW, S&VA, AM6989/3, 'Week-in-Week-out', 8 June 1999 – interview with skinheads in the Rhondda.

32 South Glamorgan Racial Equality Council, *Annual Report, 1993–4*, p. 8.

33 B. Jones, *Etholiadau'r Ganrif: Welsh Elections, 1886–1997* (Talybont, 1999), pp. 127–30, 131–2, 143–4.

34 G. Davies, 'National Front Cymru', *Planet*, 65 (October/November 1987), 109–11; G. Davies, 'National Front Cymru update', *Planet*, 66 (December/January 1987–8), 119; G. Davies, 'The far right: the activities of the Welsh redistibutivists', *Planet*, 97 (February/March 1993); *Western Mail* (7 May 1998); N. Ryan, 'England's green and unpleasant land', *Times Magazine* (10 April 1999).

35 *Wales on Sunday* (24 October 1993); *Western Mail* (March 2002).

36 *http://news.bbc.co.uk/1/shared/vote2007/welshasssembly_english/ html/region_99999.stm*; *http://www.bbc.co.uk/news/special/election2011/ constituency/html/wales.stm*; *http://en.wikipedia.org/wiki/British_National _Party_election_results*; *http://www.bnp.org.uk/news/regional/south-wales -meeting-report*; BBC Wales News (19 April 2012).

37 *http://www.theguardian.com/news/datablog/2009/oct/19/ bnp-membership-list-constituency*

38 *http://welshdefence.webs.com/31/10/13*, Wales Online (18 Oct 2009); *http://www.radicalwales.org/2010/07/do-you-believe-in-welsh-de- fence-league.html*; *http://rationalwiki.org/wiki/Casuals_United*

39 South Glamorgan Racial Equality Council, *Annual Report*, 1986–7, p. 24; *Annual Report, 1993–4*, p. 8; *Annual Report*, 1994–5, p. 1; *Annual Report*, 1995-6, p. 7.

40 *South Wales Echo* (2002).

41 *http://www.islamophobia-watch.com/islamophobia-watch/2012/11/ 26/welsh-muslims-report-widespread-racist-abuse.html*; 1 July 2013, *http://cardifflocalguide.co.uk/racist-attack-on-muslim- gravestones/*

42 *http://en.wikipedia.org/wiki/Caia_Park*; *The Guardian* (25 June 2003); *North Wales Daily Post* (18 October 2004); *Wrexham Leader* (17 June 2003); *http://www.dailymail.co.uk/news/article-185971/Shock-town- hit-riots.html*; *http://www.bbc.co.uk/news/uk-wales-north-east-wales -22978551*

43 NLW, S&VA, AM 6989, 'Week-in-Week-Out', 8 June 1999; AM 3268/3, 'The way it is', BBC2, 22 October 1996.

44 *http://welshdefence.webs.com/*; *http://www.bbc.co.uk/news/uk-wales -11916458*; *http://www.walesonline.co.uk/news/wales-news/welsh- defence-league-show-true-2076844*; *http://www.demotix.com/news/ 348554/welsh-and-english-defence-league-demonstration-cardiff*; *http://www.radicalwales.org/2010/07/do-you-believe-in-welsh- defence-league.html*; *http://casualsunited.wordpress.com/*; *http://www. edlnews.co.uk/index.php/featured-stories/derek-fender-corner/1022- casuals-united-promote-swansea-nazi-fest*; *http://rationalwiki.org/wiki/ Casuals_United*

45 In this context, see K. Chahal and L. Julienne's *'We Can't All Be White!' Racist Victims in the UK* (York, 1999), some of the fieldwork for which was carried out in Cardiff.
46 R. Geary, *Policing Industrial Disputes, 1893 to 1985* (paperback edn, London, 1986), chapter 5ff.

7

Playing the Game: Sport and Ethnic Minorities in Modern Wales

NEIL EVANS AND PAUL O'LEARY [1]

Mass spectator sport is a prominent feature of modern social and cultural life. Since the late nineteenth century it has provided a mechanism for the creation of powerful and enduring group identities, focussed on neighbourhood and municipality, region and nation, empire and race. Equally importantly, sport has been a means of socializing individuals into what it means to be men and women in a particular society at a particular juncture in history. This potent conjunction of gender, nationality and race makes a study of the relationship between ethnic minorities and sport a particularly rewarding one, because the formation of group identities is fundamentally about the drawing of boundaries between those who are considered members of the group and those who remain outside. The complexity of this process is demonstrated by the experience of Joe Calzaghe, a contemporary Welsh-Italian boxer who is widely seen as representative of an ethnically inclusive culture in Wales but who is also 'Othered' as a white European when competing against black boxers in America.[2] This chapter provides a preliminary survey of the complex relationship between ethnic groups and sport in Wales, paying particular attention to the experiences of the Irish up to the 1920s and the black population thereafter.

153

Competitive spectator sport in its modern form in the United Kingdom emerged in the late nineteenth century.[3] Like many other leisure-time activities at this time, sport was profoundly shaped by the ethos and demands of the new industrial society, including the acceptance of agreed rules and codes of behaviour, the adoption of the time discipline of industrial capitalism on the field of play and the establish- ment of hierarchical leagues for the organizing of competitions. Increasing leisure time for workers and a commensurate rise in consumer purchasing power ensured the growth and popu- larity of spectator sport as a mass activity. Moreover, mass communications facilitated this development, allowing the experiences of the sports field to be communicated to a wider population than could possibly be present in the flesh to witness a sporting event.

In such circumstances sport had the paradoxical ability to both unite and divide society: uniting in support of a team or sporting hero entailed the kind of rivalries with other teams and sporting idols that generated intense loyalties. Sport, as much as any other social activity, reflected tensions in the wider society. How did ethnic groups fare in such circumstances? Could they, too, take advantage of new forms of leisure to assert their own identities as well as utilizing them for integration? Or did the tensions between different ethnic groups in the workplace spill over into leisure-time activities?

During the mid-nineteenth century the Irish had been the object of intense ethnic antagonism, often spilling over into violence. Between 1826 and 1882 there were twenty cases of serious anti-Irish communal violence in Wales. By contrast, organized sport might have been one of the many different factors contributing to Irish integration in south Wales in the late nineteenth and early twentieth centuries.[4] Whereas in other parts of Britain sectarianism was reflected to a greater or lesser degree in sport, south Wales appears to have been remarkably free from this kind of overt ethnic tension. In

Glasgow, where soccer was divided along religious lines, sectarianism was at its worst. However, in south Wales the existence of specifically Irish rugby teams, such as the Aberavon Greenstars and the Newport Hibernians, did not represent a sectarian attitude to sport so much as an expression of community or neighbourhood identity along the same lines as other local teams, some of which were organized around particular churches, neighbourhoods or public houses.

Possibly the important distinction here is that between rugby football as the dominant sporting activity in Wales and association football (soccer), which was the popular sporting activity in England. Dai Smith and Gareth Williams have demonstrated how sport acted as a kind of cultural solvent in industrial south Wales during those years.[5] The background to this development is significant. The pell-mell expansion of the export coal industry attracted migrants from rural Wales, England and Ireland on a remarkable scale and created a new society that lacked the kind of civic institutions that might have been able to integrate newcomers. Among the significant developments was the emergence of a Welsh international side that included players from diverse cultural backgrounds, some of whom had not been born in Wales. Famously, the *Western Mail* stated of the international player Gwyn Nicholls, who was born in Gloucestershire, that 'in everything except birth, he was a true rugby son of Wales'.[6]

During the decades immediately preceding the First World War, rugby was an institution promoting social integration in particular places and for particular groups. English incomers in the south Wales coalfield benefited from the popularity of this form of leisure activity. It became a focus of allegiance that could overcome cultural distinctions. But sport could not transcend all such differences for all groups. These were also the decades during which there was communal violence against the Jews and the Chinese (1911) and the black community (Cardiff, 1919). Does the size of the minority matter as far as sport is concerned? Paradoxically, it might well be that the larger a minority, the easier it is to achieve recognition in sporting terms. Moreover, some sports have a greater capacity for integration than others. In Cardiff, baseball was widely associated with the Irish but provided few avenues of contact with the remainder of society. Furthermore, during the years either side of the First World War a new generation of migrants established Gaelic sports that had been codified as part of the Gaelic cultural revival from the 1880s, in the process creating 'Irish sporting enclaves' in some Welsh towns. This supports a view that some members of the Irish community occupied an 'intermediate' way of life, though it is questionable whether all did so.[7]

Soccer was a late arrival as a first-class game and it owed a great deal to English incomers. The emergence of Cardiff City FC as a professional club in 1910 was the tip of an iceberg of football in south Wales. By then there were 268 clubs affiliated to the South Wales Association and twelve leagues. The real growth came after 1906, when there had been only five leagues and 74 clubs. What was crucial to this process was the migration of men from north Wales, the English Midlands and south-east England into south Wales.[8] As many as 1,000 of them boarded special trains to watch Bristol City FC, so there was a clear demand for the sport in south Wales. From the 1890s Cardiff had a schools' football league, at a time when spectators jeered the game and stole the ball, but the league gathered strength and ultimately established close relations with Cardiff City. Symbolically it was a Bristolian, Bartley Wilson, who was the real founder of Cardiff City FC.[9]

Soccer, then, represented the arrival of the English in large numbers in the last surge of the expansion of the south Wales coalfield, but rugby was already in a position of sporting hegemony. Soccer drew its impetus from English incomers from the Midlands and the north, whereas rugby had come in from the west of England. Nevertheless, rugby became absorbed into the Welsh self-image,[10] whereas soccer never achieved this status, despite its substantial popular support throughout Wales.

In the case of the Irish, an aspect of rugby that had the potential to cause divisions was the onset of international contests between Ireland and Wales from the season of 1881–2. Initially, these events were ill starred, with fixtures cancelled on a number of occasions during the 1880s when relationships between the governing bodies of the sport in the two countries became strained.[11] Yet these minor hiccups failed to inflame wider passions. The matches failed to have a disrupting effect on ethnic relationships in Wales, largely because of the perceived affinity between the two countries that developed from the mid-1880s, when Welsh Liberals overwhelmingly came to support Irish nationalists in their demand for Home Rule within the United Kingdom. So pervasive was this support that when the Irish team that played against Wales at Llanelli on 7 March 1891 took the field after a series of disputed games they were greeted with sympathetic cries of 'Home Rule for Ireland'.[12] Additional evidence of rugby's integrative qualities can be found in the case of a player like William O'Neil, the son of immigrants from County Cork, who represented Wales at international level; he won eleven international caps for Wales between 1904 and 1908, during the first 'golden era' of Welsh international rugby.

The individualist sport of boxing allowed a second-generation Irishman like Jim Driscoll to achieve both personal success and the approbation of the wider community. It has been argued that boxers occupy a special position in a society during a period of transition such as that experienced by south Wales in the years before 1914 and during subsequent decades. The sport had moved away from the illegal bare-knuckled prize fighting that had been popular previously. In fact, boxing acquired a degree of respectability previously considered unthinkable. By the end of the century, the ritual violence of the Irish faction-fight was channelled into boxing as a formal and supervised (if not yet entirely respectable) leisure activity. Boxing held a particular attraction for working-class Irishmen.[13] By promoting boxing and other sports among young men, the Catholic clergy consciously strove to channel male aggression into disciplined sporting activity, thereby hoping to create a leisure culture that rejected alcohol. The widespread popularity of the sport was demonstrated by the enthusiastic welcome accorded to John L. Sullivan, the renowned Irish-American boxer, on his visit to Cardiff in January 1888.[14]

It was this working-class culture that produced an emblematic sporting hero among the Irish in south Wales, one who embraced the raw cult of masculinity that surrounded boxing and succeeded in transcending his ethnic origins to become a hero for both Irish and Welsh. 'Peerless' Jim Driscoll was without doubt the most important sporting figure in the Irish community in south Wales in the years straddling the First World War. He was born into Cardiff's 'Little Ireland' community in 1880. He progressed from the grim experience of being a fairground boxer to win the world featherweight title in 1909 and a coveted Lonsdale Belt in 1910–11. The nickname 'peerless' was bestowed on him by an uncharacteristically appreciative press in New York after his unsuccessful attempt to wrest the world boxing title from one of their own fighters; at home he was hailed as 'the prince of Wales'.[15] He was respected as an individual who maintained an allegiance to his Catholic religion, and he even turned down a lucrative fight with the French boxer Charles Ledoux because of his promise to attend an event at Nazareth House Catholic children's home in Cardiff. When he died in 1925 the city came to a standstill as tens of thousands of people lined the streets to pay their respects.[16]

By the early twentieth century the Irish community can be regarded as well integrated into south Wales society. Even some of their middle-class nationalists shared many of the assumptions about empire and imperialism that were an important feature of the political consciousness of the time.

Earlier in the nineteenth century the Irish had been the butt of hostility and violence in many south Wales communities, but now they were able to take advantage of sporting activities to cement a wider integration into the emerging male mass leisure culture of the region, the short-lived popularity of Gaelic sports notwithstanding. Among the reasons why sport had an integrative function for the Irish in Wales was that broader cultural and political developments conspired to create a situation in which it was possible for a majority of the Welsh to perceive the Irish as brother Celts with broadly compatible political aspirations within the United Kingdom. Certainly, between the 1880s and 1914 Irish Nationalists' pursuit of self-government within the United Kingdom, as opposed to separatism, allowed Gladstonian Liberals to support the cause of Irish Home Rule. In brief, before 1914 it was possible to conceive of a self-governing Ireland remaining within the empire; that political vision only ended decisively in the years 1918–22.

Imperialism and the discourse of race provide a crucial context for understanding the nature of sporting activity in Wales before 1914. Historians of rugby have emphasized the way in which ideas of Welshness were seen by the majority of people as being wholly compatible with an overarching British identity that was increasingly rooted in popular imperialism. This was demonstrated most clearly in the famous victory of the Welsh national team against the New Zealand All Blacks at Cardiff in 1905. The press considered the event to be one with imperial ramifications. The New Zealanders had remained undefeated during their tour of the British Isles and the *Western Mail* asserted that the Welsh team had 'come to the rescue of the Empire'.[17] The comment was accompanied by a remarkable cartoon by J. M. Staniforth depicting a Welshman carrying a rifle with fixed bayonet, representing the Welsh team, facing a grotesquely drawn black 'savage' wearing a grass skirt and carrying a rifle advancing on him. This black fighter has already killed the Scots, Irish and

English in their respective trenches, while the Welshman defends the final trench under a Union Jack bearing the slogan 'Home Country'.[18]

This cartoon deserves comment for several reasons. The New Zealand team was composed of members of the white settler community ('All Blacks' referred to the colour of their strip), yet Staniforth chose to depict this sporting assault on the 'Mother Country' in overtly racial and martial terms. It is a shocking reminder of the extent to which race pervaded public discussions, even when it did not surface in such a crude manifestation as this. Even the Liberal press described the match of 1905 in overtly racial terms, although in this case they referred to the Welsh – as opposed to the white – 'race'.[19] Against this background, it is important to recognize that ethnic groups such as the Irish could achieve integration in Wales partly because of the unspoken assumption that they, too, were members of the white imperial community, in spite of their Catholicism. In the version of Welsh nationality represented by sport, the nation was white and excluded groups that were deemed incompatible with the basic values of Welsh society, so there was a limit to the social role played by sport: as a powerful carrier of communal identities it can constitute meaning, but it is also influenced by other aspects of social life that limit its inclusivity. Thus, rugby became the archetypal symbol of an inclusive national identity with the capacity for uniting people of divergent backgrounds in a common identity, but it was not all-encompassing and did not transcend racial boundaries.

Viewed in this context, the Irish experience raises important questions more generally about the relationship of sport to the creation of ethnic identity and integration. Was it a question of sport promoting integration or was it a case of sport merely reinforcing a trend that already existed in other domains of society? Did sport play an active part in the process of integration or was it a passive observer of that process? After all, in the decades after 1870 the Irish experienced integration in a number of domains of social life that were, ostensibly, more important: workplace tensions began to disappear as the mass unions of the 1880s took root; in political terms, Welsh Liberals were, on the whole, much more sympathetic to Irish demands for Home Rule than were their English counterparts, who were much more seriously divided over the issue. The rise of mass spectator sport from the 1870s coincided with the period when Irish integration was taking place. Is it possible to overemphasize the role sport played in this process?

One way of addressing this general problem is by examining the extent of participation by other ethnic minorities, especially non-whites, in sporting activity in an attempt to gauge the relevant importance of sport in constituting the kinds of ethnic identities that might assist integration. It also provides an opportunity to gauge the extent of opposition to such participation. There is some evidence of an interest in sport by male members of other ethnic groups. The Jewish communities of Cardiff and Swansea played each other in an annual soccer match in the 1920s, for instance, but it is the experience of the black community that provides instructive parallels and contrasts with the Irish experience.

Irish immigrants were being integrated into south Wales society at the same time as sporting loyalties were being formed. Black newcomers, by contrast, impinged on an established situation, and consequently they found it harder to make a breakthrough. The largest black community was in Cardiff's Butetown and there is evidence of sporting interests there in the inter-war period. Photographs survive of various teams playing football, cricket and other games. Most arose from particular sections of the community and were often teams solely composed of black players. There was, for instance, a soccer team called the Cardiff All Blacks (not to be confused with the New Zealand rugby team) in the late 1930s that played annual charity matches. It was not involved in regular league or other cup competitions and it is likely that this was the most important factor preventing the emergence of racial intolerance during these games. One of the Cardiff All Blacks players had a trial for Cardiff City FC in 1938, but he was unsuccessful; it is impossible to determine whether this was because of racism.²⁰ Intriguingly, the Welsh soccer team was the first of any of the representative national teams of the British Isles to field a black player. On 5 December 1931 Chepstow-born Eddie Parris, who played for Bradford Park Avenue in the second division, represented Wales against Ireland. Some of this achievement is diminished by the fact that he was probably chosen because the Welsh Football Association had difficulty in getting English League clubs to release Welsh players for international matches. This was his only international cap.²¹

Nearer home, discrimination was far more prevalent. Many people in Butetown recalled that only racial discrimination prevented the St Lucian seaman James Ernest from playing cricket for Glamorgan, while the young Roy Francis abandoned rugby union with Brynmawr and Abertillery for the more welcoming prospect of rugby league with Barrow in 1938. Black players continued for another generation to make their way in the professional game in northern England rather than in rugby union at home in Wales.²² The professionalism of rugby league was an asset: amateur rugby union faced the problem of the need for a job and further possibilities of racism in the workplace.

There were many who made the trip to the north of England after the Second World War. Two institutions formed the basis of this progression. One was the South Church Street School. This path was blazed by Gus Risman, a man of Scottish extraction, who played only a few union games before signing for Salford in 1929. He became one of the highest-scoring kickers in the history of the game, playing until 1954 and then capping this with a successful coaching career.²³ He was following a trajectory pioneered by Jim Sullivan, from the Cardiff Irish community (but not from South Church Street

School), who dominated the rugby league world in the inter-war period and left all subsequent full backs in the game in his shadow.[24] Sullivan went to Wigan, the club of the greatest Welsh black player, Billy Boston, in the 1950s.

The second of Butetown's institutions, the Cardiff International Athletic Club (CIACs), was founded in 1946. The club represented a second generation of Butetown people, essentially those who had been born in Cardiff rather than those who had been born abroad. Its uniting of all peoples in sporting action was a reflection of this second-generation approach to community life. Butetown tended to develop unity out of the struggles against discrimination of the 1930s and the rhetoric of racial equality that characterized the Second World War.[25] Many members of CIACs were fresh from the armed services. The club quickly focussed on rugby but over the years provided cricket, soccer, baseball and basketball teams. The free-flowing rugby they played quickly built up fixture lists with second-class sides in the Valleys (there were few opponents from Cardiff) and tours in England and Ireland. The path to touring was eased by the misapprehension of some opponents that they were going to be matched against Welsh internationals! It was a community venture, sometimes taking two buses full of supporters to away fixtures. It produced many fine players and eventually a good run of success in rugby competitions, with a peak in the mid-1970s.

A crop of players emerged from this side in the 1950s who would become legendary in rugby league. Their move to that sport reveals much about racial attitudes in Wales at the time. There were no great examples of black players to follow in the union game and the only precedents were in the professional code. As early as 1888 a Maori team had toured Britain and received a cool response from the rugby teams of southern England, many of which had refused to play them. The situation was very different in the northern industrial areas that broke away in the next few years to create the Northern

Union, the ancestor of rugby league. It has been suggested that in the north the working-class players identified with the socially excluded.[26] It was Wigan, in particular, which became associated with a racially integrated team by the post-war period, having signed a Maori player as early as 1910.[27]

It was little wonder, therefore, that Billy Boston chose to go to Wigan, a club that recognized his talent and paid £3,000 for him. This contrasts starkly with the situation in Wales, where Boston was convinced he would never play for his country in the union game. Born in 1934 of West Indian and Irish parentage, he played occasionally for Neath and captained both the Welsh Boys Clubs and the Cardiff and District XV. His ambition was to play cricket for Glamorgan and rugby for Wales, but he saw little prospect of either. The cost of such attitudes of racial exclusion in south Wales was high as he was clearly one of the finest wingers (or backs in general) to come out of Wales. His scoring record is unique: more tries than he played games (571/564). In Wigan he became a civic institution who was revered for his play, his conduct and his modesty.[28]

Billy Boston was the central figure in a cluster of players who followed similar paths. About the same time Johnny Freeman went from the CIACs to play for Halifax. His achievements were immense, though not quite comparable to Boston's. He never gained an international cap, despite being rated by many the best winger in the world in his era. This, along with Wigan's infamous suspension of Boston in 1956, when he was made the scapegoat for a heavy cup defeat, and the failure of the Great Britain team to select the outstanding Roy Francis to tour colour-barred Australia in 1946, suggest that rugby league was not entirely free of racial prejudice, however much better its record was than rugby union's.[29]

Colin Dixon also took the route from Butetown to rugby league after being 'overlooked' for a youth cap in rugby union in 1961. He went on to play 715 first-class games in rugby league for Halifax, Salford, Hull Kingston Rovers, Wales and Great Britain, scoring 177 tries and one goal – a total of 533 points. His transfer to Salford in 1968 was for a world record fee of £15,000. Clive Sullivan, again from the generation below Boston and Freeman (he was born in the 1940s rather than the 1930s), reached the peak of the rugby league game, symbolized by his captaincy of Great Britain in the winning world cup side in 1972. He had overcome serious injuries as a child and had once been told he would never walk, let alone play competitive sport, at the highest level.[30]

The CIACs produced a champion in another sport – the boxer Joe Erskine. He played in the same rugby side as Billy Boston and his cousin, Johnny Freeman. His family was respected in Butetown as keepers of a seamen's boarding house. His father was a West Indian and his mother (like most in Butetown) was from the indigenous white population. Not all have recognized Erskine's mixed-race background – he was not obviously 'black' – but he was usually described at the time as coming from 'Tiger Bay', which was a way of indicating his ethnic background, and in 1964, when his career was over, he explicitly referred to himself as 'half-caste'. Erskine was introduced to boxing by his grandmother who reportedly trained and sparred with two generations of local fighters, including her grandson.

The relationship between boxing and race was complex. This was shown by the fact that a bout between the white Irishman Jack McKnight and the black Welshman Herbie Nurse in Cardiff in 1934 was advertised as 'Blacks v. Whites', indicating how racial categories frequently trumped other ethnic identities when it came to competitive sport, and especially boxing.[31] Perhaps the breakthrough for black boxers was made internationally in the 1940s. Joe Louis's fights against Max Schmelling established the right of black men to box and even to carry the hopes of racially segregated America, while in 1948 black boxers were allowed to compete for British titles.

Like Boston and Freeman, Erskine got into his chosen sport effectively through army service. From the beginning he was compared with Jim Driscoll and he carried the aspirations of his community into the ring with him. When he won the British Empire title at Maindy Stadium in Cardiff in 1956, a runner carried the news to Butetown and his success was celebrated in a calypso – written, appropriately enough in Butetown's mixed community, by twin brothers of Somali descent. Erskine's career was quite short. As a boxer he had few rivals and some who saw him compared his footwork to that of Muhammad Ali, but his punch was rarely of a knockout variety and he frequently took hard punishment on his way to his points victories. He earned a large amount of money for the time – far more than rugby players like Boston or Freeman could have done – but he spent it on drink, women and gambling. In this, too, he echoed the frailties of Jim Driscoll. He died peacefully at the age of 56 in 1990 in his lonely Cardiff flat.[32] He chose to live in Cardiff, was a frequent visitor to the haunts of his youth, and he was one of the sporting heroes celebrated on the walls of the now demolished 'Bosun' pub in Butetown, which had a display of photographs and newspaper cuttings recording achievements in many sporting fields.

By the 1970s black sportspeople were emerging on the British stage. Subsequently prominent black sportspeople in Wales did not come from the tight-knit ghetto that was 1940s Butetown. Clive Sullivan began to break the mould: he was from the Splott and Ely districts of Cardiff rather than Butetown, though he had the young Billy Boston's ability at cricket and later he played rugby league. In other sports black players were more isolated and lacked the community support that Butetown provided. Hubert 'Bull' Best (aka Tommy), who was born in Milford Haven in Pembrokeshire to a Welsh mother and a Jamaican father, made his football league debut for Chester City in October 1948. His skill on the pitch soon attracted the attention of Cardiff City FC, who secured his transfer for £7,000 and a signing-on fee of £150. He established a good rapport with spectators and claimed that racist abuse merely made him strive harder to do well. He had a schoolboy trial for the Welsh team but had been turned down. In spite of some praise for his abilities as a professional sportsman, his achievements in club competition were limited and he was never given a place in the national team.[33] Cardiff City FC's next black player came a decade later when the black South African Steve Makone was signed from the Dutch club Hercules. He stayed for only one season (1959–60), it being felt that he was not strong enough for the British game and pitches.[34] By the 1970s black players were well enough established for Clive Charles to become Cardiff's captain in 1974–5; but he came from Bow in London rather than from the local area. The brothers Dave and Gary Bennett were great crowd pleasers in the early 1980s after they were signed from Manchester City, the city of their birth.[35]

Rugby union took a long time to shake off the racism that had denied careers to Billy Boston, Johnny Freeman and Clive Sullivan. Nigel Walker gave up the game at the age of eighteen when he failed to be selected for the Wales Under 19s side, despite outclassing his opponent in the final trial. He returned to play at the age of twenty-nine when his athletics career was effectively over and he had a distinguished Indian summer for Wales. Rugby union did not open its arms to black players. From the 1960s to the 1980s there were many in the Welsh Rugby Union (WRU) who welcomed South African touring teams that were selected on the basis of race, to send Welsh tours to South Africa and even to defend that country's system of apartheid. The Springboks tour of 1970 was prevented by mass demonstrations that were bitterly resented by the rugby establishment. Unofficial tours of South Africa continued after that, though outside the auspices of the WRU. To many black people it must have seemed that rugby remained the carrier of imperial values it had been at the turn of the century. However, a breakthrough was made in the 1990s. The first black player to play for Wales at rugby union was Newport-born Mark Brown of Pontypool RFC, who represented Wales six times between 1983 and 1986.[36] During the 1980s and 1990s a small number of other players followed in his footsteps, including Glenn Webbe, Nigel Walker and Colin Charvis, although their progress in the game was not necessarily smooth. Spectators threw bananas at Glenn Webbe at some club matches (a sign of disparagement more often seen in English soccer games) and a black Cardiff RFC player, Gerald Cordle, caused an uproar in 1987 when he clashed with a spectator who repeatedly abused him in a match against Aberavon Quins in the Welsh Cup.[37] By contrast, Nigel Walker, who also played for Cardiff, claims to have experienced no such problems.[38] On the whole, overt racism among rugby spectators appears to have been less pronounced than in soccer. This is not to say the sport has not been immune to stereotyping. A survey of Heineken League players (then the highest echelon of the game in Wales) in 1993–4 revealed that fully two thirds of black players played on the wing. This remarkable statistic, which reflects the experience of black players more generally in British rugby, has been attributed to the fact that positionally the wing is situated away from the decision-making aspects of the game.[39] Nor is racist behaviour on the pitch necessarily dead.[40]

By the 1990s there were enough prominent black sportspeople in Wales for a feature in *Wales on Sunday*.[41] The four picked out as 'Welsh, gifted and black' were the athletes Colin Jackson and Nigel Walker (who had not then moved to rugby), the boxer Steve Robinson and the footballer Ryan Giggs. None of these was from Butetown. Walker was born in Cardiff of Jamaican parents and grew up in the Rumney district of the city; Jackson, also with Jamaican parents, was from Llanrumney. Giggs, whose black father, Danny Wilson, had played rugby league, is not frequently identified as a black player, though he has indicated his pride in his African background.[42] Giggs grew up in Manchester while Walker and

Jackson came from the more diffuse black immigration of the 1960s rather than the established community in Butetown. Similar points could be made about other sportsmen who represented Wales. Nathan Blake, who played for Cardiff City FC before moving to the Premier League, is from Cardiff, though not from Butetown, while Rob Earnshaw, a talented, somersaulting striker, was born in Zambia and settled in Caerphilly. A tradition of black Welsh sporting success now exists, as evidenced by Olympic athletes (Colin Jackson, Jamie Baulch, Christian Malcolm), soccer players (Nathan Blake, Danny Gabbidon, Rob Earnshaw) and rugby players (Nigel Walker, Colin Charvis, Tangaki Taulupe – 'Toby' – Faletau). What is missing from this list is female black athletes.

Sport is now a recognized avenue of achievement for black people in British society. Those players and competitors who play in Wales and in Welsh teams are in many ways doing what is expected of them, rather than breaking moulds. The rules for qualifying for representing a country in international competitions are so fluid that there is hardly any surprise that black players represent their country. This caused some frictions in the past. When qualifications shifted from birthplace alone some wondered whether Welshness remained a meaningful category. The short-lived magazine *Arcade* was insensitive (some said racist) in publishing in 1981 a photograph of the black Swansea boxer Neville Meade on its cover with the caption 'How Welsh is Welsh sport?' Bizarrely, in 2003 Labour Home Secretary David Blunkett told a Home Office anti-racism committee that the black athlete Colin Jackson had been successful 'despite being Welsh'.[43] Clearly, in the past people from different political backgrounds have had difficulty in reconciling being black with being Welsh. Only committed racists would have denied Wales the services of Colin Charvis, who qualified on the basis of a Cardiff-born mother, despite his East Midlands upbringing. The fact that he played for Wales via London Welsh, which he joined as a student, serves only to reveal the fluidity of post-nationality.

Tangaki Taulupe Faletau, who moved to Wales with his Tongan family at the age of seven, is further evidence of this trend. While he developed a successful rugby career for Wales, his New Zealand-born Tongan cousin, Mako Vunipola, who was also educated in south Wales, chose to play for England, yet in neither case are questions raised about their ability to represent their adopted nation.

The existence of professionalism in all major sports raises the question of what happens to players after their playing career comes to an end. After playing rugby league Billy Boston became a successful publican, which in his day was the summit of many players' ambitions, while others became successful coaches. It largely remains to be seen what will happen to the black players in Wales who have come to prominence in professional sport more recently, but there are encouraging signs that sporting success can lead to new careers with broader horizons: Nigel Walker entered broadcasting and became Head of Sport at BBC Wales; Colin Jackson is a prominent sports commentator; Colin Charvis, who had trained as an engineer, is a businessman; and Jamie Baulch is a successful sports entrepreneur.[44] In the twentieth century, sport proved to be a valuable avenue of progress and of community definition for ethnic minorities in Wales. The question now is the extent to which this can be sustained, extended and built upon in the twenty-first century and whether black women can emulate the sporting successes of black men.

Notes

1 Our thanks to John Jenkins, Martin Johnes, Bryn Jones and Gareth Williams for their kind help with this chapter.
2 J. Harris, 'Boxing, national identities and the symbolic importance of place: the "Othering" of Joe Calzaghe', *National Identities*, 13/2 (2011), 177–88; M. Johnes, 'On the cusp: into the Calzaghe era', in P. Stead and G. Williams (eds), *Wales and its Boxers: the Fighting Tradition* (Cardiff, 2008), pp. 193–208.

3   T. Mason, *Sport in Britain: A Social History* (London, 1988);
    R. J. Holt, *Sport and the British: A Modern History* (Oxford, 1989);
    M. Johnes, *A History of Sport in Wales* (Cardiff, 2005).

4   P. O'Leary, *Immigration and Integration: The Irish in Wales, 1798–
    1922* (Cardiff, 2000); L. Miskell, 'Reassessing the anti-Irish riot:
    popular protest and the Irish in south Wales, c.1826–1882', in
    P. O'Leary (ed.), *Irish Migrants in Modern Wales* (Liverpool, 2004),
    pp. 101–18.

5   D. Smith and G. Williams, *Fields of Praise: The Official History of the
    Welsh Rugby Union, 1881–1981* (Cardiff, 1980); G. Williams, *1905
    and All That* (Llandysul, 1991). For a different perspective, see D. L.
    Andrews and J. W. Howell, 'Transforming into a tradition: rugby
    and the making of imperial Wales, 1890–1914', in A. G. Ingham and
    J. W. Loy (eds), *Sport in Social Development: Traditions, Transitions
    and Transformations* (Leeds, 1993), pp. 77–96, and D. L. Andrews,
    'Sport and the masculine hegemony of the modern nation: Welsh
    rugby, culture and society, 1890–1914', in J. Nauright and T. J. L.
    Chandler (eds), *Making Men: Rugby and Masculine Identity*
    (London, 1996), pp. 50–69. On soccer, see M. Johnes, *Soccer and
    Society: South Wales, 1900–1939* (Cardiff, 2002).

6   Smith and Williams, *Fields of Praise*, p. 33.

7   M. Johnes, '"Poor man's cricket": baseball, class and community in
    south Wales, c.1880–1950', *International Journal of the History of
    Sport*, 17/4 (2000), 160; D. Leeworthy, 'The forgotten hurlers of
    south Wales: sport, society and the Irish, 1910–1925', *Llafur*, 11/1
    (2012), 33–48.

8   Johnes, *Soccer and Society*, pp. 19–20.

9   This section is based on an unpublished paper by Neil Evans.

10 B. Lile and D. Farmer, 'The early development of association football
    in south Wales, 1890–1906', *Transactions of the Honourable Society
    of Cymmrodorion* (1984), 213–14; M. Johnes, 'Irredeemably
    English? Football as a Welsh sport', *Planet*, 133 (February–March
    1999), 72–8.

11 Smith and Williams, *Fields of Praise*, p. 63.

12 J. Billot, *History of Welsh International Rugby* (Ferndale, 1970), p. 34.

13 O'Leary, *Immigration and Integration*, p. 240.

14 *South Wales Daily News* (4 January 1888). On J. L. Sullivan's visit to Cardiff, see M. T. Isenberg, *John L. Sullivan and His America* (Urbana and Chicago, 1994), p. 242.

15 J. O'Sullivan, 'How green was their island?', in S. Williams (ed.), *The Cardiff Book II* (Cardiff and Bridgend, 1974), pp. 20–36; D. Smith, 'Focal heroes', in his *Aneurin Bevan and the World of South Wales* (Cardiff, 1993), pp. 328–32.

16 *South Wales Echo* (3 February 1925); *South Wales Daily News* (4 February 1925); *Western Mail* (4 February 1925). For more on Driscoll, see F. Deakin, *Peerless Jim Driscoll* (Stone, Staffs, 1987); P. O'Leary, '"Peerless": the life and legend of Jim Driscoll', in Stead and Williams (eds), *Wales and its Boxers*, pp. 17–32.

17 *Western Mail* (18 December 1905).

18 The cartoon is reproduced in Andrews, 'Sport and masculine hegemony', p. 65.

19 *South Wales Daily News (18 December 1905)*.

20 Johnes, *Soccer and Society*, p. 98.

21 P. Vasili, *Colouring over the White Line: The History of Black Footballers in Britain* (Edinburgh, 2000), p. 62.

22 Conversations between Neil Evans and several older people (including James Ernest) in Butetown, 1978–80; R. Gate, *Gone North: Welshmen in Rugby League*, ii (Sowerby Bridge, 1988), pp. 43–53.

23 Gate, *Gone North*, ii, pp. 30–44; *The Independent* (19 October 1994; obituary).

24 Gate, *Gone North*, i, pp. 26–42.

25 This account of the CIACs draws on notes of an interview conducted by Neil Evans with Gerald Ernest, Butetown History and Arts Centre (21 January 2002) and the CIACs fixture list for 1990–1, which contains a short history, pp. 10–11. For the community in general see N. Evans, 'Regulating the reserve army: Arabs, blacks and the local state in Cardiff, 1919–1945', in K. Lunn (ed.), *Race and Labour in Twentieth-Century Britain* (London, 1985), pp. 68–115.

26 Tariq Ali to John Jenkins, 7 September 1998, enclosing proposal for television documentary *The Democratic Game*.

27 P. Melling, 'Billy Boston', in H. Richards, P. Stead and G. Williams (eds), *Heart and Soul: The Character of Welsh Rugby* (Cardiff, 1998), pp. 47–58.

28 This paragraph derives from Gate, *Gone North*, i, pp. 108–20, and Melling, 'Billy Boston', pp. 47–58.

29 Gate, *Gone North*, i, pp. 43–53 and 108–20; Melling, 'Billy Boston', pp. 47–58; *Sports Echo* (17 February 1996).

30 Gate, *Gone North*, i, pp. 95–107, ii, pp. 153–63; J. Latus, *Hard Road to the Top: The Clive Sullivan Story* (Hull, 1973); *The Times* (9 October 1985; obituary).

31 D. G. Williams, 'Black and white: writing on fighting in Wales', in Stead and Williams (eds), *Wales and its Boxers*, pp. 118–19.

32 This account is derived from the biographical file of cuttings in Cardiff Central Library, which includes articles from *Boxing News* and the *Empire News* as well as the Cardiff press.

33 Vasili, *Colouring over the White Line*, pp. 133–5. See also P. Stead, 'Entry of the heavyweights: Erskine and Richardson', in Stead and Williams (eds), *Wales and its Boxers*, pp. 71–86.

34 J. Crooks, *Cardiff City Football Club: The Official History of the Bluebirds* (Harefield, Middlesex, 1992), pp. 67, 145; reminiscences of Desmond Evans.

35 Ibid., pp. 99,138, 139.

36 J. M. Jenkins, D. Pierce and T. Auty, *Who's Who of Welsh International Rugby* (Wrexham, 1991), p. 27.

37 *Western Mail* (21 December 1987).

38 See the interview with Walker in M. Burley, 'Welsh gifted and black: a socio-cultural study of racism and sport in Cardiff', unpublished Cardiff Institute of Higher Education MA thesis, 1994, vol. II, appendix G, interview no. 1 (no pagination).

39 Ibid., vol. I, p. 75; J. Maguire, 'Sport, racism and British society: a sociological study of England's male Afro/Caribbean soccer and rugby union players', in G. Jarvie (ed.), *Sport, Racism and Ethnicity* (London, 1991), pp. 94–113.

40 *Western Mail* (25 February 2002).

41 *Wales on Sunday* (17 April 1994).

42 *Observer* (1 April 2001).
43 G. Jones, 'How Welsh is Welsh sport?', *Arcade* (2 October 1981); letter from R. Merfyn Jones and editor's reply, 16 October 1981. S. Brooks, 'The idiom of race: the "racist nationalist" in Wales as bogeyman', in T. Robin Chapman (ed.), *The Idiom of Dissent: Protest and Propaganda in Wales* (Llandysul, 2006), p. 159.
44 P. Stead, 'Colin Charvis', in H. Richards, P. Stead and G. Williams (eds), *More Heart and Soul: The Character of Welsh Rugby* (Cardiff, 1999).

8

Changing the Archive: History and Memory as Cultural Politics in Multi-Ethnic Wales

GLENN JORDAN AND CHRIS WEEDON

As I stood one Sunday morning in the overgrown graveyard at Llanelian, I remembered that long ago Ma had told me that there used to be a college for Black fellows in Colwyn Bay, but at the time it hadn't registered. Now it has become one of those ancient trails I retrace over and over again as if to print myself onto it ...

When I visit the graves of the Congo Boys I feel just like those pilgrims to the slave fortresses at Elmina in Ghana who stand in the ancestral spaces and recreate the past in the present. It is as though through each retraced step the slave experience is owned by them. They have to go back to make sense of themselves in the present. In one single moment they are the past, the present and the future all rolled into one — the recollection, the recreation and the restatement of the whole thing gives them a profile.

Charlotte Williams[1]

Recent years have seen the rise of widespread interest in cultural and collective memory and their relation to history, power, voice, identity and representation. This interest is shared by family, local and academic history, museums and community projects and increasingly groups that perceive

175

themselves as marginal to mainstream national and public history. The authors of this chapter have over twenty-five years of experience working with people's history and community memories. These are areas that we will argue are particularly important in multi-ethnic societies like Wales where they are tied to issues of roots, identity and belonging.

In 2007, we organized two daylong public symposia at Butetown History & Arts Centre in Cardiff Bay as part of the UK-wide commemoration of the Abolition of the Slave Trade Act of 1807. The emotionally charged contributions from Welsh people of African-Caribbean descent raised three key issues: the significance for the present of remembering marginalized, negative aspects of past national history; the affective dimensions of remembering; and the importance of how history is publicly acknowledged. The first of these issues concerns education, public history and memorialization; the second points to the importance of inclusive history to successful multi-ethnic societies; and the third questions the perspectives and voices shaping the narratives with which we remember. The history of how the transatlantic slave trade and slavery in the New World have figured in Britain offers a useful example of how history and memory are constituted by selective processes of remembering and forgetting.[2] This is the case both for public and academic histories and for cultural, collective and individual memory. The questions of whose history and memories are remembered or forgotten and how they are remembered belong to the realm of cultural politics. They involve issues of voice, agency, interests and resources. Thus the Welsh African-Caribbean people at the symposia stressed the importance of foregrounding agency, that is slave resistance in narratives about abolition, which might offer positive forms of identification, rather than images of black victims and mostly white abolitionists.

As various essays in this book have shown, narratives of

history and identity in Wales are often defined against English and wider British imperial history. The process of reshaping Welsh public history and tradition to include the country's non-white Welsh population has only recently begun. The 2007 commemorations faced specific challenges in Wales, since for most Welsh people the connections between Welsh history and transatlantic slavery had first to be made visible. The process of documenting Welsh black history for a popular audience had begun in 2005 with a three-part Welsh language documentary, *Cymru Ddu/ Black Wales*, about the history of black people in Wales.[3] In 2007, BBC Wales broadcast a documentary focussed on Wales and the slave trade and in 2010 the programme researcher, Professor Chris Evans, published a book on the Welsh and the Atlantic slave trade from 1660 to 1850.[4] Like the administrations in London and Edinburgh, the Welsh Assembly Government organized a commemorative event in 2007 – *Valuing Freedom*. This was held jointly with Cardiff Council at St David's Hall, where many seats remained empty since admission was by invitation only. Many tickets were given to black and minority ethnic community groups, implicitly suggesting that the history and memorialization of the slave trade were only really of concern to ethnic minorities.

The authority, power and resources with which to create hegemonic versions of the past – to give authoritative accounts that are available in the public domain – is largely the property of institutions. These include government departments, social science surveys, police reports, the media and museums, as well as academic history and ethnography. One of the most interesting developments in the practice of academic and public history since the mid-twentieth century has been the recovery of marginalized memories, voices and experiences – of the working-classes, women, ethnic minorities, gay, lesbian, bisexual and transgender and other groups. In Wales 'People's History' was rooted in the trade union movement with a focus on working-class history. Llafur (founded in 1970), originally known as the Society for Welsh Labour History, played a key role in recovering working class men's history, the social history of Wales and from 1983 also women's history. Since 1997 the Women's Archive of Wales has been extended and complemented this work.[5] Prior to the founding of Butetown History & Arts Centre in 1987, the history of race and minorities in Wales was pursued largely by Neil Evans whose articles on the 1919 riots were published by the journal *Llafur.*[6] In common with much people's history, Llafur from its beginning stressed the importance of how we see the past for both understanding the present and imagining the future. Both the organization and journal explicitly broadened their remit in 2002 when their subtitle changed from 'Welsh Labour History' to 'Welsh People's History'.

Since the 1960s, people's history has transformed modes of representing the past in a range of contexts, including academic and other publishing, exhibitions, museums and media programmes. In recent years it has become a mainstay of some Heritage Lottery funding programmes. When rooted in cultural democracy – that is, in practices that encourage active involvement of a broad public, including marginal-ized groups – people's history has the power to transform identities and communities and thereby people's lives. In this essay we take up issues that we have encountered in the course of more than twenty-five years of collaborative research into people's history based in the multi-ethnic dock-lands area of Cardiff. This work aims to document and make visible Wales's multi-ethnic history, thereby changing the archive and public history. The initiative began in 1987 as Butetown Community History Project, collecting oral histo-ries and photographs, and has developed into an institution – Butetown History & Arts Centre – that aims to be a national centre for the arts, history and heritage of multi-ethnic Wales.[7]

Fig. 1 Butetown History & Arts Centre,
Cardiff Bay © Glenn Jordan.

Our essay addresses questions of cultural politics, which include institutional power, public history and issues of resources, voice and representation. We also consider the importance of place and discursive context in shaping cultural and collective memory and the affective power of memorialization so clearly visible in our opening quote from Charlotte Williams. Our focus is on Wales's oldest and most famous multi-ethnic area, Cardiff docklands, which has been both the subject of multiple modes of largely negative representation and the not unrelated object of two waves of urban redevelopment. We look at the complex role of life story narratives and photography in representing a largely invisible history and reshaping both the available archive and the public face of institutions ranging from museums to BBC Wales. We argue that both the history of representations of the area and the redevelopment have shaped local memory and that changing political agendas of multiculturalism, diversity and social cohesion have affected the area's place in the Welsh imagination.

History and context

In the course of the nineteenth century, Cardiff developed rapidly into the world's leading coal exporting port. As the port expanded, it attracted sailors from Europe, the British Empire and beyond, many of whom settled in Butetown, marrying Welsh, English and Irish women. Butetown, the central docklands area, was a physically bounded community approximately a mile long and a quarter of a mile wide and became in the second half of the nineteenth century both a 'sailor town', sensationalized in the press, and the commercial and industrial centre of the city. The area was cut off from the rest of Cardiff by (now filled-in) canals, railway tracks and the Bristol Channel. Residents called the northern part of Butetown 'The Bay' or 'Tiger Bay' and the southern part 'The Docks'. Non-white minorities tended to live in Tiger Bay.

Fig. 2 Seamen from different ethnic backgrounds,
© Butetown History & Arts Centre archive

Fig. 3 Marriage of Mohamed Hassan and Katie Link, Butetown,
*c.*1924 © Butetown History & Arts Centre archive.

As Neil Evans has convincingly argued, the physical
borders of the community were reinforced after 1900 by less
tangible but equally powerful racialized boundaries that
were strengthened by the race riots of 1919.[8] In the course
of the later nineteenth century, Cardiff's 'sailor town' became
firmly associated in the popular imagination with crime and
immorality, a trope signalled in a series of fourteen feature
articles, *Darker Cardiff: Seamy Side of the Great Seaport*,
published in the *South Wales Daily News* between 22
November 1893 and 5 January 1894. This mode of
representation would surface repeatedly in the press from
the Victorian period onwards and persists into the present,
both in the form of voyeuristic nostalgia and some press
crime reports. As Evans argues in unpublished research for
an ongoing book project, it arose from the fears generated
by astonishing urban growth. There were successive moral
panics over Irish immigration, crime, prostitution, crimping
(illegal supply of sailors), drink and later over more general

181

immigration, including issues of race. A series of moral panics

> arose in 'darker Cardiff' from the 1840s until the years before
> the First World War [when] they resolved themselves into one
> about race. Moral panics were plentiful in nineteenth-century
> Cardiff but they were different in nature. It shaped Butetown
> profoundly that almost all of these could be poured into a
> racial vessel. Black people living there acquired all the vitriol
> that had been heaped on sundry miscreants for half a century
> and more. 'Darker Cardiff' had become a much more narrowly
> defined 'Tiger Bay.' The social question had become racialised.[9]

A slow process of docklands decline set in after the First
World War by which time Butetown had become an established multi-ethnic and multi-class community. By the 1960s,
the middle classes had moved out and the remaining working class community found itself in a hot spot of social
deprivation, located in the middle of a post-industrial waste-
land. Further dispersal, this time including many non-white
families, was caused by the redevelopment of the 1960s. In
this period New Commonwealth immigration was also
reshaping the ethnic profile of South Cardiff more widely.
This first regeneration scheme dispersed a large part of the
existing multi-ethnic community to council estates on the
outskirts of the city. It destroyed much of the physical fabric
of the areas, replacing both large and small Victorian houses
with council owned maisonettes, houses and tower blocks.
The second wave of regeneration, which began in 1987
under the auspices of the Cardiff Bay Development
Corporation, brought with it major Welsh institutions, a
waterfront development with restaurants, shops and luxury
housing, marinas for yachts and extensive private housing
developments. Much of this is adjacent to the old docklands
community.[10] In the words of the Cardiff Bay website: 'The
Cardiff Bay Development Corporation was set up in April

1987 to regenerate the 1,100 hectares of old derelict docklands of Cardiff and Penarth. It was part of the British
Government's "Urban Development Programme" to regenerate particularly deprived and run-down areas of British
inner cities.'[11] The new road linking the waterfront with the
city centre bypassed the existing docklands community.
Following this second wave of urban regeneration, the entire
Butetown area was renamed Cardiff Bay.

Contexts of memory: 'Tiger Bay' in the popular imagination

Butetown has always been multinational and multi-ethnic
and, since the latter part of the nineteenth century, it has had
a significant non-white population. Much of the current black
population is made up of new refugees, in particular from
Somalia. Yet, the black, Arab and other visible minority populations of Butetown have always been a minority – despite the
impression given in the1940s and 1950s by Little,[12] Drake[13]
and Collins[14] and by many subsequent social scientists. Over
several generations, from the late nineteenth to the mid-
twentieth century, Butetown developed as a cosmopolitan
community of various peoples of European, African, Middle
and Far Eastern descent. Many ethnic groups had their own
institutions and cultural practices. In the 1940s, the area is
thought to have included, in its population of circa 5,000,
people from about fifty nations and even more ethnic groups.
In the twenty-first century Butetown has continued to receive
immigrants and refugees and remains one of the most diverse
areas in Wales.

Tiger Bay has long been an imagined community and a site
of memory for older residents, their extended families and a
wide diaspora of people with links to the Bay, whose families
no longer live there or in some cases never did. Many visitors
are from outside Wales, many from overseas; they come to
Butetown History & Arts Centre looking for family roots and
connections and for streets and buildings destroyed in the

Fig. 4 Marriage of Stella Hersi to Milton Howard, American
Serviceman, early 1940s © Butetown History & Arts Centre archive.

redevelopments. A significant number of Americans, for
example, come because they have connections to Butetown
via the GI Brides who left the Bay after the Second World War.

The main source of negative representation of Cardiff
docklands over 160 years has been the local press. As we
have argued elsewhere,[15] both oral history and social science
research suggest that this history of negative representations
affected social policies towards the area, for example, as a
legitimation of the 'slum' clearance of the 1960s, of policing
policy and of the area's use by the local council as a 'dumping
ground' for problem council tenants. It has also long affected
the employment prospects of the people who live there and it
has even been shown to affect the workings of the criminal
justice system. The most notorious case of this in recent years
is that of the 'Cardiff Three' who were wrongly convicted of
murdering a mixed-race prostitute, Lynette White, in
Butetown in February 1988. In his book about the case

published in 1993, John Williams recalls how the prosecutor for the crown, Mr David Elfer, drew widely on deep-rooted stereotypes:

> He said, 'it is an upside-down society.' It is a place, he said, where people carry knives as a matter of routine, where terrible acts of violence, he implied, are no more than commonplace. The effect of this speech was simple and deadly. Suddenly it was not simply these five men who were on trial for this particular murder, it was Butetown that was on trial for having an evil reputation.[16]

During the heyday of the port, images were both negative and exoticizing. On the one hand the area was constructed as dirty, violent, diseased and immoral; on the other it was portrayed as exotic and a Mecca of 'racial harmony'.[17] These latter representational tropes continue to surface in nostalgic accounts of the past in present day articles on the Bay. The history of representations of the area comprises a complex mix of images that repeatedly cross the borders between negative, positive, romantic and nostalgic and between outsider and insider images and narratives. Oral history and photographs offer the richest insights into pre-redevelopment Butetown and how it is remembered by both those who lived there and visitors. For example, Fred Daniels, interviewed for a project on Butetown in the Second World War, tells how his family, like many others in Aberdare, took in an evacuee from Tiger Bay: 'Jimmy Lloyd you know, Maltese boy ... Every so often now, Jimmy, he used to take me down to Cardiff, down to the house. And sometimes they'd have the raids on and all that, you know. We'd be hiding under the cellars there, you know. Be bombing the Docks, you know ...'[18] His memory is not only of an exciting wartime childhood but of a harmonious multi-ethnic community, a narrative that has long been central to insider identities but has more recently surfaced in nostalgic accounts of the 'way we were' in the local press. In his oral history interview, Daniels contrasts Tiger Bay when he was young with a violent present:

> Years ago now when I used to go down to Tiger Bay and you could walk through the park there and there'd be all colours all the races imaginable and it was safe. There was no fear of anybody, you know, molesting you or that type of thing like – isn't it – you know, or raping you those days, but there were all great. Nice people everybody.[19]

Whether these references to violence refer to a present day image of Cardiff docklands or to society more widely remains unclear. What is apparent from numerous sources is that before the major re-branding of Cardiff Bay in the wake of the second redevelopment, those with no connections to the Bay often held strong preconceived ideas about Butetown.[20]

Images of Butetown in the popular imagination have been shaped by a wide range of cultural texts: 160 years of press coverage have been complemented since the mid-twentieth century by a significant number of historical and sociological studies, films, television and radio documentaries, novels, plays and short stories. Books now also include life stories and images involving local people published by Butetown History & Arts Centre. The large number of texts of all sorts about the area has made it difficult to separate 'Tiger-Bay-the-Place' from 'Tiger-Bay-the-Stories'. Increasingly this is also true of the redevelopment, as certain key individuals from the community find themselves repeatedly consulted by both media companies and students. As they repeat their stories, particular narratives become hegemonic.

The desire for voice

> Since the nature of most existing records is to reflect the standpoint of authority, it is not surprising that the judgement of history has more often than not vindicated the wisdom of the

powers that be. Oral history by contrast makes a much fairer trial possible: witnesses can now also be called from the under-classes, the unprivileged, and the defeated. It provides a more realistic and fair reconstruction of the past, a challenge to the established account. In so doing, oral history has radical impli-cations for the social message of history as a whole.[21]

People from Cardiff docklands have long been concerned with Thompson's aim of a 'more realistic and fair reconstruc-tion of the past, a challenge to the established account' and it was community responses to the first wave of redevelopment, the threat of the second redevelopment and the legacy of negative representations that led in part in 1987 to the found-ing of the community history project that became Butetown History & Arts Centre.

In response to negative, often racist and sometimes roman-tic stereotypes in the media and popular culture, the people of Butetown developed a strong, collective and emotional invest-ment in alternative narratives of the past and a concern with what Paul Ricoeur has called the 'just allocation of memory'.[22] This community feeling became apparent in 1984 to Black American cultural anthropologist, Glenn Jordan, on arrival in Tiger Bay to do preliminary research for a follow-up study to St Clair Drake's 1954 doctoral thesis on race in Britain, which dealt extensively with the Butetown area of Cardiff.[23] As Marcia Barry recalls:

I knew that we had a unique history but we hadn't realised how unique it was until someone [a Black American anthro-pologist called Glenn Jordan] came in and said, 'You *are* history and if we don't do something about it, it will be lost.' So in a way, for me, it became a crusade . . . I suddenly realised that everything around us was changing – we could actually see it – and that the elderly people were dying and lots of resi-dents had moved away through the 'slum clearance' of the 1950s and 1960s, so the community had depleted and from I

187

Fig. 5 Founding members, Butetown Community History Project,
February 1988. Back row: Selma Salaman, Olwen (Blackman) Watkins,
Kevin Haines, Marcia (Brahmin) Barry, Vera Johnson, Nino Abdi.
Front row: Glenn Jordan and Tony DeGabriel © *South Wales Echo*.

believe about 5000 in the 1950s, we're now down to two and
a half thousand . . . We realised that we had to start to do
something about it.[24]

Fig. 6 Interviewing Gerald Carey, retired merchant navy man
from Jamaica, for a BBC radio programme made by oral
historian Stephen Humphreys, 1987 © Glenn Jordan.

When he returned to begin this work in 1987, Glenn established Butetown Community History project mobilizing the desire of local people to change how they were perceived and to represent themselves and their history in ways different from dominant representations.

Remembering those early days Glenn recalls how he asked Butetown residents: 'What do you think I should be studying?' The replies essentially said two things: 'We've been studied a lot. There are always people studying us. But they don't really know much about us.' The Butetown Community History Project began collecting audio- and video-taped life histories, old photos, documents and other artefacts related to life in Butetown. Its concern with the relationship between 'Outsider' representations and 'Insider' memories and stories, together with photography, have remained at the core of Butetown History & Arts Centre's archive, exhibitions and publications.

Writing in *On Collective Memory*, first published in 1925, Maurice Halbwachs locates individual memory as 'a part of or an aspect of group memory'.[25] It is the group that provides the social frameworks for memory and these are shaped by place, time and space. How a group or society remembers changes over time and is affected by environment. In Butetown, as in many other working-class communities, it was social change and urban redevelopment that made the desire to document community memory through the collecting of oral histories and photographs so urgent. As what Pierre Nora calls 'real environments of memory (*milieux de memoire*)' disappear, new 'sites of memory' (*lieux de memoire*) such as museums, archives, monuments, festivals and anniversaries must come to replace them if they are not to be forgotten.[26] These sites of memory are concerned with narratives of history and identity that reflect cultural power in the present. As much of Butetown became subject to demolition, the need to capture the imagined and now lost places and spaces of old Tiger Bay became a motivating force behind the oral history, photography and life writing necessary to create a significant archival site of memory. The two waves of redevelopment saw canals, docks, streets, houses, pubs, gardens and so on disappear and new buildings and street names emerge.

The loss of real places and spaces of memory strengthened key tropes in the collective memory of pre-redevelopment Butetown. These include consensual narratives, similar to those found in many other working-class urban areas, such as the open houses and unlocked door that signified friendliness and honesty and the willingness to help others even poorer than oneself in times of need. Yet, in the case of Butetown, they are interwoven with a stress on the multicultural nature of the community and the lack of racism or religious-based conflict. These narratives are juxtaposed with accounts of the hostility and racism encountered once local people crossed the borders and moved beyond the community and they produce counter memory of key national events, such as the Second World War, that do not match those official narratives that stressed how 'we all pulled together'.[27] Other emotive issues also occur repeatedly in interviews; for example, the affirmation and legitimation of a black presence long before the arrival of the *Empire Windrush* in 1948. Narratives repeatedly describe cultural mixing and many individual accounts tell how children in Tiger Bay

Fig. 7 Pedro Martinez Brito (from Cape Verde) and Eleanor Rosino, Cardiff – on their wedding day, 17 January 1926 © Butetown History & Arts Centre archive.

attended all manner of religious institutions and shared each other's religious festivals.

Building an archive: questions of voice and image

> The memorial presence of the past takes many forms and serves many purposes, ranging from conscious recall to unreflected reemergence, from nostalgic longing for what is lost to polemical uses of the past to reshape the present. The interaction between present and past that is the stuff of cultural memory is, however, the product of collective agency rather than the result of psychic or historical accident.[28]

Both cultural memory and public history depend on the reservoir of texts, images and artefacts from which institutions, individuals and groups can construct narratives of the past and, as we have argued elsewhere, access to the means of cultural production is crucial to counteracting hegemonic narratives.[29] The availability of the materials with which to tell minority histories is a question of resources, funding and cultural democracy. Control of funded cultural institutions and their resources enables individuals and groups to realize for themselves particular possibilities that are denied to others. In the area of cultural memory and public history, these include the means to represent the history of one's class, community, gender or ethnic group and to define and describe self and community, for example, what it means to be a person of colour, a woman or working class, rather than being the object of definition from the outside. At stake are questions of power that include the power to name, the power to shape cultural and collective memory and the power to create those texts that constitute public history as represented in museums, monuments, educational syllabuses, documentary films and so on. The full realization of these possibilities involves both cultural and financial capital.

Fig. 8 Portrait of Somali seaman Said Ishmail Ali with
his war medals, 2001. Photograph: Glenn Jordan

As outlined above, hegemonic narratives of Cardiff docklands, accumulated over 160 years, created a common-sense perception of the area as different from 'us', in this case from the rest of Cardiff and Britain. This process of Othering promoted racism and class discrimination that affected individuals' life chances.[30] The materials collected for the Butetown History & Arts Centre archive both contest and complexify this history of negative representations via family and community counter-narratives that offer positive forms of identification, subjectivity and belonging. The recording and preservation of these narratives, as a resource for exhibitions, books and education, can be viewed as an attempt to build an archive of marginalized, invisible and disregarded memories, images and voices. Thus, the circa 7,000 photos in the archive include both images from Cardiff docklands and portraits of people in Wales from ethnically diverse backgrounds that contest racialized stereotypes. For example, the portrait of Said Ishmail Ali, together with his life story, records an unacknowledged

Fig. 9 Jack Sullivan, *Home to Tiger Bay* (oil painting) – at the Dock Gate, near where the Wales Millennium Centre is now © Butetown History & Arts Centre archive.

194

contribution by Somali seamen to mainstream British history that is largely unknown and that can help counter negative perceptions of immigrants and more recent Somali refugees.

Both photographs and narrative paintings in the archive tell of a largely marginalized past that has shaped contemporary Wales. For example, the image (Fig. 9) by local artist and docks policeman Jack Sullivan depicts a way of life that has been lost not only by the passing of time but via the physical redevelopment of the area.

In the absence of other sources, many aspects of the history of multi-ethnic Cardiff have to be reconstructed from photos, documents and oral history. Documents, for example seamen's discharge books, passports and wedding certificates, tell of the working and family lives of immigrant seamen. Yet equally interesting and telling are the unlikely names given to the seamen by the British authorities faced with the unfamiliar.[31]

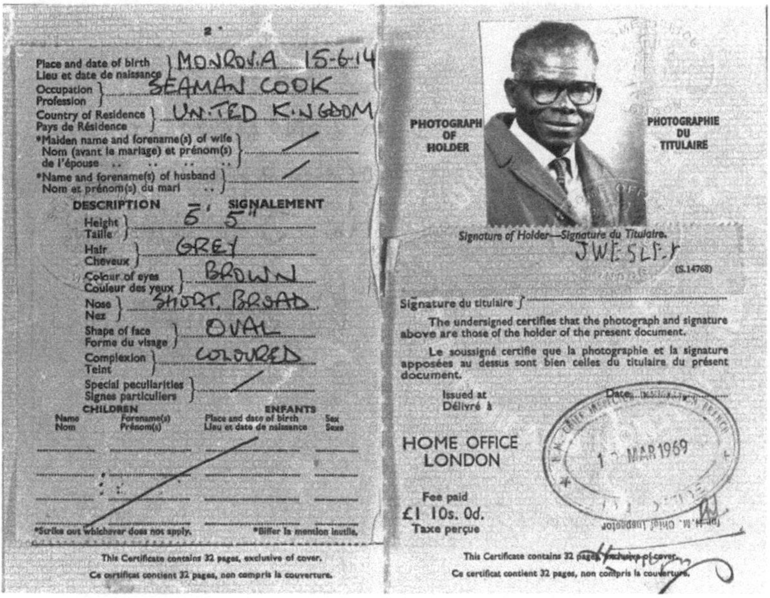
2

Place and date of birth / Lieu et date de naissance: MONROVIA 15-6-14
Occupation / Profession: SEAMAN COOK
Country of Residence / Pays de Résidence: UNITED KINGDOM
*Maiden name and forename(s) of wife / Nom (avant le mariage) et prénom(s) de l'épouse: /
*Name and forename(s) of husband / Nom et prénom(s) du mari: /

DESCRIPTION — SIGNALEMENT

Height / Taille: 5' 5"
Hair / Cheveux: GREY
Colour of eyes / Couleur des yeux: BROWN
Nose / Nez: SHORT, BROAD
Shape of face / Forme du visage: OVAL
Complexion / Teint: COLOURED
Special peculiarities / Signes particuliers: /

CHILDREN — ENFANTS

Name / Nom	Forename(s) / Prénom(s)	Place and date of birth / Lieu et date de naissance	Sex / Sexe

*Strike out whichever does not apply. *Biffer la mention inutile.

This Certificate contains 32 pages, exclusive of cover.
Ce certificat contient 32 pages, non compris la couverture.

PHOTOGRAPH OF HOLDER — PHOTOGRAPHIE DU TITULAIRE

Signature of Holder—Signature du Titulaire.
J WESLEY
(S.14768)

Signature du titulaire

The undersigned certifies that the photograph and signature above are those of the holder of the present document.

Le soussigné certifie que la photographie et la signature apposées au dessus sont bien celles du titulaire du présent document.

Issued at / Délivré à: HOME OFFICE LONDON
Date:
13 MAR 1969
for H. M. Chief Inspector

Fee paid £1 10s. 0d. Taxe perçue

This Certificate contains 32 pages, exclusive of cover.
Ce certificat contient 32 pages, non compris la couverture.

Fig. 10 Page from John Doe Wesley's certificate of identity
© Butetown History & Arts Centre archive.

The archive and exhibition resources that Butetown History & Arts Centre has produced since 1987 have relied largely on volunteer labour, donation of materials and money and small amounts of project funding. To date, this has made it impossible to fully catalogue, digitize or make fully publicly accessible existing resources or to collect other crucial source materials for the archive. Despite this the archive has become the main source for researchers at every level and for media companies requiring images and information on multi-ethnic Wales.

Why photographs and life stories?

A key question in building the archive and changing public perceptions is *how* to represent Butetown and wider, multi-ethnic Wales given limited resources, multiple rich and diverse histories, and a long legacy of stereotypes and negative perceptions of both Cardiff docklands and other immigrants and

Fig. 11 Gloria Evans (from Jamaica) with daughter Pauline Andam. From Glenn Jordan's 'Mothers and Daughters Portraits from Multi-ethnic Wales' project © Glenn Jordan.

196

refugees who have come to Wales, many since the Second World War. In the case of Cardiff docklands, collecting competing stories within the wider context of the changing physical and ethnic make-up of the area is important. Among the resources that most working-class and multi-ethnic communities possess are individual and community memories, stories, documents and photographs. If collecting these resources was a necessary starting point for the archive, our experience also suggests that they make effective and affective modes of representation. Thus empathetic documentary and reportage photographs, personal and family photographs and other documents, life stories and portraits can all challenge common-sense notions of Welshness and Britishness (as monocultural and white) counteracting those practices of inscription and representation that fail to include subjects who are visibly different and who lack wealth, status and power. While it is not uncommon to find documentary photography or documentary video being used as part of research projects or exhibitions on immigrants and minorities, portrait photography is not widely used. For us this is a question of the politics of representation. Empathetic portraits, combined with life stories, have a capacity to address audiences directly – to engage the viewer-reader offering agency to the subject who is a partner in the production of both interviews and portraits, thus giving voice to individuals who are rarely heard but able to offer privileged insights into multi-ethnic Wales.

Responses to our exhibitions and books suggest that people feel they can relate to portraits and life stories that produce an all-important affective response that is the prerequisite for meaningful change in the perception of racialized Others.

Lessons for Wales and beyond

A shared national identity depends on the cultural meanings, which bind each member individually into the larger national story. Even so-called 'civic' states, like Britain, are deeply embedded in specific 'ethnic' or cultural meanings, which give

Fig. 12 (a) and (b) Saeed Adan Yusuf and Ibrahim Ahmed
Hassan. From Glenn Jordan, *Somali Elders: Portraits
from Multi-ethnic Wales* (2004) © Glenn Jordan.

the abstract idea of the nation its live 'content'. The National
Heritage is a powerful source of such meanings. It follows that
those who cannot see themselves reflected in its mirror cannot
properly 'belong'.[32]

The sort of collaborative oral history and photographic work
described in this chapter has enabled the building of a significant resource on the past and present of multi-ethnic Wales.
The new forms of cultural and collective memory that it has
facilitated offer grounded and accessible narratives of past
experience, which speak to broad audiences and can offer
insight into the complexities of both past and present, as well
as meaningful forms of identification that may empower individuals, groups and communities and produce more inclusive
ideas of nation. Collective memory and the institutions and
practices that support it help to create, sustain and reproduce
the 'imagined communities' that give people a sense of history,
place and belonging.[33] The range of materials on which groups
can draw in constructing collective memory is a crucial
element in the process. It may include memories as related by
members of the group and narratives of history found in
books, libraries, museums, monuments, archives, photography, film and television. Important, too, are literary and visual
culture, family photos and memorabilia. It is here that the
Butetown History & Arts Centre's archive is of wider importance to multi-ethnic Wales and the UK.

Developments in new technology have enhanced the potential for the articulation and dissemination of marginalized
forms of collective memory. It is now possible to create materials on the lives of long-settled multi-ethnic communities and
on more recent immigrant and refugees that can give voice to
marginalized groups and promote intercultural understanding. Digital technology has made the means of cultural
production much more accessible and affordable. The Internet
has facilitated the articulation of cultural and collective
memory beyond the physical borders of specific communities,

Fig. 13 A Muslim/Catholic Wedding, Butetown, 1930s
© Butetown History & Arts Centre archive.

transcending geographical location. On the one hand it is creating imagined communities that can document their history via cyberspace, and on the other facilitating the dissemination of this new material. With access to the necessary funding and skills, it is now possible to make nuanced and insightful histories of minorities in Wales widely accessible in the interests of a more inclusive conception of nation in which difference is not just tolerated but understood as enriching all aspects of social and cultural life. Changing the public face of Wales through the ways in which its history and culture are represented, including an emphasis on how the past has shaped the present, is an important aspect of this struggle.

Notes

1 C. Williams, *Sugar and Slate* (Aberystwyth, 2002), p. 26.

2 For more on this see P. Connerton, '7 types of forgetting', in P. Connerton, *The Spirit of Mourning: History, Memory and the Body* (Cambridge, 2011), pp. 33–50.

3 See *Cymru Ddu/Black Wales* (S4C) and the accompanying book *Cymru Ddu/Black Wales* (2005) jointly published by S4C and Butetown History & Arts Centre (Cardiff, 2005).

4 See C. Evans, *Slave Wales: The Welsh and Atlantic Slavery, 1660–1850* (Cardiff, 2010).

5 As Neil Evans recalls, Llafur held a women's history conference in 1983, which gave rise to an issue of the journal *Llafur* with a strong women's history presence (1984). Since then the journal has published the major share of gender history in Wales.

6 See N. Evans, 'The south Wales race riots of 1919', *Llafur: Journal of the Society for the Study of Welsh Labour History*, 3/1 (1980), 5–29; and 'The south Wales race riots of 1919: a documentary postscript', *Llafur*, 3/4 (1983), 76–87. See also 'Regulating the reserve army: Arabs, blacks and the local state in Cardiff, 1919–1945', *Immigrants and Minorities*, 4/2 (1985), 68–115. *Llafur* also published Glenn Jordan's early essay on representations of Tiger Bay. See G. Jordan, 'Images of Tiger Bay: did Howard Spring tell the truth?', *Llafur*, 5/1 (1988), 53–9.

7 Butetown History & Arts Centre was founded in 1987 by Glenn Jordan and a group of local people. Chris Weedon has been involved since 1990. Based at 4 Dock Chambers, Bute Street, it has two primary aims: (1) the archives preserve and make accessible the diverse cultural history of Cardiff docklands and multi-ethnic Wales from the Victorian period to the present; (2) the galleries regularly feature visual and multimedia work by artists from diverse ethnic, racial and religious backgrounds and by women and disabled artists. The collection, exhibitions, educational workshops, publications and cultural events (e.g., public readings and other performances) seek to present counter-hegemonic histories of multi-ethnic Wales that offer alternatives to the long history of negative representations found in the press, popular culture and many academic studies.

8   N. Evans. 'From "Darker Cardiff" to "Tiger Bay": racialising the social question, 1840–1930', Cardiff University, School of English, Communication and Philosophy, 27 February 2013.

9   Ibid.

10 For more on the redevelopment see H. Thomas, 'Spatial restructuring in the capital: struggles to shape Cardiff's built environment', in R. Fevre and A. Thompson, *Nation, Identity and Social Theory: Perspectives from Wales* (Cardiff, 1999), pp. 168–88; H. Thomas, 'The local press and urban renewal: a south Wales case study', *International Journal of Urban and Regional Research*, 18/2 (1994), 315–33; and H. Thomas and R. Imrie, 'Urban policy, modernisation, and the regeneration of Cardiff Bay', in R. Imrie and H. Thomas (eds), *British Urban Policy: An Evaluation of the Urban Development Corporations* (London, 1999), pp. 106–27.

11 See *http://cardiffbay.co.uk/index.php/the-regeneration-project* (accessed 7 January 2013).

12 See K. Little, 'Loudon Square: a community survey I', *Sociological Review*, 34 (1942), 12–33; 'Loudoun Square: a community survey II', ibid, 119–46; 'The coloured folk of Cardiff – a challenge to reconstruction', *The New Statesman and Nation*, 19 (December 1942), 406; 'The psychological background of white-coloured contacts in Britain', *Sociological Review*, 35 (1943), 12–28; *Negroes in Britain: A Study of Racial Relation [sic] in English Society* (London, 1948).

13 See St Clair Drake, 'Value systems, social structure and race relations in the British Isles', unpublished doctoral thesis, University of Chicago, 1954, and 'The "colour problem" in Britain: a study in social definitions', *Sociological Review* (new series), 3 (1955), 197–217.

14 See S. Collins, 'A negro community in Wales' and 'A Moslem community in Wales', in *Coloured Minorities in Britain* (London, 1957), pp. 116–28, 116–28 and 217–27.

15 G. Jordan and C. Weedon, 'When the subaltern speak, what do they say? Radical cultural politics in Cardiff docklands', in L. Grossberg, P. Gilroy and A. McRobbie (eds), *Without Guarantees* (London, 2000), pp. 165–80.

16 J. Williams, *Bloody Valentine: A Killing in Cardiff* (London, 1993), p. 104.

17 See G. Jordan, 'Images of Tiger Bay ...' and 'On ethnography in an intertextual situation: reading narratives or deconstructing discourse?', in F. V. Harrison (ed.), *Decolonizing Anthropology: Moving Further toward an Anthropology for Liberation* (Washington, D.C., 1991), pp. 42–67.

18 Interview with Fred Daniels, Butetown History & Arts Centre (2005).

19 Ibid.

20 Many locals have their own stories about the effectiveness of negative media reporting. We can offer our own anecdote from 1991, when a city centre hotel warned hotel guests attending our wedding reception in Butetown Community Centre not to take their luggage or valuables with them to Butetown.

21 P. Thompson, *The Voice of the Past* (Oxford, 1978), p. 5.

22 In the preface to his seminal book, *Memory, History, Forgetting*, Paul Ricoeur writes of the 'just allotment' and the 'duty' of memory. He is 'troubled by the unsettling spectacle offered by an excess of memory here, and an excess of forgetting elsewhere, to say nothing of the influence of commemorations and abuses of memory – and of forgetting' (Chicago, 2004), p. xv. He proposes 'the idea of a policy of the just allotment of memory' as one of his 'avowed civic themes' (p. xv). This concept of just allocation immediately raises the question of who is responsible for such a policy and who decides what is just and who does the allocating.

23 St Clair Drake, 'Value systems, social structure'.

24 Interview with Marcia Brahim Barry, founder member of Butetown Community History Project (1996).

25 M. Halbwachs, *On Collective Memory*, trans. L. A. Coser (Chicago, 1992), p. 53.

26 See P. Nora, 'Between memory and history', *Representations*, 26, 1 (1989), 7–12.

27 See G. Jordan and C. Weedon, 'The construction and negotiation of racialised borders in Cardiff docklands', in J. Aaron, H. Altink and C. Weedon (eds), *Gendering Border Studies* (Cardiff, 2010), pp. 222–42.

28 M. Bal, J. Crewe and L. Spitzer (eds), *Acts of Memory: Cultural Recall in the Present* (Hanover, 1999), p. vii.

29 See G. Jordan and C. Weedon, *Cultural Politics: Class. Gender, Race and the Postmodern World* (Oxford, 1994), and G. Jordan, '"We never really noticed you were coloured": post-colonialist reflections on immigrants and minorities in Wales', in J. Aaron and C. Williams (eds), *Postcolonial Wales* (Cardiff, 2005), pp. 55–81.

30 For an example of this see Jordan and Weedon, 'The construction and negotiation of racialised borders'.

31 For more on this see G. Jordan, 'We never really noticed'.

32 See S. Hall, 'Unsettling "the heritage": re-imagining the post-nation', *Whose Heritage?* (London, 1999), p. 14

33 See B. Anderson, *Imagined Communities* (London, 1981).

9

Religious Diversity in Wales*

PAUL CHAMBERS

Welsh religious belief and practice has historically been associated with Nonconformity and an egalitarian religious
practice grounded in the local chapel and the Welsh language
and culture. Nonconformism emerged as a significant cultural
and social force in Welsh society in the late eighteenth century
and was consolidated in the nineteenth century. Grounded in
religious and cultural dissent and subject to constant schisms,
the religious landscape of Welsh was dotted with a patchwork
of small Protestant denominations, sects and independent
congregations. Taken individually, these groups were diverse
in matters of belief and politics. Taken together they constituted something rather more significant, what Grace Davie[1]
describes as 'established dissonance', that is, a hegemonic
cultural institution based on notions of community, respectability and resistance to the perceived threat of English cultural
and linguistic domination. As such, Welsh Nonconformism in
the nineteenth and into the twentieth century was ideally
placed to function as a significant carrier of Welsh cultural
identity.[2] This status was reinforced in the popular mind, both
by the religious census of 1851 (which demonstrated that
about 80% of the worshipping population was Nonconformist) and the growing number of Welsh politicians and
political leaders that emerged from Nonconformity.[3] Welsh
society, therefore, was historically informed by a close

206

relationship between Nonconformist religion, language and ethnicity. As with other societies in which there has been a close, hegemonic relationship between a particular form of religious expression and national identity, tolerance of religious diversity is often problematic.[4]

Historians of Wales generally agree that the population movements associated with the industrialization of Wales were a key factor in the growth and consolidation of Nonconformity in the newly industrialized regions. Industrialization also saw the migration into Wales of diverse ethnic groups.[5] In terms of ethnic affiliation to religious institutions, there were a number of outcomes. Initially, small Jewish worshipping communities were established in the seaports of Swansea and Cardiff. These communities prospered and Swansea saw its first synagogue erected in 1818 and Cardiff in 1847. By the second half of the nineteenth century, small Jewish communities were also to be found in Bangor, Llandudno, the ports of Newport and Porthcawl, and the newly industrialized Valleys of south Wales.[6] In terms of religious organization, the distinctive feature of these small, scattered communities was their reliance on the help of older larger communities.[7] While petty prejudices and intolerance were part of the daily experience of these Jewish communities, anti-Semitism rarely spilled over into the scale and type of violence associated with early Irish settlement, the Tredegar riots of 1911 being the exception.[8] While the Jewish community in Swansea numbered 1,000 members by 1914, it rapidly declined thereafter, giving way to Cardiff as the main area of Jewish settlement. In 1968 the Jewish population of Cardiff was estimated at 3,500, but this community too has declined markedly.[9] In the long term, Judaism did not prosper in Wales and this is reflected in the fact that Wales has only three operating synagogues today.

Of more significance to the religious landscape of Wales was the migration of persons of Irish and English ethnicity. The ports of Cardiff and Swansea, Newport and Port Talbot, as well as the industrial towns of the south Wales coalfield all saw extensive Irish immigration. The first wave of this migration also coincided with the process that was to lead to the restoration of the Roman Catholic hierarchy in England and Wales in 1850.[10] This Irish population was overwhelmingly Catholic and, in urban areas, tended to cluster around centres of worship such as St Joseph's in Swansea and St Peter's in Cardiff. While Irish immigration did much to restore the fortunes of the Roman Catholic Church in England and Wales, the hierarchies of each country responded very differently to the increasing identification of British Catholicism with Irish ethnicity.

In England, the Catholic authorities appeared reluctant to appoint significant numbers of Irish priests to serve parishes that were overwhelmingly Irish in ethnicity.[11] In Wales, where the growth of Catholicism was almost exclusively fuelled by Irish immigration, the appointment of Irish priests was less contentious, although in the mid-nineteenth century they still constituted a minority group among the clergy.[12] Concerns about the spiritual welfare of Irish Catholics in danger of lapsing or converting to Protestantism and fears about the effects of mixed marriages were addressed by the steady importation of increasing numbers of Irish clergy to serve the new Catholic parishes of industrial Wales.[13] By 1916 the picture on the ground had changed to such an extent that a separate Province of Wales could be established. Roman Catholicism in Wales, therefore, was of necessity initially Irish in tenor and as it prospered, successive waves of migrants from England and the Catholic countries of Europe both added numbers to the Church and confirmed its status in the popular mind as an 'alien' church.

This was reflected in the cultural and social experience of the Roman Catholic Church in what was an essentially Nonconformist Wales. D. Densil Morgan comments:

> Bereft of any indigenous working class tradition such as that of Lancashire and other parts of the north of England ... Catholicism was viewed in Wales with hostility and fear. Its

mores were strange, its rituals mystifying, and the presence among its faithful of thousands of virtually peasant Irishmen and their rough families put the church well beyond the pale. For most Welsh Christians it was a foreign and vaguely sinister institution.[14]

Irish Catholic communities in the period 1826–82 were subjected to sporadic outbursts of organized violence, not infrequently leading to many injuries and even some deaths. While these disturbances were primarily fuelled by the Irish Catholics' position as a reserve army of labour and were not unique to Wales, undoubtedly the prevailing climate of religious bigotry also played its part.[15] Gwyn A. Williams suggests that, by 1900, the Irish population were well on their way to being assimilated into Welsh culture and society,[16] but Trystan Owain Hughes characterizes the experience of Catholics, even well into the twentieth century, as one of hostility and prejudice from non-Catholics.[17]

For Irish Catholics in Wales, their patterns of settlement offset this to some extent. Residential stability facilitated the work of parish priests and, combined with the increasing establishment of Catholic schools, a pattern of religious socialization based on minimal levels of religious conformity and loyalty to tribal institutions emerged. Catholics had to struggle in the face of sustained discrimination for acceptance in all areas of life. For example, the concept of Catholic education was bitterly resisted in some areas of Wales. The Nonconformist hegemony in local government meant that Free Church opposition to Catholic schools could effectively delay or block the establishment of new schools and isolated examples of this practice were to continue even after the 1944 Education Act.[18] Sectarian denunciations of 'the religion of Rome' appeared to be rooted as much in ethnicity as theology. The Church was frequently described as 'alien' and 'foreign' and even the possibility of a 'Welsh' Catholicism was frequently derided.[19] Again, the close association of

Nonconformity with Welsh identity frequently led to converts to Roman Catholicism being accused of denying not only their faith but also their Welsh identity.[20] Fears about the 'dilution' of Welsh ethnicity and identity were further fuelled by the continued growth of the Catholic Church and its emergence as the second largest denomination in Wales. Indeed, as late as 1949, at a meeting of the General Assembly of the Presbyterian Church of Wales in Cardiff, the Principal of Aberystwyth Theological College stated: 'We are a reformed Church and cannot sit back and allow our country to be taken over to the Roman Catholic faith without some protest.'[21] Nevertheless, by the 1950s, the credentials of the Roman Catholic Church in Wales were becoming established within the national religious sphere.

While the Irish identity of the Church remained strong, immigration of groups of non-Irish ethnicity (notably Italian and Polish), intermarriage and assimilation with indigenous Welsh people and culture, social and geographic mobility, and progressive secularization, were all eroding Catholicism's perceived 'ghetto' status. The Church's own relaxation of its claims to exclusivity opened the way for ecumenical initiatives with Welsh religious institutions and the promotion of the Welsh language and culture within the Church did much to counter accusations of its 'alien' status. The high-profile conversions of prominent figures in Welsh elite circles had also contributed to an increasing recognition of the 'Welsh' nature of the Church. This transformation of Catholicism's fortunes in Wales was, however, coloured by the fact that, historically, the progressive waves of Catholic immigrants had made little or no attempt to assimilate or embrace the Welsh language and culture. Given the close identification of that culture with Nonconformity and the hostility of Nonconformism to Catholics, this is understandable. Trystan Owain Hughes suggests that, ultimately, 'this Irish identity was not replaced by a specifically Welsh consciousness but rather with an anglicized one instead'.[22]

Indeed, if there was a threat to indigenous religious institutions, it did not come from Rome, but from England and from the creeping anglicization of religion. Wales was the only region of Britain to experience net immigration between 1860 and 1914, with the majority of migrants settling in Glamorgan and Monmouthshire.[23] Immigration brought anglicization, first within the commercial world but ultimately within the religious sphere.[24] For a triumphant Nonconformity that had helped shape a distinctive oppositional Welsh culture grounded in language and dissent, anglicization posed a threat to its cultural identity and linguistic independence. The Nonconformist establishment reacted in a number of ways. Politically, it sought the disestablishment of the Anglican Church in Wales, damned as it was in the popular mind by its association with landlordism and English culture.[25] The Presbyterian Church of Wales was a prime mover in this project, but was also instrumental, through the foundation of the Forward Movement in 1885, in trying to engage with the increasingly anglicized proletariat of south-east Wales in their own language. Welsh Baptists and Independents as denominations were not so accommodating and this was reflected in the increasing emergence of English Congregational chapels catering for the new anglicized middle-class and English Baptist congregations, many sited in Monmouthshire and Glamorgan and more proletarian in character. It was becoming increasingly apparent in the industrialized regions that the use of the English language in chapel services was becoming commonplace[26] and by 1895 the English chapels were confident enough in their own strength to hold their own separate conferences.[27] The last great religious revival of 1904 can be seen as a reaction both to the increasing secularization of Welsh society and the increasing anglicization of Nonconformity in Wales. Ultimately, it failed to halt, or even slow, either process. The inheritors of the spirit of the revival were the myriad small sects of the Evangelicals and Pentecostals, English in culture and outlook and increasingly divorced from the everyday lives of Welsh people.

The political influence of Welsh Nonconformity reached its zenith in the years 1881–1920, bracketed by the Sunday Closing (Wales) Act 1881 and the Welsh Church Act 1914. The disestablishment of the Anglican Church in 1920 was a hollow victory, however. The new Church in Wales was able to make a relatively smooth transition to becoming a major Welsh institution,[28] while Nonconformity increasingly struggled to maintain its social, cultural and political hegemony in Welsh life.[29] From 1920 on, and against the background of a marked decline in public religious observance, Nonconformity found itself in increasing crisis. While it still retained a strong presence and influence in Welsh society until the 1950s, the steady erosion of the Welsh language and the progressive anglicization of Wales raised significant questions about the traditional association between Nonconformism and Welsh identity. Both Anglicanism and, to a lesser extent, Roman Catholicism were able to draw on notions of a 'Celtic Church' to affirm their Welsh identity,[30] while for the new evangelical sects and denominations that were springing up, identity was primarily a question of identification with the community of the 'saved' rather than the 'nation'. In 1930 the first Welsh mosque was opened in Butetown, Cardiff. Built with a combination of local authority money and funding from the local Islamic community, it heralded the first shoots of official recognition of a new religious diversity that was increasingly to characterize parts of Wales in the second half of the twentieth century.[31] Crucially, and within the context of the preceding discussion, it opened up the possibility of new types of identity formation based on new understandings of what it is to be Welsh and religious.

If the nineteenth century was a period of religious growth, the twentieth century was largely characterized by the progressive secularization of Welsh society. Whereas the 1851 religious census suggested that approximately 50% of the

212

population attended either church or chapel, the Welsh Churches Survey of 1995 suggested that approximately 9% of the population then attended a place of worship.[32] Decline has been most marked in those religious institutions most closely associated with the Welsh language and culture.[33] In the period 1970–95, the Presbyterian Church of Wales closed 350 chapels and experienced a 51% drop in membership, the Union of Welsh Independents closed 166 chapels and membership fell by 49% and the Baptist Union of Wales closed 163 chapels and membership fell by 58%.[34] These losses are far higher than those of their nearest denominational counterparts elsewhere in Britain. Decline was less marked in the Church in Wales. Adopting a different unit of measurement, the number of Easter communicants as a percentage of the general population over the age of fourteen years declined from 7.4% in 1970 to 4.6% in 1990, a drop of 38% overall.[35] Conversely, the story of Roman Catholics in Wales has been one of growth and consolidation until 1970, after which decline set in.[36] Undoubtedly, the fortress model of a church forged in conditions of prejudice and discrimination, continuing ties of ethnicity, continued migration from the European Union and a higher than average birth rate, all worked to partially offset the effects of secularization in Welsh society. A series of interviews[37] carried out with Roman Catholic clergy in 1995–6 illustrated the recent decline in mass attendance and the virtual demise of Catholic social clubs. Social and geographical mobility associated with embourgeoisement, the resultant loss of social cohesion and the loosening of ties of ethnic identity were all seen as contributing factors in the weakening of a distinctive religio-ethnic subculture.

One response to this pervasive religious decline within the mainstream denominations has been a move towards ecumenicalism and greater cooperation between Christian faith groups. Beginning in the 1950s, various indigenous cooperative networks have emerged to offset the growing weakness of individual denominations. The Evangelical Movement of

Paul Chambers

Wales and Associating Evangelical Churches of Wales emerged from the evangelical community, while the mainstream denominations (including the Roman Catholic Church) came together in what was eventually to become CYTÛN (Churches Together in Wales).[38] Welsh ecumenicalism can be seen as both a defensive strategy in the face of secularization and as the institutional recognition and acceptance of the diversity and difference increasingly characterizing the religious sphere.

D. Densil Morgan suggests that, 'Just as there is no longer a single Welsh cultural identity, pluralism has become an undoubted characteristic of the religious life of the new Wales.'[39] Within the Christian sphere, new groupings of evangelical character, notably neo-Pentecostals and house churches, have become a vibrant and growing part of the religious economy.[40] Outside of the Christian sphere many world faiths are now present in Wales: Bahaism, Buddhism, Hare Krishna, Hinduism and Sikhism, and, most visibly, Islam. While it would be misleading to suggest that these non-Christian religions constitute a numerically significant presence in Wales, nevertheless they constitute a growing sector within the religious economy.[41] Islam constitutes the largest non-Christian faith group in Wales, with 24,000 Muslims recorded in the 2001 census. Figures for the 2011 census only give statistics for England and Wales and have yet to be disaggregated. Cardiff (Butetown and Riverside) and Newport (Corporation Road) have long been home to significant Muslim communities and in recent years Swansea (St Helens) has also become home to a vibrant and visible Muslim community. While these Islamic communities have until recently been phenomena associated with cities, in 1991 new mosques were established in the county boroughs of Bridgend and Rhondda Cynon Taff, starting a trend that now encompasses most medium conurbations in Wales. In 1997 a Welsh-based Association of Muslim Professionals was established, furthering the institutionalization of Islam into Welsh culture and society. In 2003 a Muslim Council of Wales was

214

established, representing fifty-three Muslim organizations and mosque associations. Many of these smaller groups have established close working relations with local authorities, police forces and non-governmental organizations as well as Plaid Cymru and the Welsh Labour Party.[42]

In many ways, what we are now seeing in Wales in relation to Islam echoes the prior experience of Irish Catholics. Within the urban areas Muslim communities and businesses tend to visibly cluster around places of commerce and worship and communities have not been free from hostility and prejudice and even violence. This raises questions about just how pluralistic Welsh society really is, and whether a recognition of diversity is necessarily the same thing as a full acceptance of ethnic minority faith groups into the cultural and civic life of Wales. In terms of cooperation, or even communication, between Christian and non-Christian faith groups, there was little evidence up to 2003 of any meaningful contact other than localized interfaith initiatives that have been dependent on the goodwill of individuals.[43] This changed with the sponsorship of the National Assembly of Wales for an Interfaith Council of Wales, which was established in 2002. Despite this development non-Christian faith groups can appear to be marginalized, both within the religious sphere and within the sphere of civic society. The discussion below, drawing from interviews with thirty faith group leaders,[44] will offer evidence of the Christocentric nature of Welsh civic society.

The process of political devolution, culminating in the establishment of the National Assembly for Wales, has given Wales the wherewithal to begin developing its own civic culture. Devolved government, it was claimed, would bring greater levels of 'accessibility, representativeness, legitimacy, openness, participation, innovation, inclusiveness and accountability'.[45] A key element in this project has been the emergent partnership between the National Assembly and the voluntary sector.[46] As voluntary associations, faith groups are an integral part of civil society.[47] In terms of their structural

Paul Chambers

position within Welsh civic society, some faith groups are both working with government to deliver key services in Wales and seeking to work with politicians towards the common good.[48] In general, faith groups in Wales have welcomed political devolution and the potential opportunities it has opened up for them in terms of their public role. Indeed, sections of the Christian community (notably the Welsh-speaking denominations) enthusiastically campaigned for devolution in the run-up to the 1997 referendum.

Compared with England and Scotland, cooperative relations between faith groups and government, both formal and informal, are far more developed. The mainstream Christian denominations, represented by CYTÛN, have a seat on the Third Sector Partnership Council and monthly 'prayer breakfasts' held in Cardiff bring faith group leaders, politicians and civil servants together. Some of the interests of those non-Christian faith groups associated with ethnic minorities are articulated through the Equality and Human Rights Commission in Wales, which also has a seat on the TSPC. In terms of formal links, evangelical Christians are less well served as a group, reflecting both the fragmented nature of Welsh evangelicalism and the well-documented reluctance of many evangelicals to engage with political institutions.[49] In terms of informal contacts between the personnel of faith groups and the Assembly, these were overwhelmingly characterized by faith group leaders as 'good'.

One factor that has contributed to a sense of engagement with the National Assembly has been its geographical proximity to the headquarters of many faith groups operating in Wales and its small size compared with Westminster. Another factor has been the willingness of Assembly Members (including the previous and present First Ministers) to make themselves accessible to faith group leaders. However, both formal and informal relations have tended to follow the historic contours of Welsh civic society. Both those historic denominations associated with a specifically Welsh brand of

Nonconformist Protestantism and the Anglicans have better access than those faith groups that have historically been considered 'foreign'. The Assembly also appears to favour dialogue with the larger institutions over the type of loose organizational structures that characterize both sections of the evangelical community and non-Christian faith groups. A further dilemma (or, more properly, a set of dilemmas) for those non-Christian faith groups associated with ethnic minorities lies in the current nature of their links with the Assembly.

Despite the historic presence of non-Christian faith groups in Wales, we cannot talk about them being embedded in civic life in the same manner as some Christian faith groups. Also, as noted above, these groups do not conform organizationally to historically recognized structures such as 'church' or 'denomination', making communication difficult, although the development of indigenous organizations such as the Muslim Council of Wales or the Hindu Cultural Association (Wales) allows some faith groups to partially articulate their concerns. The most cited dilemma was the absence of any direct formal religious representation in the Assembly. While the EHRC can, within its secular remit, represent their interests, it is *not* a faith-based organization. In terms of *direct* faith group participation, non-Christian religions are effectively excluded from the VSPC. Furthermore, where the Assembly engages with these groups, it largely does so primarily on the basis of ethnic cultural identity or 'race' rather than religious identity (and this includes relations with the Muslim Council of Wales). As Chaney and Williams have noted elsewhere in this volume, it is effectively a race equality agenda that drives relations between the Assembly and ethnic minority groups. While not belittling the importance of this agenda, non-Christian faith groups, as *faith groups*, feel excluded from the Assembly in terms of their potential contributions and marginalized in terms of their specific religious identities. The vexed question of religious versus ethnic identity has

recently been rehearsed elsewhere,[50] but suffice it to say that
non-Christian faith group leaders in Wales still perceive this
state of affairs, when compared with their Christian counterparts, as discriminatory. Unsurprisingly, these same leaders
were supportive of the establishment of an Assembly-
sponsored, and quasi-political, Interfaith Council for Wales,
as were some evangelical Christian groups who also felt
excluded from political institutions.

The interface between religious and political institutions
in Wales is also taking place within the wider stage of the
European Union. Growing religious diversity in Europe has
been accompanied by an increasing climate of Islamophobia
and civil unrest in many European cities, and a growth in
state-sponsored 'anti-cult' legislation.[51] In Britain, the
'Rushdie affair' and the public discourse surrounding
non-Christian faith schools reveals a secularized society
apparently ill at ease with the presence of an Islamic minority
and often ignorant of the religious life and needs of ethnic
minority groups.[52] In France, incidents such as the *affaire du
foulard* suggest that religious tolerance and pluralism are not
self-evident or taken-for-granted propositions. Throughout
Europe, sporadic outbursts of organized violence, both
directed at ethnic minority faith groups and communities
and, increasingly, emanating from those communities, serve
to highlight these issues. Religious discrimination is not
merely an issue of 'race', as the experience of new religious
movements attests. Scientologists and Jehovah's Witnesses
(and other faith groups deemed 'cults') throughout mainland
Europe have been subjected to limitations on their religious
liberty. The German, Italian, French, Belgian, Swiss and
Greek governments have all produced negative assessments
of these groups and, in many cases, hostile legislation has
followed.[53] In the case of the Scientologists, members in various European states have been imprisoned, denied
employment, denied basic freedoms of religious association
and thought and have been subjected to a background of

routine exclusion and discrimination.[54] For both ethnic minority faith groups and new religious movements, the right to freedom of conscience and religion and the right to non-discrimination on religious grounds, as protected by the existing Articles 9 and 14 of the European Convention on Human Rights, appear easily circumvented by member states and regional parliaments and assemblies. Little appears to have changed with the introduction of new European directives on religious discrimination[55] and the track record of states and particularly of some regional governments arguably remains poor. This makes it all the more important for the National Assembly for Wales to live up to its rhetoric of inclusivity and democratic accountability, if minority faith groups in Wales are not to be discriminated against.

Overall, religious groups in Wales have cautiously welcomed political devolution, both in terms of its potential to transform their position within civil society, and in terms of the National Assembly's stated intention to work towards a more democratic and inclusive Wales. Devolution has taken place against the background of a growing religious diversity in Welsh society, which, while not as marked as that witnessed in England or other parts of Europe, is nevertheless a reality. In common with other societies where there has been a historically close relation between religious institutions and 'national' identity, religious tolerance of minority faith groups has often appeared to be only grudgingly extended. Discrimination, intolerance and even violence have all at some time formed the background to the growth of religious diversity in Wales. At the very least, followers of minority religions have been treated as second-class citizens within the Welsh religious and civic spheres. While the progressive decline of mainstream Christianity throughout the twentieth century has opened up spaces for a more diverse religious landscape to emerge in Wales, the full acceptance of these groups remains elusive. Welsh society and institutions remain largely Christocentric in character and orientation. This is illustrated well by the current struggle of non-Christian groups to engage with political institutions on the basis of their various religious rather than cultural identities. A recognition of a religiously pluralistic Wales is one thing and a tolerance of ethnic diversity is perhaps another, but only an unqualified acceptance of the right of minority faith groups to participate within civil society can truly be termed religious tolerance.

Notes

* The research on which parts of this chapter are based was funded by the Glamorgan Policy Centre, at the former University of Glamorgan, Wales.

1 G. Davie, *Religion in Modern Britain* (Oxford, 1994), p. 95.

2 P. Chambers, 'A very religious people? Religious decline in Wales and the consequences for Welsh identity', in G. Davie and L. Woodhead with P. Heelas (eds), *Predicting Religion: Mainstream and Margins in the West* (Aldershot, 2002).

3 P. Chambers and A. Thompson, 'Public religion and political change in Wales', *Sociology*, 39:1 (2005), 29–46.

4 For example, see I. Merdjanova, 'In search of identity: nationalism and religion in Eastern Europe', *Religion, State and Society*, 28/3 (September 2000), 233–63.

5 N. Evans, 'Immigrants and minorities in Wales, 1840–1990: a comparative perspective', *Llafur*, 5/4 (1991), 5–26 (reprinted in chapter 1 of this volume).

6 J. G. Campbell, 'The Jewish community in Britain', in S. Gilley and W. J. Sheils (eds), *A History of Religion in Britain* (Oxford, 1994), pp. 436–87.

7 U. R. Henriques, 'The conduct of a synagogue: Swansea Hebrew congregation, 1895–1914', in Henriques (ed.), *Jews of South Wales* (Cardiff, 1993), pp. 85–110.

8 A. Glaser, 'The Tredegar riots of August 1911', in Henriques (ed.), *Jews of South Wales*, pp. 151–76; G. Alderman, 'The anti-Jewish riots of August 1911 in south Wales', *The Welsh History Review*, 6/4

(1972), 190–200; W. D. Rubinstein, 'The anti-Jewish riots of 1911 in south Wales: a re-examination', *The Welsh History Review*, 18/4 (1997), 667–99.

9   See Campbell, 'Jewish community'.

10 M. Hornsby-Smith and R. M. Lee, *Roman Catholic Opinion: A Study of Roman Catholics in England and Wales in the 1970s: Final Report* (Guildford, 1979), p. 14.

11 Ibid., p. 21.

12 P. O'Leary, *Immigration and Integration: The Irish in Wales 1798–1922* (Cardiff, 2000), pp. 223–4.

13 The Welsh hierarchy was undoubtedly helped in this by the fact that prior to mass Irish immigration, the Roman Catholic Church in Wales consisted of little more than a few recusant families living in the border areas. See D. D. Morgan, 'The essence of Welshness? Some aspects of Christian faith and national identity in Wales, c.1900–2000', in R. Pope (ed.), *Religion and National Identity: Wales and Scotland c.1700–2000* (Cardiff, 2001), p. 151.

14 Ibid., pp. 150–1.

15 P. O'Leary, 'Anti-Irish riots in Wales, 1826–1882', *Llafur*, 5/4 (1991), 27–35.

16 G. A. Williams, *When was Wales? A History of the Welsh* (Harmondsworth, 1991), p. 179.

17 T. O. Hughes, *Winds of Change: The Roman Catholic Church and Society in Wales 1916–1962* (Cardiff, 1999), pp. 1–5.

18 Ibid., pp. 131–57, 223–5; G. E. Jones, *Which Nation's Schools? Direction and Devolution in Welsh Education in the Twentieth Century* (Cardiff, 1990), p. 100.

19 T. O. Hughes, 'Continuity and conversion: the concept of a national church in twentieth century Wales and its relation to "the Celtic Church"', in R. Pope (ed.), *Religion and National Identity: Wales and Scotland c.1700–2000* (Cardiff, 2001), pp. 123–38.

20 Hughes, *Winds of Change*, pp. 81–5.

21 Ibid., p. 151.

22 Ibid., p. 180.

23 P. Jenkins, *A History of Modern Wales: 1535–1990* (Harlow, 1992), pp. 236–8.

24 E. T. Davies, *Religion and Society in the Nineteenth Century* *(Llandybïe, 1981), pp. 68–71.*

25 Williams, *When was Wales?*, pp. 228, 234.

26 J. V. Morgan, *The Welsh Religious Revival 1904–5: A Retrospect and Criticism* (London, 1909), pp. 254–5.

27 W. R. Lambert, 'Some working class attitudes towards organised religion in nineteenth-century Wales', in G. Parsons (ed.), *Religion in Victorian Britain*, iv, *Interpretations* (Manchester, 1988), pp. 110–12.

28 C. Harris and R. Startup, *The Church in Wales: The Sociology of a Traditional Institution* (Cardiff, 1999), pp. 1–6.

29 R. Pope, *Building Jerusalem: Nonconformity, Labour and the Social Question in Wales, 1906–1939* (Cardiff, 1998), passim.

30 Hughes, 'Continuity and conversion', 123–38.

31 Chambers and Thompson, 'Public religion'.

32 Bible Society, *Challenge to Change: The Results of the 1995 Welsh Churches Survey* (Swindon, 1997).

33 D. G. Evans, *A History of Wales 1906–2000* (Cardiff, 2000), pp. 179–88.

34 P. Chambers, *Religion, Secularization and Social Change in Wales* (Cardiff, 2005), p. 17.

35 Harris and Startup, *Church in Wales*, p. 22.

36 Ibid., p. 21

37 Chambers, *Religion, Secularization and Social Change*, pp. 63–5.

38 Chambers and Thompson, 'Public religion'.

39 Morgan, 'Essence of Welshness', p. 159.

40 See, for example, P. Chambers, 'On or off the bus: identity, belonging and schism: a case study of a neo-pentecostal house church', in S. Hunt, M. Hamilton and T. Walter (eds), *Charismatic Christianity: Sociological Perspectives* (Basingstoke, 1997).

41 D. P. Davies, 'A time of paradoxes among the faiths', in D. Cole (ed.), *The New Wales* (Cardiff, 1990).

42 P. Chambers, 'Secularisation, Wales and Islam', Journal of Contemporary Religion, 21:3 (2006), 325–40.

43 Chambers and Thompson, 'Public religion'.

44 Ibid.

45 P. Chaney, T. Hall and A. Pithouse, 'New governance – new democracy', in P. Chaney, T. Hall and A. Pithouse (eds), *New Governance – New Democracy? Post-Devolution Wales* (Cardiff, 2001), p. 3.

46 B. Dicks, T. Hall and A. Pithouse, 'The National Assembly and the voluntary sector: an equal partnership?', in Chaney, Hall and Pithouse (eds), *New Governance – New Democracy?*, pp. 102–25.

47 See, for example, the arguments of A. Shanks, *Civil Society, Civil Religion* (Oxford, 1995), or R. Wuthnow, *Christianity and Civil Society* (Valley Forge, 1996).

48 A. Edwards, *Transforming Power: A Christian Reflection on Welsh Devolution* (Bangor, 2001), p. 23.

49 P. Broadbent, 'Evangelicals and social justice', in C. Bryant (ed.), *Restoring Faith in Politics* (London, 1996), pp. 30–44.

50 P. Weller, A. Feldman and K. Purdam, *Religious Discrimination in England and Wales*, Home Office Research Study, No. 220 (London, 2001).

51 For an excellent discussion of these issues, see G. Davie, *Religion in Modern Europe* (Oxford, 2000), pp. 115–37.

52 This being true before the events of New York, 11 September 2001; the stakes have certainly been raised since.

53 Davie, *Religion in Modern Europe*, pp. 117–21.

54 Information on human rights violations against Scientologists in Germany, France and Belgium, including a document sent in 1999 to the Country Based Support Scheme Commissioner (Strasbourg). (The CBSS is sponsored by the European Union, European Instrument for Democracy and Human Rights.) See both European Human Rights Office, *Church of Scientology, Discriminatory Actions and Proposed Measures Against Minority Religions by the French Government* (Brussels, n.d.), and European Human Rights Office, *Church of Scientology, Human Rights Violations: Belgium* (Brussels, n.d.).

55 Two new directives under Article 13 of the Treaty of Amsterdam 1997 provided, for the first time, an enforceable, common legal framework of minimum protection against religious discrimination.

10

Extending the Parameters of Social Policy Research for a Multicultural Wales

ROIYAH SALTUS AND CHARLOTTE WILLIAMS

In the two-hundredth edition of *Planet* Neil Evans posed the interesting question: 'are we getting the social science we need in order to understand Wales in an era of devolved government?'[1] This question provokes a complex set of considerations and debates, not least the relationship between government and academia, between knowledge production and policy making and their links with wider social and political movements.[2] This debate is pertinent to a consideration of the extent to which social policy research might be harnessed toward the Welsh Government's political ambition of equality, more specifically, race equality in Wales.[3] The question demands a consideration not only of the nature of the evidence base and its significance to policy making in an era of self-government, but suggests this evidence as fundamental to an understanding of Wales itself.

The attention given to the importance of exploring both the concept, and how best to operationalize ethnicity in research in the UK remains embryonic, in contrast to the USA, for example, where ethnic minority perspectives are a mandatory consideration in all government funded social research. Salway et al.'s review of the state of play in the UK[4] concluded that:

There is a need both to convince a wider audience of social researchers of the need to address ethnicity within their work, and also to encourage those researchers who already work in the field of ethnicity to reflect on and improve their current practice.[5]

Salway et al. cite UK-wide evidence[6] that indicates the majority of social research is focused on the white population and does not consider minority ethnicity as a variable. This immediately begs the question as to whether social research in Wales can engage more wholesomely with these considerations to produce real sustainable change to the wellbeing of ethnic minorities.

In this context we would suggest at least five important justifications for increased engagement with these issues that do not amount to a case for privileging minority ethnicity but argue for it on the basis of principle. First, this contention is based on the self-evident argument that Wales – irrespective of particular locales – *is* a multicultural society, indeed it is 'superdiverse'[7] and thus not easily readable as a conglomeration of discrete communities but more an amalgamation of highly differentiated peoples who, for the sake of convenience, we categorize into ethnic minority groups. Although caution is needed when comparing census ethnicity data over the ten-year intervals due to changes and increases in tick boxes, changes to how the ethnicity question is worded and the ethnic categories used, what these data reveal is telling. The 2011 census indicates that the number of people from black ethnic minority backgrounds increased to 135,203 (approximately 4.0% of the total population) since the last census, an increase from 2.1% (61,5800) in 2001 and 1.5% (41,551) in 1991.[8] Since 1991, in Wales there have been steady increases in the proportions of African, Indian, Pakistani, Bangladeshi and Chinese people, and increases in the number of people who classified themselves according to one of the several mixed ethnicities categories.[9] Based on the latest census, there have been notable increases in these same groups, with the 'African', 'Mixed' ethnic groups and 'Other White' groups being the fastest growing population groups and those under the umbrella of 'Others', including new migrants, also being numerically significant.

Another important particularity is the fact that the ethnic minority populations in Wales remain highly concentrated geographically in south-east Wales cities and moreover contin-ues to comprise great heterogeneity both between and within the different population groups based on socioeconomic status, gender, migration history, employment, skills and language proficiencies. The common denominator, however, is that ethnicity forms one of the major social divisions of modern Britain *sic* Wales, such that it remains important to consider the impact of structural discrimination and racism.[10]

Thirdly, a review of the evidence in particular policy fields demonstrates the need for even more fine-tuned data to tell the story of black and ethnic minority groups in Wales. It highlights the limitations of some of the more conventional apparatus of national social surveys and the issues of confi-dentiality and validity that small and deep data sets present. It highlights a paucity of evidence in some crucial areas of well-being. Linked to this is the oft heard policy discourse of 'Welsh solutions to Welsh social problems', that is, the need for a better understanding of the patterns and causes of issues in as much as they are specific to Wales and Welsh policy making. We need to know more about what the specific factors of place are that contribute to racial disadvantage. Appropriate responses are too often hampered by lack of good quality research in this respect, as this chapter illustrates.

Of equal importance is the fact that research on ethnicity and race cannot be said to be a specialist pursuit. Besides the fact that we all possess an ethnicity, there are important and evident intersections to be considered and to be controlled for if we are to understand at all the role of ethnicity. Thus, rather than over emphasizing ethnic minority differences and distinctiveness, an inclusive approach is needed that addresses the role of similarities (for example, in terms of class, locality, gender) as causal/contributing factors. Otherwise we engage in ethnic essentialism that gives ethnicity the fundamental causal role and serves to define research in this area as a marginal specialism, at once peripheral and excluded from mainstream policies.[11]

Lastly, even putting aside all the legal duties and requirements of responding appropriately to minority populations and all the political aspirations of equality of opportunity in Wales,[12] there must be a political (small 'p') argument that points to researchers' responsibilities towards wider society of which they are a part. It is worth reiterating Wilkinson and Pickett's *The Spirit Level*[13] dictum on unequal societies: that more inequality is more socially damaging and societies characterized by high rates of inequality have higher rates of distress and lower levels of life expectancy, educational attainment, social mobility and of course trust. These are concerns that affect the population as a whole.

This chapter explores the available evidence on the position of racialized minorities in Wales across a number of key policy domains. The chapter draws on Winckler et al.'s 2009 review[14] of the key equality strands, and Davies et al.'s quantitative analysis of economic inequality in Wales in 2011.[15] We show that in the last decade disparities continue to exist for black and ethnic minority people across a range of policy domains. While more evidence has been gathered over the last decade that sheds light onto the lives of people from ethnic minority groups, we conclude by arguing for the need for a sustained mainstreaming of these concerns within social policy research in Wales.

Health and social care

It remains the case across the UK that disparities exist within the health and social care system, with differences such as 'race', ethnicity, socioeconomic status and geographic location impacting on the level of access to information, treatment and care, and on the utilization, experience and satisfaction of health and social care provision.[16] In addition, for a disproportionate number of people from black and ethnic minority backgrounds in the UK, poverty and socioeconomic positioning, often exacerbated by (among other things) societal and institutional racism and discrimination, continue to impact negatively on their health and social outcomes.[17] Although research shows that black and ethnic minority groups are diverse in terms of socioeconomic status, language, generation, culture and lifestyles (diversity that is reflected in their health status, disease patterns, lifestyles, social capital and health behaviour), it is clear that a disproportionate number of people from black and ethnic minority backgrounds are at an increased risk of comparatively poor health and reduced access to, and benefit from, a range of health and social care services.

The evidence in Wales is accumulating from a very low starting point. Neither the Welsh Health Survey carried out in the mid-1990s nor the Atlas of Health Inequalities in Wales from 1998 gave any information on ethnic minority population groups. During this period, the NHS Equality Unit study in 1998 found considerable variability in the collection of ethnic data, making any attempt to understand the prevalence and treatment of ill health difficult.[18] What emerged from these studies was a pervasive univeralism that permeated service delivery to the neglect of black and ethnic minority people and a paucity of alternative provision.[19] For example, a study conducted in 2000 by the Policy Research Institute on Ageing and Ethnicity (PRIAE) highlighted a major difference between England and Wales being the relative absence of voluntary specialist organizations for older people from minority communities.[20]

The evidence base on the health and social care needs of the ethnic minority population in Wales, although better than it was a decade ago, nevertheless remains patchy. Access to health and health related services, and explorations on how to improve services remains a research preoccupation.

228

Recent studies, for example, have sought to identify the health and health promotion needs of black and ethnic minority groups in Wales;[21] the mental health and treatment needs of black and ethnic minority groups;[22] the accessibility of services carers,[23] and the health and social care needs of unaccompanied children seeking asylum.[24] What is evident is that these are ongoing issues and there remains an apparent lack of information on access to care for black and ethnic minority populations in Wales.[25] A few studies have been undertaken that focussed exclusively on specific groups, for example on the experiences of Bangladeshi patients in primary care settings,[26] the incidence of active tuberculosis in children,[27] the emotional wellbeing of Bangladeshi mothers living in Wales and their perceptions of the postnatal period,[28] the views and perceptions of Gypsy Travellers,[29] and the understanding and beliefs of people with diabetes from the Bangladeshi community.[30] Although adding to the evidence base, providing insights into the perceptions, experiences and expectations of various population groups, these studies taken as a whole do not represent any concerted effort to bridge the knowledge gap and are more a reflection of the predilections of individual researchers than any strategic approach to addressing health inequities.

Not having a necessary evidence base in which to shape policy and secure funding to develop services and programmes is replicated in the field of social care. In the past decade, statistical reviews[31] and a number of local, regional and national studies have been conducted, many of which have been commissioned via funding strands within Welsh Government departments. This empirical evidence includes studies exploring the views and perceptions of older ethnic minority groups in terms of their understanding of dignity and their care expectations,[32] as well as studies exploring the experiences of carers, the wellbeing of unaccompanied young people, the views of particular Muslim groups, the impact of substance misuse, and domestic violence[33] conducted by

229

academics and research-active third sector organizations. Among the themes that emerge from this research data are the ongoing high levels of hidden and unmet need, low levels of knowledge of existing services, difficulties in accessing services, the competencies of care professionals, the difficulties in operationalizing the duties and practices underpinning the various equality frameworks, and the policies and practices underpinning health and social care delivery in Wales. Other key challenges included those posed for service providers by the dispersal of minorities across Wales with obvious implications for the design and delivery of services in rural areas.

It is important to note however some large-scale programmes gaining funding during the last decade that have included a specific focus on improving the health and social wellbeing of ethnic minority groups in Wales. These included the Barefoot Health Workers Project, funded by the inequalities in health fund and the Sustainable Health Action Research Programme of the Welsh Assembly Government from 2001 until 2007, which worked with the African-Caribbean, Bangladeshi, Pakistani, Somali and Yemeni communities of south Cardiff to identify health needs and to develop and deliver culturally appropriate activities to address their needs.[34] Also funded by the Sustainable Health Action Research Programme was the Triangle Project that worked to support Local Health Alliances in Cardiff, Merthyr and Powys in tackling health inequalities for black and ethnic minority communitites, focusing on action research and community engagement.[35] Over the last decade there has also been a drive to develop regional and national strategies linked specifically to the health needs of ethnic minority groups (for example, mental health), as well as strategies linked to specific issues such as the needs of refugees.[36]

There remain gaps, however, in our understanding of the health and social care needs of ethnic minority populations in Wales. In his systematic review of databases and other statistical sources reporting on ethnic groups and their potential to enhance the evidence base on health promotion, Peter Aspinall identified the major gaps in national Welsh studies, such as the Welsh Health Surveys, and the unreliability of ethnicity data, for example the Patients' Episode Database for Wales (PEDW), in highlighting the needs of black and ethnic minority groups.[37] Moreover, a study conducted in 2005 that scoped the then current health and health-related research and clinical practice activity taking place in Wales found that stand-alone research activities account for the majority of activity; not one all-Wales study with a fully representative sample of black and ethnic minority participants was found.[38] Recommendations from the study proposed the establishment of a research infrastructure aimed at enabling regional and all-Wales research to be reviewed and prioritized and to provide a dedicated research and development context in which to link issues of ethnicity and race to the key biomedical, clinical and healthcare research under way. Such a programme ran from 2005 until 2010 and represented the first strategic Wales-wide approach aimed at the development of research priorities for Wales's ethnic minority population.[39] Although short-lived, the programme offered great potential in providing a coherent infrastructure to underpin research rooted in addressing health and social inequities in Wales.

Housing

Housing is one of the key indicators of social exclusion, impacting on people from ethnic minority backgrounds in Wales, in different ways and to varying extents. A recent exploration of the equalities policy context in relation to housing[40] reveals a building initiative focussed on the housing needs of ethnic minority groups and other disadvantaged groups. Key developments that have taken place in the last decade include the passing of legislation in relation to the management of groups of people who qualify as being in 'priority need', as well as a range of national strategies and action plans that focus on specific population groups, including ethnic minority groups, lesbian, gay and bisexual people, disabled people, women, older homeless people, refugees and asylum seekers, Gypsy Travellers and children and young people.⁴¹ This included, in the early 2000s, the development of a requirement of social landlords to consult with black and ethnic minority groups on their housing needs, and of local authorities to have separate housing strategies for ethnic minority groups. More latterly these specific interventions have now been fully integrated.

Research analysing housing statistics identify the impact of the above policies, as well as to explore the housing needs, provision and experiences of ethnic minority population groups. This includes analysis of the 2001 UK census (the latest census figures have yet to be fully analysed). The 2001 data reveal a lot about the family composition of various ethnic groups and indicates that household composition makes a significant difference to the risk of income poverty. In 2001 the majority of households in Wales, irrespective of the ethnic background of the Household Reference Person (HRP), were composed of one family. One-person households are most apparent among Black Caribbeans (approximately 40%) while over a fifth of Bangladeshi households are composed of more than one family, more than three times the rate for households headed by white people.⁴² Married-couple households were the most common type of family composition among all ethnic groups. Mixed Caribbean-headed households have the highest proportion of lone-parent households of any ethnic group, a family type most vulnerable to poverty. Lone-parent households and cohabiting households are least common among households headed by Asians including, Bangladeshi, Indian and Chinese.⁴³

In Wales pensioner households are around a third as common among black and ethnic minority groups compared with white population groups. They are least common for Asian households, including Indian, Chinese and Bangladeshi. The small percentage of pensioner families in many black and ethnic minority ethnic groups indicates that in these ethnic groups, older people are more likely to live in households headed by younger relatives. Joint and extended family forms are common among Bangladeshi communities. The ageing demographic of most black and ethnic minority groups will mean increasing numbers of pensioner households over time.[44] However, demographic and generational shifts that occur over time will alter ethnic minority group family structures. It has been suggested, for example, that the tradition of extended families is weakening in Indian and Chinese families.[45] The impact this may have in terms of people who are already at risk of poverty has yet to be explored.

The data suggest that black and ethnic minority households in Wales are much more likely to be living in overcrowded conditions than the average household.[46] For all black and ethnic minority groups the proportion of households that are overcrowded is higher than the average and also higher than all white households. Based on the 2001 census, we know that households headed by a person of Bangladeshi origin have the highest proportion of overcrowding (26.9%), while the Chinese ranked third highest among ethnic groups for overcrowding (18.8%). Those from Caribbean backgrounds had higher than average overcrowding but the lowest proportion of people living in overcrowded circumstances of all non-white ethnic minority groups.[47]

Owner-occupation is nevertheless high among some ethnic minority groups. Data from the 2001 census indicate that the Chinese population in Wales ranked the second highest ethnic minority group for owner-occupied housing. Yet the evidence indicates that Chinese people disproportionately live in poorer quality, private rented and often tied accommodation.[48] Relatively high levels of owner-occupied housing was also apparent among Bangladeshi and Indian people. More people owned houses than rented among Black Caribbeans, yet for Mixed Caribbeans, renting was more apparent than home ownership.[49] This may reflect the relatively young age structure of this population.

There is some evidence of a growing awareness of the particularities of housing for ethnic minority groups.[50] Lack of access to information, poorly maintained accommodation and discriminatory practices, alongside evidence of some innovative and effective policies and practices were themes emerging from research on the experiences and views of refugees.[51] What is evident is that the housing circumstances and needs of black and ethnic minority groups is characterized by diversity, with some groups experiencing relative advantage in the housing and labour markets compared with others.[52] As with other areas explored in this chapter, the evidence base in this policy field remains patchy, a fact exacerbated by the lack of official data or monitoring information, the tendency not to evaluate policy interventions and the lack of research that extends beyond an exploration of specific housing needs to the shifting perceptions and experiences of housing provision and services. The outcomes of the 2011 census provide an important point of comparison and indicate any specific patterning over time.

Education

A lack of qualifications and basic skills can produce negative outcomes in terms of employment, income and standard of living. Educational disadvantage starts from a very young age and is closely linked to one's social economic position as well as shaped by differences such as ethnicity. This has long been accepted by the Welsh Government and its programmes have sought to raise education standards from the very early years; for example, with the introduction of the Scandinavian model of a Foundation Phase for all children between the ages of three and seven prior to the start of the national curriculum. The continuation of a non-selective comprehensive school system, the abolition of testing up to Key Stage 3 (age fourteen) and Welsh baccalaureate are other distinct features of Welsh education. There has also been the establishment of an administrative framework that covers all levels of education (curriculum development, monitoring and assessment), as well as the activities of the further education, skills and training sector.[53]

There has also been a concerted effort to promote and embed equal opportunities and diversity within all areas and strands of education and training. In her recent review of education and equalities in Wales, Anita Pilgrim argues that things have moved on significantly over the last decade, in some areas more so than in others.[54] There has been a raft of legislation and guidance on equalities and education in Wales and in guidance on inspecting primary and secondary schools, equality issues have been thoroughly embedded.[55] Perhaps of great importance has been the development of a comprehensive capturing and evaluation of statistical data on equalities in education, which allow for a clearer picture of education pathways of different groups of students than was possible a few decades ago, although the robustness and populating of the data sets remains a contested issue.[56]

Pilgrim's 2011 review of education in Wales[57] reveals that the statistics show a gradual rise in the numbers of school pupils from an ethnic minority background, with higher figures at present in primary schools. She states that in 2006/7, 93.2% of pupils in primary schools were white and 4.9% were from an ethnic minority background.[58] A similar breakdown is evident in secondary schools (94.2% white and 3.8% from ethnic minorities) and in special schools (93.3% white, 4.4% from ethnic minorities). In terms of attainment, the review draws out several other key facts from the emerging evidence base. This includes evidence published in 2003 to show that ethnic minority pupils in Wales have a lower attainment at Key Stages 1–4 by substantial margins (although there is wide variation between ethnic groups), an English as an Additional Language Association of Wales (EALAW) report that found that low achievement for most ethnic minority groups is more pronounced in secondary than in primary school, and figures compiled by Welsh Assembly Government figures for 2007 that indicated that a higher percentage of pupils from a Chinese or Chinese British ethnic background achieved the Core Subject Indicator (CSI) than any other ethnic group at all the Key Stages; the Black ethnic group has the lowest percentage of pupils achieving the CSI at each Key Stage.[59]

According to Pilgrim,[60] it is evident that the issue of skills levels in the wider ethnic minority population also remains of concern. There are marked differences in the qualification level of different ethnic minority groups. While the proportions of people from Caribbean backgrounds and Chinese people without qualifications are close to the white population and the average for Wales, Indian people have substantially fewer people without qualifications while Bangladeshi have substantially more.[61] More recent research by Davies et al.[62] shows that in both Wales and England, Bangladeshi males and Pakistani females have the highest proportion without qualifications of ethnic groups, while Indian and Chinese males are among the best qualified. Moreover, fewer black and ethnic minority people in Wales hold at least level 2 qualifications than the population as a whole (55% compared with 68%); however, black and ethnic minority people are equally likely to hold degree-level qualifications as the population as a whole.[63] Bangladeshi people have the lowest proportion of all ethnic groups who have a higher level qualification, while Indians have the highest proportion of all ethnic groups. Chinese people have a higher than average number of people who have higher level qualifications. Those from Caribbean backgrounds are on the lower end of the spectrum for ethnic groups in terms of higher level qualifications.[64]

Analysis of annual population data for Wales by Davies et al.[65] shows that the majority of Indian men holding a degree possess a postgraduate degree, while the majority of Chinese men holding a degree possess an undergraduate degree. Indian and Chinese women are similarly well qualified with the highest percentage of graduates among females, but there appears to be a relatively high proportion of Chinese females with postgraduate degrees. In this study they performed multivariate analysis to determine the individual contribution of a range of factors, including ethnicity, on the relative likelihood of an individual attaining high or low level of educational attainment. They found that in relation to ethnicity, controlling for other factors, such as age, disability, housing tenure and religion (and also mindful that such a substantial variation may possibly reflect the relatively small sample size of some ethnic minority groups), Indian males in Wales are 400% more likely to possess a degree compared with white males.[66] This differential is larger than that which exists in other areas of the UK where the relative differential is estimated to be 60%. Moreover, they found that among both men and women, Bangladeshi people, as a group that experiences some of the most profound disadvantage in Wales, are 85% less likely than white people to have a degree.[67]

These recent analyses, conducted by Pilgrim, Davies et al. and others indicate clearly that educational attainment among ethnic minority populations varies and that attention must be given to the differences and similarities within, as well as between, ethnic groups. In terms of primary and secondary education, research conducted in the last decade has highlighted ongoing concerns regarding educational attainment, evidence of ongoing barriers faced by students,[68] inadequacies in terms of ethnic monitoring in schools and in the training and confidence among teachers in terms of cultural diversity and dealing with racism.[69] More research is clearly needed on early years education. A key theme of many of the studies is the relationship of poverty to educational attainment, which must be of concern.[70]

Labour market participation

Educational achievement is fundamentally linked to labour market participation but so too are the types and nature of economic opportunities available. Over a decade ago, the statistical profile on the labour-market participation of ethnic minorities indicated for both ethnic minority men and women lower economic activity rates as compared with whites, less likelihood of being employed, higher levels of self-employment than whites, higher rates of unemployment and high youth unemployment.[71] A comparison with evidence from contemporary Wales reveals a similar picture of disadvantage for many ethnic minority groups. In the Davies et al. study,[72] with the exception of the Black Caribbean group, the male full-time employment rate fell below those classed as white, with self-employment rates among the Pakistani working-age population, and to a lesser extent those also of the Bangladeshi working-age population, notably higher than those of the white population, and also notably higher than in other parts of the UK. This may be a reflection of a lack of employment opportunities in Wales, the particular settlement patterns in Wales, or the strategies and underpinning social networks and pathways to employment undertaken by those from ethnic minority backgrounds.[73]

In general women are disadvantaged in the labour market and there is more dramatic variation in employment between ethnic groups when considering females. Data from the 2001 census indicated that Caribbean and Chinese women were more likely than white women to be in the labour force, while Indian women had similar rates of economic activity compared with white women overall. Bangladeshi women were shown to have a lower than average participation rate with less than a quarter of Bangladeshi women aged 16–74 in the labour force and the highest rate of unemployment of all ethnic groups.[74] Both Chinese and Indian women had a substantially higher than average rate of self-employment; Bangladeshi women had a slightly higher than average rate while women from Black Caribbean backgrounds had lower than average rates of self-employment.[75] Today, in almost all population groups, women face an above-average incidence of non-employment. This is particularly the case for some ethnic minority groups in Wales, notably women of Indian,

Bangladeshi and Pakistani and Chinese ethnicity.[76] Women from these backgrounds are also at a greater risk of being exposed to economic disadvantage and poverty because they tend to engage in a range of unpaid work activities that revolve around caring within the home and this has implications for financial security in later life with regard to pensions and savings.[77]

Evidence suggests that younger UK-born Bangladeshi women are increasingly accessing higher education and valuing paid employment while still retaining a strong sense of family, but there is some evidence that these women still face discrimination in the labour market.[78] For older women, a number of factors may contribute to their relative economic inactivity including their first generation immigrant status, lack of British qualifications and fluency in English, and lack of accessible educational opportunities.[79]

There are particular vulnerabilities incurred for children of black and ethnic minority families living in Wales given the nature of economic activity. For example, households in which there are dependent children but no economically active adults may be more at risk of child poverty.[80] Over a fifth (21.9%) of black and ethnic minority children, compared with 13.6% of white children, live in households in which the head has not worked for some time, or has never worked. This figure rises to a quarter for children from Caribbean households and is around one fifth for the Bangladeshi ethnic group but is lower for Indian (9.1%) and Chinese (7.6%) households.[81] About two fifths of all dependent children have household heads from the lowest occupational groups (semi-routine and routine occupations) or who are out of the workforce, exceeding half of Caribbean children and reaching nearly three fifths for Bangladeshi children.[82] In contrast, only a quarter of dependent Indian and Chinese children live in such households. Indian and Chinese children are most likely of all ethnic groups to live in households with two or more economically active adults. Caribbean children are more likely than most groups to live in households in which there are no economically active adults.[83]

The evidence suggests a horizontal segregation of the labour market for black and ethnic minority groups. Representation of ethnic minority groups in various sectors and occupations in Wales indicates that particular black and ethnic minority groups tend to be overwhelmingly concentrated in certain sectors. Winckler et al.'s review revealed that ethnic minority populations tend to be concentrated in sectors associated with poor terms and conditions and low pay, such as health and social care (20.4%), hotels and catering (16.9%) and in wholesale and retail trade and repair of motor vehicles (16.8%).[84] So, for example, over a third of Indian women and approximately a fifth of Black Caribbean populations work in the health and social care sector. A large proportion of this group is employed in public sector services and as a consequence vulnerable to the impacts of recession. The majority of employed Chinese and Bangladeshi men and women are heavily concentrated in the hotels and catering sector and nearly a third of the Chinese population work in skilled trade occupations. Interestingly, however, the proportion of ethnic minority groups working in professional careers is higher than for the white population and slightly higher for black and ethnic minority men and women working as managers or senior officials. People of Indian origin are especially likely to work in professional occupations.[85]

What is evident overall is that employment prospects in each minority community relate to a range of factors, including migration histories, the perception of employees of particular minority groups, the economic and cultural resources of that community and the geographical or local labour-market influences on demand for employees.

Discussion

From this brief review of the range of policy domains it is possible to identify a number of challenges facing researchers and policy-makers in the coming decade. It is evident that there is a heightened awareness of the issues of race and ethnicity on the political agenda and an apparent commitment on the part of politicians to equality mainstreaming as key to the development of policy strategies.[86] The Welsh Government's programme for government (2011–16)[87] commits the Government to advance equality of opportunity and to tackle discrimination. The Welsh Government's Strategic Equality Plan[88] details how the Government is fulfilling the general duty in the Equality Act 2010 and the Wales-specific equality duties. The Strategic Equality Plan sets out outcome-focussed equality objectives that put the spotlight on the practical differences that are needed to be made to people's lives. What remains key is the importance and need to underpin this policy framework with rigorous, linked-up social science evidence that will shape, drive and evaluate programmes of action. How this is done in the context of the key preoccupations underpinning this chapter remains a pressing question. The evidence base is growing and strides are being made in our understanding and knowledge of ethnic minority population groups in Wales, but there are still significant gaps in our knowledge.

We would argue that advances in the evidence base will require mainstreaming of these considerations into the social science research effort per se. Research commissioners and funders, including the National Institute for Social Care and Health Research (NISCHR) as the core government instrument of research development in Wales, will need to require those they fund to address ethnic minority impacts, alongside other equality dimensions, within the context of their research considerations. That does not mean that they will all have to include a specific ethnic minority dimension to their research but it does mean that they will have to justify the research design against such considerations, that is, to know when and how to include an ethnic minority dimension in their work.[89]

Beyond these mainstreaming issues there are clearly considerations and challenges posed by pragmatic obstacles, capacity, specificity and attrition of evidence to consider in relation to the state of play of research on race and ethnicity. Limited capacity on all fronts means that race/ethnicity specific research in Wales will struggle to be more than an interesting sideline. The strength of the caucus of researchers interested in these issues will always be self-limiting as will the capacity at grass-roots level. If you place this within the broader picture of black and ethnic minority research networks across the UK there remains cause for concern. The exercise conducted by the Centre for Evidence in Ethnicity, Health and Diversity (CEEHD) highlights the fact that in England at present there are very few established and centralized sources of best practice guidance and evidence or established standards and professional support. Attempts at local and regional level in England to develop networks and establish groups to share information and best practice have, for the most part and for a number of reasons, been short lived.

We are mindful that responding to ethnic diversity is a complex issue not least because of competing definitions of ethnicity. Ensuring standards and consistent definitions between different data sources is not straightforward. Further ethnic categories may not be the most useful way of responding to need in certain circumstances and may not be the key determining factor in differential use of and access to services. Social disadvantage itself has a pervasive impact on equal outcomes. What the evidence does highlight is that the ethnic minority experience in Wales is considerably diverse and not coupled with disadvantage and discrimination in consistent ways. It is likely that more sophisticated analysis of the relative position of different groupings will be required to produce effective responses to inequality.

There is a wealth of guidance from the literature on 'doing race research'. As Salway et al. note, 'there is more material that is concerned with how to conduct research on ethnicity than when or why attention should be given to ethnic diversity'.[90] They further conclude that although the need for social research to respond to multi-ethnic nature of UK society is increasingly recognized, 'it appears there are few mechanisms currently in place to encourage or support researchers in this direction and little in the way of quality assurance checks within the research cycle'.[91]

There is a need to specify and prioritize what it is that is Wales-specific about such research when, for example, conditions such as diabetes, eye care, the incidence of certain conditions in the minority population would be factors irrespective of place, yet issues of access to services, discrimination, quality of service delivery would not. Moreover, clarity is needed on motivations, assumptions, analytical understandings that underpin ethnicity research and the meanings of the ethnic categories in use. What, for example, is the significance of place for understanding minority ethnicities and their wellbeing? Is the geographical limitation of Wales useful in terms of understanding the issues facing ethnic minorities? How can we theorize the intersections between race and other lines of social division within the Welsh context?

What is evident is that tackling ethnic and racial inequality is much more than providing descriptive set of statistics, useful as they are for monitoring trends, changes and gaps. Indeed, over the last decade the Welsh Government has sharpened its focus on development of data collection. However, without monitoring and intervention based on an understanding of why such inequalities persist, what processes or what types of intervention will work to improve the situation, we are in stasis.

Notes

1   N. Evans, G.Day and C. Aull Davies, 'Understanding Wales', *Planet*, 200 (2010), 36–49.

2   G. Day in 'Understanding Wales', ibid., 37.

3   See C. Williams and P. de Lima, 'Devolution, multicultural citizenship and race equality: from laissez-faire to nationally responsible policies', *Critical Social Policy*, 26/3 (2006), 498–522.

4 S. Salway, R. Barley, P. Allmark, et al., 'Ethnic diversity and inequality: ethical and scientific rigour in social research', Joseph Rowntree Foundation (2011).

5 Ibid., p. 6.

6 A. Oakley, 'Ethnicity and research evaluating interventions: issues of science and ethics', in J. Y. Nazroo (ed.), *Health and Social Research in Multiethnic Populations* (London, 2006), pp. 142–64.

7 See S. Vertovec, 'Super-diversity and its implications', *Ethnic and Racial Studies*, 29(6) (2007), 1024–54 and S. Fanshawe and D. Skriskandarajah, *You Can't Put Me In A Box – Super Diversity and the End of Identity in Britain* (London, 2010). See *http://visit. lincoln.ac.uk/C7/C5/Equality/ED%20Annual%20Reports/You%20 Can't%20Put%20Me%20in%20a%20Box.pdf* (accessed 5 August 2013).

8 Centre on Dynamics of Ethnicity, *Area Profiler for Ethnic Diversity and Related Variables* (2013). See *http://www.ethnicity.ac.uk/census/* (accessed 5 August 2013).

9 Wales Statistical Directorate, *A Statistical Focus on Ethnicity in Wales*, Welsh Assembly Government (WAG) (Cardiff, 2004).

10 R. Davies, S. Drinkwater, C. Joll, et al., *An Anatomy of Economic Inequality in Wales*, Equality and Human Rights Commission (Cardiff, 2011).

11 K. Atkin and S. Chatoo, 'The dilemmas of providing welfare in an ethnically diverse state: seeking reconciliation in the role of a "reflexive practitioner"', *Policy and Politics*, 35 (2007), 379–95, and J. Nazroo, *Health and Social Research in Multiethnic Societies* (Basingstoke, 2006).

12 Williams and de Lima, 'Devolution, multicultural citizenship and race equality'.

13 R. G. Wilkinson and K. Pickett, *The Spirit Level: Why More Equal Societies Almost Always Do Better* (London, 2009).

14 V. Winckler (ed.), S. Gale, S. McClalland, A. N. Pilgrim and t. Stirling, *Equality Issues in Wales: A Research Review*, Equality and Human Rights Commission and the Bevan Foundation (Manchester, 2009).

15 R. Davies et al., *An Anatomy*.

16 NHS Wales Equality Unit/Commission for Racial Equality, *A Survey*

of Current Secondary Health Care Practice – Health Services for Ethnic Minorities in Wales (1998).

17 J. Nazroo, *Health and Social Research in Multiethnic Societies* (Basingstoke, 2006).

18 NHS Wales Equality Unit, *Meeting the Health Needs of Ethnic Minority People in Wales: A Survey of Current Secondary Health Care Practice* (Cardiff 1998).

19 For example, E. Coyle, I. Harvey and L. Shah, *The Health and Social Care Needs of Ethnic Minorities in South Glamorgan* (Cardiff, 1993); A. Jamal, 'An assessment of the "felt" health needs of minority ethnic groups in West Glamorgan and the opportunities for health promotion', unpublished M.Sc. dissertation, University of Wales Swansea (1995); M. Coulton and S. Roberts, *Unequal Access to Health Care: The Experiences of Black and Ethnic Minorities in Swansea, Neath and Port Talbot* (Swansea, 1997).

20 Policy Research Institute on Ageing and Ethnicity (PRIAE), *Hope and Care: Black and Ethnic Elders in Wales*, National Assembly for Wales (Cardiff, 2000).

21 Ethnos, *The Secondary Health Care Needs of Ethnic Minority Communities in Wales*, All Wales Ethnic Minority Association (Swansea, 2003)., I. Papadopoulos and M. Lay, *Enhancing the Health Promotion Evidence Base on Minority Ethnic Groups, Refugees/Asylum Seekers and Gypsy Travellers*, Welsh Assembly Government (Cardiff, 2005), and I. Papadopoulos and M. Lay, 'The health promotion needs and preferences of Gypsy Travelers in Wales', *Diversity in Health & Social Care*, 4 (2007), 167–76.

22 R. Saltus and K. Kaur-Mann, 'Black and minority ethnic mental health service users in Wales: a snapshot of their views', *Mental Health Nursing*, 25/5 (2005), 4–7, and R. Saltus, C. Downes, P. Jarvis and S. Duval, 'Inpatients from black and minority ethnic backgrounds in mental health services in Wales: a secondary analysis of the Count Me In census, 2005–2010', *Diversity and Equality in Health and Care*, 10/3 (2013), 165–76.

23 J. Merrell, F. Kinsella, F. Murphy et al., 'Accessibility and equity of health and social care services: exploring the views and experiences

of Bangladeshi carers in South Wales, UK', *Health & Social Care in the Community*, 14 (2006), 197–205.

24 T. Hewitt, N. Smalley, D. Dunkerley and J. Scourfield, *Uncertain Futures: Children Seeking Asylum in Wales* (2005). See *http://www. savethechildren.org.uk/sites/default/files/docs/uncertain_futures_-_ report_1.pdf* (accessed 5 August 2013).

25 Winckler (ed.), *Equality Issues in Wales: A Research Review*.

26 K. Hawthorne, R. Pill, J. Chowdhury and L. Prior, 'Understanding family, social and health experience patterns in British Bangladeshi families: are people as diverse as they seem?', *Primary Health Care Research and Development*, 8 (2007), 333–44.

27 B. Fathoala, M. Evans, I. Campbell, J. Sastry and M. Alfaham, 'Active surveillance for tuberculosis in Wales: 1996–2003', *Archives of Disease in Childhood*, 91 (2006), 900–4.

28 J. Hanley, 'The emotional wellbeing of Bangladeshi mothers during the postnatal period', *Community Practitioner*, 80 (2007), 347.

29 P. Niner, *Accommodation Needs of Gypsy-Travellers in Wales: Report to the Welsh Assembly Government* (Cardiff, 2006), and *Physical Condition Survey Accommodation Needs of Gypsy-Travellers in Wales: Report to the Welsh Assembly Government* (Cardiff, 2006).

30 S. Choudhury, S. Brophy and R. Williams, 'Understanding and beliefs of diabetes in the UK Bangladeshi population', *Diabetic Medicine: A Journal of the British Diabetic Association*, 26 (2009), 636–40.

31 Wales Statistical Directorate, *A Statistical Focus on Ethnicity in Wales*.

32 R. Saltus and E. Folkes, 'Understanding dignity and care: an exploratory qualitative study on the views of older people of African and African-Caribbean descent', *Quality in Ageing and Older People*, 14(1) (2013), 36–46.

33 All Wales Ethnic Minority Association (AWEMA), *Challenging the Myth – They Look After Their Own: Carers Services: Access Issues for Black and Minority Ethnic Carers in Wales* (Swansea, 2003); J. Merrell, F. Kinsella, F. Murphy, S. Philpin and A. Ali, 'Support needs of carers of dependent adults from a Bangladeshi community', *Journal of Advanced Nursing*, 51/6 (2005), 549–57; M. Mahoney and S. Taj, NHS Wales Equality Unit, *Meeting the Health Needs of*

Ethnic Minority People in Wales: A Survey of Current Secondary Health Care Practice (Cardiff 1998). A. Ali and R. Cifuentes, *Ethnic Minorities & Substance Misuse*, Swansea Substance Misuse Action Team (Swansea, 2006), available at *http://www.swansea.gov.uk/ media/pdf/5/4/EM_Research-Study-Conference_Report_05-06.pdf*; Welsh Assembly Government/All Wales Saheli Association, *Muslim Women Talk* (Cardiff): R. Lee, 'A social audit of the Muslim community in Wales', *Statistical Article*, Welsh Assembly Government (Cardiff, 2007), available at *http://wales.gov.uk/docs/statistics/2007/070509socialmuslimen.pdf*; T. Threadgold, S. Clifford, A. Arwo et al., *Immigration and Inclusion in South Wales*, Joseph Rowntree Foundation (York, 2008).

34   S. Toner, *'Barefoot' Health Workers Project – Final Report* (2007). See *http://www2.nphs.wales.nhs.uk:8080/LPHTeamsDocs.nsf/ ($All)/194478D1AF7BC7F28025755100546C19/$File/ Barefoot%20Project%20Final%20Report%20Feb%2008%20. pdf?OpenElement* (accessed 6 August 2013).

35   S. Cropper, A. Porter, G.Williams, R Moore, A. Porter, *Community Health and Well-Being:* Action Research on Health Inequalities (London, 2007).

36   Welsh Assembly Government, *Refugee Inclusion Strategy* (2008). See *http://wales.gov.uk/topics/housingandcommunity/communitycohesion/ publications/refugeeinclusion/?lang=en. (accessed 15 September 2014).*

37   P. Aspinall, *Health ASERT Programme Wales: A Review of Databases and Other Statistical Sources Reporting Ethnic Group and their Potential to Enhance the Evidence Base on Health Promotion*, Welsh Assembly Government (Cardiff, 2007).

38   R. Saltus, *Scoping Study to explore the Feasibility of a Health and Social Care Research and Development Network covering Black and Minority Ethnic Groups in Wales. Final Report*, University of Glamorgan (Pontypridd, 2005).

39   C. Williams, J. Merrell, J. Rance, G. Olumide, R. Saltus and K. Hawthorne, 'A critical reflection on the research priorities for improving the health and social care to black and minority ethnic groups in Wales', *Diversity in Health and Social Care*, 4 (2006), 193–9.

40   Winckler (ed.), *Equality Issues in Wales: A Research Review.*

41 See Wales Statistical Directorate, *A Statistical Focus on Ethnicity in Wales*.

42 Ibid.

43 Ibid.

44 Ibid.

45 R. Davies et al., *An Anatomy*.

46 See Wales Statistical Directorate, *A Statistical Focus on Ethnicity in Wales*.

47 Welsh Assembly Government, *Profile of the Housing and Socio-Economic Circumstances of Black and Minority Ethnic People in Wales in 2001* (Cardiff, 2005).

48 See Wales Statistical Directorate, *A Statistical Focus on Ethnicity in Wales*.

49 See, for example, P. Brown, A. Steele and S. Pugh, *The Experiences and Usage of Services in Housing, Social Care and Health of Black and Minority Ethnic (BME) Elders in Wales. Final Report for the National Assembly for Wales*, Salford University Housing and Urban Studies Unit (Salford, 2006).

50 See, for example, *Profile of the Housing and Socio-economic Circumstances of Black and Minority Ethnic People in Wales, 2001*, Welsh Assembly Government Housing Directorate research report HRR 4/05, *www.wales.gov.uk/dsjlg/research/0405hrr/reporte.pdf?lang=en* (accessed 15 September 2014), P. Brown, A. Steele and S. Pugh, *The Experiences and Usage of Services in Housing, Social Care and Health of Black and Minority Ethnic (BME) Elders in Wales. Final report for the National Assembly for Wales*, Salford University Housing and Urban Studies Unit (Salford, 2006); D. Dunkerley, J. Scourfield, T. Maegusuku-Hewett and N. Smalley, 'Children seeking asylum in Wales', *Journal of Refugee Studies*, 19, 4 (2006), 488–508; T. Threadgold, S. Clifford, A. Arwo et al., *Immigration and Inclusion in South Wales*, Joseph Rowntree Foundation (York, 2008), *http://www.jrf.org.uk/publications/immigration-and-inclusion-south-wales* (accessed 15 September 2014)

51 Winckler (ed.), *Equality Issues in Wales: A Research Review*.

52 Ibid.

53 Ibid.

54 For example, the United Nations Convention on the Rights of the
    Child was formally adopted by Wales in January 2004. Key policy
    include: Welsh Assembly Government, *The Learning Country – A
    Paving Document: A Comprehensive Education and Lifelong
    Learning Programme to 2010 in Wales* (Cardiff, 2001), and Welsh
    Assembly Government, *The Learning Country 2: Delivering the
    Promise* (Cardiff, 2008). Also ACCAC (Qualifications, Curriculum
    and Assessment Authority for Wales), *Equal Opportunities and
    Diversity in the School Curriculum in Wales* (Birmingham, 2001),
    and ESTYN, *Equal Opportunities and Diversity in Schools in Wales.
    Survey on the Implementation of ACCAC Guidance on the Promotion
    of Equal Opportunities and Diversity (2001) and the Effectiveness of
    Schools and LEAs in Meeting Statutory Duties under Race Relations
    Legislation* (Cardiff, 2005).

55 A. Pilgrim and J. Scourfield, 'Racist bullying as it affects children in
    Wales: a scoping study', *Contemporary Wales*, 20 (1) (2007), 144–58.

56 Pilgrim, A. N. 'Eduction' in Winckler et al., *Equality Issues in Wales:
    A Research Review*.

57 Ibid, p. 136.

58 Ibid, p. 136.

59 Ibid, .p. 156.

60 Ibid, p. 156.

61 R. Davies et al., *An Anatomy*, p. 151.

62 Welsh Government 2007, cited in Winckler et al, *Equality Issues in
    Wales*, p. 156.

63 R. Davies et al., *An Anatomy*, p 151.

64 Ibid, p. 3.6

65 Ibid, p. 36.

66 Ibid, p. 36.

67 For example, H. Gardner and K. Lanman, 'Living in rural Wales: the
    experiences of black and minority ethnic people in Carmarthenshire
    and Montgomeryshire', Dyfed Powys Race Equality Network, unpub-
    lished report (2005), and L. O'Neill, *Barriers to Learning Among
    Selected Communities*, Welsh Assembly Government (Cardiff, 2007).

68 English as an Additional Language Association of Wales (EALAW),
    English as an Additional Language Wales: The Achievement of

Ethnic Minority Pupils in Wales, National Assembly for Wales (Cardiff, 2011), and Pilgrim and Scourfield, 'Racist bullying as it affects children in Wales'.

69 D. Egan, *Poverty and Low Educational Achievement in Wales: Student, Family and Community* (2013). See *http://www.jrf.org.uk/sites/files/jrf/wales-education-poverty-summary.pdf* (accessed 12 September 2013).

70 C. Williams, G. Day, T. Rees and M. Standing, *Equal Opportunities Study for the Inclusion in European Structural Fund Programme Document 2000–2006: A Report for the National Assembly Office*, National Assembly for Wales (Cardiff, 1999).

71 R. Davies et al., *An Anatomy*.

72 Ibid.

73 Welsh Assembly Government *Profile of the Housing*.

74 Ibid.

75 R. Davies et al., *An Anatomy*.

76 E. Brittain, H. Dustin, C. Pearce et al., *Black and Minority Ethnic Women in the UK*, The Fawcett Society (London, 2005).

77 Brittain et al., *Black and Minority Ethnic Women*.

78 Ibid.

79 R. Davies et al., *An Anatomy*.

80 Brittain et al., *Black and Minority Ethnic Women*.

81 Ibid.

82 Welsh Assembly Government (2005).

83 Winckler (et al.), *Equality Issues in Wales: A Research Review*.

84 Ibid.

85 Williams and de Lima, 'Devolution, multicultural citizenship and race equality'.

86 Welsh Government, *Programme for Government* (2011), *http://www.cynnalcymru.com/sites/default/files/Programme%20for%20Government.pdf* (accessed 3 December 2013).

87 Welsh Government, *Strategic Equality Plan and Objectives 2012–2016* (Cardiff, 2011).

88 Salway et al., 'Ethnic diversity and inequality'.

89 Ibid., p. 19.

90 Ibid., p. 9.

11

Experiencing Rural Wales

CHARLOTTE WILLIAMS

The link between rural Wales and notions of authentic Welshness has been a long-standing theme in both the academic literature and in popular representations. The Welsh countryside and its imagined characteristics hold a very privileged place in dominant constructions of national identity. Myths of a peaceable and tolerant nation, deeply embedded in the national imaginary are rooted in an idealized Welsh rural community life that summons the trope of the *gwerin*, a particular form of localized communitarianism to express the values of egalitarianism, classlessness and internationalism. Myths are of course important to nation building but they also function as a powerful exclusionary force. Welsh imaginings of the countryside as the heartland of Welsh language and culture have fostered not only a sense of cultural purity and cultural homogeneity but have rendered rural territory as the site for the protection of very exclusive constructions of national identity. These 'ideologies of place', as Cloke[1] refers to them, form an important intersection with issues of difference and diversity that can be illustrated through a consideration of 'race' and racialized subjects living in rural communities.

This chapter considers the available evidence on the experience of black and minority ethnic people in rural Wales. From a body of work that primarily focussed on

251

exploring the issues of rural racism, popular interest and research has grown considerably in recent years, illustrating the changing nature of rural communities and rural identities and contributing to wider understandings of contemporary multiculturalism. Challenging the myths of rural Wales as homogeneous, white and not multicultural and as open, tolerant and non-racist has been central to this endeavour. This critical interrogation of the Welsh rural community and its selective representations has, I will argue, had the wider impact of challenging exclusive conceptions of national identity and national myth making. In tracking the contours of the development of what might be called the rural/race axis, this chapter considers the particularities of Wales and the contextual factors that shape the ways in which we understand the field. It then proceeds to a consideration of rural studies in Wales and illustrates how these have contributed to the development of the wider literature on race/ ethnicity and rurality. It concludes by assessing what these debates suggest for ideas of multicultural citizenship and changing identities in Wales.

Rural/race debates

Academic research and theorizing on rurality and ethnicity has advanced at a pace since Jay's seminal study *'Keep them in Birmingham'*.[2] Jay provided the first empirical analysis of the constellation of factors that mark out the phenomenon of rural racism in his study of the south-west of England, and the 1990s saw a number of studies across the English countryside replicate and consolidate the evidence that racism in areas with low ethnic minority concentrations is no less prevalent than in areas of concentration and that low numbers do not equate with low needs in terms of service provision.[3] The characteristic story of rural race issues describes a situation in which the racialized rural subject experiences high levels of isolation, is communicated a sense of unbelonging or *othering* at everyday banal levels, experiences no small amount of discrimination and racisms and struggles to access appropriate services in the face of sluggish and unresponsive service delivery. Ethnic minority individuals are both visible and invisible in this context: visible by virtue of their difference and invisible in commanding attention to their needs from service providers. The resounding story of *no problem here* has echoed across the rural landscapes of Britain and provided the rationale for neglecting needs and failure to address racisms or promote social cohesion by local authorities and other public bodies. However, several attempts have been made to share good practice and delineate a policy orientation more attuned to the needs of diverse rural communities.[4]

In an examination of the ways in which debates on rural racism has progressed in earlier work[5] I identified three distinct but interrelated analytical trajectories based on concerns with *representations, relations* and *rights. Representations* relates to a theme in writings that critiqued the ways in which primarily the English countryside is represented to refract with deeply embedded notions of exclusive British national identity. Such accounts explored the ways in which the countryside had become synonymous with whiteness and ideas of white safety, rendering the countryside as somehow pure and uncontaminated by racial difference. This has effectively produced a 'passive apartheid'[6] in which racialized minorities feel not only 'out of place' in the countryside but, as the research indicates, they lack access to it for recreation and leisure.[7] They are effectively excluded by a powerful representation of the countryside that suggests it is not for them.

Other studies hold as their key focus the nature of social *relations* in communities and point to the ways in which community cohesion and a sense of belonging is hampered for the ethnically different individual via banal racisms and/or their inability to form communities of co-ethnic association.[8]

And finally a number of studies take a *rights*-based approach and focus on policy development pointing to fundamental inequalities experienced by ethnic minority rural dwellers in the exercise of their rights as citizens, most notably in encounters with service providers.[9]

While the research of the 1990s illuminated the extent and nature of rural racism 'from John O'Groats to Land's End',[10] it contained a number of weaknesses. Robinson and Gardner's work in Powys[11] advanced the field by pointing to the issues of differentiation. They argued that there is more than one rural racism and that not every person living in a rural area suffers equally from this. Their contention was that much of the rural race research had had the unwitting effect of conveying black and minority ethnic individuals in rural areas as 'unhappy, regretful, isolated, rejected and vulnerable victims of racial harassment, whose experiences are unremittingly negative'.[12] Robinson and Gardner challenged this stereotype by demonstrating diverse experiences of rural living and opened the way for a consideration of rural subjectivities in more nuanced analysis.

It was also becoming more apparent that factors specific to place required explication and analysis – that the simple urban/rural divide masked discernible differences between rural racisms, place to place. The connection of these rural/race analyses to national context was, however, still tenuous. Nation featured in as much as it was connected to images of the rural idyll but the notion that articulations of 'race' and racism within the particular political, social and cultural national contexts had a bearing on localized responses to issues of diversity and integration was underexplored. Indeed, as I argued[13] the debates on rural racism had become divorced from wider discourses of British multiculturalism, in the process somehow reaffirming the countryside as not multicultural. New ethnicities and changing perceptions of nation and national identity in a post-devolution era would be factors that disturbed constructions of the rural and paved the way for more a detailed analysis of ethnic minority experiences in rural areas. Rural/race studies could no longer be seen as distinct from their national contexts.[14]

Ideologies of place: the distinctiveness of Wales

In seeking to define and delineate rural racism as an issue distinct from metropolitan race relations research studies had paid little attention to the 'ideologies of place'.[15] Academic theorizing on race and racism in Scotland, Ireland and Wales in the 1990s had taken that very trajectory in aiming to develop an understanding of race as an intersection with ideas of place, culture, nation and national identity,[16] but little attempt was made to reconcile these findings with the literature on the rural. In many ways this was an omission and especially given that large parts of Wales are rural. The population of rural Wales at 960,000 makes up almost one third of its total population. It is a nation of low population density in British terms made up of small towns, settlements and villages of no more than 20,000 people beyond the large conurbations of Cardiff, Swansea and Newport.[17] Areas of rural Wales are culturally distinct with higher densities of people speaking Welsh and as evidence in this volume and elsewhere reveals, Welsh rural communities have never been as wholly monocultural as imagined.[18] Cloke points to the importance of taking into account the 'significance of nationhood in fashioning ... the ruralities of Wales and Scotland'[19] and there is clearly a constellation of factors that is peculiarly the preserve of Wales and that forms a particular intersection with issues of race and ethnicity in this context.

In a seminal essay[20] I proposed a challenge to prevailing ideas of Welsh tolerance (a notion to which I return for review in the concluding chapter of this book). I explored how particular myths of Welsh national identity have been sustained that promote the notion of a society characterized by harmony, hospitality, internationalism and openness to incomers. The roots of the tolerance sentiment are multiple and, while laudable and aspirational, furnish a dominant myth of nation that has served to inhibit a consideration of the facts of racial intolerance historic and present (see chapter 13). The Welsh rural heartland and its community life provide the spiritual home for these ideas. The enduring nature of the *gwerin* imaginary and all its cultural paraphernalia continues to hold a powerful symbolic force such that Day asserts: 'the existence of a classless *gwerin* provides the foundations for one of the dominant versions of Welshness and Welsh nationhood, and it makes frequent appearances more or less at the margins of social science writing on Wales'.[21]

The exclusionary force of this imagining has fed into ideas about who does and who does not belong in the Welsh countryside. The *gwerin* construct, central to the Welsh rural idyll, communicates a bedrock assumption that to be Welsh is to be Welsh speaking and by and large this has conventionally been equated with being white. But as a portrayal of the Welsh countryside it has also generated a particular spin on the *no problem here* mantra so familiar to accounts of rural racism, underpinned as it is by a culture of disbelief, denial and deflection.[22] *No problem here* in the Welsh sense speaks to a disbelief in the existence of a multicultural rural society and a view of the Welsh countryside as monocultural. It reflects a denial of the facts of racism, even when faced with the evidence, by referring to the tolerance ideas. It offers a convenient deflection of the blight of racism as an import of English settlement in Wales. Taken together, these interrelated themes have provided a powerful rationale for inaction and complacency in responding to the experiences of ethnic minority rural subjects.

Further, any examination of ethnic relations in Wales needs to consider Wales as a bilingual nation and the interface of issues of race and racism with struggles to protect the survival of the Welsh language. The Welsh language and its culture is the most fundamental marker of Welsh distinctiveness. By far the biggest ethnic boundary marker in Wales is the English/ Welsh axis. The English as an ethnic group form the largest significant *other*, and both historically and in contemporary Wales a racially marked discourse has been deployed on both sides of the axis: on the one hand to express fears of English colonization and cultural contamination of the Welsh-speaking heartlands on the other to demarcate the Welsh as a racialized *other*. This narrative, which engages the full conceptual apparatus of racial imagery, has been effective in displacing any concern with other forms of ethnic cleavage in Wales. It has been the narrative of race relations in the Welsh countryside.

The intersection of the politics of language and the politics of ethnic minority race relations is not straightforward, however, and they can be seen as spatially marked with particular localized areas/spaces of Welsh language use producing a differentiated set of experiences for ethnic minority groups. I have suggested that a particular spatial imagining of 'race' has prevailed in Wales that operates to map a crude geography of 'race', containing the narrative of race to identifiable cities in the south and leaving unmarked a broad rural landscape regarded as fundamentally not multi-cultural.[23] There are indeed no large concentrations of minority groups beyond the metropolitan areas of south Wales, and ethnic minorities in the rural landscape are inter-nally highly differentiated, dispersed and often isolated as individuals, families and small groups. Their ability to mobi-lize as a community of interest is severely limited, although with sponsorship a number of ethnic minority organizations have emerged and are active in rural Wales. This calls for a focus on the local – on particular articulations of issues of diversity and difference, on localized politics and how they are played out in understandings of identity and belonging. It demands attention to the level and degree of ethnic minority mobilization in particular localities and to localized strate-gies to respond to diversity.

The perceptible 'presence' of ethnic minority peoples in rural Wales has increased considerably over the last decade. Rural Wales is changing rapidly. Most recently it has experienced international labour migrations following EU expansion in 2004. Since May 2004 over 10,000 migrant workers have been documented as arriving in rural Wales, most notably from Poland. In the post-devolution era other groups in the rural landscape have become more visible in public policy terms, including asylum seekers (see chapter 12), Gypsies and Traveller peoples, Muslims and other religious minorities, and migrants of all kinds. As constituencies they form counter-publics, demanding recognition, actively multiculturalizing areas and contributing to contestations of the traditional rural voice. An alternative cultural politics of the countryside has emerged – as transrural, breaking down the essentialized dualisms of rural/urban, home/away, cohesive, bounded/ porous and reflecting the characteristics of difference, dynamism and dystopia, to use Cloke's terms.[24] Research studies from rural Wales illustrate the salience of the national story of multiculturalism in the making and attest to the ways in which the Welsh rural landscape is changing.

Research studies on rural/race in Wales

Research in the rural community has been a long-standing feature of Welsh social science and continues to be so. A recognized contribution of this early Welsh rural sociology are the community studies that marked a clear departure from essentialist typifications of the rural idyll in their willingness to depict diversity, division and dissent in Welsh community life and challenge the notion of *gwerin*.[25] While academic writing developed to address a number of forms of *othering* in Welsh community life,[26] the intersection with 'race' and diverse ethnicities emerged on the agenda not by reference to black and minority ethnic groups but in the depiction of English/Welsh ethnic relations. It is this axis that deployed the language of metropolitan race relations to characterize the potential cultural contamination of the Welsh heartland by putative English colonial interlopers. The pervasive and sustained myth of Welsh tolerance accordingly cast manifestations of racism in the community as an English import and the preserve of English incomers.

The focus of early studies in Wales on the experiences of the visible difference of black and ethnic minorities aimed to capture and explore the prejudice and racist sentiment of the majority community. Vaughan Robinson's work in Swansea in the 1980s raised the spectre of majority racial prejudice toward refugees[27] which he later extended to work in other parts of Wales. In the first edition of *A Tolerant Nation?*, Robinson reported on a quantitative study undertaken in 2001 of residents living in rural Powys surveying their attitudes toward 'race' and immigration.[28] This groundbreaking study was funded by Victim Support Powys which sought to give an evidence base to its experience of calls to its helpline from a range of ethnic minority individuals. The callers reported verbal racist abuse, physical attacks, criminal damage to property, bullying of children, exploitation at work among other issues. Robinson interestingly notes the frustrated efforts of Victim Support to raise funds for this initiative, which he attributes to the pervasive culture of disbelief and denial underpinning thinking about race in Wales:

> One potential funder suggested there was no need for the initiative since there 'are no ethnic minorities in Ystradgynlais', even though he was at the time standing outside an Indian take-away, next to a filling station owned by an Asian businessman, opposite a Pakistani-owned mini-market, and facing a Chinese restaurant.[29]

Robinson found local inhabitants capable of considering themselves as more tolerant than the UK norm while at the same time prepared to express racist sentiments that were indeed as extreme or more so than elsewhere in the UK. His study graphically illustrated the experiences of rural racism for Powys' ethnic minority residents, including a sense of being made to feel out of place, a sense of isolation, differential treatment and overt racism, and a lack of understanding of their cultures. He concluded that rural racism in Wales is shot through with myths and contradictions and that the Welsh imaginings of tolerance were just that – imaginings.[30]

In the second part of this Powys study Robinson – with a colleague Hannah Gardner – extended the data collection to include in-depth qualitative interviews with some forty black and minority ethnic residents living in rural Powys and brief interviews with a stratified sample of 300 local residents who were surveyed on their attitudes to British and local dimensions of race and immigration.[31] The qualitative data revealed a rich picture of diversity of experience of exclusions in a rural community and how this is manifest through stereotyping and gossip, experiences of verbal and physical abuse, hate mail and public avoidance or simple cliquishness. Robinson and Gardner found many of their respondents identifying a particular 'rural mindset' that served to excuse potentially racist behaviour as innocent or unintended.[32] While many of these issues are common to the phenomenon of rural racism irrespective of place, this study did attempt to consider these issues in the context of sensitivities relating to Welsh language and culture and the notion of a distinctive Welsh tolerance. In a consideration of the quantitative data the researchers probed the controversial question: 'who perpetrates racism in rural Wales: the Welsh, the English or both?',[33] with the aim of testing the notion of Welsh tolerance. What the reported evidence suggests is a very mixed picture, signalling both the inclusionary and the exclusionary potential of 'Welshness', including the Welsh language, as perceived and articulated by the respondents. While these categories are necessarily clumsy, their findings do suggest some discernible differences between the English and the Welsh in their attitudes to ethnic minorities, in favour of the idea of Welsh tolerance. However, the researchers explain this by reference to the fact that few of Powys' Welsh residents had any contact with black and minority ethnic residents in their daily lives, and their professed tolerance was accordingly hypothetical rather than actual. Their presumed tolerance, however, was clearly shown to be limited, with respondents expressing overtly prejudicial and stereotyped views of English incomers.

The 'outsider' status of the English as the largest ethnic *other* in Wales has formed the basis of identity studies in post-devolution Wales.[34] While the English/Welsh boundary is the biggest marker of ethnic distinction, the experiences of those who had migrated from England has been little documented. Day et al. critically explore the notion that migration into Wales from England represents a continuing challenge to the maintenance of distinctive Welshness and provide evidence to throw light on the characteristics and experiences of this dominant minority. Their study questions the veracity of the most frequently voiced criticism of English migrants' attitudes to settlement in Wales and assesses their impact on local communities. They find the majority of migrants attempting to integrate into Welsh life, socially and politically, some even learning to speak Welsh and in general not conforming to the stereotype colonial interloper.

Thus not all ethnic groups experience the rural in the same ways. The visibilities and consequent vulnerabilities of *certain* ethnic groups are clearly identified in the available literature in Wales. Studies ranging from Robinson's early studies of asylum seekers and refugees to the more recent research[35] indicate in particular the ramifications of dispersal policies, for example. The Caia Park estate riots in Wrexham in semi-rural north-east Wales in 2003 saw two nights of rioting in a conflict between local residents and asylum seekers that had to be quelled by over 200 riot police drafted in from neighbouring Merseyside. Albeit sporadic, this rioting was no small affair and whatever the causal factors represented a blatant challenge to ideas of Welsh tolerance.

The complexities of what is too easily called rural racism are not however confined to public attitudes. Studies from Wales show public services as being ill equipped or reluctant to respond to minority needs such that access to rights is severely curtailed.[36] In addition, minority groups themselves may be less likely to utilize services because of the perception that they are aimed at a white client group. What has come to be called 'institutional racism'[37] focusses on the lack of responsiveness of public agencies to the needs of racialized minorities. A number of studies undertaken in Wales illustrate these shortcomings. For example, the Black and Ethnic Minority Support Team (BEST) Report,[38] commissioned as part of the then National Assembly for Wales's Communities First programme, which aimed to get local people in the most deprived wards in Wales involved in improving their own areas and prospects, involved a needs-based study across the six county boroughs of north Wales. The study aimed to map the profile of ethnic minorities in the area and consider what specific support structures were available to them. Published in 2004, the report confirmed the constellation of factors familiar to the matrix of rural racism. It noted sluggish and misguided institutional responses, poor data collection and poor ethnic monitoring, high levels of ignorance in designing responses to diverse needs and the lack of specific ethnic provision/services. Despite the requirements of the Race Relations (Amendment) Act 2000, reports continued to demonstrate public authorities struggling to deliver responsive services for increasingly diverse communities and with poor consultation mechanisms for reaching out to so-called 'hard to reach groups'.[39] This institutional lethargy on the part of rural authorities and its effects has been noted in relation to other migrant groups.

The longitudinal study conducted by the Wales Rural Observatory (WRO)[40] reported on an earlier scoping of public authorities' response to the more recent migration of EU migrant populations. They found local authorities taking one of three positions:

> those that consider there is no significant migrant workforce within their area; authorities that are conscious of the presence of an overseas workforce, but have taken no action to date; and those that are aware of the growing number of Central and Eastern European economic migrants and are taking action to support their needs.[41]

Subsequently, the ebb and flow of this economic migration has been the subject of some considerable research in the last decade. The WRO report noted over a third of all migrant workers move to live and work in rural areas of Wales.[42] Many of these migrations have been chain migrations with families and friends following pioneer migrants often from rural areas of Eastern Europe to migratory hot spots across Wales. Settlement has been in particular areas, for example Llanelli, Betws y Coed and Llanrwst in Conwy, Welshpool in Powys and Milford Haven in Pembrokeshire. Collectively, these studies have illustrated the nature and extent of EU migrations to Wales and the impacts of this migration on migrants and their families and on the receiving communities.

By far the largest ethnic group among migrant workers in Wales are the Polish. Seven in every ten migrant workers in Wales are from Poland.[43] The oft-cited claims that Polish migrants have infused diversity into local populations, brought entrepreneurship, invigorated Catholic Church attendance and integrated into the community have been subject to empirical testing. Thompson et al.'s study[44] finds to the contrary. Their study of Llanelli suggests the local Polish population as 'largely un-integrated with the town primarily because of language barriers, but also because of choice . . .'[45] Only those families with children in local schools appeared eager to integrate with the local population. For the rest, life outside the workplace appeared rather more focussed on family and friends in Poland. Their research indicated that the Polish migrants had been unwilling or unable to contribute anything to the life of the local Catholic congregation despite the best efforts of the clergy and laity, with indifference and even antagonism toward the church being expressed by their respondents.[46] The WRO study also found poor levels of integration, with only one in ten of the respondents involved in organized activities in their area of settlement.[47] They found social contacts between migrant workers and the local community weakly developed with migrants tending to socialize among themselves. Language, money, working hours and racism were cited as the reasons. All the available evidence points to the difficult working and living conditions of many of the migrant workers studied. The WRO study highlighted that these migrants were subject to generally low pay, long working hours and living in lower quality housing, and it is obviously more difficult to be generous with time and community spirit when you live and work in such oppressive circumstances.

Overall a picture of self-reliance emerges. The WRO study concludes that:

> Overall the picture is one of numerous yet weak ties between the migrant population and local communities in most parts of rural Wales. Many of the migrant workers surveyed said they knew people in their local area, spoke fairly frequently with their neighbours, and socialised with local people. Yet few counted people as close friends, few participated in local organised activities and most lived only with people of the same nationality and relied on social networks of people of the same nationality.[48]

In spite of this, the study reported that most of the respondents had relatively positive views of their local communities.

They saw their contribution as not simply economic but also as cultural.

Paula Hamilton's work on the children of migrant workers and schooling in Wales[49] also reveals these frustrated attempts at integration and provides a complex picture of needs and resilience within communities in transition. Hamilton takes as her focus the preparedness of schools in Wales to respond to the rapid and significant influx of migrant workers to predominantly rural areas following European Union expansion in 2004. While Hamilton's work illustrates the familiar disruptive impacts of migration on these children in terms of their social and emotional wellbeing, she highlights the far-reaching changes needed to promote the wellbeing and learning of these children, including changes to pedagogic practices of schools, the building and fostering of home-school relationships, practices that acknowledge and accommodate language diversity, and teacher practitioners that can take a critically reflective approach to their practices and develop an outreach mentality.[50]

Many of these families face isolation and ostracism in their communities. Hostile reactions to Polish migrants has been an ongoing concern and local authority initiatives have been geared toward achieving greater community cohesion. In the WRO study a quarter of respondents reported discrimination, including verbal abuse, bullying and harassment but generally the respondents did not regard their communities as hostile.[51]

There is little, therefore, to suggest the assuaging of the characteristic constellation of factors documented as rural racism. Ethnic minority communities are not homogenous and typically across Wales do not live in strong collectivities but as individuals, families or small groups. Factors of age, gender, length of settlement and other factors prescribe their experiences. For example, the picture of ethnic minority children's needs in largely white communities is best glimpsed from Scourfield et al.'s studies and later book on childhood identities in Wales.[52] A study reporting in 2002 of children's experiences in what the authors termed 'predominantly white areas' poignantly characterizes these children's day-to-day experiences in Wales.[53] Although not strictly based in rural Wales this study typifies the challenges to young people growing up in areas of low ethnic minority density. The study focussed on the views expressed about quality of life, sense of community, leisure activities, experience of racism and dealings with institutions. The authors revealed a complex picture of a variety of experiences related to factors of class, gender, age and location. Their findings challenged positive renditions of Welsh community life as tolerant and inclusive but also the notion of wholly negative experiences of racism. While racism in all its manifestations was found to be an ever-present reality for these children, including verbal abuse and bullying, many of the children in the study were deploying creative ways of responding to their situation and several spoke optimistically of their lives in such areas. In concluding that 'Racism is an everyday reality for many parents and children but it is not overwhelming',[54] perhaps the authors understate the heavy penalty these daily negotiations and acts of resilience can have on these children.

Later research by Scourfield et al. with school children in middle childhood provides more evidence of these daily negotiations.[55] This study used qualitative methods to explore children's talk of their experience of identity building. The majority of ethnic minority children in their sample showed a reluctance to claim Welshness based on racialized and exclusive conceptions of national belonging, but nevertheless they actively engaged in reworking ideas about exclusive Welsh identities.

What these studies of childhood in Wales reveal is not solely the increasing diversity of communities but the ways in which adjustment and change is being accommodated both within minority groups and within the majority community and mainstream institutions. They provide a litmus test of the inclusivity and social cohesion ambitions of the Welsh

Government, revealing the extent to which investments in the future are being made and the extent to which the impact of changing perceptions of national identity are being realized.

Themes of poor service delivery, mislabelling of needs, contestation over official categorizations and issues of lack of visibility feature in the literature on more obscured minority identities in rural areas. Research is emerging in Wales on the position of numerous other less visible 'not quite whites' and 'discrepant others',[56] including Gypsy and Traveller peoples and Muslims.

Studies of these groups in Wales are thin on the ground but there have been audits[57] and reviews of government activity in respect of this group[58] and the Welsh Assembly Government developed its strategy for Gypsies and Travellers in 2011.[59] Gypsies and Traveller communities are among the most disenfranchised and marginalized in Wales. They experience the highest levels of inequality and profound spatial marginalization. Most Gypsy and Traveller sites are located on the edges of villages and towns at a distance from local amenities, often being physically bounded at the perimeter and subject to vocal and uninhibited opposition from local residents. Chiesa and Rossi[60] interestingly argue, however, that the official orientation to the issues facing Gypsies and Travellers is based on a perception and categorization of them as a 'poverty issue', evoking interventions aimed at a redistribution of resources and assimilation of this group toward settled ways of life. Thus the ways in which this group becomes officially recognized is by virtue of its problematic behaviour as a low status ethnic group. Chiesa and Rossi argue that these external ascriptions of the Gypsy way of life devalue and denigrate individual and collective self-esteem and represent a political misuse of Gypsy-Traveller culture. They call for a paradigm shift in the thinking about Gypsy-Travellers, for analytical and interventive frameworks that eschew the stigmatic status of Gypsies and Travellers in favour of an exploration of their self-designated assertions of identity and appropriate redistributive responses that build from dialogue and 'affords identities untainted by stratified patterns of misrecognition'.[61] By and large Gypsies and Travellers remain invisible to inhabitants of rural areas and the validity of their movements and mobilities are contested.

The theme of visibilities and invisibilities is taken up by Rhys Jones in his examination of Muslims in rural west Wales.[62] He notes how particular groups are excluded by a discursive absence in the representations of the rural community, being written out of rural space. Constituting just 0.2% of the region's population, Jones describes how this small community negotiates what he calls 'visible absence on the one hand, but physical presence on the other'.[63] He illustrates how Muslims in rural communities are often less visible than their counterparts in more urban areas by virtue of the fact that fewer wear religious dress and that their religious spaces are not purpose-built mosques but invariably premises originally used for other purposes. He uses the adopted term 'storefront' mosques to describe how Muslims in rural areas make use of a variety of everyday spaces such as empty classrooms, old gymnasiums, church halls or spaces above shops as sites to perform their religious identities. This tactical appropriation of everyday spaces provides a base for small but vibrant networks of Muslims to thrive and assert presence. In these networks Muslim residents can 'normalise the experiences of being Muslim in the region',[64] combat isolation and creatively negotiate the absence of Islamic services and food – in Jones's words 'making-do'.[65] Jones argues that in this way they form a pioneer group, operating in the context of lack of precedent to negotiate an existence that opens up an expression of their Muslim identities. They are, he argues, actively engaged in recreating and shaping the rural space rather than being passive subjects of a homogenized rural experience. Jones's study contributes to an understanding of rural transformations, illustrating aspects of negotiating settlement, cohesion and presence through acts of citizenship.

These small acts and everyday negotiations require public space and public imaginings of the rural community to be more inclusive and to engage in a politics of acknowledgement and acceptance.

Conclusion

Considerable ground has been made in encapsulating the experience of the rural from the perspectives of a variety of ethnic minority groups and in demonstrating the ways in which the rural idyll has been disturbed by the increasing presence and claims-making of these populations. The perceptible absence of non-white people from the rural landscape that led to a collapsing of whiteness, Welshness and national identity as the dominant symbolism of the rural community has been undermined. This myth, both quietly assumed and at times more conspicuously subject to exploitation by right-wing political parties such as the BNP, has provided a powerful exclusionary force that is daily contested in the politics of recognition, attachment and belonging being played out in rural communities. Issues of identities, belonging, difference, locality, hybridity and complex and evolving articulations of subjectivities have opened up the debates on rurality and race and ethnicities beyond an examination of the dimensions of rural racism. This is not to understate the continuing evidence of racism in rural communities, both banal and institutional, and one reading of these studies suggests ongoing low-level antagonism, hostilities, banal racism and sustained institutional lethargy that minorities have just learned to live with.

Alongside this the evidence points to ethnic minorities in rural communities as active citizens, displaying resilience, coping strategies, maintaining vibrant co-ethnic networks of support and specialized service delivery, at the same time as actively contributing to the life of their localities. Ethnic minorities were too readily conceptualized and written up as rural *others* with too little attention given to commonalities, contributions and reciprocities. There are clearly a variety of experiences crucially mediated by factors such as length of settlement, age, class, gender and community status among others that deserve further consideration. There is work to be done on civic association and engagement and on the political mobilization of voice and choice in areas of sparse minority populations that could usefully add to the debates about transformations in rural areas. There is work to be done on the labour market access and workplace relations in these areas. Critically, the intersection with the Welsh language remains largely underdeveloped, particularly in relation to migrant languages and motivations toward language learning. Pat Harrison's study of Polish children's schooling experience hints at this interface.[66] Tunger and Viger's work[67] opens this debate by exploring the role of language as constructed by policies for the acculturation of migrants in competing discourses of national belonging, drawing on evidence from what they call the 'highly charged linguistic environments'[68] of Wales and Switzerland where work opportunities exist for migrants in rural areas and where non-state language groups pursue vigorous revitalization policies.

Contributions to the understanding of this broad range of movements and mobilities have come from a multidisciplinary body of theory drawing on scholarly work in Wales within sociology, social geography, cultural theory and social policy among others. This work has served to challenge the formulaic dichotomies of rural/urban, traditional/modern by contesting singular notions and experiences of the rural and pointing to plural and differentiated countrysides.[69] The urban as multicultural and the rural as monocultural has been refuted and overtaken by theorizing the *transrural* relationships that difference and diversity necessarily bring. It is no longer possible to conceive of 'the rural' as a distinct geographical space but more as a series of overlapping *social* spaces reflecting multiple imaginings, meanings and social constructions and experiences. Such a transrural[70] approach accommodates both the specificities of place but at the same time permits a focus on other connections of scale – national, regional, transnational – and their interconnectivity. So, for example, the work on EU migrants in Wales speaks to processes of international migration impacting on the rural, to personal and collective connections with the country of origin and country of settlement – virtual and actual. Similarly Jones's work on Muslims in Wales hints at their interconnections with the wider politics of Islam, regionally, nationally and internationally, criss-crossing spatial divides in satisfying needs, mobilizing supports and contributing to community. Beyond linear conceptualizations of movement into or out of rural areas by minority groups, theorizing rurality vis-à-vis ethnicities has opened up a consideration of multicultural place making, rural identities and permits a view of how national and transnational processes form part of people's experiences and constructions of the rural.

Challenges to the particular absences and presences in hegemonic ideas about rurality and rural people have also emerged as the result of broader changes in national politics. The big-P politics brought about by devolution has gradually led to a revisionist view of national identity, foregrounding civic over ethnic constructions of national identity and committing to a more inclusive politics (see chapter 13 and concluding chapter). Over the past decade the Welsh Government has rolled out a number of reforms related to multicultural policy making that place duties on the local state irrespective of place.[71] Local authorities must monitor ethnic presence in their localities, consult and engage and formulate responsive policies in collaboration with minority groups. The curriculum and school practices must reflect the multicultural realities of Wales and a number of discrete strategy papers exist to protect and promote the rights of particular groups such as Gypsies and Travellers and asylum seekers. This politics is more than the sum of its parts. It has served to

locate the rural within wider debates on national multiculturalism and indeed British multiculturalism as notions of both
Britishness and Welshness have been critically examined.

Notes

1   P. Cloke, 'Contextualising rural racism', in N. Chakraborti and
    J. Garland (eds), *Rural Racism* (Devon, 2004), p. 27.

2   E. Jay, *'Keep them in Birmingham': Challenging Racism in South-
    West England* (London, 1992).

3   For an overview, see P. de Lima, 'John O'Groats to Land's End: racial
    equality in rural Britain?', in Chakraborti and Garland, *Rural Racism*,
    pp. 36–61.

4   See, for example, G. Craig, B. Ahmed and F. Amery, '"We shoot them
    in Newark!" The work of the Lincolnshire Forum for Racial Justice',
    in P. Henderson and R. Kaur (eds), *Rural Racism in the UK: Examples
    of Community-Based Responses* (London, 1999), pp. 22–32.

5   C. Williams, 'Revisiting the rural race debates: a view from the Welsh
    countryside', *Ethnic and Racial Studies*, 30/5 (2007), 741–65.

6   Ibid., 741.

7   C. Philo, 'Neglected rural geographies: a review', *Journal of Rural
    Studies*, 8/2 (1992), 197–9.

8   See, for example, L. Ray and K. Reed, 'Community, mobility and
    racism in a semi-rural area: comparing minority experiences in East
    Kent', *Ethnic and Racial Studies*, 28/2 (2005), 212–34.

9   Henderson and Kaur (eds), *Rural Racism in the UK*; M. Dhalech,
    Challenging Racism in the Rural Idyll: Final Report, National
    Association of Citizen's Advice Bureaux (Exeter, 1999).

10 de Lima, 'John O'Groats to Land's End'.

11 V. Robinson and H. Gardner, 'Place matters: exploring the distinc-
    tiveness of racism in rural Wales', in S. Neal and J. Agyeman (eds),
    *The New Countryside? Ethnicity, Nation and Exclusion in
    Contemporary Rural Britain* (Bristol, 2006).

12 Ibid., p. 88.

13 Williams, 'Revisting the rural race debates'.

14 Neal and Agyeman (eds), *The New Countryside?*

15 Cloke, 'Contextualising rural racism'.

16 See, for example, R. Miles and A. Dunlop, 'The racialisation of politics in Britain: why Scotland is different', *Patterns of Prejudice*, 20/1 (1986), 23–32; B. Fanning, *Racism and Social Change in the Republic of Ireland* (Manchester, 2002); C. Williams, 'Race and racism: some reflections on the Welsh context', *Contemporary Wales*, 8 (1995), 113–31.

17 G. Halseth, S. Markey and D. Bruce (eds), *The Next Rural Economies: Constructing Rural Place in Global Economies* (Oxfordshire, 2010).

18 G. Day, *Making Sense of Wales: A Sociological Perspective* (Cardiff, 2002).

19 Cloke, 'Contextualising rural racism', p. 20.

20 Williams, 'Race and racism'.

21 Day, *Making Sense of Wales*, p. 142.

22 C. Williams, 'Strange encounters: lifting the lid on race in Wales', *Planet*, 157 (Spring 2003), 19–24.

23 Williams, 'Revisting the rural race debates'.

24 Cloke, 'Contextualising rural racism'.

25 See, for example, R. Frankenburg, *Village on the Border* (London, 1957); I. Emmett, *A North Wales Village: A Social Anthropological Study* (London, 1964). See also later work: G. Day, 'A community of communities? Similarity and difference in Welsh rural community studies', *Economic and Social Review*, 3 (July 1998), 233–57.

26 See, for example, F. Bowie, 'Wales from within: conflicting interpretations of Welsh identity', in S. MacDonald (ed.), *Inside European Identities: Ethnography in Western Europe* (Oxford, 1993) on non-Welsh speakers, and R. Crwydwen, 'Welsh lesbian feminist: a contradiction in terms?', in J. Aaron, T. Rees, S. Betts and M. Vincentelli (eds), *Our Sisters' Land: The Changing Identities of Women in Wales* (Cardiff ,1994).

27 V. Robinson, 'A study of racial antipathy in south Wales and its social and demographic correlates', *New Community*, 12 (1985), 116–24.

28 V. Robinson, 'Exploring myths about rural racism: a Welsh case study', in C. Williams, N. Evans and P. O'Leary (eds), *A Tolerant Nation? Exploring Ethnic Diversity in Wales* (Cardiff, 2003), pp. 160–78.

29 Robinson, 'Exploring myths about rural racism', p. 166.

30 Ibid.

31 Robinson and Gardner, 'Place matters'.

32 Ibid., p. 56.

33 Ibid., p. 64.

34 G. Day, H. Davis and A. Drakakis-Smith, "There's one shop you don't go into if you are English": the social and political integration of English migrants into Wales', *Journal of Ethnic and Migration Studies*, 36/9 (2010), 1405–23.

35 H. Crawley and T. Crimes, *Refugees Living in Wales: A Survey of Skills, Experiences and Barriers to Inclusion* (Swansea, 2009).

36 C. Williams, J. Borland, A. Griffiths, G. Roberts, H. Bradshaw and E. Morris, Snakes and Ladders: Advice and Support in Employment Discrimination Cases in Wales (2003). Report available at *http:// www.equalitiesandhumanrights.com* (accessed 1 September 2013).

37 The Race Relations (Amendment) Act 2000 defines this term.

38 C. Williams, S. Turunen and J. Jeffries, *Ethnic Minorities in North Wales: A Mapping Exercise*, commissioned by Black and Ethnic Minorities Support Team and Welsh Assembly Government. Report available at *http://www.mewn-cymru.org.uk/ResourceReports.php* (accessed 1 September 2013).

39 C. Williams and T. Hong Baker, *Developing Effective Engagement for Consultation with Black and Ethnic Minorities in Rural Areas* (2009). Rural Action Research Programme Briefing Series, see *http:// www.ruralgateway.org.uk/en/node/1066?page=5* (accessed 12 June 2009).

40 M. Woods and S. Watkin, *Central and Eastern European Migrant Workers in Rural Wales*, report 20, Wales Rural Observatory (2008).

41 Ibid., p. 3.

42 Ibid.

43 Ibid.

44 A. Thompson, P. Chambers and L. Doleczek, '"Welcome to Llaneski": Polish migration in south west Wales', *Contemporary Wales*, 23/1 (2010), 1–16.

45 Ibid., 13.

46 Ibid., 14.

47 Woods and Watkin, *Central and Eastern European Migrant Workers in Rural Wales*, p. 44.

48 Ibid., p. 53.

49 P. Hamilton, 'Including migrant worker children in learning and social context of the rural primary school', *Education 3–13*, 41/2 (2011), 202–17. See also P. Hamilton, 'It's not all about academic achievement: supporting the social and emotional needs of migrant worker children', *Pastoral Care in Education*, 31/2 (2012), 173–90, and P. Hamilton, 'Fostering effective and sustainable home-school relations with migrant worker parents: a new story to tell?', *International Studies in Sociology of Education*, 23/4 (2013), available at *http://dx.doi.org/10.1080/09620214.2013.815439* (accessed 4 September 2013).

50 Ibid.

51 Woods and Watkin, *Central and Eastern European Migrant Workers in Rural Wales*.

52 J. Scourfield, J. Evans, W. Shah and H. Beynon, 'Responding to the experiences of minority ethnic children in virtually all white communities', *Child and Family Social Work*, 7 (2002), 161–75. See also J. Scourfield and A. Davies, 'Children's accounts of Wales as racialised and inclusive', *Ethnicities*, 5/1 (2005), 83–107, and J. Scourfield, B. Dicks, M. Drakeford and A. Davies, *Children, Place and Identity: Nation and Locality in Middle Childhood* (London, 2006).

53 Scourfield et al., 'Responding to the experiences of minority ethnic children'.

54 Ibid., 174.

55 Scourfield and Davies, 'Children's accounts of Wales as racialised and inclusive'.

56 D. Sibley, *Geographies of Exclusion* (London, 1995).

57 P. Niner, *Accommodation needs of Gypsies and Travellers in Wales*, report to the Welsh Assembly Government (2006), available at *http://wales.gov.uk/docs/dsjlg/publications/equality/140407-gypsy-accommodation-needs-en.pdf* (accessed 4 September 2013).

58 S. Cemlyn, M. Greenfields, S. Burnett, Z. Matthews and C. Whitwell, *Inequalities Experienced by Gypsy and Traveller Communities: A Review* (Manchester, 2009). See chapter 8: 'Wales and Scotland',

pp. 202–6, *http://www.equalityhumanrights.com/sites/default/files/documents/research/12inequalities_experienced_by_gypsy_and_traveller_communities_a_review.pdf* (accessed 4 September 2013).

59 Welsh Assembly Government, *'Travelling to a Better Future'* – A *Gypsy and Traveller Framework for Action and Delivery Plan* (Cardiff, 2011).

60 F. Chiesa and E. Rossi, 'Contested identities and spatial marginalization: the case of Roma and Gypsy-Travelers in Wales', in S. Moroni and D. Weberman (eds), *Space and Pluralism* (Budapest, 2013).

61 Ibid., p. 21. Available online at *http://papers.ssrn.com/sol3/papers.cfm?abstract_id=2187089* (accessed 5 September 2013).

62 R. D. Jones, 'Negotiating absence and presence: rural Muslims and "subterranean" sacred spaces', *Space and Polity*, 16/3 (2012), 335–50. See also R. D. Jones, 'Islam and the rural landscape: discourses of absence in west Wales', *Social and Cultural Geography*, 11/8 (2010), 751–68.

63 Jones, 'Negotiating absence and presence', 335.

64 Ibid., 342.

65 Ibid., 335.

66 Hamilton, 'Fostering effective and sustainable home-school relations with migrant worker parents'.

67 V. Tunger and D. Vigers, 'Migration in contested linguistic spaces: the challenge for language policies in Switzerland and Wales', *European Journal of Language Policy*, 2/2 (2010), 181–95.

68 Ibid., 181.

69 See Wales Institute of Social and Economic Research (WISERD), Language, Citizenship & Identity research grouping: *www.wiserd.ac.uk* (accessed 4 September 2013).

70 K. Askins, 'Crossing divides: ethnicity and rurality', *Journal of Rural Studies*, 25 (2009), 365–75.

71 C. Williams and P. de Lima, 'Devolution, multicultural citizenship and race equality: from laissez-faire to nationally responsible policies', *Critical Social Policy*, 26/3 (2006), 498–522.

12

'This is the place we are calling home': Changes in Sanctuary Seeking in Wales

ALIDA PAYSON

The 1999 Immigration and Asylum Act, following closely on devolution, 'marked not only a sea-change for British asylum policy but also . . . for Wales' and for people seeking sanctuary here.[1] The Act, one in a series of Acts from 1993 to 2009 to redraft asylum policy, is understood principally to have transformed the number and diversity of sanctuary seekers in Wales. For the first time, as part of a policy of 'no-choice dispersal', the United Kingdom Government ordered asylum applicants receiving housing support to move to housing sites across Britain, including to Cardiff, Newport, Swansea and Wrexham.[2] While Wales has a long history of hosting refugees at local scales, estimates suggest that after 1999 the population of sanctuary seekers living in Wales more than tripled, from estimates of about 3,565 to 12,500 in 2009.[3] With rising numbers came a rise in diversity: one profile showed that, in March 2004, the 2,605 asylum seekers in Wales under the aegis of the National Asylum Support Service (NASS) belonged to seventy-four nationalities, most numerously Somali, Pakistani, Iraqi and Iranian.[4] Yet dispersal did not simply amplify the numbers and diversity of sanctuary seekers in Wales. In effect, the 1999 Act, together with others, also enmeshed Wales – sanctuary seekers, local communities and the Welsh Government – in an increasingly

277

hostile and corrosive set of UK policies on asylum that have eroded rights and degraded conditions for sanctuary seekers in Britain. These changes have corresponded with widespread national media stories that 'scapegoat', 'stereotype' and 'criminalize' sanctuary seekers, with terms like 'illegal' and 'bogus', 'parasites', 'scroungers', 'would-be immigrants' and 'cheats'.⁵ In fact, since 1993 the situation for many sanctuary seekers in the UK and in Wales has grown increasingly precarious, especially through UK policies of dispersal, detention, deportation and destitution.⁶ The consequences of these transformations for sanctuary seekers building new lives in Wales, along with ensuing community responses, have been profound.

Sanctuary seekers to Wales flee war, violent displacement and persecution. They seek asylum in Wales either under the 1951 United Nations Convention on the refugee, which defines a refugee as someone seeking protection 'owing to a well-founded fear of being persecuted for reasons of race, religion, nationality, membership of a particular social group or political opinion', or under Article 3 of the European Convention on Human Rights, 'prohibiting torture, or inhuman or degrading treatment or punishment'.⁷ Despite the protections promised by these laws, UK border statecraft since the 1990s has constricted refugee status and created new, more precarious classes for people at its margins.⁸ The question of terms has therefore become contentious. Instead of 'victims' of persecution deserving state protections, since the 1990s sanctuary seekers have been recast 'as perpetrators of insecurity' warranting state policing.⁹ Because of the way terms like 'asylum seeker' and even 'refugee' have been confused and freighted with stigma, Oxfam uses the term 'sanctuary seeker' as an 'overarching term to encompass refugees, asylum seekers' and all others seeking protection due to persecution, whatever their immigration status.¹⁰ This chapter adopts the same usage, reserving other terms to distinguish a specific immigration status.

In the current hostile political setting, the story of contemporary sanctuary in Wales is not one of fleeing persecution elsewhere for protection and the free, full exercise of rights and citizenship in 'a tolerant nation'. Rather, people seeking sanctuary in Wales find themselves buffeted by global patterns of displacement and marked out by entrenched racism and discrimination in immigration law. They have also been constrained by two decades of policies that have progressively criminalized asylum and redacted rights to permanent protections, to work, to citizenship, to legal representation and appeal, among others.[11] Manifold community responses include substantial research into the lived experiences and concerns of sanctuary seekers in Wales since dispersal began to take effect. This chapter charts this research and contextualizes it critically in terms of patterns in refugee movements and rights around the world, legacies of EU and UK immigration policy and the history of refugees in Wales. The chapter also investigates some of the forms of community response to sanctuary seekers' evolving concerns. Finally, this chapter sketches recent mobilizations by coalitions of sanctuary seekers and citizens that challenge and work to re-imagine sanctuary in Wales.

The fates and experiences of sanctuary seekers in Wales, and the communities in which they live, are of particular concern given the wider purview of this book. The Welsh Refugee Council estimates that refugees and asylum seekers make up 'approximately 30[%] of Cardiff's ethnic minority population', and refugees live across Wales.[12] Not all sanctuary seekers are racialized as non-white, yet as a writer from the Southall Black Sisters explains, 'immigration law is at the cutting edge of black communities' experience of racism at the hands of the state'.[13] Taken more broadly, sanctuary seekers in Wales are at the 'cutting edge' of contests over rights, citizenship and contemporary belonging that resonate across communities. The next section of this chapter takes up some of the historical and geographical roots and 'routes', as Paul

Gilroy might put it, connecting the current circumstances of refugees in Wales to forces of displacement and forms of 'racism at the hands of the state'.[14]

Asylum in context: forced displacement and immigration discrimination

Patterns in who has sought sanctuary in Britain, and why they have done so, reflect global patterns of forced migration and rising millions of refugees that have in turn precipitated sharp changes in UK immigration policy.[15] According to the United Nations High Commissioner for Refugees (UNHCR), the number of officially recognized refugees around the world rose from 2.4 million in 1975 to 10.4 million in 2011, with 24.1 million additional displaced 'people of concern'.[16] The causes forcing people to flee their homes at these scales are myriad and complex. While most refugees originate from less economically developed nations in the global South – Afghanistan, Iraq, Somalia, Sudan and the Democratic Republic of the Congo account for almost half of all refugees in 2011 – scholars emphasize how the root causes of displacement may originate in the political, economic and historical practices of more developed countries in the global North, including the UK.[17] The wars in Afghanistan and Iraq, Cold War and colonial legacies, deepening rifts in economic inequality perpetuated by trade agreements, development loans and debt burdens, all contribute to rising numbers of displaced people around the world.[18] Despite these connections, Europe, North America and Australia have since the 1980s fortified their borders and policies into 'an exclusionary regime, designed to keep out asylum seekers from the South'.[19] The restrictive measures of 'Fortress Europe' range from tall razor wire-topped fences between Spain and Morocco to prisons in Turkey for potential asylum seekers, including children.[20] These policies have 'produced asylum migration as almost the only possible opportunity for migration from less developed countries', while systematically criminalizing those who seek it.[21]

Policies on asylum in the UK, beginning with the 1993 Asylum and Immigration Appeals Act, recapitulate the strategies of Fortress Europe. In the UK, however, these laws also draw from and bolster a century of racially discriminatory immigration policy whose colonial roots predate even the 1905 Aliens Act.[22] As a 2008 report on immigration and social cohesion policy in south Wales states: 'migration policy in the UK has consistently involved forms of elite racism and classism which privilege English speaking, whiteness, education and economic capital'.[23] In addition to immigration laws that explicitly restricted numbers for Asian, Caribbean and African migrants, people settled and working in Britain were subject to 'delays, indignities and separation that would not have been tolerated had they been imposed on white families'.[24] More recently, the 1981 British Nationality Act eliminated birthright to citizenship 'so as to exclude black and Asian populations' and further fracture and limit access to citizenship.[25] Not all asylum seekers are racialized as non-white, but elite and structural racism in UK immigration law finds contemporary form in asylum policy. It is perhaps not incidental that UK policy began eroding refugee rights over the same period that more people began seeking sanctuary in Britain from Sri Lanka, Iran, Pakistan and Uganda, instead of from Communist Europe, such that the public image of the asylum seeker became racialized and 'taken to mean people who are visibly different and culturally distinct'.[26] Indeed, along with 'ignorance of human rights law' and failing to offer a fair hearing for asylum seekers, the UNHCR has criticized the UK Home Office for 'racial stereotyping' in its processes and decisions on asylum claims.[27]

This critical history and context serves to complicate what in 2000 Conservative leader William Hague called Britain's 'proud tradition': the cultural mythology around sanctuary in the UK.[28] Asylum in Britain became dramatically politicized from the late 1990s, as the UK experienced a brief and dramatic rise in applications for asylum accompanied by vitriolic, widespread and misinformed media coverage.[29] Subsequent political backlash has reduced applications to a quarter of those levels, with 19,804 new asylum applications in the UK in 2011.[30] Britain has recently been castigated by international bodies for reducing the numbers of people offered sanctuary regardless of legitimacy or need.[31] While Wales has a distinct history with respect to sanctuary, which the next section considers, global interconnections, historical legacies and contemporary politicized fervour set the tone and context for contemporary sanctuary seekers in Wales.

Sanctuary seekers in Wales

To say that Wales has a long history of welcoming and hosting refugees is something of a truism. Welsh politicians invoked the idea of a 'Welsh welcome' as dispersal policies bringing asylum seekers to Wales began to take effect around 2001.[32] While this history is, perhaps, too mythologized, and the reality more ambivalent, small numbers of refugees did come to and sometimes settle in Wales throughout the twentieth century. The stories of these refugees, many of them extraordinary, form a powerful part of Welsh 'folk memory' of hospitality and welcome for people seeking sanctuary from persecution.[33] In addition to hosting some refugees during and between both World Wars, from the 1950s relatives and friends fleeing post-war and post-colonial conflicts joined long-established ethnic minority communities in Wales.[34] Thus, while UK Government-sponsored dispersals settled all but a few of tens of thousands of refugees outside of Wales until 1999, sanctuary seekers have a rich and long-standing – if sporadic – presence in Wales.[35] The dramatic recent changes in sanctuary in Wales take shape as part of a complex story of community connections, migration and mobilization.

Early sanctuary for refugees in Wales took place at local, even intimate, household and community scales. In the 1890s, Jewish people fleeing pogroms in Eastern Europe settled across the south Wales Valleys, later concentrating in Cardiff.[36] In 1914, a fleet of fishing trawlers carrying Belgian refugees docked in Milford Haven, where initial offers of hospitality overflowed; other Belgian refugees among the 250,000 officially resettled in Britain were dispersed to Merthyr, Aberdare, Mountain Ash, Pontypridd and elsewhere in Wales, where they were supported by local charity and civic leaders.[37] Advocacy and support for refugees often drew from organizing and activism, sometimes by trade unions and political bodies but also by religious and women's groups.[38] In 1937, following civic outrage over the bombing of Guernica, some 230 Basque children fleeing the ravages of the Spanish Civil War settled in four special group homes in Wales.[39] As the British government provided nothing for their care, the children were supported by neighbourly charity, an extraordinary commitment given the scale of poverty in many Welsh towns in 1937. Small numbers of Jewish children also found homes in Wales from the late 1930s via the *kindertransport*.[40] This local advocacy for and generosity on behalf of refugees mixed over the same period with riots and xenophobic violence directed towards other migrants and ethnic minority groups, as addressed elsewhere in this volume.

While few Government-settled refugees such as the Ugandan Asian or Kosovar groups came to Wales between 1950 and 1999, with the exception of a few hundred Vietnamese refugees in 1979, others arrived through existing ties to Wales.[41] Research by the Butetown History & Arts Centre and the Runnymede Trust suggests that long-established ethnic minority communities in south Wales informally drew upon and supported family members seeking sanctuary from conflicts that included Indian Partition and civil war in Somalia, Sudan, the Democratic Republic of Congo and the Yemen.[42] The ties that drew friends and family fleeing conflict to south Wales were often multigenerational and extensive: in the early twentieth century people from more than fifty nationalities called the Butetown neighbourhood in Cardiff home.[43] Smaller communities in Newport, Swansea and some Welsh towns held similar connections. These established communities offered innumerable visible and invisible supports, from grocery shops to places of worship and informal job networks, which were and continue to be vital to the early resilience of many sanctuary seekers in Wales.

To consider just one example, conflict in Yemen after 1994 led to flight to join 'friends and family' in south Wales, where Yemeni seamen had developed a strong community, 'marrying local people' and establishing the first mosque in the UK in the early 1940s.[44] Around 2,000 Somali refugees fleeing civil war in the late 1980s–1990s made up the largest group of refugees drawn by ties of family and community to Wales, however.[45] The diverse, heterogeneous Somali community in Cardiff – about 2,000 people in 1994, now about 8,000 – was first established at the end of the nineteenth century by Somali merchant seamen and attracted and supported the new sanctuary seekers.[46] A 1994 Save the Children report into the experiences and concerns of the new arrivals noted that, in addition to aid from relatives, friends, mosques and organizations such as the Somali Advice and Information Centre, these newly arrived refugees required additional support (such as interpretation and culturally sensitive service provision) to navigate institutions and authorities.[47] Such networked support suggests that some sanctuary in Wales has followed patterns of family reunification and traced interconnected geographies that also shape how contemporary sanctuary seekers make their lives here.

Despite the presence of thousands of refugees in Wales in 1997, survey research of service providers at the end of the 1990s displayed what Vaughan Robinson termed 'cultures of "ignorance", "disbelief" and "denial"' about the existence and needs of refugees or the relevance of their services to them.[48] In 1999, the UK Government passed legislation that would provoke a 'sea-change' in the patterns of sanctuary seeking in Wales and likewise in community responses.[49] Researchers lament the lack of reliable demographic data on sanctuary seekers in Wales, but information from NASS on 2,322 asylum seekers in 2009 offers a telling snapshot. Nearly three quarters came from Afghanistan, China, Eritrea, Iran, Iraq, Pakistan, Somalia, Sudan or Zimbabwe.[50] The vast majority lived in the four dispersal cities of Cardiff (57%), Swansea (24%), Newport (16%) and Wrexham (3%).[51] With the dramatic increase in the number of sanctuary seekers in Wales – estimated to have risen from 3,565 in 1997 to 12,500 in 2009 – came an increase in diversity among sanctuary seekers. Refugees in Wales now originate from at least sixty countries and speak more than forty languages.[52] Class, gender, age, sexuality, occupation, parenthood, legal status, languages and fluency, employment and religion, especially, modulate sanctuary seekers' identities, community connections and relationship to the state.[53] Refugee community organizations, coalitions and programmes have grown to respond to this 'sea-change' and to help sanctuary seekers rebuild their lives in Wales. A decade of research collaborations has delved into their lived experiences and concerns. The research reveals some common struggles, some of which trace their origins directly to UK Government policy on asylum.[54] The next section treats the dramatic effects of some of these policies.

Policies of dispersal, criminalization and destitution

Since 1993, as asylum has become increasingly politicized in Britain, ten distinct Acts of Parliament have transformed the rights and condition of sanctuary seekers. The term 'asylum seeker' hardly featured in popular, media or political discourse before the 1990s, but as Imogen Tyler argues, by creating a new category of person with undecided status (the 'asylum seeker') the state could 'manoeuvre around' protections and entitlements due to refugees.[55] These 'manoeuvres' in the UK have progressively restricted sanctuary seekers' rights to appeal, work, settle permanently, unite with family or become British citizens, along with access to adequate healthcare, housing, education and legal representation.[56] They extend from refusing entry to those without papers – often inevitable for those in flight – to policies of 'enforced dispersal, detention, deportation and destitution' once in the UK.[57] Scholars write that such policies have become 'normalized', and framed as 'essential' instruments in the on-going attempt to control or manage immigration in Britain.[58] These laws have successively criminalized the asylum process, punishing violations of civil immigration law by imprisoning and deporting tens of thousands of people, all while undercutting access to legal representation and fair process. Dispersal policies now push asylum seekers into a series of disruptive removals and into 'hard-to-let' housing in places they do not choose. One refugee in a Cardiff focus group commented: 'they weren't actually told their rights, they don't know their rights, they live in kind of poor conditions and they don't know what to do about it'.[59] Finally, these laws have enforced, as a strategy of 'deterrence', acute destitution for many sanctuary seekers while cutting access to vital services. The United Nations and refugee organizations in Britain have censured these policies as contravening human rights law.[60] They have had dramatic local consequences.

The criminalization of asylum and widespread use of detention and deportation are novel strategies of immigration control that permeate experiences of asylum in Wales. In 2012, some 13,161 asylum seekers out of 27,486 total asylum applicants were detained for some period of time, suggesting that 'roughly half' of all asylum seekers in the UK will experience detention.[61] People are detained in a series of special-built, privately contracted 'detention centres', 'induction' and 'removal centres' near many airports that operate 'virtually unconstrained by the procedural safeguards' afforded to citizens in the criminal justice system.[62] Further, while before the 1990s forced deportation had been reserved as a policy of last resort and seen to be a 'traumatic and coercive use of state power', in 2006 the UK deported 18,235 'refused' asylum seekers, and 10,077 in 2011.[63] Constance, a sanctuary seeker in Wales from Cameroon, described 'the moral torture' of 'living with the threat of being snatched and removed at any time'.[64] Some deportations appear to violate the principle of *non-refoulement*, a vital tenet of the UN Convention on the refugee, which forbids returning a person to a country where he or she may be in direct danger.[65] Precarity and criminalization, in addition to sometimes violating human rights law, also causes unusually high rates of depression and ill health in asylum seekers.[66]

Novel dispersal and related housing policies, enforced under the aegis of 'spreading the burden' of support for asylum seekers away from the south-east, have had profound effects on people and communities in Wales.[67] Prior to 1999 forced dispersal had been used only in exceptional cases to settle large groups of refugees seeking sanctuary at once.[68] Most asylum seekers arriving in the UK chose to live near friends, relatives and in already-established communities with a shared culture or language.[69] In one 2009 study in Wales, almost 80% of refugees described 'significant housing problems'; these included impermanency, structures in poor repair, housing infested with vermin or insects, damp, dilapidated and over-crowded spaces, 'problems with neighbours and community' and high cost.[70] Due to housing pressure, others find themselves allocated to temporary housing in hostels where 'the accounts of the standard of living ... are very disturbing'.[71] The vagaries of the asylum process often entail not one but many displacements and removals. One woman explained through a translator: 'She's saying coming to the UK she thought it was going to be a better life for her, but moving back and forth from one house to another, not knowing where she is, is almost as difficult as being there'.[72] This movement often proves especially disruptive for sanctu-ary-seeking children and young people, whose schooling is interrupted or even suspended as a result.[73]

Dispersal has also troubled sanctuary seekers' safety and sense of belonging, and exacerbated experiences of racism. Some asylum seekers to Wales must live in neighbourhoods 'outside urban centres where they lack support services and that are ethnically homogenous, where often they are the only visibly different foreigners and where they become targets for abuse and violence'.[74] While local community leaders stress that much has changed in the intervening decade, in 2003 two nights of violence erupted on a Wrexham housing estate following an attack by white Welsh residents on an Iraqi Kurd asylum seeker who fractured his skull.[75] Dispersal has some-times had isolating effects even in an urban centre like Cardiff, as asylum seekers have been required to accept housing in 'rough areas' and majority-white neighbourhoods away from community and the conveniences of the city centre, and where, as one Somali refugee in Cardiff put it, there are 'abso-lutely no mosques, no any kind of halal shops, no even black people around'.[76] Fully half of the sanctuary seekers in a 2009 research study reported experiencing 'negative public atti-tudes and racism' of some kind in Wales, including from institutions and public officials.[77] Many also report routinely insensitive and discriminatory treatment from both NASS officials and private landlords.[78] Perhaps most seriously, the precarious and changeable asylum process increasingly forces people into homelessness, staying on friends' couches, in churches and even on the street.[79]

In addition, UK immigration legislation has increasingly imposed destitution for sanctuary seekers. Asylum seekers awaiting a decision on their claim, with rare exception, are not allowed to work, and levels of state support perpetuate rather than prevent destitution. If asylum seekers receive support, they receive less than £6 per day; this is 70% of the established income support for citizens, which itself is 'normally considered a minimum for survival'.[80] Others have no support whatsoever, such as those who do not claim asylum immediately upon entering the country, or who have exhausted the appeals process but may judge it too dangerous to return to their country of origin. Together these policies, which were adopted ostensibly to 'deter' other asylum seekers, can lead to conditions of deep poverty and destitution. Indeed, the 2007 Joint Committee on Human Rights has warned that the combination of forbidding work and restricting support 'breaches the Article 3 [European Convention on Human Rights] threshold of inhuman and degrading treatment'.[81] UK support for asylum seekers, rather than being exceptionally generous, is one of the lowest in the EU. Moreover, for some this survival support is accessed through a much-maligned voucher system. An extensive study produced by a coalition of refugee councils revealed that due to the voucher system 'people are unable to buy enough or appropriate food [and] ... essential non-food items' or to reach 'essential services, including legal advice and medical care' and finally that 'the payment card causes anxiety and distress ... and promotes stigma'.[82] Asylum seekers in Wales describe going hungry, being unable to buy basic supplies for themselves or their babies and children, and being 'stuck', even from travelling to appointments related to their asylum claim.[83] For sanctuary seekers with no claims to support – for example, those who decline vouchers offered only on the condition of deportation – the situation can be desperate: research by the Scottish Poverty Information Unit found that 'hundreds' of non-status asylum seekers were 'living in Scotland on less than the UN's global poverty target of 77 pence ... a day'.[84] Refused and destitute asylum seekers across Britain describe similarly desperate circumstances. Indeed, few other groups in the UK have all options for support stripped away to this extent.[85]

The consequences of forbidding asylum seekers from working can prove severe and enduring, causing 'poverty, deskilling, loss of self-esteem and significant under- and unemployment' for sanctuary seekers.[86] As one sanctuary seeker in Wales who had been a lawyer in Zimbabwe put it: 'I find it really hard being unable to work. I have always been very active ... without work you don't have any money and without any money you can't do anything.'[87] Not working also contributes to ongoing stigma for sanctuary seekers, who are presented as a 'cost' for communities, and are sometimes perceived to be a 'threat' to service provision for citizens.[88] While many sanctuary seekers do voluntary work, all of the relevant research in Wales commented on the importance of paid work to improving livelihoods, building 'language and broader cultural competence' and cultivating 'social connections'.[89] In one study, a 'professionally qualified refugee' pointed to the way that belonging in Wales is in many ways contingent on finding a job, because 'if you can't participate you can never be integrated'.[90] Once granted a decision and legally permitted to work, refugees experience substantial barriers to finding employment, including difficulties transferring qualifications and pervasive reported discrimination in hiring.[91]

While two thirds of sanctuary seekers in Wales had been employed in their countries of origin, a startling two thirds to three quarters were unemployed in Wales.[92] In their home countries, sanctuary seekers had been 'teachers, drivers, restaurateurs, electricians, soldiers, farmers, nurses, civil engineers, journalists, geophysicists, accountants and flight crew'.[93] While some, often for reasons of gender, have been 'denied education' in their countries of origin, in general sanctuary seekers tend to be proportionately better qualified than their British counterparts: 76.4% in one study held a secondary education certificate, 28.5% had a university degree and 8.9% a postgraduate degree.[94] Yet even highly qualified refugees often experience profound barriers to full employment. One internationally qualified doctor, who had participated in the Wales Asylum Seeking and Refugee Doctors (WARD) programme and had passed three sets of exams to be recertified in the UK, said: 'I'm still waiting for a job, nothing so far, that's my history, worked in takeaway for a long time'.[95] In Wales, those who find work often resort to what scholars have referred to as 'survival employment' – low-wage, low-skilled, precarious work where sometimes, as scholars observed of Cardiff, 'exploitation and discrimination appear to be endemic'.[96] Unemployed refugees in one research study reported being willing to take 'any' kind of job.[97] Furthermore, in Wales in particular, where rising proportions of low-income families continue to be poor despite being in work, sanctuary seekers may find themselves entrenched in regional patterns of low-wage, part-time jobs that provide no route out of poverty.[98]

In recommendations to the Welsh Government, researchers noted that 'areas of UK Government Policy on asylum have negative impacts on the entire process of integration/inclusion and social cohesion' for people seeking sanctuary in Wales.[99] In particular, the report criticizes policies that enforce destitution and threaten detention and deportation, which 'drive asylum seekers underground', dispersal processes that uproot and disrupt everyday life and belonging, voucher systems that perpetuate destitution and policies that strand young people 'who complete school and have nowhere to go'.[100] Their research charts concrete, disturbing examples of the effects of such policies. Yet the same policies have also provoked multi-faceted responses and mobilizations across communities in Wales at a range of levels.

Mobilization, care and protest

This chapter has shown that the past decade has transformed not only the number and diversity of sanctuary seekers in Wales, but also the scales and varieties of harm and injustice perpetrated by policies of detention, dispersal, deportation and destitution. In response, sanctuary seekers and the heterogeneous communities in which they have come to live in

Wales have organized and mobilized. They have done so to make the effects of these policies visible, to challenge stereotypical myths and stigmas about sanctuary seekers, and to bridge gaps in basic support for survival and human rights. Groups have taken up strategies of direct response, care, advocacy and protest. In this, groups in Wales join 'an explosion of "immigrant protest"' and activism globally.[101] Indeed, as scholars have noted, 'refugee activism has become a significant political force in its own right, with coalitions of citizens and non-citizens engaging in various forms of advocacy and resistance' to protest and temper 'deteriorating conditions', state 'violence', and hostile media and political discourse ringing sanctuary seekers in neo-liberal states.[102]

In Wales, the Welsh Government's commitments to racial equality and to refugee inclusion themselves suggest forms of resistance – within the law – to some of the principles behind and effects of UK Government immigration law. As such, the Welsh context reflects the insight of immigration scholars Davide Però and John Solomos in 2010, who emphasize that the 'state' is not a 'compact and coherent anti-immigrants engine which is strongly committed to and fully effective in enforcing government policy', but rather a 'vast and heterogeneous entity' within which individuals and groups can and do make choices against and changes to the intentions of the 'policy makers' on any given issue.[103] In providing key services and support to sanctuary seekers, yet without devolved control over immigration or asylum legislation, the Welsh Government has in general worked in contradistinction to harsher policies in England and to mitigate harm from UK immigration law. Indeed, the Welsh Government is vocally committed 'to support and enable refugees to re-build their lives in Wales and make a full contribution to society'.[104] The All Wales Refugee Policy Forum, convened in 2003, led to a range of research projects that worked closely with sanctuary seekers to identify key concerns, and ultimately to a broad commitment to a substantial refugee inclusion strategy in

2008.[105] The Wales Migration Partnership, a coalition of local government offices and community organizations, serves as an important watchdog, link and emissary to 'enable strategic and political oversight on asylum', monitor policy, communicate with the Home Office and help promote strong service delivery for sanctuary seekers and other migrants in Wales.[106]

Welsh Government interventions to support sanctuary seekers are too extensive to cover in depth here, but include measures for health, language learning, interpretation, education, housing and other opportunities for intercultural exchange. In England, for example, since 2004 refused asylum seekers must pay prohibitive private fees for all but emergency healthcare services, but not in Wales. In 2007, the deleterious effects of the UK-wide policy prompted the Welsh Assembly Government to restore access to free secondary healthcare for all sanctuary seekers regardless of decision status.[107] Another crucial intervention has been funding for free English-language learning provision for sanctuary seekers.[108] The Welsh Government's race equality scheme works to address wider discrimination and integration issues. While sanctuary seekers may still experience steep barriers to access services and may be delayed by long waiting lists, government in Wales, as in Scotland, bears out a commitment to sanctuary seekers' equality and rights.

Yet in Wales, as elsewhere, to map the contours of this mobilization requires breaking out of a 'narrow and formal understanding of politics' and to attend instead to the gestures by which sanctuary seekers and advocates resist the worst of state policy and practice, demand rights and build alternative systems of mutual support. The Independent Asylum Commission, for example, conducted a vigilant 'citizens' enquiry' into the UK asylum system from 2006 to 2008, producing 180 'recommendations to safeguard people who seek sanctuary here, while restoring public confidence in the UK's role as a place of sanctuary'.[109] Mobilization takes many different forms, but can be loosely grouped into three: first,

professional support and service provision by refugee community organizations and other established third-sector
organizations that serve sanctuary seekers; secondly, small,
grass-roots generosity and projects bringing together advocates and sanctuary seekers around common interests and
concerns; and thirdly, direct action protest to resist specific
cases of deportation, destitution and detention. Scholars of
migrant protest and activism have described the 'forms of
mutual support and care which create social spaces below the
radar of existing political structures' as a vital but often invisible aspect of mobilization. These forms include 'mutual
cooperation, friendships, favours that you never return, affective support, trust, care for other people's relatives and
children, transnational relations of care, the gift economy
between mobile people'.[110]

Much of this 'care' comes from networks of family and
friends who open up rooms and offer food and shelter,
particularly when other support has been withdrawn. This
care can be quite straightforward, and as one person from the
focus groups in Cardiff put it: 'I went straight to where the
Somalis were just asking people, as soon as I went there, they
took me to the advice centre . . . and they advised me really
where to go'.[111] But it can also be more extensive. For example, in a book of sanctuary seekers' accounts from Wales,
Seeking Sanctuary: Stories of Despair and Hope, each of the
seven women featured describes turning to friends for a place
to stay or other vital support when their circumstances
became desperate. Such dependent relationships may be
fraught and conflicted, as sanctuary seekers express feeling
burdensome, and these relationships may sour or even turn
abusive under stress.[112] Too often, also, this displaces the
burden of care onto those in the community who can least
afford it.

This grass-roots 'care' does not only operate among sanctuary seekers, but also between sanctuary seekers and local
communities. A 2005 Save the Children report *Uncertain*

Futures: Children Seeking Asylum in Wales noted that local communities have often responded to new arrivals with gifts, information and hospitality. One refugee recounted: 'when we first came here there was a problem with the gas and they helped us, and we didn't have a TV and they gave us a TV, and sometimes they give us a lift to do the shopping'.[113] Established refugee community organizations like the Welsh Refugee Council, Displaced People in Action and Oasis Cardiff, along with smaller projects such as SHARE Tawe efforts in Swansea, among many others, all help organize this kind of direct support, including 'offers [of] hospitality, in the form of accommodation, meals, a warm welcome and solidarity, to destitute asylum seekers'.[114] Among the grass-roots coalitions bringing together concerned 'citizens and noncitizens' are groups like the Women Seeking Sanctuary Advocacy Group Wales and the Llanishen Refugee Women's Group. Small-scale community groups based on shared culture, language or country of origin, such as the Sudanese Community Association or Kurdi Cymru, also provide a variety of forms of care, from advice and help adjusting to life in Wales to community celebrations and events.[115] Faith-based organizations in Wales also play a critical survival and advocacy role: churches in Wrexham, Newport, Swansea and Cardiff offer non-denominational support and even emergency refuge. One sanctuary seeker reported: 'some people in the church try to give us what we can survive with'.[116] Taken together, these forms of mutual and neighbourly activism, care and protest show an extensive, richly diverse local response to the ways sanctuary seekers have been stigmatized, criminalized and forced into destitution by state policy in the UK.

Finally, it is worth mentioning that over the past decade, Wales has also seen vocal advocacy and direct action protests over the treatment of sanctuary seekers. The groups No Borders South Wales, Strangers into Citizens Campaign and No One is Illegal have protested against specific incidents of deportation. In 2012, to protest the deportation of the Saleh family to Egypt where the family feared for their safety, a No Borders witness describes protesters arguing with immigration officials, sitting in the road and chaining themselves to the axle of the bus carrying the family to the airport.[117] Some sanctuary seekers, in acts of desperation that are also acts of protest, have engaged in self-harm as a last resort against forced deportation. These forms of mobilization seek to address, as scholars Imogen Tyler and Katarzyna Marciniak put it, 'the violence engendered by border controls' that often proceeds, hidden from public view, by making that violence visible and political.[118]

Conclusion

The story of refugees in Wales thus cannot be told simply as a passage from persecution elsewhere to sanctuary and citizenship in Britain. For a variety of political and historical reasons, sanctuary seekers have become symbolic, scapegoated bodies whose rights and status have been eroded and diffused across a complicated and messy hierarchy of legality, citizenship and belonging. In this, they join a long history of discriminatory policy from the state, join a rising trend of superdiversity and cosmopolitanism in international migration patterns to and from Wales, and join broader mobilizations to reclaim the rights of displaced people. Refugee issues take a unique and often hyper-local shape in Wales but are nonetheless part of a larger contestation. As one sanctuary seeker acknowledged in research in Wales, '[while] maybe we were dispersed, not by our choice, but by the government policy', Wales has become home, often through the efforts of a wildly diverse cohort of new friends, connections, advocates and asylum seekers themselves: 'this [is] the place where we are calling home, because this is the place where we find our friends, this is the place where we are working, this is the place where we are doing what we can do'.[119] The future welcome and vitality of that home, 'where we are doing what we can do', depends on the ongoing contest between policies that objectify and punish sanctuary seekers and the myriad forms of mobilization that reshape and reinvent the meaning of sanctuary in Wales.

Notes

*   I would like to thank Kerry Moore for her invaluable guidance, edits and comments, and Paul Bowman, Jenny Kidd, Chris Weedon, Meg Brown Payson and Eli Lazarus for their helpful suggestions and support.

1   V. Robinson, *Mapping the Field: Refugee Housing in Wales* (Cardiff, 2006) p. 6.

2   Ibid.

3   Ibid., pp. 4–7; V. Winckler (ed.), *Equality Issues in Wales: A Research Review*, Equality and Human Rights Commission and the Bevan Foundation (Manchester, 2009), p. iii.

4   Robinson, *Mapping the Field*, pp. 4–7.

5   G. Philo, E. Briant and P. Donald, *Bad News for Refugees* (London, 2013), pp. 1–3.

6   I. Tyler, *Revolting Subjects: Social Abjection and Resistance in Neoliberal Britain* (London, 2013), p. 143.

7   Institute of Race Relations, *Asylum Statistics* (London, 2013). See *http://www.irr.org.uk/research/statistics/asylum/* (accessed 21 August 2014).

8   A. Bloch, 'The importance of convention status: a case study of the UK', *Sociological Research Online*, 6/1 (2001), 1–10, see *http://www.socresonline.org.uk/6/1/bloch.html* (accessed 21 August 2014); L. Schuster and J. Solomos, 'Asylum, refuge and public policy: current trends and future dilemmas', *Sociological Research Online*, 6/1 (2001), 1–11, see *http://socresonline.org.uk/6/1/schuster.html* (accessed 21 August 2014).

9   UNHCR, 'Chapter 3: addressing refugee security', in *The State of the World's Refugees 2006 – Human Displacement in the New Millennium* (Geneva, 2006), p. 64. See *http://www.unhcr.org* (accessed 21 August 2014).

10   J. Maman and H. Muggeridge, *Best Practice Guide: For Community Organisations Working with Sanctuary Seeking Women in Wales*

(Cardiff, 2011), p. 3. See *http://policy-practice.oxfam.org.uk/publications/best-practice-guide-for-community-organisations-working-with-sanctuary-seeking-197790* (accessed 21 August 2014).

11   Philo et al., *Bad News for Refugees*, pp. 20–4.

12   Welsh Assembly Government (WAG), *Refugee Inclusion Strategy Scoping Report* (Cardiff, 2005), p. 24. See *http://wales.gov.uk/dsjlg/research/refugeescoping/report.pdf?lang=en* (accessed 21 August 2014).

13   P. Joshi, 'Jumping through hoops: immigration and domestic violence', in R. Gupta (ed.), *From Homebreakers to Jailbreakers: Southall Black Sisters* (London, 2003), p. 133.

14   P. Gilroy, *The Black Atlantic: Modernity and Double Consciousness* (London, 1993), p. 19.

15   S. Castles and M. Miller, *The Age of Migration: International Population Movements in the Modern World*, 4th edn (Hampshire, 2009), p. 188.

16   Ibid., p. 190; UNHCR, *UNHCR Statistical Yearbook 2011* (2012; online edn, 2013), p. 6. See *http://www.unhcr.org/statistics* (accessed 21 August 2014).

17   UNHCR, *UNHCR Statistical Yearbook 2011*, p. 28.

18   Philo et al., *Bad News for Refugees*, pp. 13–19.

19   Castles and Miller, *Age of Migration*, p. 193.

20   Ibid., p. 192; P. Mason, 'The EU is ignoring the human rights abuses behind Morocco's razor wire', *The Guardian* (2 September 2013). See *http://www.theguardian.com/commentisfree/2013/sep/02/eu-ignoring-rights-abuses-morocco* (accessed 20 November 2013).

21   T. Threadgold and G. Court, *Refugee Inclusion: A Literature Review* (Cardiff, 2005), p. 10.

22   B. Parekh (ed.), *The Future of Multi-Ethnic Britain: The Parekh Report* (London, 2001), pp. 205–23; Philo et al., *Bad News for Refugees*, p. 20; L. Schuster and J. Solomos, 'Race, immigration and asylum': New Labour's agenda and its consequences', *Ethnicities*, 4/2 (2004), 267–70.

23   T. Threadgold et al., *Immigration and Inclusion in South Wales* (Cardiff, 2008), p. 30.

24   Parekh (ed.), *Future of Multi-Ethnic Britain*, p. 208.

25   Tyler, *Revolting Subjects*, p. 54.

26   V. Robinson, R. Andersson and S. Musterd, *Spreading the 'Burden'? A Review of Policies to Disperse Asylum Seekers and Refugees* (Bristol, 2003), pp. 5–7.

27   Philo et al., *Bad News for Refugees*, p. 37.

28   Ibid., p. 32.

29   T. Speers, *Welcome or Over Reaction? Refugees and Asylum Seekers in the Welsh Media* (Cardiff, 2001), p. 33.

30   Ibid., p. 28.

31   Castles and Miller, *Age of Migration*, p. 190; Philo et al., *Bad News for Refugees*, pp. 24–5.

32   Speers, *Welcome or Over Reaction?*, p. 33.

33   H. Davies, *Fleeing Franco: How Wales Gave Shelter to Refugee Children from the Basque Country During the Spanish Civil War* (Cardiff, 2011), pp. 10–23.

34   C. Bates, 'The hidden story of partition and its legacies', *BBC History* (3 March 2011), *http://www.bbc.co.uk/history/british/modern/partition1947_01.shtml* (accessed 21 August 2014); Butetown History & Arts Centre (BHAC), *Migrant Memories: The Indian Partition and Settlement in Southeast Wales* (film, 23 minutes) (Cardiff University Centre for Critical and Cultural Theory and BHAC, 2013).

35   Robinson, *Mapping the Field*, pp. 4–6.

36   N. Evans, 'Immigrants and minorities in Wales, 1840–1990: a comparative perspective', in C. Williams, N. Evans and P. O'Leary (eds), *A Tolerant Nation?: Exploring Ethnic Diversity in Wales* (Cardiff, 2003), p. 18.

37   Davies, *Fleeing Franco*, pp. 10–23; Evans, 'Immigrants and minorities in Wales', p. 18.

38   H. Jones, 'National, community and personal priorities: British women's responses to refugees from the Nazis, from the mid-1930s to early 1940s', *Women's History Review*, 21/1 (2004), 121–51.

39   N. Benjamin, 'Foreword', in H. Davies, *Fleeing Franco*, pp. v–vi.

40   E. Davies, *Kerry's Children: A Jewish childhood in Nazi Germany and Growing up in South Wales* (Bridgend, 2004).

41   Robinson, *Mapping the Field*, p. 4.

42 Runnymede, *Cardiff Migration Stories: Making Histories* (London, 2012). See *http://www.makinghistories.org.uk/uploads/Cardiff%20 Migration%20Stories%20210x210%2020pp%20v3.pdf* (accessed 21 November 2013).

43 S. Gilliat-Ray and J. Mellor, 'Bilā-d al-Welsh (Land of the Welsh): Muslims in Cardiff, south Wales: past, present and future', *The Muslim World*, 100/4 (2010), 453; G. Jordan, '"We never really noticed you were coloured": postcolonialist reflections on immigrants and minorities in Wales', in J. Aaron and C. Williams (eds), *Postcolonial Wales* (Cardiff, 2005), p. 60.

44 Runnymede, *Cardiff Migration* Stories, p. 12; Gilliat-Ray and Mellor, 'Bila-d al-Welsh (Land of the Welsh)' pp. 457–9.

45 Save the Children, *The Somali Community in Cardiff* (Cardiff, 1994).

46 Runnymede, *Cardiff Migration Stories*, p. 4; Threadgold et al., *Immigration and Inclusion in South Wales* pp. 15–19, 33–4, 48–51.

47 Save the Children, *Somali Comunity in Cardiff*, pp. 4–20.

48 V. Robinson, 'Cultures of ignorance, disbelief and denial: refugees in Wales', *Journal of Refugee Studies*, 12/1 (1999), 78–87.

49 Robinson, *Mapping the Field*, pp. 4–10.

50 Ibid.

51 H. Crawley and T. Crimes, *Refugees Living in Wales: A Survey of Skills, Experiences and Barriers to Exclusion* (Swansea, 2009), p. 1. See *http://www.swansea.ac.uk/media/media,41835,en.pdf* (accessed 21 August 2014).

52 WAG, *Refugee Inclusion Strategy*, p. 2.

53 S. Vertovec, 'Super-diversity and its implications', *Ethnic and Racial Studies*, 30/6 (2007), 1024–54; Threadgold et al., *Immigration and Inclusion in South Wales*, pp. 3–4.

54 Information Centre about Asylum and Refugees (ICAR), 'Mapping the UK, Cardiff, Services' (London, 2009). See *http://www.icar.org. uk/index.html@lid=9987.html* (accessed 21 August 2014).

55 Tyler, *Revolting Subjects*, pp. 83–4.

56 Philo et al., *Bad News for Refugees*, pp. 20, 13–28.

57 I. Tyler and K. Marciniak, 'Immigrant protest: an introduction', *Citizenship Studies*, 17/2 (2013) 143–4; Tyler, *Revolting Subjects*, pp. 83–4.

58 A. Bloch and L. Schuster, 'At the extremes of exclusion: deportation, detention and dispersal', *Ethnic and Racial Studies*, 28/3 (2005), 491–2.

59 T. Threadgold and S. Clifford, *Focus Groups with Refugees: Report to the Welsh Refugee Council* (Cardiff, 2005), p. 14.

60 Philo et al., *Bad News for Refugees*, pp. 37–45.

61 British Refugee Council, *Refugee Council Information: Detention in the Asylum System April 2013* (London, 2013), p. 2. See *http://www. refugeecouncil.org.uk/assets/0002/7333/130326Detention_in_the_ Asylum_System.pdf* (accessed 21 August 2014).

62 Tyler, *Revolting Subjects*, pp. 75–103; L. Weber, 'Down that wrong road: discretion in decisions to detain asylum seekers at airports', *The Howard Journal*, 42/3 (2003), 249.

63 Philo et al., *Bad News for Refugees* pp. 43–5; Institute of Race Relations, *Asylum Statistics*.

64 P. Barrera (ed.), *Seeking Sanctuary: Journeys of Despair and Hope* (Cardiff, 2011), p. 16.

65 M. Gibney, 'Asylum and the expansion of deportation in the United Kingdom', *Government and Opposition*, 43/2 (2008), 147; Philo et al., *Bad News for Refugees*, p. 43.

66 Z. Steele et al., 'Two year psychosocial and mental health outcomes for refugees subjected to restrictive or supportive immigration practices', *Social Science & Medicine*, 72 (2011), 1149–56.

67 Robinson et al., *Spreading the Burden?*, pp. 103–45.

68 Bloch and Schuster, 'At the extremes', 505–8.

69 Ibid.

70 Crawley and Crimes, *Refugees Living in Wales*, pp. 17–19.

71 Threadgold and Clifford, *Focus Groups with Refugees*, p. 56.

72 Ibid., p. 55.

73 T. Hewett, N. Smalley, D. Dunkerley and J. Scourfield, *Uncertain Futures: Children Seeking Asylum in Wales* (Cardiff, 2005) pp. 1–6.

74 Bloch and Schuster, 'At the extremes', 505–8.

75 Robinson, *Mapping the Field*, p. 7; BBC Wales, 'Caia Park race riot: "Big changes" seen in 10 years' (online edn, 21 June 2013), *http:// www.bbc.co.uk/news/uk-wales-north-east-wales-22978551* (accessed 21 November 2013).

76   Threadgold and Clifford, *Focus Groups with Refugees*, p. 58.

77   Crawley and Crimes, *Refugees Living in Wales*, p. 5; Threadgold and Clifford, *Focus Groups with Refugees*, pp. 17–20.

78   Threadgold and Clifford, *Focus Groups with Refugees*, pp. 54–8.

79   Ibid., p. 31.

80   Philo et al., *Bad News for Refugees*, p. 46.

81   Ibid., pp. 40, 46.

82   S. Reynolds, *Your Inflexible Friend: The Cost of Living without Cash*, British Refugee Council and Asylum Support Partnership (London, 2010). See *http://www.refugeecouncil.org.uk/assets/0001/7057/ASP_-_azurecard-v4.pdf* (accessed 21 August 2014).

83   Barrera, *Seeking Sanctuary*, p. 48.

84   M. Gillespie in Philo et al., *Bad News for Refugees*, p. 47.

85   K. Dorling, M. Girma and N. Walter, *Refused: The Experiences of Women Denied Asylum in the UK*, Women for Refugee Women (London, 2012), pp. 12–20.

86   H. Crawley, *Chance or Choice? Understanding Why Asylum Seekers Come to the UK* (London, 2010), p. 49.

87   Barrera, *Seeking Sanctuary*, p. 48.

88   Speers, *Welcome or Over Reaction?*, p. 33

89   Crawley and Crimes, *Refugees Living in Wales*, p. 27.

90   Threadgold et al., *Immigration and Inclusion in South Wales*, p. 32.

91   Crawley and Crimes, *Refugees Living in Wales*, p. 28.

92   Ibid.

93   Ibid., p. 27.

94   Ibid., p. 22.

95   Ibid.

96   G. Creese and B. Wiebe, '"Survival employment": gender and deskilling among African immigrants in Canada', *International Migration*, 50/5 (2012), 56–76; Threadgold and Clifford, *Focus Groups with Refugees*, pp. 38–53.

97   Crawley and Crimes, *Refugees Living in Wales*, p. 28.

98   Joseph Rowntree Foundation, *Monitoring Policy and Social Exclusion in Wales 2013* (York, 2013), p. 2.

99   Threadgold and Clifford, *Focus Groups with Refugees*, p. 76.

100 Ibid.

101 Tyler and Marciniak, 'Immigrant protest', 143–4; D. Però and J. Solomos, 'Introduction: migrant politics and mobilization: exclusion, engagements, incorporation', *Ethnic and Racial Studies*, 33/1 (2010), 2.

102 Tyler and Marciniak, 'Immigrant protest', 143.

103 Però and Solomos, 'Introduction', 14.

104 Welsh Assembly Government, *Refugee Inclusion Strategy* (Cardiff, 2008), p. ii.

105 WAG, *Refugee Inclusion Strategy Scoping Report*.

106 Wales Migration Partnership, *Enabling a Rights Based Approach to the Inclusion of Asylum Seekers, Refugees and Migrants in Wales: Strategic Objectives* (16 December 2012). See *http://www.wsmp.org.uk/Home.asp?id=SX136E-A77FEE67* (accessed 21 August 2014).

107 P. Aspinall and C. Watters, *Refugees and Asylum Seekers: A review from an Equality and Human Rights Perspective*, Equality and Human Rights Commission, research report 52 (Manchester, 2010), pp. 114–15. See *http://www.equalityhumanrights.com/uploaded_files/research/refugees_and_asylum_seekers_research_report.pdf* (accessed 21 August 2014).

108 Barrera, *Seeking Sanctuary*, pp. 11–49.

109 Independent Asylum Commission, *Citizens for Sanctuary Campaign to Make Independent Asylum Commission's Recommendations a Reality* (London, 2008). See *http://www.independentasylumcommission.org.uk/* (accessed 21 August 2014).

110 D. Papadopoulos and V. Tsianos, 'After citizenship: autonomy of migration, organizational ontology and mobile commons', *Citizenship Studies*, 17/2 (2013), 178–96.

111 Threadgold and Clifford, *Focus Groups with Refugees*, p. 14.

112 Dorling et al., *Refused*, pp. 14–15.

113 Hewett et al., *Uncertain Futures*, p. 36.

114 Maman and Muggeridge, *Best Practice Guide*, pp. 20–2.

115 For an extensive list of many of the groups active across Wales, see Welsh Refugee Council, *Refugee and Asylum Seekers Service Directory* (Cardiff, 2012), pp. 6–51.

116 Threadgold and Clifford, *Focus Groups with Refugees*, p. 31.

117 No Borders South Wales, 'Saleh Family – Action Report and Update'
     (Cardiff, 2012). See *http://noborderswales.wordpress.com/2012/10/26
     /saleh-family-action-report-and-update/* (accessed 21 August 2014).
118 Tyler and Marciniak, 'Immigrant protest', 143–4.
119 Threadgold and Clifford, *Focus Groups with Refugees*, p. 22.

13

Getting Involved: Public Policy Making and Political Life in Wales

PAUL CHANEY

Introduction

A quarter of a century ago a UK-wide study concluded that 'non-white access to the political agenda in Britain remains minimal and problematic'.[1] Contemporary analysis suggests that for some this is still the case. It states there remains 'worrying evidence that . . . citizens of Black Caribbean heritage do not feel that the British political system has treated them fairly . . . A just and well-functioning democracy requires that all citizens have fair access to the political arena'.[2] The academic literature also underlines that 'ethnicity is a social construct specific to a social and historical context';[3] thus a key question that this chapter will engage with is: how has devolution in Wales affected ethnic minorities' political engagement? This is an appropriate locus of enquiry not least because several of the 'big ideas' that underpinned constitutional reform were packaged in the buzzword 'inclusiveness'.[4] For ethnic minorities this was particularly resonant – for their experience of government in Wales had always been about exclusiveness and marginalization.[5]

In the 1980s and 1990s pro-devolutionists were keen to underline that constitutional reform presented the opportunity to address past failings. Thus, after the 1997 general election the Secretary of State for Wales pledged that 'ethnic and other minority issues should have a high profile in the National Assembly for Wales'.[6] Many doubted this, and few in Wales's ethnic communities were surprised when, subsequently, no black or Asian candidates were elected to the Assembly. As one black councillor put it: 'we knew this before the candidates ever went out for selection – unfortunately'. Centuries of political marginalization were not to be undone by inclusive rhetoric alone. However, leading politicians continued to make the case for a new relationship between ethnic groups and government. For example, just weeks after assuming office in May 1999, the new First Minister stated that 'the Assembly needs to address and relate to the aspirations and needs of black and ethnic minority communities throughout Wales ... I believe very strongly that we need to build the partnership with Black and ethnic minority groups.'[7]

Thus, if the public pronouncements of politicians are to be believed, devolution is about discontinuity with the past. Certainly the years since the Assembly began its work have brought seismic changes in the structures of governance, yet in respect of 'ethnic' participation they continue to present many questions. For example: what has been the nature of black and Asian people's involvement in the process of government? How do the measures taken by the political parties, Welsh Government and National Assembly measure up to the need to ensure effective participation from ethnic minorities? In attempting answers to these questions this chapter is structured as follows: first, it explores the political parties' records on ethnic minority representation; secondly, it examines ethnic minorities' engagement with the Welsh legislature and government; and thirdly, it discusses the findings in the context of current academic debate and thinking.

Political parties' record on ethnic minority representation

In this section we examine the record of the political parties with regard to how they shape black and minority ethnic political participation, specifically: (1) descriptive representation (this is sometimes called the 'politics of presence')[8] and refers to having black and minority ethnic individuals present as political representatives. This is an appropriate focus because, despite the major changes in the institutions and law making associated with devolution, ultimately it is the parties that determine the extent to which ethnic minorities participate in political life as elected representatives; and (2) using the concept of 'issue-salience' the following discussion also considers the attention that parties have afforded to policy needs of Wales's ethnic minorities in their election manifestos.[9] This is an important aspect of political participation because political theory asserts that the more an issue is emphasized by a party (making it 'salient'), the greater the probability it will engage voters who share concerns on the matter.[10] In turn, this affects black and ethnic minority turnout, accountability and the legitimacy of government.

According to the 2011 census the estimated black and ethnic minority population of Wales is approximately 4.3%.[11] Notwithstanding this fact (and the earlier political rhetoric on inclusion), the first two Assemblies (1999–2003 and 2003–7) had no black and ethnic minority Assembly Members (AMs). It took until 2007 for the first black and ethnic minority Assembly Member to be elected. In the fourth Assembly there are two black and ethnic minority Assembly Members (one born in Zambia, the other in Pakistan). This constitutes 3.3% of the total (and compares with 1.6% in the Scottish Parliament and 4.3% in the House of Commons).[12] It is a history that points to systemic failings on the part of the parties in Wales. It is confirmed by analysis of the candidates that the four main parties put forward at the 2011 elections. Just 2.7% of the total was from a black and ethnic minority background. Plaid Cymru[13] and the Welsh Liberal

Democrats[14] fielded one black and ethnic minority candidate a piece, Welsh Labour two,[15] and the Welsh Conservatives three.[16]

Analysis of internal party debates reveals awareness of the problem of black and ethnic minority under-representation, and in some quarters at least, a desire to address it. For example, Welsh Labour activists drafted the following resolution for the party's 2006 conference: 'not a single Assembly Member, nor any Member of Parliament representing a Welsh constituency, belongs to an ethnic minority. Conference believes that this situation undermines the legitimacy of both the Assembly and Parliament as bodies claiming to represent the people of Wales ...'[17] Successive initiatives have attempted to increase ethnic minorities' presence in parties. Prominent affirmative action measures include the Operation Black Vote shadowing scheme that ran in the National Assembly during 2007–8 (whereby black and ethnic minority people accompanied AMs and their staff in aspects of their work in order to gain greater understanding of their roles – and, it was hoped, would subsequently be encouraged to stand for office equipped with such knowledge), and the broadly similar Step Up Cymru scheme supported by the National Assembly and the Welsh Government in 2009–10.

Participants in the latter scheme spoke of it in a positive manner. One reflected: 'I think the mix of training and mentoring has made me much more aware of the opportunities that my community group can take to influence policy for the benefit of my community'; while another said: 'I came into this scheme with minimal knowledge of the political process. I came away from the scheme with a vast amount of knowledge, which now enables me to make choices and decisions relating to politics in a way I would never have thought before'.[18] Although participants' comments attest to the inherent value in such affirmative action initiatives, the schemes' small scale and limited duration limits their impact, and, as the academic literature suggests, crucially they fail to address the underlying cultural and structural causes of black and ethnic minority marginalization in contemporary politics.[19]

Another salient aspect of ethnic minorities' participation in political life is grounded in electoral politics. In setting out details of prospective policies, manifestos perform a multiplicity of functions. At one level they provide useful benchmarks of the progress made towards, and future aspirations for, 'race' equality and pluralism in public policy making.[20] Crucially, they also provide a yardstick by which to check parties' delivery on earlier promises in relation to 'substantive representation' – a term that, in this context, denotes advancing ethnic minorities' needs and wants in public policy making.[21] Manifesto attention matters not only in terms of equality and democracy but because, as a key study has underlined, 'ethnic minority voters accept that many issue areas have a latent race dimension to them'.[22] Thus, as noted, the political science literature on 'issue-salience' emphasizes that party programmes that include attention to the substantive representation of ethnic minorities probabilistically increase the propensity of black and ethnic minority communities to participate in political life via the ballot box.

Content analysis of party manifestos for the first devolved elections in 1998–9 shows that Wales lagged behind Northern Ireland and Scotland in the number of policy proposals on the representation of ethnic minorities (22.2% of the overall 'devolved'-elections total, compared with 53.7% and 24% respectively). In the first elections to the National Assembly for Wales party manifesto pledges related to a mean of just three policy areas per election (the two principal frames were anti-discrimination and participation in policy and decision making). There were statistically significant party differences in issue salience (or, as noted, in the amount of attention afforded to the substantive representation of ethnic minorities).[23] Plaid Cymru made most references (41.7% of the all-party total in the 1999 elections to the Assembly, compared with 33.3% for Welsh Labour and 25% for the Welsh Liberal Democrats). The Welsh Conservatives failed to make any proposals in their manifesto. Plaid's lead in the first devolved elections replicates the pattern in the other devolved nations where 'regionalist' parties also predominated (the Scottish National Party made 42% of the all-party total in Scotland; the Ulster Unionists 40% and the SDLP 60% in Northern Ireland). As noted, examination of the nature of the policy proposals in the 1999 vote reveals that ethnic minority participation in public and political life is a prominent trope in the discourse. For example, under the heading 'Liberal Democrats Wales' better government guarantees' it states that they would establish 'a Partnership Committee of members of minority ethnic communities and Assembly Members'.[24]

When the 2011 Welsh, Scottish and Northern Irish elections are compared with the 1999 vote a significant shift is apparent. The greatest number of policy proposals on the representation of ethnic minorities was made in the Welsh election (50% of the meso-level elections total), followed by the Scottish (32%) and Northern Irish (18%) ballots. In terms of party contribution, Labour advanced the greatest number of proposals in the Welsh elections (44.1% of all proposals) compared with the Welsh Liberal Democrats and Plaid Cymru (32.4% and 17.6% respectively). Again underlining a Left-Right cleavage, the Welsh Conservatives accounted for just 5.9% of the total. In the 2011 election greatest cross-party attention was afforded to proposals on 'race' equality for refugees and asylum seekers. Examples of this discourse include: 'Plaid's civic nationalism celebrates tolerance, mutual understanding and difference. We condemn the point-scoring used by other parties and the pandering to unfounded xeno-phobic prejudices in the debate on immigration'.[25] This was followed by promoting 'race' equality (for example, Welsh Labour 'want[s] to ensure that the different needs of people from different ethnic groups ... are recognised and catered for, especially in key public services such as education and social care').[26] When the 1998/9 and 2011 Welsh elections are compared, it is notable that there is a threefold increase in issue salience in the party programmes as a whole. Accordingly, this provides some evidence of a reprioritization of the substantive representation of ethnic minorities in devolved electoral politics.[27]

A 'participatory democracy'?[28]

In this section we explore four aspects of black and ethnic minority participation in policy making and political life: government funding of civil society organizations and policy networks; black and ethnic minority participation in public administration with reference to staff diversity at the National Assembly and Welsh Government; black and ethnic minority representation via two of the Assembly's institutional procedures purposively designed to foster inclusive governance (the Third Sector Partnership Council and the standing Committee on Equality of Opportunity); and civil society black and ethnic minority groups' experience of engaging in public policy making .

There has not been a post-national and universal norm that has driven political engagement and advanced the representation of ethnic minorities. Yet, viewed from an international perspective, legislative attempts to uphold 'race' equality and underpin ethnic minority participation in the conduct of public business are a common feature of contemporary governance. In this regard Wales is no exception. Examples derive from domestic legislation (UK/GB and Welsh statutes)[29] and international measures (such as European Commission Directives).[30] Despite this, progress has been limited. This can be seen in the number of black and ethnic minority people employed in the legislative and executive branches of government. In the case of the National Assembly for Wales Commission; in 2010–11, just 4.4% (or fifteen individuals from a staff of 343 people) identified themselves as being from an ethnic minority (this compares to 4% in the British civil service).[31] In turn, the Welsh Government has a worse record on staff diversity. In

2011–12, just 2.1% of the 5,000 employees that disclosed details of their ethnicity were 'non-white'.[32]

Recruitment data also suggest that under-representation is an issue that will take a significant period of time to address. For example, in 2011–12 just 1.7% of 1,400 applicants to externally advertised, non-senior civil service posts were from an ethnic minority.[33] Equally concerning is the fact that none of the 100 applicants to twenty-three externally advertised senior civil service posts was from an ethnic minority.[34] Such factors underpin the government's failure to meet its own staff diversity target (as set out in its earlier diversity delivery plan, circa 2008) for black and ethnic minority staff to constitute 3.1% of staff in the feeder grades and 2.5% in senior grades by 2008.[35]

The underlying causes of low levels of ethnic minority employment include communication issues. When asked about access to employment opportunities in the Assembly, interview data show that ethnic minority respondents 'did not regularly see ... jobs advertised, or know where to look for a job with the organisation'. Moreover, 'cultural awareness and equality of opportunity were [also identified as] important factors to encourage job applications from ethnic minority people'. In addition, 'the lack of visible ethnic minority staff, the need for specific qualifications, lengthy applications forms and discrimination and harassment' were also identified as potential barriers to applying for job, at the National Assembly.[36]

From the outset of devolution in Wales, successive administrations have espoused a 'mainstreaming' approach to 'race' and other modes of equality. For example, the current government's *Strategic Equality Plan and Objectives 2012–2016* is aimed at 'mainstreaming equality, human rights, diversity and inclusion across the Welsh Government'.[37] It is an approach internationally defined as 'the (re)organisation, improvement, development and evaluation of policy processes, so that an equality perspective is incorporated in all policies at all levels and at all stages'.[38] Contrasting models can be identified.[39] In Wales, the language employed in official strategies is broadly consistent with the participative-democratic model. This aims to move beyond traditional 'expert-bureaucratic' public administration (whereby key decisions are largely made by officials and the political elite) and encourage civil society organizations to advance equality claims on government through active participation in policy work.[40]

'Participation' here can be defined as the full range of formal and informal means employed by individuals and groups to influence the aims, scope, design and implementation of public policy.[41] In this regard the Welsh Government's mainstreaming strategy is unambiguous and states: 'good communication with relevant stakeholders is vital to successful policy making ... [officials need to] facilitate effective engagement and consultation'.[42] Latterly, this ambition that has been placed on a statutory footing for 'engagement' is one of the Wales-specific requirements of the public sector equality duty developed under the regulatory framework of the Equality Act 2010. This compels listed public bodies in Wales to

> involve people who it considers representative of one or more of the protected groups and who have an interest in how an authority carries out its functions ... engagement must take place in relation to setting equality objectives, preparing and reviewing a Strategic Equality Plan [... and] assessing the likely impact on protected groups of any policies or practices being proposed or reviewed'.[43]

In order to promote the political participation of ethnic minorities successive devolved administrations have invested significant sums of public money in developing policy networks and capacity among civil society organizations. Thus, for example, data for 2010/12 show that a total of twenty-five ethnic minority organizations received £6.65 million.[44] Such interventions engage with an enduring academic debate, namely whether government can intervene successfully to create or enhance policy-oriented social capital. The latter can be viewed as a democratic resource allied to pluralism. It refers to the norms and networks of trust and reciprocity that unite social groups in advancing policy claims on those in power. Critics argue that demand to engage in policy work is something that cannot be fostered by government action because it is 'organic', innate and embedded in communities. Yet, existing analysis of devolved governance in Wales indicates that there is some evidence that states that intervention of this type can facilitate the political participation of ethnic minority groups in civil society.[45] However, there are also key questions that attach to the extent, quality and sustainability of this participation.

It should also be noted that governments' pursuit of ethnic minority participation was dealt a significant blow by what a Welsh Government report described as 'fundamental weaknesses' in relation to a flagship consultative body, the All Wales Ethnic Minority Association (AWEMA). Over the years the Welsh Assembly Government's payments to AWEMA totalled £7.15 million, with a further £3.01 million having been committed in principle'.[46] Now dissolved, its core aims included the goal of fostering participation in the policy process and developing the capacity and skills of the multi-ethnic communities. Inter alia, subsequent official investigations have highlighted shortcomings in AWEMA's 'governance arrangements ... management; financial controls and processes; [and] an absence of key policies and procedures'. The foregoing developments have undermined trust and caused reputational damage to government efforts to encourage black and ethnic minority participation. In consequence, following the closure of AWEMA, a series of new Welsh Government funded bodies has been created including the Hindu Council of Wales[47] and the Wales Race Forum. Both were established in 2012–13. The latter was hailed by the Government as 'the start of a new two way process of engagement [... a] Forum [that] will help the Welsh Government to understand the key issues and barriers within black and ethnic minority communities and will enable the Welsh Government to engage on an on-going basis rather than just consulting on specific issues'.[48] The extent to which this ambition is realized will in large measure depend on whether appropriate lessons have been learned from the AWEMA debacle.

Neo-institutionalist analyses emphasize how the design of legislatures such as the National Assembly matter because they shape the nature and extent to which different groups are able to influence public policy making.[49] Accordingly, the Assembly has a series of mechanisms designed to foster the engagement of a diversity of social interests in policy making. These give an insight into black and ethnic minority engagement in the work of devolved government. The first example considered here is the Third Sector Partnership Council (TSPC). This is a forum aimed at fostering civil society participation and it stems from the statutory requirement that Ministers publish and lay before the Assembly a formal third sector scheme. Crucially, this states 'the goal is the creation of a civil society which has a duty to promote equality of opportunity to all its members'.[50] At its heart is a series of state-sponsored policy networks. These facilitate periodic meetings between sector representatives and government ministers. Analysis of the transcripts of the second Assembly reveals that, while the promotion of equalities took place in the majority of meetings, 'race' equality and the substantive representation of ethnic minorities only ranked fourth among equalities issues. It was discussed in under a third (29%) of meetings. In contrast, gender equality issues received the greatest attention (and were discussed in 40% of meetings), followed by disability (36%) and language (33%). Notwithstanding this, the deliberation on the substantive representation of ethnic minorities was wide-ranging in nature and included: voluntary sector concerns over schools' awareness of diversity matters ('especially within schools with a low number of black and ethnic minority pupils who sometimes refuse to report racial bullying when it occurs'),[51]

315

discussion of the need for government support for a 'race' equality network,[52] concerns over the standard of the government's Race Equality Scheme,[53] and the promotion of 'race' equality in healthcare.[54] On one level the TSPC provides some evidence of how devolution may institutionalize ethnic minority representation in policy work. Yet it is also the case that this nexus is bureaucratic in nature and, as noted, that the substantive representation of ethnic minorities has not secured as much attention as some other equalities issues.

The Assembly's equality committee was a further key institutional mechanism designed to secure progress against the earlier political rhetoric of inclusive governance (it was superseded by a revised committee structure following the 2011 elections). As a cross-party policy development forum it was concerned to scrutinize government and engage external interests in policy making. A key way in which the latter was achieved was through the calling of 'invitees' to give evidence and advice. Accordingly, analysis of who appeared before the committee over its twelve years of existence provides a valuable index of political participation. However, notwithstanding official acknowledgement by the Committee that 'members of Black and minority ethnic communities in Wales have a lot of advice to offer the Assembly and Members want to see their knowledge being fully utilised',[55] analysis of the transcripts and minutes of 126 meetings held during the life of the Committee (1999–2011) reveals that invitees from ethnic minority organisations attended just 9.5 per cent of meetings. Analysis of the transcripts and minutes of 126 meetings held during the life of the committee (1999–2011) reveals that invitees from ethnic minority organizations attended just 9.5% of meetings.[56] Discourse analysis of the committee proceedings reveals some civil servants lacked basic familiarity with 'race' equality issues and engaging with black and ethnic minority communities. For example:

> Staff in the Assembly w[ill] be fully involved in the consultation process [for the Assembly's 'race' equality scheme] to help their

understanding of the issues and facilitate more effective implementation of the scheme. The process was also designed to
enhance senior officials' understanding of what mainstreaming
racial equality really involved, and they w[ill] be attending
consultation events to engage directly with representatives of
the BME (black and minority ethnic) communities.[57]

Notwithstanding such issues, the data reveal that the committee had the potential to be an effective nexus between ethnic
minority organizations and AMs. Examples of this include
the appearance of a race equality network that made a powerful case to politicians to address a litany of equality issues
faced by people from ethnic minorities in north Wales. The
minutes of the meeting record state:

> It was reported that there was a lack of ethnic monitoring, no
> reliable statistics, a lack of investment in training of staff and
> politicians and numerous examples of institutional racism.
> The practice of local advertising of posts meant that they
> reached very few ethnic minorities and public bodies were not
> setting appropriate targets for dealing with these issues
> correctly ... public bodies were not recognising their failure
> in these areas and on the issue of racism generally ...[58]

Overall, and in contrast to the TSPC, analysis of the committee
proceedings shows that significant attention was paid to ethnic
minority representation. Its transcripts and minutes show that
such matters featured in almost three quarters (73%) of all
meetings (1999–2011). It is argued that the principal significance of this is that they reveal the limited nature of direct
ethnic minority participation in the first years of the Assembly,
even in the work of the one committee purpose-built to secure
such engagement. It shows that the Assembly generally
employed an 'expert-bureaucratic' model of mainstreaming
'race' equality, whereby decisions were largely determined by
the internal deliberations of the political elite. It also shows

ethnic engagement to be reliant on a small number of organizations. As such, the evidence here resonates with earlier work that concluded: 'far from promoting integration [such] frameworks may rather perpetuate a condition of institutionalised marginality'.[59] A further key point emerging from this study is that, while over its first decade the Assembly (and government) espoused participation and engagement with *civil* society, the evidence shows that in reality much of the engagement was with *civic* society. This distinction is a crucial one. The former is comprised of community and voluntary groups. The latter is part of (or closely associated with) the state.

Earlier work has thrown some light upon the reasons why black and ethnic minority policy engagement has been so limited.[60] It has highlighted an information gap for 'the majority of ethnic minority people questioned were not ... aware of how to find information about the National Assembly and how to contact Assembly Members'. Despite academic work highlighting the democratizing potential of communication technologies,[61] a significant number of black and ethnic minority groups 'did not have the internet or the skills to use it. Those that had used [the Assembly's] website, found it too formal and not very user-friendly'. Yet there was also a call for 'more outreach work with ethnic minority people [this, it was felt,] was necessary to increase understanding of the work of the National Assembly and to encourage people to apply for jobs within the organisation'. It is also the case that, with the noted exception of one ethnic minority AM, 'few respondents were aware of local AMs' surgeries, most did not know how to contact their Assembly Member. Many [said that they] only see their AM during election campaigns'. The political science literature also emphasizes the role of effective communication in underpinning participation,[62] in this regard the evidence suggests that further work remains following devolution. Asked about access to National Assembly proceedings some said that they had watched Assembly business in the Senedd but 'many were not aware that they could, or thought it too inaccessible'. Moreover, despite law-makers' efforts to employ new means to reach out, among the black and ethnic minority organizations 'there was very little knowledge about web-casting or the petitioning system'.

Interviews, the internal literature of civil society organizations and research studies reveal further insights into ethnic minorities' views on engagement in politics and policy making. They show a general level of frustration in attempts to get 'race' equality on the policy agenda.[63] One disaffected interviewee spoke of 'business as usual ... being given the same old run-around when you try and talk to some of them [that is, politicians], unreturned calls – the regular stuff'.[64] Another said, 'I question what difference it's made [that is, devolution], I know folk who feel let down ... there were hopes in the early days, but I don't think they [politicians/policy-makers] want to listen'.[65] Another spoke of 'being left behind ... right now I think we've fallen back, you get the impression ... some groups have made gains – we were already behind ... that gap's grown'.[66] Such views raise questions about the impact of mainstreaming strategies on the most marginalized equalities constituencies such as ethnic communities. The heart of this issue lies in a conceptual tension, namely as to 'whether and to what extent the notion of sameness (e.g. equal participation) and difference (special action ...) [are] included in ... mainstreaming strategies'.[67] The need for effective engagement was outlined by one organization thus: 'groups which are empowered are able to do so on their own terms and contribute ... Disempowered groups need support so that they do not end up being folded back into project types which reflect and serve the ways of life of other mainstream groups'.[68]

Others expressed concerns about under-representation in public life in a manner that links to existing work on the importance of the descriptive representation of ethnic minorities.[69] Thus, the manager of a non-governmental organization (NGO) complained: 'we campaigned so hard to have a Black woman elected, that did not happen ... for our members

that's a massive setback'.[70] A further concern expressed by
one black and ethnic minority policy network centred on the
way that government engaged with them: 'when consulta-
tions are undertaken and the exercise is complete, no attempt
is made to feed back on the findings . . . This is absolutely
necessary to ensure transparency and accuracy of reporting.'[71] Another black and ethnic minority organization was
highly critical of what it saw as pervasive inequalities in
power and resources associated with its experience of partic-
ipating in the work of government:

> 'Partnership' has become rhetoric for the Welsh Assembly
> Government . . . to order to justify control and the distribu-
> tion of limited funding. It seems to also be fashionable to talk
> about 'partnership work'. However, effective partnerships are
> not evidenced, resulting in disillusion and apathy of smaller
> community groups. Key policy and decision-makers must
> realise the reality of community work through effectively
> listening to those from a grassroots level and ensure effective
> evaluation of all partnership work.[72]

Another manager made a similar point: 'there is insufficient
support afforded to local groups. Through practical engagement with local groups we see them struggling to survive simply
because they are neglected and marginalized because of the lack
of resources and support mechanisms.'[73] An additional point is
'that because many BME organisations are comparatively small,
some of the capacity issues . . . apply disproportionately to
them'. A further concern was the dearth of official data:

> there has been limited or no statistical information relating to
> ethnic minority women and the number of women who have
> accessed, and are continually benefiting from, the ethnic
> minority women's voluntary sector and the services provided
> in Wales. It is therefore argued that greater efforts must be
> made by the Welsh Assembly Government.[74]

Aside from this plethora of concerns there is also evidence that black and ethnic minority groups demand to participate in political life and policy making. For example, one organization argued that it is 'imperative [the Welsh Government] play a key role in determining the direction of future activities and directives in relation to developing a stronger engagement with Muslim communities'.[75] This organiszation's manager added: 'greater effort needs to be made to reach ... local project workers and community members. WAG needs to reassess the way it reaches Muslim communities and consider alternative and non-traditional methods of engagement.'[76]

Discussion

Some earlier studies suggest that 'certain issues are conditioned by ethnic and racial components, [such that] minorities in Britain have formed a consciousness of solidarity'.[77] While this may be the case, it is also true that in Wales ethnic mobilization remains weak and fragmented. There has not been sustained political activism spanning ethnic minority groups and centred on the new, national tier of Welsh Government. While governance practices in twenty-first century Wales are more democratic and transparent than in the pre-devolution era, the institutional mechanisms to engage a diversity of social interests in policy making have only made modest gains. Similarly, successive governments' attempts to boost social capital among ethnic minorities and encourage participation in policy making have had mixed results. The views of civil society organizations suggest a demand to be involved. Yet they also point to communication barriers and limited awareness of how to engage. A further problem is that ethnic minority communities themselves are not immune to the same pathologies that undermine the effectiveness of other groups in civil society. These include internal divisions founded on mistrust, ineffective organizational leadership and the negative consequences of competition for power, influence and resources.

In terms of symbolic politics,[78] the parties' poor record on the number of black and ethnic minority candidates and AMs is a major disappointment. Weighed against the inclusive rhetoric of the 1990s it marks a singular failure to secure necessary cultural change.[79] It also has practical implications for 'substantive policy can be communicated, implemented, or averted by symbolic politics'. Thus the number of Black and Asian elected representatives is significant because they are probabilistically more likely than their parliamentary peers to advance the interests of ethnic minorities when making policy and law.[80] Accordingly, the presence of just two black and ethnic minority Assembly Members restricts opportunities for the positive benefits that descriptive representation can bring. Specifically, the way in which black and ethnic minority representatives can act as catalysts for change and enrich and inform political debate by drawing on first-hand, situated knowledge of 'race' issues.

In electoral politics there has been a degree of progress in the form of a threefold increase in the issue salience of ethnic minorities in the policy programmes of the parties of the Left. The significance of this is its potential impact on ethnic minority participation via the ballot box. The latter outcome is explained by mandate and accountability theories.[81] Both are fundamentally concerned with the connection between political representation and policy responsiveness.[82] Thus, mandate theory asserts that when in government parties should implement the policies that they promised when running for office. According to this view, party programmes in liberal democracies should feature proposals aimed at meeting the needs of all ethnic groups. It is a relationship underlined by accountability theory that asserts that elections are, in practice, 'opinion polls' on the performance and policy record of the party or parties forming the previous administration. Notwithstanding this, it is also the case that the modest gains made by the parties of the Left are negated by the scant attention the Welsh Conservatives have paid to ethnic minority issues.

The post-1999 period also links with debates over liberal versus legislative mainstreaming regimes. Weighed against the inclusive rhetoric that accompanied the creation of the National Assembly – and, importantly the heightened expectations of black and ethnic minority communities at that time[83] – progress can again be judged disappointing. A liberal mainstreaming context has prevailed whereby successive administrations' espousal of ethnic minority participation has not progressed far beyond the discursive sphere. Many of the measures to foster participation have been discretionary in nature (such as funding ethnic minority civil society organizations and policy networks). They have not been backed by legally enforceable rights to participate in policy making. Potentially, the 'engagement clause' in the Welsh public sector equality duty introduced in 2011 offers the prospect of change for it provides a legal route to challenge public bodies, including government, should they fail to secure the participation of black and minority ethnic people in the exercise of public functions.

In attempting to assess progress it should be noted that the move to devolved government has provided the means to resist Westminster policies that may have a negative impact on 'race' equality and ethnic participation in a way that was not previously possible. A recent example is the Welsh Government's commitment to retain equality impact assessments (EIAs). These are a technical policy tool that requires policy-makers to identify and avoid any potentially negative impact that new policies might have on ethnic minorities. Crucially, this is to be done via direct engagement with black and ethnic minority groups themselves.[84] In 2013 EIAs were abolished by the centre-Right UK government at Westminster, yet retained in Wales, a decision lauded by the Wales Race Forum as 'beneficial for all endeavouring to ensure racial equality'.[85] However, EIAs also point to a wider issue, namely the need for an effective equalities monitoring and enforcement regime. Here it should be noted that the regulatory authority, the Equality and Human Rights Commission, has been subject to significant funding cuts over recent years. These are unlikely to have left its regulatory capacity unaffected.

Overall, while it would be unrealistic to expect that, in a little under a decade-and-a-half, all aspects of the centuries-old marginalization of ethnic minorities would be swept away, it is the case that devolution is transforming aspects of governance in Wales. There is limited evidence that new institutional structures and the territorialization of electoral politics have the potential to promote substantive representation and foster the participation of ethnic minorities. However, the inescapable reality is that progress to date has been disappointing. An expert-bureaucratic rather than participatory-democratic model of mainstreaming 'race' equality has prevailed and ethnic minority participation in political life remains limited. Policy making has often been determined by the deliberations of the political elite and been overly reliant on engagement with civic rather than civil society. This is a key concern. Vibrant democracy depends on political engagement with *civil* society because it enhances accountability, legitimacy and trust – as well as being more responsive to citizen needs in conditions of increasing social diversity. If allowed to endure, the practices seen to date will perpetuate a condition of institutionalized marginality for ethnic minorities. The challenge is to learn from the Assembly's first years and take swift action to address the issues discussed in this chapter and broaden and deepen participation in public policy making and political life.

Notes

1   D. Studlar and Z. Layton-Henry, 'Non-white minority access to the political agenda in Britain', *Review of Policy Research*, 9/2 (1989), 273–93.

2   A. Heath and O. Khan, *Ethnic Minority British Election Study* (London, 2002), pp. 1–2.

3 R. Afkhami, *Ethnicity: Introductory User Guide: ESDS Government* (Manchester, 2012).

4 P. Chaney and R. Fevre, 'Ron Davies and the cult of "inclusiveness": devolution and participation in Wales', *Contemporary Wales*, 14 (2001), 131–46.

5 C. Williams, 'Race and racism: some reflections on the Welsh context', *Contemporary Wales*, 8 (1995), 113–33.

6 R. Davies, 'Shaping the vision', *Red Kite* (June 1995), 14–17.

7 Alun Michael in a speech at the launch of the All Wales Ethnic Minority Association, Pierhead Building, Cardiff, 24 July 1999.

8 See A. Phillips, *The Politics of Presence* (Oxford, 1995).

9 The classic text here is D. RePass, 'Issue salience and party choice', *American Political Science Review*, 65 (1971), 389–400.

10 D. Robertson, *A Theory of Party Competition* (New York, 1976).

11 This is the proportion of 'non-white' respondents to the census and includes people with mixed and multiple ethnic heritages. See Office for National Statistics, *2011 Census: KS201EW Ethnic Group*, Local Authorities in England and Wales (2012), *http://www.ons.gov.uk/ons/publications/re-reference-tables.html?newquery=*&newoffset=0&pageSize=25&edition=tcm%3A77-286262* (accessed 8 June 2013).

12 Cf. R. Cracknell and House of Commons, *Ethnic Minorities in Politics, Government and Public Life*, Standard Note: SN/SG/1156, Social and General Statistics Section, 5 January 2012 (London, 2012), p. 4.

13 Victor Babu.

14 Liz Musa.

15 Vaughan Gething; Mari Rees.

16 Natasha Asghar; Mohammad Asghar; Altaf Hussain.

17 Welsh Labour Grassroots: Gwreiddiau Llafur Cymru, *WLG Newsletter*, 4 (December 2005/January 2006), p. 2.

18 National Assembly for Wales Commission, *Step Up Cymru Mentoring Scheme: Evaluation Report* (Cardiff, 2011), p. 32.

19 Cf. P. Chaney, *Equality and Public Policy* (Cardiff, 2011).

20 R. Pelizzo, 'Party positions or party direction? An analysis of party manifesto data', *West European Politics*, 26(2) (2003), 67–89.

21 S. Tamale, *When Hens Begin to Crow: Gender and Parliamentary Politics in Uganda* (Boulder, 1999).

22 S. Saggar, *Race and Representation: Electoral Politics and Ethnic Pluralism in Britain* (Manchester, 2000).

23 P= <0.001, Chi Squared = 26.0; df = 2; p= 0.00000226

24 Welsh Liberal Democrats, *Guarantee Delivery: Liberal Democrat Manifesto for the National Assembly for Wales* (Cardiff, 2009), p. 6.

25 Plaid Cymru, *Ambition is Critical: A Manifesto for a Better Wales* (Cardiff, 2011), p. 19.

26 Welsh Labour, *Standing Up for Wales* (Cardiff, 2011), p. 64.

27 As such it is consistent with international studies of the impact of devolution on other marginalized groups – see, for example, C. Ortbals, M. Rincker and C. Montoya, 'Politics close to home: the impact of meso-level institutions on women in politics', *Publius*, 42(1) (2012), 78–107.

28 National Assembly Advisory Group, *National Assembly Advisory Group Recommendations* (Cardiff, 1998), p. 6, paras 1.09, 1.10. Also P. Hain, *A Welsh Third Way?* (London, 1999).

29 Such as the Equality Act 2010 and the earlier Race Relations (Amendment) Act 2000.

30 Racial Equality Directive 2000/43/EC.

31 A further 5% (seventeen staff) chose not to identify themselves against any specific group. Request for information disclosure ref. 328, April 28 2011, *http://www.assemblywales.org/abthome/abt-nafw/abt-foi/disclosure-log-month-view/ati_328_-_response_redacted.pdf?langoption=3&ttl=The%20position%20of%20Black%20and%20Ethnic%20Minorities%20staff* (accessed 1 June 2013).

32 Welsh Government (WG), *Welsh Government: Employer Equality Report, 2011–2012* (Cardiff, 2012), p. 35. (Total: 5,330. Of these 200 said 'prefer not to say' and 130 did not respond to the survey.) The issue of double counting is acknowledged here (Welsh Government civil servants are also included in the British civil service total – yet the latter employs 460,000 staff, thus the relative proportion of BME staff is unlikely to be significantly affected).

33 Sixty did not disclose their ethnicity. See WG, *Employer Equality Report, 2011–2012*, p. 26.

34 Ten did not disclose their ethnicity. See ibid., p. 28.

35 WAG, *Race Equality Scheme Action Plans (Revised) – All Departments (2006–2008)* (Cardiff, 2008), p. 74.

36 National Assembly for Wales Commission, *Equality Scheme 2008-2011: Summary of Responses to the Consultation and Involvement Exercise* (Cardiff, 2008) p. 74.

37 WG, *Strategic Equality Plan and Objectives 2012–2016* (Cardiff, 2012), p. 114.

38 Council of Europe, *Gender Mainstreaming: Conceptual Framework Methodology and Presentation of Good Practices* (Strasbourg, 2008), unpaginated.

39 T. Barnett Donaghy, 'Mainstreaming: Northern Ireland's participative democratic approach', *Policy and Politics*, 32 (1) (2003), 49–62.

40 S. Nott, 'Accentuating the positive: alternative strategies for promoting gender equality', in F. Beveridge, S. Nott and K. Stephen (eds), *Making Women Count: Integrating Gender into Law and Policymaking* (Aldershot, 2000), pp. 247–76.

41 B. Hogwood and L. Gunn, *Policy Analysis for the Real World* (Oxford, 1984).

42 WAG, *Mainstreaming Strategy* (Cardiff, 2006), pp. 7–12.

43 Equality and Human Rights Commission, *The Essential Guide to the Public Sector Equality Duty: An Overview for Listed Public Authorities in Wales* (Cardiff, 2011), p. 6.

44 Ministerial answer to written Assembly question WAQ61409. See *http://www.assemblywales.org/bus-home/bus-business-fourth-assembly-written-questions/gwyych20121026-2.pdf?langoption=3&ttl=Information%20Further%20to%20WAQ61409%20%28PDF%2C%20235KB%29* (accessed 19 August 2014).

45 For a discussion see P. Chaney, 'Social capital and the participation of marginalized groups in government: a study of the statutory partnership between the third sector and devolved government in Wales', *Public Policy and Administration*, 17, 4 (2003), 22–39.

46 Wales Audit Office, *The Welsh Government's Relationship with the All Wales Ethnic Minority Association* (Cardiff, 2012), p. 18.

47 See *http://wales.gov.uk/newsroom/equalityanddiversity/2013/130415-hindu-council-wales/?lang=en* (accessed 28 May 2013).

Paul Chaney

48 See *http://wales.gov.uk/topics/equality/rightsequality/race/walesrace-forum/?lang=en* (accessed 8 June 2013).

49 E. Clemens and J. Cook, 'Politics and institutionalism: explaining durability and change', *Annual Review of Sociology*, 25 (1999), 441–66: 'the analysis of institutional change rests on an appreciation of the heterogeneity of institutional arrangements and the resulting patterns of conflict or prospects for agency and innovation' (p. 460).

50 National Assembly for Wales, *Voluntary Sector Scheme* (Cardiff, 2000), p. 7.

51 6 February 2006.

52 19 May 2005.

53 15 November 2004.

54 14 November 2004; 18 July 2007.

55 quality of Opportunity Committee, *Minutes* (EOC(2)-03-05), 17 March 2005, Para 3.12.

56 This ignores the attendance at each meeting of representatives of the Commission for Racial Equality (and its successor body, the Equality and Human Rights Commission) as 'standing invitees' – a practice that ended in 2007.

57 Committee on Equality of Opportunity, *Minutes*, EOC(2)03-03 (2 October 2003), para. 3.1: 'Race Equality Scheme'.

58 Committee on Equality of Opportunity, *Minutes*, EOC-04-01 (9 May 2001), presentation by North Wales Race Equality Network (NWREN).

59 D. Griffith, N. Sigona and R. Zetter, 'Integrative paradigms: marginal reality – refugee community organisations and dispersal in Britain', *Journal of Ethnic and Migration Studies*, 15(4) (2006), 501–18.

60 National Assembly for Wales Commission, *Equality Scheme 2008–2011: Summary of Responses to the Consultation and Involvement Exercise* (Cardiff, 2008), p. 78. Subsequent attention has been paid to some of these issues.

61 R. K. Gibson, P. G. Nixon and S. J. Ward, *Political Parties and the Internet: Net Gain?* (London, 2003).

62 Cf. J. Mcleod, D. Scheufele and P. Moy, 'Community, communication, and participation: the role of mass media and interpersonal

discussion in local political participation', *Political Communication*, 16 (3) (1999), 315–36.

63 For a discussion see P. Chaney, 'New legislative settings and the application of the participative-democratic model of mainstreaming equality in public policy making: evidence from the UK's devolution programme', *Policy Studies*, 33, 5 (2012), 455–76.

64 Interview, 4 September 2007.

65 Interview, 7 July 2003.

66 Interview, 4 November 2008.

67 L. Mósesdóttir and R. Erlingsdóttir, 'Spreading the word across Europe', *International Feminist Journal of Politics*, 7(4) (2005), 513–31.

68 Black Environment Network, *Working with Black Environment Network for Ethnic Participation and Representation: Summary of a Presentation by BEN to the National Assembly for Wales* (n.d.).

69 A. Krizsán and V. Zentai, 'Gender equality policy or gender mainstreaming?', *Policy Studies*, 27, 2 (2007) 135–51, 136.

70 Interview, 23 April 2004.

71 Independent Commission to Review the Voluntary Sector Scheme, *Final Report* (Cardiff, 2004), p. 48.

72 Minority Ethnic Women's Network [MEWN] Cymru, *Voices from Within Report* (Cardiff, 2007), p. 36.

73 Independent Commission to Review the Voluntary Sector Scheme, *Final Report*, p. 36.

74 MEWN Cymru, *Voices from Within Report*, p. 51.

75 All Wales Saheli Association/Welsh Assembly Government, *Muslim Women Talk Wales Project Report* (Cardiff, 2006), p. 4.

76 Ibid.

77 M. Kittilson and K. Tate, *Political Parties, Minorities and Elected Office: Comparing Opportunities for Inclusion in the U.S. and Britain* (Oxford, 2004), pp. 1–21, p. 7.

78 U. Sarcinelli, 'Symbolic politics', in W. Donsbach (ed.), *The International Encyclopaedia of Communication* (Oxford, 2008), pp. 165–8.

79 A. Brysk, '"Hearts and Minds": bringing symbolic politics back in', *Polity*, 27, 4 (1995), 559–85.

80 P. Chaney, 'Critical actors vs. critical mass: the substantive representation of women in the Scottish Parliament', *The British Journal of Politics & International Relations*, 14 (2012), 441–57.

81 See, for example, T. Royed, 'Testing the mandate model in Britain and in the United States: evidence from the Reagan and Thatcher eras', *British Journal of Political Science*, 26(1) (2006), 56–69; J. Fearon, 'Electoral accountability and the control of politicians: selecting good types versus sanctioning poor performance', in A. Przeworski, S. C. Stokes and B. Manin (eds), *Democracy, Accountability, and Representation* (Cambridge, 2003), pp. 55–98.

82 J. Stimson, 'Party government and responsiveness', in A. Przeworski, S. C. Stokes and B. Manin (eds), *Democracy, Accountability, and Representation* (Cambridge, 2003), pp. 68–81.

83 See C. Williams and P. Chaney, 'Inclusive government for excluded groups: ethnic minorities', in P. Chaney. T. Hall and A Pithouse (eds), *New Governance – New Democracy?, Post-Devolution Wales* (Cardiff, 2001), pp. 78–101.

84 They were developed in 2005 (in cooperation with the then Commission for Racial Equality) and have been subsequently updated, under the title 'Inclusive Policymaking Guidance'.

85 See *http://wales.gov.uk/topics/equality/rightsequality/race/walesrace-forum/?lang=en* (accessed 8 June 2013).

14

Claiming the National: Nation, National Identity and Ethnic Minorities

CHARLOTTE WILLIAMS

In over a decade of devolution Welshness has been reclaimed and reworked in new and interesting ways. Debates about nation and national identity may have always been a Welsh preoccupation but devolution has served to focus them more sharply in academic research and writing, in the arts and literature and in the public consciousness. The achievement of a measure of self-governance by a small but highly self-conscious nation was bound to carry symbolic significance in terms of Welsh identity, perhaps more so than the disruptions of constitutional reform itself. Counter narratives have emerged that have challenged dominant versions of Welsh national identity and served to complicate the easy English/Welsh divide that has so significantly framed ethno-cultural relations. The cultural space has been opened up to contestation from a number of angles, not least to accommodate the social, cultural, political and economic contributions of ethnic minorities. There has undoubtedly been a perceptible shift in the ways in which nation is portrayed and imagined post devolution and the ideas of Welsh tolerance once so central to an understanding of national character, and which engaged us in the first edition of this book, have been consistently challenged.

Wales is a divided nation. It is also a diverse nation. The two are not synonymous. Long-standing cleavages between north

331

and south, east and west, urban/rural, Welsh-speaking/English-speaking, indigenous/in-migrant, working class/'taffia' are cleavages that mark the experiences of ethnic minority communities as well as the majority population. This differentiation inevitably raises a number of questions about Welsh nationhood and identity. On what basis do we invest in Wales as a nation-state? How is nation discussed and realized? What are the dominant conceptions of Welshness? Can and do ethnic minority communities claim any sense of belonging and ownership to the nation? What is it that binds us other than the border of Offa's Dyke? The ways in which these issues are debated and addressed tell the story of how multiculturalism is being fashioned and developing in the part self-governing Wales.

Understanding nation as a site of attachment and belonging for ethnic minorities has been much discussed in relation to the broader reframing of Britishness.[1] In debating the *Future of Multi-Ethnic Britain*, for example, Bikhu Parekh argued for a re-imagining of the national story,[2] demonstrating the ways in which a multi-ethnic, multi-faith Britain required a reconceptualization of nation itself. What is less considered are the ways in which these issues are played out for black and ethnic minorities at the level of the sub-state nation. Indeed the assumption of many prominent multicultural theorists at the time of devolution was that constitutional change was set to disenfranchise such dispersed minorities from the 'black' constituency and further marginalize their identity claims.[3] Parekh, however, did ask the provocative question of a multi-national Britain: what do the separate countries stand for?[4] This spur was to some thinking about how these nations, Scotland, Ireland and Wales, would re-imagine themselves. Would they be able to square the claims of ethnic nationalism on which so much of the devolutionary imperative rested with the realities of contemporary multiculturalism?

One of the clear implications of devolution was the opportunity to rework discourses of race and ethnicity, to reconfigure the narrative of nation and national identity and to re-imagine Wales in deliberate and conscious ways rather than as a product of drift or uncontested 'common sense'. This was acknowledged at the outset.

Ron Davies, the recognized architect of the National Assembly for Wales, declared:

> Once the Assembly is established it must reflect the diversity and plurality of Welsh social, political and cultural life. By doing that we will have a greater status for the Assembly as a national institution; we can give a clearer focus for the development of our Welsh sense of identity.[5]

In 1999 Paul Murphy, the then Secretary of state for Wales, spoke of:

> a new sense of citizenship – where the Bangladeshi community in Swansea and the Somali community in Cardiff have the same stake in our new democratic Wales as it has for me, the great grandson of Irish immigrants ... who crossed the Irish sea 130 years ago, looking for a better life in Wales.[6]

This chapter considers how these issues have played out. It considers the impact of attempts to reframe ideas about Welshness and national identity. It asks whether proximities of scale have had an effect on ethnic minorities' sense of belonging and identity and concludes with some consideration of the state of play of Welsh multiculturalism. The concluding argument suggests that in many respects we may have gone for the easy win, foregrounding issues of identity claims over the deeper and more troubling issues of ethnic inequalities.

Challenges to the tolerance thesis

A central theme of this book has been the tolerance thesis that at its heart proposes Wales as somehow distinct by reference at least to its immediate neighbour in terms of the nature of public attitudes to immigrants and minorities. This thesis suggests the national character as welcoming and egalitarian and by extension positions Wales as more receptive to immigration than other parts of Britain and as more accommodating of difference and diversity. Wales is not alone in this type of claim; indeed the other Celtic nations have similarly proclaimed such sentiments, often without empirical testing of the reality underpinning these claims.

Ideas of tolerance and inclusion have featured highly in the Welsh government's progressive political agenda. In *One Wales*[7] and more recently in *Getting on Together: A Community Cohesion Strategy for Wales*[8] the government commits to the promotion of Wales as a bilingual and multicultural society. The Welsh Government has taken active steps to promote civic and inclusive conceptions of nation and national identity via such policies, via political speech making and via the celebration of a vibrant multiculture as part of the cultural life of Wales. The symbols and tone of early proclamations to inclusiveness have been actively translated into a number of explicit policy measures to reflect engagement with the principles of progressive universalism (see chapter 10). Yet multiculturalist policies, important as they are in providing the framework for change, are not the only touchstone and in post-devolution Wales evidence has been emerging to qualify the tolerance claims.

Perhaps the most noticeable exception in populist claims to tolerance relates to anti-English attitudes. What is perhaps surprising in relation to the tolerance thesis is the extent to which this latter type of sentiment *is* justified and tolerated. The English are by far the biggest ethnic grouping in Wales and sustained and significant levels of in-migration mean they continue to command considerable political attention. English monoglot speakers form over 80% of the Welsh population and while two thirds of the Welsh describe themselves as Welsh this is in a context in which almost a third of the population were born outside Wales, mostly in England.[9] The legacy is that some 40% of today's total Welsh population were either born in England or have one parent born in England.

English/Welsh conflict has surfaced regularly on the political agenda, from debates about the 2001 census categories when the identification 'Welsh' was denied to ongoing debates about English colonization and transformation of the socio-linguistic nature of rural Wales. This latter debate in particular has served to heat up the boundaries of the English/Welsh axis to the extent that this divide has been viewed as 'racialized' and has drawn heavily on the conceptual framework of race talk.[10] As Mann and Tommis pertinently observe:

> Occasional flares bring these debates into the public arena. . . .
> These debates clearly indicate that the 'race problem' in Wales
> is not defined simply in terms of colour, as is the case else-
> where in the UK, but significantly on the front of the generalized
> 'other' as English or English-speaking.[11]

It is of note that the police forces in Wales include English/Welsh animosities as part of racially motivated crime statistics. Nowhere else in the UK is this the case.

The heated nature of these debates has not dissipated in the post-devolution era. Mann and Tommis's study, for example, investigating public sentiments towards different types of immigrants and minorities, notes that those respondents with more 'narrow' interpretations of national identity display greater opposition to immigration of all kinds.[12]

There is passing reference to the nature of these ethno-cultural relationships in a plethora of studies, most notably as they relate to issues of Welsh language and culture. The interface of the so-called 'language issue' with race issues has a particularly uncomfortable history.[13] The language issue has served in the past to deflect attention away from issues of race on the political agenda, which in turn fuelled the myth that 'there is no problem here' in terms of race relations. It is not

---

surprising that this terrain has been fraught. A number of factors contributed to some considerable confusion over the issues. Prior to the first Welsh Language Act 1993 and the establishment of the Welsh Language Board, the main mechanism for settling disputes of language discrimination was the Race Relations Act 1976. This piece of legislation was always found wanting in relation to the satisfaction of claims, not least because it was seen to be fuzzy over the fundamental issue of whether the Welsh were indeed a race or not,[14] an issue that was often interpreted as a denial of a separate identity. This institutional mechanism in itself was responsible for contributing to the construction of the language debate within racialized terminology. In the absence of any other discourse, this became the way to view the issue and offered the terms with which to discuss it.

Alongside this, there is evidence, both historically and in contemporary Wales, to suggest that in popular imagining the oppression of the Welsh was frequently paralleled with the plight of the black man.[15] This parallel was typically used as a type of shorthand concept for depicting the exploitation of the Welsh by the English not simply in economic terms but also in the negative perceptions of the Welsh by the English as 'dark strangers'. Note, in this vein, controversy over A. A. Gill's description of the Welsh as 'ugly pugnacious trolls',[16] and in 2001, the outcry over the BBC broadcaster Ann Robinson commenting that the Welsh are 'useless'.[17] Again this serves to invite the use of racist and emotive terminology. It is well known that the nationalist organization Cymdeithas yr Iaith Gymraeg frequently used the term 'white settlers' to describe English incomers, explicitly evoking racist categories in which the Welsh white majority are aligned with the 'black' oppressed. The legacy of these tendencies is that valid concerns over threats to the vibrancy of small Welsh communities in terms of protecting a minoritized culture and language have been overlaid with all the imagery, fears, threats and terminology of racism in the way that the problem is both perceived and described. This type of discourse constructs 'the Welsh' and 'the Welsh community' as fixed and immutable both culturally and linguistically and in the antipathy towards the *other* – the English are also constructed as a monolithic block. Within this bilinear construction of 'us' and 'them', there existed little space to locate black and ethnic minorities. They were destined to become neither English, nor Welsh – just an inconvenient complexity to the debate.[18]

The incomer debates, most specifically as applied to the more rural areas of Wales, have a number of spin-offs for any discussion of race and national identity in Wales. First, they present a homogeneous and static picture of the Welsh community. It can be argued that communities in Wales, and indeed in rural Wales, are much more internally diverse than is purported and sustained in these arguments (see chapter 9) and that they are subject to wider forces of economic development, globalization and Europeanization in changing their demographic profile. They cannot and will not stand still in the ways we may wish in order to preserve linguistic enclaves – other mechanisms will be needed to counter the impacts on linguistic integrity of migrations in and out. The movement of labour, considerable youth out-migration, the dispersal of asylum seekers and other 'push and pull' factors of geographical mobility will necessarily affect Welsh communities. Secondly, this discourse has a tendency not only to present an idea of Welsh national identity in fixed and static ways but also to contribute to widely internalized ideas about 'proper' Welsh identities and cast other claims as somehow spoiled or lacking. Too often the word 'Welsh' has been used synonymously to denote Welsh speaker, both in popular and political parlance, leaving the non-Welsh-speaking Welsh with 'not', 'lost' or 'apologized' identities. Ideas of 'Welsh Wales' that have been academically demarcated on the basis of empirical evidence[19] feed into everyday ideas about who belongs and who does not belong, who can settle and who cannot. The bipolar nature of the incomer debates has served to deny the complexity and variety of Welsh identities. A study by Day, Davis and Drakakis-Smith[20] is significant in this respect in that it directly sought to explore the impact of English migration in a geographical patch of Wales commonly regarded as the Welsh heartland. This work serves to challenge and make complex the dynamic of ethno-cultural relationships, pointing not only to the absurdity of the constructions of the English as a homogenous and monolithic *other* but also to demonstrate their motivations and efforts at integrating in Welsh communities. In 'There's one shop you don't go into if you are English', Day et al. argue that

> many adapt by adopting new or alternative definitions of national belonging, including being British, claiming to be 'really' Welsh, becoming more 'Welsh,' or assuming some hyphenated identity. A minority find themselves more conscious of their Englishness, and unable to integrate into a Welsh community.[21]

As one touchstone of the tolerance thesis, therefore, the nature of these relationships indicates that there is some way to go in achieving the harmonious integration appealed to in the Welsh Government's cohesion strategy.[22]

Anti-English sentiments aside, it could be argued that the 'tolerance' thesis in relation to racialized minorities has not yet been fully tested in many parts of Wales. Most of Wales has not been characterized by the mass immigration of minorities from the Commonwealth as is the case in several English cities. Across Wales as a whole the presumption of the tolerance is countered by no small amount of evidence of racism and xenophobia experienced by ethnic minorities, new migrants, refugees, Gypsies and others marked out as incomers (see chapter 9). Moreover, there is ample evidence to suggest that those long-settled ethnic minorities of second, third and fourth generation and more experience daily racisms, often banal but nevertheless poignant. Scourfield et al.'s study of ethnic minority children growing up in predominantly white areas[23] finds these children managing racism on a day-to-day basis and a study by Threadgold et al. startlingly notes:

> Across all the minority communities and groups encountered in this project our research findings show that racism, institutional racism and discrimination are significant factors in producing social exclusion, and inhibiting both economic integration and community integration. Racist and class based discrimination stops people from enjoying their full civil rights and participating fully in society, leads to poor delivery of services and keeps people from feeling they belong. Our research suggests that this creates marginalized subcultures where people come to feel at best frustration at what is happening to them and at worst hopelessness, and where they express real fear of leaving their communities for white environments.[24]

The Threadgold et al. study explicitly tests out ideas of tolerance and inclusion in relation to newer migration and across several areas of Wales addressing the central question of community cohesion – can we get along together? They sought to tap into how integration and community cohesion is imagined and enacted in these contexts.[25] What they find includes a very mixed picture of different stages and kinds of integration. They argue, importantly, that social class and disadvantage play a key role in any understanding of cohesion and their evidence suggests critical barriers to inclusion as related migrant status, both new and more established.

Thus, in the post-devolution era, the 'myth of tolerance' has been subject to much discussion, debate and no small amount of empirical testing – a significant shift from the position apparent when we put together the first collection of *A Tolerant Nation?* Mann and Tommis's evidence finds no support for the particularity of Wales in relation to tolerance. Indeed they state: 'Looking at regional differences across the UK, there appears no less "opposition" towards immigration amongst people living in Wales compared to people living in England'.[26] However much it is contested, it nevertheless remains an important 'myth' of Welsh nationhood, one that can be evoked with both positive and negative connotation and therefore one that continues to have significance.

Identities and nationhood

The ways in which such racist and xenophobic attitudes and behaviours interact with ideas of nationalism and national identity are a key consideration in unpacking this myth.[27] Theorists of nationalism have hotly debated the relationship of racism to nationalism. For Nairn,[28] writing in the context of British politics, racism is inevitably a derivative of nationalism. He argues that the post-war resurgence of racism was possible because of the lack of any major mobilizing myth of nationalism in a post-imperial Britain. Thus the politics of Britain became racialized in the post-war period in tandem with economic decline and 'black' immigration. Other writers have developed this thesis, arguing that racism is embedded in British nationalist ideology.[29] By contrast, Anderson rejects any axiomatic relationship between the two ideologies, suggesting both race and nation as imagined communities: 'on the whole racism and anti-Semitism manifest themselves, not across national boundaries, but within them'.[30] For Anderson, nationalism and racism are not synonymous and can be articulated as distinct discourses. While there are obviously points of theoretical disagreement, writers such as Anthias and Yuval-Davis[31] have suggested more broadly that most ethnicities of hegemonic national collectivities contain elements of racist exclusion within their symbolic orders, and that particular boundaries become racialized. Since the early 1990s, writers such as Paul Gilroy, Stuart Hall and Tariq

Modood have not only contributed to making public and
political the relationship between Britishness and racism but
have significantly challenged dominant notions of Britishness
and British identity, giving evidence of new and emerging
black British identities.[32] Prior to devolution few such attempts
had been made to theorize these issues at the level of the Celtic
nations – to ask to what extent Welsh/Scottish/Irish nationalism contains racist and exclusionary elements.[33]

In the first edition of this volume Williams and Chaney
offered an analysis of the extent to which Welsh nationalism
rose to the challenge of an 'inclusive' politics based on civic as
opposed to ethnic allegiance.[34] Political parties, not least Plaid
Cymru – the Party of Wales, the principal nationalist political
party – charted a way from overtly ethnic nationalism to the
promotion of civic nationalism with attempts to achieve a
constructive form of engagement with minority groups and
individuals (see chapter 12). In the Williams and Chaney early
study of ethnic participation and the National Assembly,[35]
issues of national identity were raised almost incidentally and
suggested an ambivalent and uneasy relationship of minority
communities to the majority Welsh society. Respondents
grappled with identification with an institution that apparently had little meaning or relevance for them. The demand
for a National Assembly, associated as it was with Welsh
distinctiveness based on ethno-cultural nationalism, may well
have provided its *raison d'être*, but basing Welsh governance
on exclusively ethnic criteria would be potentially alienating
to the ethnic minority constituency. Yet even at that time, this
study also revealed responses containing strong expressions
of attachment to things Welsh and to Welsh identity especially
evoked by reference to long settlement in localities such as
those within the Cardiff area.

Commenting on the perspectives of Scottish devolution
from the minority viewpoint, Grant[36] found a much more
unequivocally positive connotation with the word 'Scottish'
as did Hussein and Millar[37] in their examination of

multicultural nationalism. While this comparison is interest-ing it could be argued that one of the key differences between Wales and Scotland is the relatively weak affiliation to 'Welshness' articulated in the population as a whole by contrast with stronger national identification in Scotland.

Attempts to politically manipulate popular conceptions of Welsh identity are everywhere apparent. Guidici's analysis[38] considers media portrayals of Italian immigration to Wales in the post-devolution era and uses the term 'model minority' to illustrate how Italians have been constructed in media report-ing as an ideal type to reinforce and mobilize an inclusive rhetoric. The Italian immigrant has been narrated in history as a successful model of integration and this Guidici argues has been used politically as a banal reinforcement of the toler-ance myth. Thus the immigrant past portrays an inclusive Wales ratcheting up an image that serves contemporary polit-ical ends. By contrast, the Threadgold et al. study finds the media culpable of doing the exact opposite in relation to *othered* minorities such as the Somalis.[39]

The imposition of objective, institutionally contrived iden-tities is all too frequently out of step with subjectively experienced localized identity formation,[40] the realm of what can be called 'banal' interactions – borrowing from Billig's term 'banal nationalism'.[41] Billig's analysis is significant because he shifts attention from the traditional focus of polit-ical theory to a consideration of how ideas of nation and the language of nationhood are reproduced at the level of routine social practices – how we in our everyday lives construct inclusions and exclusions, how we speak about and experi-ence belonging and how we communicate our perceptions of who belongs and who does not. Billig's banal nationalism provides an interesting theoretical framework from which to pursue the interface of race and nationalism at the level of specific localities and communities. To what extent does, for example, Wales and Welshness remain an abstraction to those who identify as Butetown black? To what extent are specific territorial areas of Wales seen as multicultural such that ethnic minorities in 'white' Wales remain and are contained as 'outsiders' to be tolerated? What types of identifications with Welshness and Wales do minorities seek and/or attain?

A glimpse of the complexities of these issues comes from a small handful of studies. Scourfield et al.'s study[42] of children in the Valleys (formerly the south Wales coalfield) found a variety of responses to questions of Welsh identity. Although most of the children in their study saw themselves as different from other Valleys children, they offered a variety of identity affiliations, some based on religion (Muslim), some based on other nationalities (Pakistani) and among their dual heritage respondents' identifications with Welsh Valleys culture were at times strongly expressed, at other times not. The study concludes that identity is not especially problematic for any one type of family. What is potentially problematic for any of these children is growing up in such an overwhelmingly white environment, with substantially limited access to alternative sources of cultural affirmation.[43] In a later study, Scourfield and Davies[44] explore the construction of localized and national identities among eight- to eleven-year-olds in six primary schools across Wales and find in their 'talk' constructions of Welshness as racialized. They find 'aspects of the children's talk that pose a barrier to the development of an inclusive Welsh citizenship and also aspects that support it'.[45]

Rhys Jones's study[46] of Muslims in Wales also points to the negotiation of new and interesting identifications among a minority community analyzing their positioning as a counter-public engaged in making representations for place, presence and recognition in the shaping of their identities within Wales. Scourfield's work on children and Rhys Jones's work on Muslims are but two examples in an emerging area of academic interest. Perhaps the greatest impact on the reshaping of Welsh national identity, however, has come from within the arena of arts and literature, with numerous examples giving voice to the ways in which identifications are changing, developing and being claimed (see introduction).

Ethnic minority affiliation to Welsh nationhood is necessarily mediated by a number of factors. Migrant communities are neither homogeneous nor static; indeed, the demographic profile of Wales's black and minority ethnic population reveals considerable diversity not only in terms of ethnicity but also according to length of settlement, migration pattern, age, socioeconomic status, and so on. In addition, minority communities mobilize their ethnic identification in complex patterns, referencing country of origin, country of settlement, country of onward settlement as well as cultural distinctiveness.[47] The identifications of second- and third-generation black Welsh will be quite different from those who have more recently migrated for work from English cities. It is also apparent that gender and age mediate identity quite significantly. New concerns and points of identification are emerging among youth in Wales that defy the more conventional identifications of previous generations, as Grant noted in the Scottish context:

> The truth is that in terms of a redefining of Scottish identity, devolution has missed the boat. Already young Scots, glued to the Internet and digital television, think in global rather than national terms. They identify not by haggis but by haircut ... Few of them read *The Scots Magazine*, idolise Sean Connery or listen to Holyrood debates ... young Scots are happier defining themselves individually through contemporary consumer fads than through anything traditionally defined as Scottish.[48]

These influences are no less felt on second- and third-generation minority ethnic youth in Wales who, by now, are experienced cross-cultural navigators. The expansion and strength of black British identity, and indeed more global black or faith identifications, are also key contextualizing influences.

What these developments indicate is that it is not useful to speak about simple identification but of multiple identifications across a number of axes. Neither is it reasonable to talk simply of the Welsh identity in either aspirational or empirical terms. More useful is the concept of Welsh plural identities. As Day and Suggett correctly suggested:

> the question we ought to address is not that of the real 'nation' or national identity which lies behind concepts employed in political life, but that of the formation, articulation and propagation of the concepts themselves. Nationalist ideas, myths and definitions have to be deconstructed. This means that we need to treat 'Wales' as it has figured in successive, rival discourses, and consider the question 'How many Wales?' or 'How many ways of being Welsh?'[49]

The mobilization of more pluralist nationhood is well under way. Academic studies are augmented by the numerous cultural offerings, blogs, writings, performances and representations that extend identity themes, manipulate and reshape formulations of sub-state national identities and demonstrate creative ownership of the plurality that is Welshness. Ethnic minorities are actively engaged in mobilizing nation as a site of attachment and identity formation, transforming the nation-building process not dislodging it.

Wales and multiculturalism

Nations and nationalisms necessarily seek homogenizing norms, symbols and identifications. Flags, anthems, prizes and awards, slogans, images and more suggest one nation and mobilize a pride in nation. These gestures vary considerably in the ways in which they seek to engage with diversity and the realities of a multicultural public and in terms of their operational principles of inclusion and exclusion. In this respect the new Wales evidences a perceptual change.

Charlotte Williams

From a very low base the notion of a Welsh multiculturalism emerged and was given a platform by the politics of devolution. It found a place on the public policy agenda and in the cultural life of Wales and deliberate efforts have been made to construct and reflect the realities of a multicultural, multi-faith and multi-ethnic society. An analysis of why this happened could point to a number of factors: the efforts of a political class anxious to open up its appeal beyond the narrowing effects of a politics of Welsh ethnic nationalism; the campaign of a political caucus concerned with issues of equality for women and therefore by extension equality for other disadvantaged groups; an acknowledgement of the broader impacts of globalization and economic development and/or indeed the efforts and campaigns of ethnic minority groups themselves to claim recognition. There are a number of explanations for the apparent shift in the 'race'/ethnic politics of Wales that can be documented over a 150-year period and more, as this book attests. Today we may call it multiculturalism to denote the actions by governments and the turbulence from below that reflect a diverse set of peoples working out how to live together within a given territory. Tomorrow this term may become irrelevant simply by virtue of the fact that nations are not, nor never have been, as homogenous as imagined. Wales will axiomatically be referred to as a plural nation and Welshness embraced in plural ways.

Notwithstanding this, multiculturalism has come to mean many things. There must be caution about any empty celebration of diversity that offers a thin rhetorical mask to gloss over both the difficulties of the notion of a national community, both normatively and experientially, and disguises the fact that different groups have very unequal resources: economically, socially and politically. There will be many that continue to point to the enduring and systemized nature of social disadvantage among many ethnic minority groups in Wales (see chapter 10) and their relative powerlessness. There is ample evidence of racism, discrimination, both overt and banal, that proves to be as resilient as ever. The contemporary concern must be with the achievement of substantial citizenship and all that this entails in terms of rights, redistribution, recognition and feelings of belonging.

On the positive side there is evidence that the infrastructure of governance aimed at promoting the inclusiveness of ethnic minorities has had some impact and that constitutional change has had a galvanizing effect on the mobilization of the minority voice (see chapter 12). There is evidence of a clear policy agenda pitched at addressing issues of ethnic diversity and issues of cohesion and integration and this includes an agenda in the arts and culture.

Nevertheless, in the public sphere there is still a considerable way to go if the measure is outcomes rather than inputs. Wales is still a very closed society comprising a small number of elite networks with overlapping membership. Political representation of ethnic minorities in the Welsh Government, within the civil service and in public appointments remains woefully low (see chapter 12). Gains made easily are too easily reversed. The 2013 figures on diversity in public appointments, for example, show ethnic minorities making the biggest losses with only fifty-six appointments and reappointments of a total of 1,087 appointments (5.5%) compared with the 2011/12 figures when they held 119 positions (7.2%).[50] By any measure ethnic minorities do not feature large among those who rule Wales. In addition, despite long settlement and a high degree of intermarriage as compared with other areas of Britain, there is no commensurate degree of economic integration for ethnic minorities in Wales,[51] nor evidence to support the claimed high degree of social integration particularly at the levels where it counts, as this book has illustrated.

So what can be said about the current multicultural settlement? Welsh multiculturalism remains a curious bundle of contradictions and a project in the making. The opportunities provided by devolution have been immense, some

captured and others squandered. Attention to ethnic difference has found a place in mainstream politics and practice
over the past decade, if rather tentative, a little crude and
underdeveloped. There is little doubt that the politics of
recognition has had more returns for all than the politics of
redistribution. Debates that pivot around the emergence of
new ethnicities and identities at the level of the sub-state
have become more sophisticated and risen to ascendency
over debates that focus on ethnic disadvantage. A range of
counter-publics, minorities old and new, have been engaged
in challenging the myths of Welshness and in reworking the
national story. Their contributions are immense, if not wholly
recognized, to the economic, social and cultural life of Wales.
Their presence, in a way that reflects a long history, places
Wales in the global network on interconnections, movements
and mobilities.

Notes

1   See B. Parekh, *The Parekh Report: The Future of Multi-Ethnic Britain*
    (London, 2000), and T. Nairn, *Gordon Brown 'Bard of Britishness'*
    (Cardiff, 2006).
2   Parekh, *Future of Multi-Ethnic Britain*.
3   Y. Alibah Brown, *Imagining the New Britain* (New York, 2001).
4   Parekh, *Future of Multi-Ethnic Britain*, p. 15.
5   R. Davies, 'Shaping the vision', *Red Kite* (June 1995), 17.
6   Speech by Rt Hon. Paul Murphy MP, Secretary of State for Wales,
    Bournemouth, 29 September 1999.
7   Welsh Assembly Government (WAG), *One Wales: A Progressive
    Agenda for the Government of Wales* (Cardiff, 2007).
8   WAG, *Getting on Together: A Community Cohesion Strategy for
    Wales* (Cardiff, 2012).
9   Wales Statistical Directorate, *Welsh Language*, Welsh Government
    (Cardiff, 2013).
10 C. Williams, 'Strange encounters: our assumptions about race',
    Planet, 158 (2003), 19–24.

11 R. Mann and Y. Tommis, *Public Sentiments Towards Immigration in Wales* (Bangor, 2012), p. 30.

12 Ibid.

13 See D. Denny, J. Borland and R. Fevre, 'Racism, nationalism and conflict in Wales', *Contemporary Wales*, 4 (1991), 150–65, and C. Williams, '"Race" and racism: some reflections on the Welsh context', *Contemporary Wales*, 8 (1995), 113–31.

14 See, among others, Richard Townsend-Smith for a discussion of case law in *Wales Law Journal*.

15 Williams, 'Strange encounters'.

16 Ibid., p. 21.

17 Ibid.

18 Ibid.

19 D. Balsom, 'The three Wales model', in J. Osmond (ed.), *The National Question Again* (Llandysul, 1985).

20 G. Day, H. Davis and A. Drakakis-Smith, 'Being English in north Wales: inmigration and inmigrant experience', *Nationalism and Ethnic Politics*, 12/3–4 (2006), 577–98, and G. Day, H. Davis, A. Drakakis-Smith, 'There's one shop you don't go into if you are English: the social and political integration of English migrants into Wales', *Journal of Ethnic and Migration Studies*, 36/9 (2010), 1405–23.

21 Day et al., 'There's one shop', p. 1405.

22 Ibid.

23 J. Scourfield, H. Beynon, J. Evans and W. Shah, 'The experience of black and minority ethnic children living in the south Wales valleys', unpublished report, Cardiff School of Social Sciences (2002), p. 31.

24 T. Threadgold, S. Clifford, A. Arwo et al., *Immigration and Inclusion in South Wales*, Joseph Rowntree Foundation (York, 2008), p. 42.

25 Ibid., p. 63.

26 Mann and Tommis, *Public Sentiments*, p. 30.

27 R. Fevre and A. Thompson (eds), *Nation, Identity and Social Theory: Perspectives from Wales* (Cardiff, 1999).

28 T. Nairn, *The Break-Up of Britain: Crisis and Neo-Colonialism* (London, 1977).

29 P. Gilroy, *There Ain't No Black in the Union Jack* (London, 1987).

30 B. Anderson, *Imagined Communities: Reflections on the Origins and Spread of Nationalism* (London, 1983), p. 136.

31 F. Anthias and N. Yuval-Davis, *Racialised Boundaries: Race, Nation, Gender, Colour and Class in the Anti-Racist Struggle* (London, 1996).

32 T. Modood and P. Werbner (eds), *Debating Cultural Hybridity: Multicultural Identities and the Politics of Anti-Racism* (London, 1997); S. Hall, 'Attitude and aspiration: reflections on black Britain in the nineties', *New Formations*, 33 (Spring 1998), *http://www. newformations.co.uk/abstracts/nf33abstracts.html* (accessed 8 September 2013); Gilroy, *There Ain't No Black*.

33 See Denny, Borland and Fevre, 'Racism, nationalism and conflict in Wales'; C. Williams, 'Passports to Wales? Race, nation and identity', in R. Fevre and A. Thompson (eds), *Nation, Identity and Social Theory*, pp. 69–89; R. Miles & A. Dunlop, 'The racialisation of politics in Britain: why Scotland is different', *Patterns of Prejudice*, 20/1 (1986), 22–3; and P. Hainsworth, 'Politics, racism and ethnicity in Northern Ireland', in P. Hainsworth (ed.), *Divided Society: Ethnic Minorities and Racism in Northern Ireland* (London, 1998), pp. 33–52.

34 See also C. Williams and P. Chaney, 'Inclusive government for excluded groups: ethnic minorities', in P. Chaney, T. Hall and A. Pithouse (eds), *New Governance – New Democracy? Post-Devolution Wales* (Cardiff, 2001), pp. 78–101.

35 Ibid.

36 K. Grant, 'The dull consensus of Scottish identity', *Soundings*, 18 (2001), 146–53, 150.

37 A. Hussein and W. Millar, *Multicultural Nationalism: Islamaphobia, Anglophobia and Devolution* (Oxford, 2006).

38 M. Guidici, 'Immigrant narratives and nation-building in a stateless nation: the case of Italians in post-devolution Wales', *Ethnic and Racial Studies* (2012), 1–19.

39 Threadgold et al., *Immigration and Inclusion in South Wales*.

40 See, for example, A. Thompson and G. Day, 'Situating Welshness: "local" experience and national identity', in Fevre and Thompson, *Nation, Identity and Social Theory*, pp. 27–47, on how local experience of national identities diverge from public and political

identifications; R. Mann and S. Fenton, 'The personal contexts of national sentiments', *Journal of Ethnic and Migration Studies*, 34/3 (2009), 317–34.

41 M. Billig, *Banal Nationalism* (London, 1995).

42 J. Scourfield, J. Evans, W. Shah and H. Beynon, 'Responding to the experiences of minority ethnic children in virtually all white communities', *Child and Family Social Work*, 7 (2002), 161–75.

43 Ibid., 166.

44 J. Scourfield and A. Davies, 'Children's accounts of Wales as racialised and inclusive', *Ethnicities*, 5/1 (2005), 83–107.

45 Ibid., 83.

46 R. D. Jones, 'Negotiating absence and presence: rural Muslims and "subterranean" sacred spaces', *Space and Polity*, 16/3 (2012), 335–50. See also R. D. Jones, 'Islam and the rural landscape: discourses of absence in west Wales', *Social and Cultural Geography*, 11/8 (2010), 751–68.

47 C. Williams and P. Chaney, 'Devolution and identities: the experience of ethnic minorities in Wales', *Soundings*, 18 (2001), 169–83.

48 Grant, 'The dull consensus', 149.

49 G. Day and R. Suggett, 'Conceptions of Wales and Welshness: aspects of nationalism in nineteenth century Wales', in G. Rees, J. Bujra, P. Littlewood, H. Newby and T. L. Rees (eds), *Political Action and Social Identity* (London, 1985), p. 96.

50 Operation Black Vote, *http://www.obv.org.uk* (accessed 8 September 2013).

51 R. Davies, S. Drinkwater, C. Joll et al., *An Anatomy of Economic Inequality in Wales*, Equality and Human Rights Commission (Cardiff, 2011).

Index

Aberavon Greenstars 155
Aberavon Quins 168
Abercraf 26
Aberdare 31, 130, 185, 283
Aberfan 39
Aberriw 70
Abertillery 162
Aberystwyth 30, 210
Aberystwyth Theological College
    210
abuse 141, 145–7, 167, 168, 259,
    260, 265, 266, 288
ACCAC (Qualifications,
    Curriculum and Assessment
    Authority for Wales) 249
Afghan war 280
Africa 52–3, 56, 70, 79, 87, 95, 97,
    99, 105, 106–27, 167, 168,
    176, 183, 225, 226, 230, 281
African Institute (Colwyn Bay); see
    also Congo Institute 117, 118,
    119, 122
African Times 120
Africans 12–13, 108, 111–12,
    114–15, 119
Afro-Caribbeans; see also West
    Indians 173, 176, 230, 232,

    233, 236, 238, 239, 240, 282,
    305
Agbebi, Mojola (D. Brown Vincent)
    118
Agyeman, J. 272
Alderman, Geoffrey 24
Alfred Jones Institute 121
Ali, Muhammad 166
Aliens' Act (1905) 281
Aliens' Act (1914) 30
Aliens Order (1915) 35
All Wales Ethnic Minority
    Association (AWEMA) 314–15
American Baptist Missionary
    Union (ABMU) 116
Amsterdam Treaty (1997) 4, 223
Anderson, Benedict 3
Anglican Church 211, 212, 217
Angola 111
Anthias, F. 340
Arabs 32
Arcade 169
Asians 141, 145, 232
    Ugandan Asians 283
Assam 69, 70, 71, 75, 77, 80
Associating Evangelical Churches
    in Wales 214

Association of Muslim
    Professionals 214
asylum seekers *see* refugees
Atlas of Health Inequalities in
    Wales 228
Australia 5, 56, 164, 280
Autobiography of Elizabeth Davis,
    The 60

Baartmann, Saartje 54
Bahaism 214
Bala 51
Banana (Congo) 108
Bangladesh *see* East Pakistan
Bangladeshis 6, 15, 225, 229–30,
    232–3, 236–40, 333
Bangor 207
Baptist Missionary Society (BMS)
    107–27
Baptist Union of Wales 213
Baptists 107-27, 211
Bardi (Emilio-Romagna) 28
Barmouth 29
Barrow 162
Barry 34, 135
baseball 156, 163
basketball 163
Basu, Aparnu 80
Baynes, Alfred H. 107, 108, 109,
    117
Bayneston 108
Beddoe, John 98, 99
Belfast 35, 36, 37, 38, 44
Belgians 29, 30
Belshella, Alan 144
Bengal 69, 71, 72, 74, 77, 80
Bennett, Dave 167
Bennett, Gary 167
Berlin Conference (1884–5) 108
Best, Hubert 'Bull' (Tommy) 166
Bethelsdorp 52

Billig, M. 342
Birmingham 252
Black Environment Network 329
blacks 31, 32, 35, 41, 108, 115,
    143
Blaina 130
Blake, Nathan 169
Borneo 59
Boston, Billy 163, 164, 165, 166,
    167, 170
Bottomley, Horatio 118, 120, 121
boxing 157, 158, 165
Bridgend 31, 214
Bristol 137, 156
Bristol City FC 156
British Honduras 56
British National Party (BNP); see
    also National Front 142
Brixton (London) 137
Brown, Mark 168
Brynmawr 33, 130, 162
Buddhism 214
Burton, Eli 29
Butetown (Cardiff) 11, 18, 31, 32,
    40, 42, 131, 135, 137, 161,
    162–6, 169–9, 176–205, 214,
    284, 342
Butetown History and Arts Centre
    11, 176–205, 283

Cadoxton (Neath) 138
Cadwaladyr, Betsy *see* Davis,
    Elizabeth
Caernarfon 72, 120
Caerphilly 6, 169
Caia Park estate 146, 261
CAJEX 33
Callaghan, Jim 32
Calvinistic Methodists 12, 69, 71,
    75
Cameroons 108, 117, 122

Index

Cape Colony 51, 53, 54, 56
Cape Town 52
Capel y Beirdd 107
Cardiff 6, 11, 25, 26, 28, 29, 31–4,
    37–42, 112, 122, 130–6, 138,
    142, 145, 146, 155, 156, 158,
    159, 162–9, 177–205, 207,
    208, 210, 212, 214, 216, 230,
    255, 277, 279, 283–6, 288,
    291, 294, 295
Cardiff All Blacks 161, 162
Cardiff and District Citizens'
    Union 136
Cardiff and District XV 164
Cardiff and Merthyr Guardian 134
Cardiff Bay 176, 182–3, 186
Cardiff City FC 156, 162, 166,
    167, 169
Cardiff International Athletic Club
    (CIACs) 163, 164, 165
Cardiff RFC 168
Cardiganshire; see also Ceredigion
    27
Carmarthen 142
Carmarthenshire 30
Caribbean 15, 70, 233
Cathedral Road Synagogue
    (Cardiff) 33
Cenhadwr, Y 72, 73, 75, 78, 80
census (1851) 206, 212; (1911) 26;
    (1951) 31; (2001) 232, 233,
    238, 335; (2011) 2, 5, 6, 14,
    214, 225–6, 234, 307
Centre for Evidence in Ethnicity,
    Health and Diversity (CEEHD)
    242
Ceylon 56
Chaney, P. 16, 217, 341
Charles, Clive 167
Charvis, Colin 168, 169, 170
Chepstow 162

Chester City FC 166
Chicago 132
Children 12, 26, 30, 22, 53, 56, 66,
    74, 75, 78, 116, 118, 119, 158,
    191, 229, 232, 234, 239,
    259–60, 265–6, 270, 280, 283,
    284, 288, 289, 294, 295, 339,
    343, 349
China 56, 70, 108, 114, 285
Chinese 6, 15, 32, 133–5, 155, 225,
    232–3, 236, 238–40, 259
'Chosen One, The' 86
Christianity 15, 62, 65, 73, 77, 78,
    80, 107, 114, 219
Christianity and the Race Problem
    79
citizenship 10, 19, 252, 268, 279,
    281, 296, 333, 343, 347
Clash of Colour, The 80
Clausewitz, Karl von 34
colonialism 12, 59, 86
Colour Bar Act (1926) 31, 115
Colwyn Bay 13, 106–27, 175
Combat 18 142, 145
Commission for Racial Equality
    (CRE) 139
Commonwealth Immigration Act
    (1962) 40, 43
Communities First project 262
Congo, the 106–27, 175, 280, 283
Congo Institute; see also African
    Institute 106–27
Congo Institution Committee 111
Congo Training College 109
Congregationalists 211
Connery, Sean 344
Conrad, Joseph 62
Conservative Party 41, 281, 308,
    309–10, 322
Cordle, Gerald 168
Core Subject Indicator (CSI) 236

cricket 161, 162, 163, 164, 166
Crimea 61
Cronicl Cenhadol, Y 71
cultural democracy 178, 192
cultural memory 192
Cuvier, Georges 87
Cymdeithas Cyfamodwyr Cymru
    Rhydd 143
Cymdeithas yr Iaith Gymraeg 336
Cymru Fydd 63–4
CYTÛN (Churches Together in
    Wales) 214, 216

Daniels, Fred 185–6
Davie, Grace 206
Davis, Elizabeth (Betsy
    Cadwaladyr) 60
Davies, Rhys 86, 98, 100
Davies, Ron 333
De Winton, Sir Francis 108–9
Dennis, James 78
deportation 278, 286–7, 288–9,
    291, 294, 295
destitution 278, 285–6, 288–9,
    291, 294, 295
detention 278, 286, 291, 294
devolution vii, 8, 15, 16, 215, 216,
    219, 254, 258, 261, 271, 277,
    305–7, 312, 316, 318, 319,
    321, 324, 331–48
*Dictionary of Welsh Biography,
    The* 123
discrimination 9, 13, 14, 162, 163,
    194, 209, 213, 218–9, 223,
    226, 228, 239, 241–3, 253,
    265, 279–80, 290–1, 293, 309,
    312, 336, 339, 346
dispersal 15, 40, 182, 230, 261,
    277–9, 282, 285–8, 291, 337
displacement 136, 278–80, 287
Dixon, Colin 164–5

Dringo'r Andes 65
Driscoll, Jim 157–8, 166
Drysorfa, Y 71
Dyfed Powys Police 139-40

Earnshaw, Rob 169
East India Trading Company 51,
    60
East Pakistan (Bangladesh) 69, 73
ecumenicalism 14, 213–14
Edinburgh 177
Edmunds, Dilys 73
education 16, 26, 29, 41, 43, 64,
    78, 107, 115, 122, 176, 192,
    194, 209, 227, 234–7, 239,
    281, 286, 290, 293, 310
Education Act (1944) 209
Education and Lifelong Learning
    Committee 249
Edwards, Thomas Charles 75-8
Ely (Cardiff) 138, 156
employment 33, 40, 41, 131, 141,
    184, 218, 226, 234, 238–40,
    285, 290–1, 312
Emrys ap Iwan *see* Jones, Robert
    Ambrose
England 2, 4, 10, 17, 18, 28, 30,
    40, 43, 55, 64, 86, 99, 113,
    117, 142, 144, 145, 146, 147,
    155, 156, 162–3, 170, 208,
    211, 216, 219, 228, 242, 252,
    261, 292, 293, 334–5, 340
English 2, 10, 18, 25–7, 38, 40,
    42–3, 55, 58, 59, 60, 61, 62,
    64, 65, 79, 94, 111, 155, 156,
    160, 162, 168, 180, 206, 207,
    211, 235, 239, 252, 253,
    256–61, 231–8
English as an Additional Language
    Association of Wales (EALAW)
    235

Index

English Football League 166
equality/equalities 16, 18, 19, 34, 79, 123, 147, 163, 217, 224, 227, 228, 230, 235, 241–3, 267, 280, 292–3, 309–13, 315–19, 323–4, 346
Ernest, James 162
Erskine, Joe 165–6
Esteban, M. 27
Ethé, Herman 30
European Convention on Human Rights 219, 278, 289
European Union 4, 213, 218, 265
evacuees 30
Evangelical Movement of Wales 213–14
evangelicals 12, 70, 74, 211, 212, 214, 216, 217, 218
Evans, Ann 52–5
Evans, Benjamin 116
Evans, Evan 51, 54–5
Evans, Margiad 86, 89
Evans, Neil 10, 12, 13, 14, 15, 98, 178, 181, 224
Evans, Steve 141

Fed, The: A History of the South Wales Miners in the Twentieth Century 24
Fiji 56
First World War 11, 26, 29, 30, 44, 78, 135, 155, 156, 158, 182
Forward Movement 211
France 70, 113, 143, 218
Francis, Hywel 24
Francis, Roy 162, 164
Frankenstein 85
Franklin, John Lionel 119
Freeman, Johnny 164-7
Freetown 118
Friend of Sylhet 72

Friend of Women in Bengal, The 72
Frongoch mine (Ponterwyd) 27
Frythones, Y 80

Gadlys 116
Gandhi, M. K. 73
Garndolbenmaen 107
gender 13, 80, 85–105, 226–7, 265–6, 270, 285, 290, 315, 344
German Baptist Missionary Society 117
Germans 30, 31, 108, 122
Germany 117
Ghose, Hridesh Ranjan 73
GI Brides 184
Giggs, Ryan 168
Gilman, Sander 88
Gilroy, Paul 280, 340
Glamorgan 26, 31, 41, 133, 145, 162, 164, 211
Glasgow 35, 36–7, 38, 42, 44, 155
'Glaw, Y' 74
globalization viii, 8, 4, 9–11, 13, 15, 16, 337, 346
Grangetown (Cardiff) 40
'Great Chain of Being, The' 87
'Great God Pan, The' 86, 93, 96
Greeks 8, 33, 133
Gwalia in Khasia 70
Gwent police 139, 140
Gwerin 24, 251, 256, 258
Gymraes, Y 59
Gypsy Travellers 8, 29, 100, 229, 232, 267

Halifax 164,165
Hall, Stuart 340
Hare Krishna 214
Havel, Vaclav 24
health 227, 228

Heineken League 168
Hildebrandt, H. 88
Hindu Cultural Association 217
Hinduism 214
Holmes, Colin 24, 35
Hottentots; see also Khoikhoi 51
Household Reference person
    (HRP) 232
housing 97, 146, 182
Hughes, Claudia 123
Hughes, Katie 109
Hughes, Katie (née Jones) 109
Hughes, Stanley 109
Hughes, Trystan Owain 209, 210
Hughes, William 13, 106–27
Hull Kingston Rovers 165
human rights 4, 216, 219, 223

Ieuan Gwynedd *see* Jones, Evan
Immigration Advisory Service 145
Immigration and Asylum Act
    (1999) 277
imperialism 12, 13, 51, 55, 59, 60,
    62, 66, 75, 76, 87, 121, 122,
    143, 158, 159
Independents 211, 213
India 51, 56, 60–2, 66, 69, 70,
    72–5, 77, 79, 80, 88, 106, 108,
    113–15
Indian Independence Bill (1947) 79
Indians 80, 236, 65
in/exclusion 260, 291, 292, 307,
    312, 334, 339, 342, 345
Institute of Race Relations 150,
    297, 301
Interfaith Council of Wales 218
internationalism 12, 24, 69, 70,
    251, 255
Iraqis 146, 277, 280, 285, 288
Iran 285, 281
Iranians 277

Ireland 18, 32, 35–6, 37, 63–4,
    113, 131, 155, 157–9, 162–3,
    255, 332
Irish 5, 8, 14, 18, 24–6, 30, 32,
    36–9, 58, 63, 64, 129–31,
    133–4, 136, 153–61, 164,
    180–1, 207–10, 215, 310
Islam; see also Muslims 3, 214,
    215, 271
Italians 5, 27, 28, 31, 33, 342

Jackson, Colin 168–70
Jamaica 189, 196
Jamaicans 166, 168
James, J. Spinther 117
Jay, E. 252
Jefferson, Thomas 93
Jehovah's Witnesses 218
Jenkins, Daniel J. 116
Jenkins, Nigel 70, 76
Jews 11, 28, 33, 34, 63, 134, 135,
    137, 145, 155
John Bull 118–21
Jones, Ann *see* Evans, Ann
Jones, D. G. Merfyn 70
Jones, Evan (Ieuan Gwynedd) 59,
    149
Jones, Hugh 108
Jones, J. Arthur 74
Jones, John Pengwern 72, 74
Jones, Katie *see* Hughes, Katie
Jones, Margaret 63
Jones, Merfyn 36
Jones, Michael D. 62
Jones, Philip 40
Jones, Robert Ambrose (Emrys ap
    Iwan) 62
Jones, Thomas 70

Karimganj (India) 73, 74
Keating, Joseph 38

Khasia, Khasi Hills 12, 56, 57, 70, 78
Khoikhoi, the 51–5
Kinkasa 108–10
Kosovars 283
Ku Klux Kian 142, 143
Kullar, Mohan Singh 138
Kurds 146

Labour Party 215
Lagos Weekly Record 118
Lancashire 36, 37, 38, 112, 208
Landana (Congo) 111
Landore (Swansea) 25
Larsing, U 78
Le Pen, Jean-Marie 143
League of Nations 79
Ledoux, Charles 158
Lela, Chundra 73
Leopold II, king of Belgium 108, 121
Lewis, Sir Herbert 71
Lewis, Mostyn 71
Lewis, Sir Samuel 118
Lewis, Thomas 110
Liberal Democrats 308–10
Liberal Unionism 37, 38
Liberalism 37
Liberia 117
Link, The 72
Liverpool 13, 30, 35–7, 39, 42, 44, 108, 109, 112, 117, 132, 137
Livingstone, David 107
Llais Llafur 27
Llandudno 112, 119, 207
Llanelian 110, 116, 175
Llanelli 31, 132, 134, 145, 157, 263
Llangollen Baptist College 108
Llanidloes 51, 53
Llanrumney (Cardiff) 168
Llanrwst 51, 263

Llantrisant 130
Llanystumdwy 107
Llon a Lleddf 56
Lloyd, E. M. 75
Lloyd George, David 78
London 2, 25, 26, 38, 57, 86, 87, 91, 93, 97, 102, 110, 135, 137, 145, 177
London Missionary Society 51
London Welsh 169
Louis, Joe 165

Machen, Arthur 86, 93
Madagascar 56
Madras 61
Maesteg 144
Malacca 56
Malchow, H. L. 85, 86, 97
Makone, Steve 167
Manchester 42, 107, 168
Manchester City FC 167
Manchester Guardian 74, 115
Marx, Karl 45
Matadi (Congo) 108
Matthews, Basil 79
Meade, Neville 169
Meibion Glyndŵr 143
Merseyside 10, 261
Merthyr Tydfil 26, 38, 129, 143, 230, 283
Merthyr Vale 39
migrant workers 258, 263, 265
migration 30, 36, 129, 130, 156, 207, 208, 213, 226, 246, 258, 261, 263, 265, 271, 280, 281, 282, 296, 334, 337, 338, 339, 344
Miles, Robert 42
Milford Haven 166, 263, 283
Miners' Federation of Great Britain 26

Index

Minimum Wage Act (1912) 27
Miskell, Louise 131
missionaries 11, 18, 51, 66, 69–80,
    106, 108, 111, 114, 115
Missionary Herald, The 107
Mobilization 15, 257, 270, 279,
    282, 291, 293, 294, 296, 297,
    321, 345, 347
'Modest Adornment, A' 86, 89, 92,
    97
Modood, Tariq 340–1
Mold 25
Monmouthshire 31, 95, 133, 211
Moody, Dwight Lyman 116
Moolenaar, H. K. 108
Moore, Lisa 88
Morford, Ernestina 120
Morgan, D. Densil 208, 214
Morgan, Eluned 64, 65
Morocco 63, 280
Morriston 25
Mountain Ash 38
multiculturalism 1–9, 17, 18, 180,
    254, 258, 272, 332, 333, 345,
    346, 347
Munster 38
Murphy, Paul 333
Muslims; see also Islam 15, 145,
    214, 258, 267, 268, 271, 343
Mussolini, Benito 31
Myfanwy, the 64

Nairn, Tom 340
Nantyglo 130
Natal 56
National Assembly for Wales (NAW)
    4, 215, 219, 306, 309, 333;
    Commission 311; Communities
    First Programme 262
National Asylum Support Service
    (NASS) 277, 285, 288

National Front; see also British
    National Party 142, 143
National Institute for Social Care
    and Health Research
    (NISCHR) 241
national identity 2, 3, 5, 70, 112,
    160, 197, 207, 251–5, 267,
    269, 271, 331–5, 337, 340,
    341, 343, 345
nationalism 43, 64, 310, 332,
    340–2, 345
neo-Nazi groups; see also British
    National Party, Combat 18, Ku
    Klux Klan, National Front
    139, 142
New Calabar (Nigeria) 17, 120
New York 3, 145, 158
New Zealand All Blacks 159
Newfoundland 54
Newport 6, 26, 135, 142, 145, 168,
    207, 214, 255, 277, 284, 285,
    295
Newport Hibernians 155
Newtown (Cardiff) 32
NHS Equality Unit 228
Nicholls, Gwyn 155
Nightingale, Florence 61
N'Kanza 108, 109
Nonconformity 14, 69, 77, 206–12
Normans 11
Northern Ireland 4, 6, 10, 44, 309,
    310
Notting Hill 39
Nottingham 39
'Novel of the Black Seal, The' 86,
    93–4, 97

Oldham, J. H. 79
O'Leary, Paul 24
O'Neil, William 157

Pakistanis 6, 138, 225, 230, 236, 238, 239, 259, 277, 343
Pan-Africanism 12
Parekh Report 1, 332
Paris 63, 87
Parris, Eddie 162
Parry, Jon 24
Patagonia 64–5
Patients' Episode Database for Wales (PEDW) 231
Pembrokeshire 39, 166, 263
Pentecostals 211
Persecution 278, 279, 282, 296
Philipps, Norah 63
Philipps, Wynford 63
Plaid Cymru 30, 66, 215, 307, 309, 310, 341
Poles 8
Polish 210, 263, 264, 265, 270
Policy Research Institute on Ageing and Ethnicity (PRIAE) 228
Pontlottyn 130
Pontypool 130
Pontypool RFC 168
Pontypridd 142, 283
Port Talbot 207
Porter, Andrew 76
Porth 146
Porthcawl 207
Powys 6, 144, 230, 254, 259, 260, 261, 263
Presbyterian Church of Wales 69, 210, 211, 213
Price, Watcyn M. 79
protest 12, 27, 60, 129, 136, 145, 210, 291, 292, 295, 296,
Protestantism 36, 38, 208, 217
Punjab 60

Races of Britain, The 98, 99

race 1, 7, 8, 13, 18, 42, 43, 79, 80, 85, 89, 91–6, 106, 114, 122, 123, 139, 141, 153, 160, 165, 167, 178, 182, 186, 187, 217, 218, 226, 227, 231, 232, 254–60, 269, 278, 309–12, 322, 335–7, 340, 342, 344 ; 'discourses of race' 159; race 'thinking' 9; and *passim*
Race Relations Act (1976) 376
Race Relations (Amendment) Act (2000) 262
Racial Attacks 13, 18, 141, 147
racism 4, 8, 10, 15, 42, 87, 97, 98, 114, 138, 141, 142, 162, 167, 168, 190, 194, 226, 228, 237 (see also riots); discrimination 9, 13, 14, 162, 163, 194, 209, 213, 218, 219, 226, 228, 239, 241–3, 253, 265, 279, 280, 290–1, 292, 312, 336, 339, 346; equality 16, 315–17, 319, 323, 324; harassment 254, 265, 312; rural racism 17, 251–72 ; stereotypes 13, 14, 85, 86, 91, 101, 185, 187, 194, 196; and *passim*
Rastafarians 42
Rebecca riots 131
'Red Dragon' revolt 26
Rees, Sarah Jane (Cranogwen) 80
refugees 15, 29, 132, 144, 183, 195, 197, 200, 230, 232, 234, 239, 261, 277–80, 283–7, 290–2, 296, 310, 338
Refugee Inclusion Strategy 292
Report of the Foreign Mission 71
Rhondda 38, 130, 132, 142, 146, 214
Rhondda Cynon Taff 214
Rhosllanerchrugog 63

Rhyl 30
Risman, Gus 162
riots 3, 13, 24, 25, 30, 32, 36, 38, 39, 42, 122, 128, 129, 130–9, 145, 147, 178, 181, 247, 261, 283
Riverside (Cardiff) 214
Roberts, E. A. 74
Robinson, Ann 336
Robinson, Steve 168
Robinson, Vaughan 254, 259, 260, 261, 284
Roman Catholicism 208, 210, 212
Rowlands, Helen 72–4
rugby league 162–8, 170
rugby union 162, 164, 167, 168
Rumney (Cardiff) 168
rural/race 252, 255, 258

St Helens (Swansea) 214
Salford 162, 165
Salvation Army 131
sanctuary 15, 277–97
sanctuary seeker 277–9, 282, 284–97
Sao Salvador 107
Sankey, Ira David 116
Save the Children 284, 294
Schmelling, Max 165
Scientologists 218
Scotch Cattle 131
Scotland vii, 2, 4, 6, 10, 18, 37, 38, 42, 43, 216, 255, 289, 293, 309, 310, 332, 342
Second World War 2, 30, 34, 39, 74, 78, 162, 163, 184, 185, 194, 197
Senghennydd 133
Seren Cymru 116
sexuality 86, 88, 90–2, 285
Shelley, Mary 85
Shillong (Khasia) 74

Sierra Leone 117
Sierra Leone Weekly News 118
Sikhism 214
Sikhs; Bhuttra Sikhs 40, 60
Silchar (Khasia) 75
slavery 60, 93, 108, 115, 121, 176, 177
Smith, Dai 155
soccer 155, 156, 161, 162, 163, 168, 169
social care 16, 227–30, 240
Solomon a Gaenor 19, 139
Somali 166, 193, 195, 198, 230, 277, 284, 288, 294, 333, 342
Somali Advice and Information Centre 284
South Africa 87, 115, 167
South Africa Bill (1909) 115
South Church Street School (Cardiff) 162
South Glamorgan 145
South Glamorgan Community Relations Executive 41
South Shields 34, 136
South Wales Anti-Fascist Organization 143
South Wales Association (football) 156
South Wales Miners' Federation 29
Spanish Aid movement 32
Spain 280
Spaniards 27, 65
Spivak, Gayatri Chakravorty 55
Splott (Cardiff) 166
sport 2, 14, 153–70
Springboks 167
Staniforth, J. M. 159, 160
Stanley, Henry Morton 107, 109, 120, 121
Steffens, A. 117
Stoddard, Lothrop 79

Strobel, Margaret 80
Sudan 56, 280, 283, 285
Sudanese 295
Suggett, R. 345
Sullivan, Clive 165–7
Sullivan, Jim 162
Sullivan, John L. 158
superdiverse 225
superdiversity 2, 296
Swansea 6, 25, 26, 28, 29, 31, 34,
    41, 133, 144, 145, 147, 161,
    169, 207–8, 214, 255, 259,
    277, 284, 285, 295, 333
Swansea Valley 26
Sylhet (Bengal) 70, 72, 74, 76

Tagore, Rabindranath 73
Tahiti 56
Third Sector230, 315
Third Sector Partnership Council
    216, 311, 315
Thomas, David 79
Tiger Bay; see also Butetown 11,
    165, 180–8, 190, 191
Tonypandy 31, 38, 129, 132, 134
Toxteth (Liverpool) 137
Transatlantic Slave Trade 176
Tredegar 24, 38, 39, 130, 131, 133,
    137, 207
Trinidad 56
Turkey 280
Tynged yr laith 43

Ulster 35–8
    unionists 310
Uncle Tom's Cabin 119
Underhill (Congo) 108
Union of Welsh Independents 213
United Nations High
    Commissioner for Refugees
    (UNHCR) 280

University College of Wales,
    Aberystwyth 30

Valleys, the 130, 133, 134, 140–7
Victim Support Powys 259
Vietnamese 283
VSPC 217

Wales on Sunday 168
Wales Rural Observatory (WRO)
    262–5
Walker, Nigel 167–70
Warneck, Gustav 78
Webbe, Glenn 168
Welsh (language) 5, 8, 9, 12, 30,
    44, 57, 66, 73, 75, 80, 85–102,
    107, 109, 206, 210, 212, 213,
    216, 255–7, 260, 270, 332,
    335
Welsh Baptist College; see also
    Llangollen Baptist College 107,
    108
Welsh Baptist Gymanfa 118
Welsh Baptist Union 213
Welsh Boys Clubs 164
Welsh Church Act (1914) 212
Welsh Churches Survey (1995) 213
Welsh Government 16, 224, 229,
    234, 241, 243, 271, 277, 291,
    292, 293, 306, 308, 311–15,
    321, 323, 334, 338, 347;
    Strategic Equality Plan 241
Welsh Football Association 162
Welsh Health Survey 228, 231
Welsh Language Act (1993) 336
Welsh Language Board 336
Welsh language movement 66
Welsh Outlook 29
Welsh Refugee Council (WRC)
    279, 295
Welsh Rugby Union (WRU) 167

Index

Welsh Women's Liberal Association 63

West Indies 56, 135, 136

West Indians 40

Western Mail 155, 159

Westminster 26, 323

Wigan 163–4

Wilberforce, William 60

Williams, Charlotte 5, 16, 17, 175, 179

Williams, Elizabeth 73

Williams, Gareth 155

Williams, Gwyn A. 209

Williams, Jane 60

Williams, W. R. 79

Wilson, Bartley 156

Wilson, Danny 168

Women 3, 26, 52, 59, 64, 70, 73, 77, 78, 80, 88–90, 92, 96–8, 114, 122, 153, 170, 177, 180, 232, 236–43, 283, 294, 320, 346

Wrexham 106, 145, 146, 261, 277, 285, 288, 295

Yemen 135, 283, 284

Ynys (Caernarfonshire) 107

Young Wales movement; see also Cymru Fydd 78

Young Wales 63, 64

Ystradgynlais 259

Yuval–Davis, N. 340